QUEEN

QUEEN LIVE

A CONCERT DOCUMENTARY BY GREG BROOKS

FOREWORD BY BRIAN MAY

OMNIBUS PRESS

London / New York / Paris / Sydney / Copenhagen / Berlin / Madrid / Tokyo

Exclusive Distributors
Music Sales Limited,
8/9 Frith Street,
London W1D 3JB, UK.

Music Sales Corporation,
257 Park Avenue South,
New York, NY 10010, USA.

Macmillan Distribution Services,
53 Park West Drive,
Derrimut, Vic 3030,
Australia.

To the Music Trade only:
Music Sales Limited,
8/9 Frith Street,
London W1D 3JB, UK.

Every effort has been made to trace the copyright
holders of the photographs in this book but one or
two were unreachable. We would be grateful if
the photographers concerned would contact us.

Printed and bound in Singapore

A catalogue record for this book is available from
the British Library.

Visit Omnibus Press on the web at
www.omnibuspress.com

Queen Live

CONTENTS

"People are giving you two hours of their time, so you have to give them EVERYTHING for those two hours. We want every person to go away from a Queen concert feeling they got their money's worth, and we use every possible device to achieve that."
Brian May.

Foreword

By Brian May

The first edition of this book was published in large format paperback in 1996, the result of a prodigious amount of work by a young Greg Brooks, who at that time had no *inside* access to us, Queen, which makes his achievement all the more remarkable. *Queen Live: A Concert Documentary* has never been out of print since then.

When I first saw this incredibly ambitious work, I was amazed that someone I had never even met seemed to know more about my touring life than I did!

I asked Greg why he was driven to write the book. He said: "I wrote it because I had been a fan since 1976 and had amassed tons of information on Queen live, but there was not a book to refer to, to answer the questions I and many other fans were asking: When was Queen's first gig in Australia? / Did Queen ever play in Mexico or at the Marquee in London? / Who were Queen's support acts? / Did Queen ever play 'It's Late', 'March Of The Black Queen' or 'White Man' live? / What cover versions did Queen perform? / What did Freddie and Brian say during concerts? / Is it true that Queen smuggled their equipment out of Argentina on a jumbo jet, just before it could be impounded? And so on.

"*None* of these things were in any book. Very very little was documented on Queen concerts. Also, I had a bit of a reputation as being an *expert* on Queen live, so the Fan Club staff would often ring me with questions, fans would write to me, TV and Radio researchers would sometimes ask me to view footage and identify it, and Jim Beach's office would call up with the odd concert related question too. So I decided to offer *all* the information I had accumulated, in one body of work – which turned into a book.

"I also wanted to tie up some of the copious loose ends on the bootleg situation - which was at that time rather messy and confusing."

Greg was at this time working full-time for the Civil Service, and researching and writing only in his limited spare time, with no access to any information which might exist in our vaults (supposing we even had vaults!) and, almost unimaginably now, with no Internet! His only resources were his own notes (and those of fellow enthusiasts) and the devotion of a true fan to his goal; the completion of The Book. Greg explains: "I wrote 80 percent of it that way, and then I jacked in my job so I could finish it – I lived on cheese on toast for eight solid months. It took me 18 months to gather together 20 years worth of data from every country Queen ever toured in. The info came from fan club mags, letters from pen-friends, setlists I kept from the concerts I attended, and those of other fans, and tons of anecdotes that people sent me. I gathered data from wherever I could find it."

Greg's determination and perfectionism paid off. The book has become the standard reference work on Queen's live appearances … a copy to be found on the bookshelves of fans all around the world. The book is always to hand in my studio too, for those moments when we are trying desperately to remember where we heard *that* particular ad-lib from Freddie.

So what has changed since then? What is new in this revised edition? Well, Greg's life changed dramatically, to say the least. We were so impressed by the depth of his knowledge and his dedication to our history that we offered him a job. Since 1997 he has become our trusted archivist, patiently working his way through all our relics … the relics from within … after all, we were actually *there* at every one of those concert s … a strange thought!

Greg has been able to compile anew, using Queen's (and my) own documents, tapes, notes, and anecdotes, and these days he joins us in creating our modern day Queen history. In addition, Greg says: "Because of the internet there are hundreds of setlists *out there* which I have now been able to cross reference with. There are more anecdotes to add, new bootlegs to update, slight errors to correct, new interesting information and pictures to drop in. Some of the photos in the original book are in the wrong years, so we have put that right. The book is now 99 percent accurate, I think, as opposed to 90-something percent."

Flicking through this necessarily summarised account of every Queen gig, everyone who was ever there will be triggered into remembering their own special viewpoint and feelings at the time. My own recollections are mainly from a position just stage left of centre, in that *pole position* I, as lead guitarist, was privileged to occupy, usually just a little behind our amazing singer, giving him a power-base to work off. Roger and John and I expounded our energies, whether it was in a tiny club in the early Seventies, or in front of thousands of fans in a football stadium in the Eightie, and often it seemed as if our combined forces were channeled directly through Freddie – our unique and fabulous link with the people out there. Freddie had his own view of the proceedings, and so did you, no matter where you may have been, sitting, or standing, or even if you were busy elbowing your way to the hot dog stand! Greg's book places all this in a framework we can share.

The book is now prefaced by a new introduction by Greg which makes clear what is new and amended in this much improved second edition. So there you have it. Here is a work which we can rely on. I've ordered my copy already!

Brian May – December 2004.

INTRODUCTION TO 2005 EDITION

Since the original pressing of this book, in 1996, new information has emerged about Queen concerts that was not known (or accessible) back then, or else it could not be verified then. I have endeavoured to include all that material in this revised edition and have even reluctantly sacrificed photographs here and there in order to squeeze it in. However, a good deal of the data brought to my attention in recent years could not be confirmed and is therefore not included. Alas, too much Queen live mythology must therefore remain so. Only that which could be corroborated - from at least three separate sources - has been introduced here.

Certain individuals were aggrieved that I should challenge the validity of that which they insisted I put in, yet they offered not one single piece of substantiating evidence. I asked only that two other sources could verify their data, and in the absence of that my original text survived. The outcome of all this was the inclusion of much new data – a lot it significant - and confirmation of details I suspected in 1996 but could not then offer as fact. Now, finally, I have been able to hear many of the tapes and confirm those nagging details. I have rectified the niggling errors that inevitably crept into the original text, as well as making clearer certain points that some readers felt were misleading. I hope it is now the case that anything even remotely ambiguous before, is absolutely clear now.

The most significant aspect of this revision, and still the most important element of the entire book, to you AND me, I guess, is the inclusion of new information on setlists which was previously inaccessible to me. Access to the band's audio archive (and Brian's personal tapes specifically), combined with information meticulously assembled on a couple of first-rate fan-made web sites, has enabled me, for example, to offer accurate setlist data on the much loved European leg of the 'Live Killers' tour – and several of the

Crazy UK gigs later that year which I'd never heard before, not even on bootlegs. Indeed, we now have a full and accurate picture, for the first time, of which performances on Queen's first live album came from which shows – even down to Freddie's unforgettable adlibs, banter and 'Death On Two Legs' dedicated to's ...'

The 'Live Killers' tour is dear to me, and many other fans too, so herein at last are accurate accounts of those legendary shows. I have not always specified exactly which song, adlib or particular Freddie/Brian audience address came from which show, because there is good reason to save that information for a bigger, better future (official) Queen Live release. I have, however, let you in on which concerts (the particular nights) featured on the LP, and which did not. One day (sooner than later, I think) you will discover exactly where each 'Live Killers' recital came from; You'll find out exactly where Freddie uttered, "The things you have to do for money!" and "This is called 'Spread Your Wingsa'!" We do now, finally, have Freddie's coments for nearly every show on that leg of the tour, including Zagreb, Zurich, Saarbrucken and all three nights in Paris.

A credible volume of data documented by the fans (including me) indeed remains proven and accurate, other stuff is close but not quite there, and some things are just wrong. I learned, for instance, that John Etchells only began recording the 'Killers' shows from Brussels onwards (January 26, 1979), and so the German shows from the week prior to that could immediately be dismissed. Details like that would have been invaluable a decade ago when first I researched that material. Whoever it was that suggested anything on the first live LP came from Bremmen, was mistaken ... but he meant well!

Actually, when all said and done, considering what relatively little we've all had to work with over the years (official *inside* confirmation of basic facts, figures and speculation being so thin on the ground, I mean), we did a pretty good job. Certainly *most* of what we believed happened at gigs - for which there is little or no bootleg representation - *did* happen. Queen did play *those* songs and *those* medleys, covers and encores, and Freddie *did* say all those wonderful things he was reported to have said. I generally found – as I dissected each page for amendments - that the most frequent errors in the first pressing were merely songs in the wrong sequence or a song missing from an encore or medley. There was nothing in the original text that was outrageously wide of the mark, just the odd inexact setlist - so that can't be too bad!

A (nearly) final thought, if you will indulge me. I would ask you keep in mind that it is definitively NOT the case that every Queen concert was recorded from the mix desk and kept in the archive for prosperity – as is so often suggested. Sadly, tragically, that just didn't happen. Many shows *were* recorded, of course, but not ALL – not by a very long way. There is not seven hundred and something full and unedited concerts, of fantastic mix-desk sound quality, lurking in the vaults. In truth, there is probably less than ten percent of that; some of it audio only, some video only, and some a little of both - and not necessarily all in usable quality, as many people also believe.

This I mention because of course it means that I am still unable to verify too much of the data I offered in 1996. Despite the emergence of the all-knowing and all-powerful World Wide Web, I note with interest that there remains to this day a great many loose ends to tie up. Speculation and guesswork, some if outrageously wide of the mark, thrives still, among the same old experts that were debating these same issues twenty years ago. A voluminous number of posters, flyers, ticket stubs and other concert memorabilia has surfaced from this vast global forum, and some of it is great stuff, but in terms of actual significant facts, earth-shattering anecdotes, Queen concert revelations, relatively little has emerged in recent times.

Probably the most exciting find in recent years, in terms of concert memorabilia, is that of Freddie's original handwritten setlist for a gig at the King's college Hospital on March 10, 1972. This remarkable item pinpoints precisely the material Queen were playing at that time, without ambiguity. We know now the songs and order in which they were played. We can be certain that 'Hangman' and 'Stone Cold Crazy' do indeed date back that far, and we even ascertain that both 'Jesus' and 'The Night Comes Down' were definitely performed live, as we had suspected but had no way of proving.

This revised work is the most extensive scrutiny of Queen's live concerts you will find. It is bigger and better, more fluent, and the oversights have been addressed. The pictures have been placed in the correct sequence and even the mispelled Japanese venues are correct now (thanks to a friend). The unclear is clearer, the jacket and format is new, and we've even updated the live product Discography and Bootlegs sections to incorporate post-1996 CDs and (official) live DVDs. Further, you will note the brand new addition of the 'Typical Concert Setlist' element – offering useful at-a-glance summaries of the songs played on each tour. And, as you will no doubt have noticed, Brian May has kindly written a Foreword.

Though this is the story of Queen Live, it is not, of course, told from *their* unique perspective – I never pretended otherwise. That particular delight awaits us – and what a book that will be! No, this is the story from the *other* side. I like to think of this work as *our* story, not just mine. These pages represent Queen on stage as seen from the fans equally unique perspective, for I was, and I remain, exactly that; a fan - first and foremost, and always.

It seems we must wait a while longer for the *real* inside story of Queen live. Only three people can offer that, and I'm not one of them. I hope this will *do* in the meantime.

Greg Brooks – January 2005

Introduction to 1995 Edition

As one the world's most innovative and exciting live acts, Queen were expected to tour frequently, and they did. Compared to most bands, there is a generous quantity of live recordings and videos on the market. Three live albums, close to a dozen videos, and two exceptional DVDs (each containing the full length show; Wembley 1986, Milton Keynes 1982), with more planned, is significant concert representation by any standards. However, few of these products come even remotely close to capturing the true atmosphere and energy that Queen generated in concert. Fans and collectors regard the album output, especially, as far from sufficient. Most are only too aware of the wealth of material known to exist within the band's own archive and which still awaits proper release.

Although many fans regard *Live Killers* (issued in 1979) to be the best concert representation so far released, even that has curious omissions. 'Somebody To Love', 'If You Can't Beat Them', 'Fat Bottomed Girls', and 'It's Late' are all AWOL. At the time of its release *Killers* even met with criticism from within the band. Indeed, two of them made public their contempt for it, as well as for live albums generally. I have always regarded the criticisms aimed at *Killers* as unfounded. In my opinion it is an exceptional compilation - by far the most exciting and complete account of a Queen tour yet to have emerged, officially. I say officially because many great shows (too numerous to list) have surfaced via unofficial channels, but still await a proper home video/DVD release.

Having sifted my way through many hours of concert material from the *Live Killers* period (Europe 1979), and a good deal more again towards the end of 2004, it is clear the album is a far better representation of events than its two successors ever were – and the less said about *Live Magic* the better. The versions of 'Don't Stop Me Now', 'Spread Your Wings', 'Love Of My Life', 'Now I'm Here', 'Dreamer's Ball', '39' and Roger's blistering 'I'm In Love With My Car', were in my view never surpassed at any other venue on that tour. Queen and John Etchells really did offer us the best recitals.

It is perhaps ironic that despite such relatively few recordings being available to fans, there does exist (in the Queen archive) a volume of material that warrants release – though it is not as simple as I had imagined back in '96, now that I better understand some of the sound issues afflicting certain audio and video tapes.

Shows known to exist on video include Hammersmith Odeon (1975), Hyde Park (1976), Houston, Texas (1977), Paris, Hammersmith and Japan (1979), Brazil and Argentina (1981), Frankfurt and Austria (1982), Japan and Sydney (1985), not to mention the much acclaimed Earls Court performance of June 1977). None of these concerts have ever seen the light of day (legitimately), and none it seems are likely to - in the foreseeable future at least. The Hammersmith Odeon show came very close to being issued on home video at one point, but was ultimately shelved.

The response from fans to the *Rare Live* video compilation of 1989 was a good deal less than enthusiastic. To suggest it was lukewarm would be to overstate it. Although the idea was sound enough, the end result was not. At best the compilation was disappointing, and at worst wholly inadequate and a travesty. Despite some slick editing, the snippets of shows do Queen's live performances little justice, chopping and changing randomly from one concert to another. Watching this video is like watching a television drama while someone else continually flicks around the channels with the remote control.

Fortunately or unfortunately - depending on which side of the music industry fence your sympathies lie - bootleggers were almost always at Queen shows. They have ensured over the years that shows which would otherwise have been enjoyed only by those present at the time are available (in part at least) for all of us to experience. Such unauthorised recordings are illegal, of course, and responsible for colossal losses in revenue each year within the music industry. They can also be a source of great disappointment to fans, as many offer notoriously poor sound quality. Some are so bad as to be completely inaudible. Despite vast numbers having been seized over the years, many continue to flood the market. The current wave of bootlegs are DVDs. Some are surprisingly good, some are even great (Live, the Japan '79 disc), and others are dire. Collectors are advised to exercise caution before buying.

While bootlegs are frowned upon by the music industry as a whole, they are the only means by which fans can gain access to material which would otherwise be unavailable to them. In Queen's case, bootlegging was inevitable. The restricted officially sanctioned concert product gave collectors little choice but to resort to unofficial alternatives. Though it is not my business to condone bootlegs, I also make no apology for the numerous references to them in this book. Without them, this project would have been impossible. Furthermore, had I only the official issues from which to refer, originally, the end result would have lacked details which are the very essence and heart of the Queen live show. A huge wealth of information is available from bootlegs. The performance is heard in all its glory, warts and all, unedited, and exactly as it happened. The listener hears the concert (or most of it) as it was supposed to sound, and did sound, to the audience then present, not a polished studio interpretation.

In 2004, Queen Productions took the unprecedented (I think) step of playing the bootleggers at their own game. Using the official Queenonline web site as a base, the plan offered the top 100 best and most significant Queen

bootlegs as mp3 downloads. I was involved in selecting these titles (with fellow experts Frank Palstra, Andreas Voigts and Frank Hazenberg) and together we chose only the most interesting and with the best sound quality. The first downloadable batch is already available as I write, with the remaining 90 or so to follow over the coming months … or years!

Queen never repeated the same evening's entertainment on two nights running. Although the basic setlist might be similar from one night to the next, the delivery and manner in which certain songs were executed could differ enormously, and frequently did. The same song could very well be performed in a number of different ways, depending on numerous factors: the atmosphere within each venue, the mood within the band and, especially, the rapport between Freddie and the audience.

Many of the setlists herein were compiled using information sent to me by fellow collectors over a 16-year period. As most of them originate from an assortment of bootleg recordings - which are notorious for offering only an edited account of the show they represent, and rarely a complete one - it is likely that some lists, especially early ones, are marginally incomplete or appear in slightly the wrong sequence.

In most cases I was able to cross reference any list which appeared implausible or incomplete, and make the appropriate amendments. However, since there is no definitive Queen concert list to consult, nor anything remotely like it, and given that many shows have not one single bootleg relating to them, it was occasionally necessary to offer instead the most likely setlist. In those instances, details from shows of a similar period which are known to be accurate, were used to compile a very close approximation as to what Queen performed, or to fill in any missing gaps.

Despite having access to over 400 separate fan and collectors' lists from all around the world, I typically encountered the same shows time and time again. While details relating to one show, gained from several different sources, can precisely determine most of the true setlist of a given performance, at the same time, few recordings offer a full show. An educated guess at the entire set is all that can therefore be offered.

In some cases collectors who submitted lists were unaware that some examples they forwarded contained false or misleading information. This was not deliberate. Great numbers of bootlegs do not feature the material they purport to, or they include music recorded from another performance entirely. Such tapes are usually put together to exploit new or unsuspecting fans. The inclusion of one or two rare songs that were not actually performed on a specific night are used to inspire additional sales of a bootleg, sales which would otherwise not have occurred. In extreme cases, material from several shows is strung together and issued as an *enigmatic* recording. Freddie and Brian's between song banter is cunningly excised to make the ploy almost impossible to detect. For this reason, it can be dangerous to rely too heavily upon some information, no matter how credible the source seems.

To confuse the issue yet further, Queen often performed the same songs on two or three consecutive nights, but not always in the same sequence. A song which was not performed in its usual allotted position, will therefore *appear* to be misplaced, but may not be. An illustration of this is the legendary Christmas Eve show of 1975.

Because the band inadvertently missed out 'Seven Seas Of Rhye' during the main set, they instead fitted it in after 'In The Lap Of The Gods', at the end of the show. The bootleg sleeve note details would seem to be inaccurate, especially when compared to other listings of the period, but are in fact correct. Likewise, the addition of (part of) ''39' in the middle of a Magic Tour gig, July 19, 1986, seems greatly conspicuous, until you realise that Brian May celebrated his 39th birthday of that day. Thus, all is seldom what it seems in the spurious and murky world of bootlegs.

There is no foolproof method to determine which lists are accurate and which are unreliable. While the majority of setlist information hereafter is entirely accurate, I do not claim that to be the case in every instance. Where possible the data has been cross referenced six or seven times – and revisited in yet more detail for this extended edition.

In conclusion, I should point out that while some tours (or legs thereof) have huge bootleg representation, others have comparitively little - or none. This factor accounts for the general imbalance of information throughout these pages. I apologise in advance, therefore, for the many entries which appear with little or no accompanying text. It was, even with access now to the full Queen audio archive, entirely unavoidable.

Greg Brooks - August 1995

Freddie Mercury

Prologue

When 'Let Me Entertain You' materialised in 1978, on the *Jazz* album, the lyrics captured in a few short verses the very essence of the Queen live show. The song expresses exactly - though tongue in cheek, as is often the case with a Freddie composition - the atmosphere, theatricality, spectacle and sheer unparalleled excitement one experienced when confronted by Queen live on stage.

Freddie's brief yet faultless summary (invented phrases and all) leaves little to the imagination. He welcomes all ladies and gentlemen, has them dancing in the aisles. With jazz and razzmatazz and a little bit of style, he pulls them and he pills them, he even *crueladevilles* them, and to thrill them he'll use any device. Later he boasts of crazy performance, and grounds for divorce. With sound and amplification and a lot of pretty lights, the piece de resistance, and a tour de force - of course. When Freddie says they'll breakfast at Tiffany's and sing to us in Japanese, he means it.

With this vivid picture he paints, we the fans are transported back in time to the first or last show we attended. Or, if we never got to see Queen in concert, left pondering over what might have been.

Those of us that *were* there, know it all to be true; everything Freddie promised us, Queen delivered – and then some!

We *were* the crueladevilled! Those that were not … those that missed out on the Queen live KILLERS … well … you have the videos and DVDs.

Preface

In a career which spanned three decades, Queen inspired innumerable articles, books and television and radio interviews. Every aspect of their history has been explored in one form or another; every fact, figure, quote, misquote and anecdote used and re-used time and time again, in biographies, newspaper articles and documentaries. As most information on the band was exhausted years ago, predicting the content of each new publication – even before the first page has been turned – has become absurdly, infuriatingly simple.

Despite an extensive library of printed matter, however, very little focuses specifically on Queen's live performances. It was partly for this reason that I first decided to compile this book. What began as a project purely for my own use quickly snowballed into what most people around me regard as a book – though I *still* prefer to call it a Live Study. Although I had anticipated the project would occupy some considerable time,

I did not envisage it taking six years to complete. It was a labour of love from beginning to end.

In undertaking a project such as this, there is a danger of going into too much detail and bordering on monotonous or boring. It is immensely difficult to know exactly where to draw the line between that which is relevant and interesting information, and that which is unnecessary and tedious. I apologise should any of the following text fall into the latter category. In my experience, however, nothing relating to Queen and their concerts, however trivial it might seem, is ever considered boring by the typical fan.

I hope, if nothing else, that this book (now revised) offers an insight into what made Queen such extraordinary concert showmen. It is an avenue of Queen's career which has for too long been overlooked, yet which was such a fundamental part of the band's evolution … as much a part of Queen as 'Bohemian Rhapsody' and black nail varnish.

*This book is dedicated with much love to the
memory of Louise Blake and Phil (Bruce) Cross*

*Both remain a constant source of support
and inspiration - wherever they may be*

Acknowledgements

I am indebted to many individuals who were kind enough to assist me with additional background and cross-referencing for this book (the first pressing and this revised edition). Almost without exception everyone I contacted responded with material used in some form or another. I am grateful to each and every one.

I offer sincere thanks to Ayumi Akahori, Celia Diego Alvarez, Andy Armitage, Basje Asselbergs, Paul Barrett, Walter & Renate Bazen, Paul Bird, Miklos Borbely, Angela Brown, Ron Buczko, Giancarlo Calo, Tom Crossland, Luca Cuoghi, Stan Dwelback, Neil French, Vinnie Garstroke, Richard Guibault, Frank Hazenberg, Colin Humphries, Jon James, Jim Jenkins, Steve Jesson, Inma Pacheco Jimena, George & Shalva Kokochashvili, Keith Lambert, Ernst Larson, Martin Latham, Justin Leiter, Paul Lynas, Jeanette Lea, Richard Mace, Grenville Madison, L. Mattending, Val Moss, Luke Mullens, Colin Naylor, Gary Nolan, Frank Palstra, David Parr, John Bendy-Pett, Mike Phillips, Andrew Reid, Darren Robins, Hannie Roggeveen, Paul Ryan, Mike Skunk-Salter, Antonio Henrique Seligman, Erwin Sijbrands, Skinner, Carole Smith, Jacky Smith, Dylan Taylor, Kim Thomson, Jeffrey Tratliff, Ian Trenfield, Adam Unger, Lee Watkins, Becky Welham, Rinus & Marijan Walstijn, Ron Wheeler and S. Peacock, in Hull (for reasons you might spot in the text?).

Special thanks to Arthur Hardy (for invaluable guidance and encouragement from day one), Greg (Teraitch) Hardy, Carl (Monty) Tyson, Vanessa Florey, BB, Andy Broad (the person responsible for bringing Queen to my attention in the first instance), Iain Wright (for restoring my computer back to a usable state after I had rendered it useless), Beverley, Chris, Charlotte, Emily & Francesca Ludlow, and most especially my mother Rosemary (whose wallpaper and paintwork my copious Queen posters destroyed through the years)

Further thanks and appreciation for help on this revised edition to Chris Charlesworth, Frank Palstra, Frank Hazenberg, Andreas Voigts, Gary Taylor, Mark Hodkinson, Martin Scully, Bob Wegner, Robert Moon, Bill Brown, Chrystel Bandreigh, the mighty Jim Stevenson, Ian Murray, Yuko Terado, Dean Whittaker, Chris Whittaker, Justin Shirley-Smith, Kris Fredriksson, Richard Gray, Wayne Bowtrout, Jeanathon Howard, William Page, JP (Ginger) Page.

And to the inimitable Brian May (for access to a wondrous archive and for his encouragement and kind Foreword).

Extra special thanks to Marie Whittaker for exemplary work on this revised edition above and beyond the call of duty. Genuine appreciation and recognition to you MW.

A proportion of incidental information in this book was extracted from Queen Fan Club magazines. Contact Jacky or Val at:

THE OFFICIAL INTERNATIONAL QUEEN FAN CLUB
The Old Bakehouse, 16a Barnes High Street, Barnes. London SW13, ENGLAND
Tel: 0208 392 2800

Queenonline.com- The official Queen web site

Brian May's personal website can be found at **Brianmay.com**
The site includes the ever popular Brian's Soapbox; a two-way dialogue with correspondents from all around the world, plus Queen and BM news and features, as well as comment on a host of other topics. Updated every day.

BREAKTHRU - The Queen Online Community
A fun and friendly fan site - with weekly chat nights.
http://groups.msn.com/BreakthruTheQUEENonlinecommunity

KEY

● A quote (excluding Freddie, Brian and Roger's on-stage audience addresses)

❖ A product is released

■ A concert setlist (× 309)

● An author's note

◀» A BBC Session (× 6)

↗ A newspaper review

♫ A notable concert (a favourite among fans – and/or a widely bootlegged gig) (× 123)

① This concert was Queen's first in this country (× 27

Queen's very first live performances are regarded not so much as concerts, but as informal gatherings of friends, fellow students and college acquaintances. Unlike conventional shows, tickets are distributed only to individuals who can be relied upon for constructive critical feedback. The band encourage feedback, good and bad, from all who attend.

It is not until February 1971, after three bassists have been tried and found wanting, that John Deacon joins the band. The first, Mike Grose, leaves in early August 1970, after just three shows.

● "I left Queen because I'd had enough of playing, basically. I had just got to that point. We weren't earning any money to speak of, and we were living in squalor. I just didn't want to be part of it any more. Brian had another year of his studies to go, and so did Roger, and I thought 'to hell with it'."

Mike's departure is amicable. As Queen have a gig pencilled in for August 23, a replacement is required urgently, and it comes in the form of London-based Barry Mitchell, who remains for six months. His last performances are on January 8 and 9, 1971, when Queen play alongside Genesis as support to Kevin Ayres and The Whole World Band.

● Barry Mitchell: "The band struck me as being heavily into Led Zeppelin and Hendrix and in some respects they sounded a lot like Zeppelin. I was *in* straight away, after the first rehearsal. They just checked me out to see whether I could play or not.

"I didn't think they were going anywhere. It never struck me as being great. It never felt like that for me. They were striving for something that was already there - Led Zeppelin. But I didn't want to go there, I wanted to do something different."

The next bass player, Doug Bogie, lasts only two performances before being sacked for stealing the coveted centre stage position at the show on February 20.

By late February, it seems unlikely that a compatible bassist will be found. Salvation comes when Brian, Roger and a friend, John Harris, meet John Deacon at a local disco. John auditions at Imperial College soon thereafter and is hastily recruited, thus completing the quartet that would ultimately remain together for three months short of twenty-one years.

● Brian: "It was a question of not being able to find the right man at the beginning. We tried a few people. Deacy was just a natural, really. We thought he was a spectacular bass player. We were really pleased."

Four months of intensive rehearsals follow before the new line-up is ready to perform its first shows in July. The gigs are typically attended by sixty or seventy people and provide Queen with an opportunity to gauge valuable audience reaction and comment. An invitation for one show asks guests to attend *'a good time with good music, from a band who desperately need an opinion.'*

Precise details regarding the material Queen perform during this period, are sketchy. Very little is documented and recollections from those who were there are similarly vague. They play a combination of their own compositions and covers of other peoples' material - as Smile had done at their shows. These covers include songs by Buddy Holly, James Brown, The Everly Brothers, The Yardbirds and The Rolling Stones, all of whom had been major musical influences on the four band members, especially, in Brian's case, Eric Clapton. Brian would much later dedicate a solo composition to him ('Bluesbreaker' on the 1983 'Star Fleet' project).

Queen also play material by Elvis Presley, Gene Vincent, Little Richard, Rick Nelson, Shirley Bassey, Bill Haley and The Spencer Davis Group. Only when a satisfactory following has been established, and they regard themselves as completely ready, do they introduce more of their own material – which does exist, even at this time.

● Brian: "You can only get so far in playing to

audiences who don't understand what you're doing, so we did more heavy rock'n'roll with the Queen delivery to give people something they could get hold of... get on, sock it to 'em, get off. If you go on stage and people don't know your material, you can get boring."

Although a great many cover versions feature in the set (typically: 'Jailhouse Rock', 'Be Bop A Lula', 'Shake Rattle And Roll', 'Stupid Cupid', 'Bama Lama Bama Loo' and 'Big Spender'), the band also include two of their own (original) compositions and segments of experimental material which had worked best during rehearsals. One of these pieces began life during Ibex days - Freddie Mercury's pre-Queen group. 'Lover' is developed slowly and eventually emerges with the new title 'Liar' – which makes it onto the debut album two years later.

Another song, which the band use to open show, is called 'Stone Cold Crazy', and this too surfaces later on an album; in a significantly honed form on *Sheer Heart Attack*, 1974, where it credited to all four members of the band - the first time this occurred. Evidently, the track underwent so many changes during its development that no-one could recall who actually wrote which parts.

Queen experiment with early arrangements of songs that will one day feature on albums, and other pieces which will ultimately fall by the wayside. In addition to well-known songs like 'Keep Yourself Alive' and 'Doing All Right' (a song written by Brian May and Tim Staffell, and actually recorded by Smile), the band frequently perform an enigmatic song called 'Hangman'. This features only in early concerts (up to April 1976) and never surfaces on any album - it does not even survive on any studio session tape. It does, however, feature on numerous bootlegs, such as *Queen Invite You To A Night At The Budokan*, *Mercury Poisoning* and *Year Of The Opera*.

The track 'Shag Out', which occasionally appears on collectors' lists, and always causes confusion, is not actually a song as such, but a segment from 'Hangman'. At some stage a short Queen live guitar/drum extract (without vocals) is featured on a bootleg, and it is likely that the bootleggers invented the title 'Shag Out' then.

With the emergence in May 1991 of Freddie's biblical tale 'Mad The Swine' (a track left off the début album because of a difference of opinion between Queen and producer Roy Thomas Baker), and the so called 'Long Lost' re-take of 'Keep Yourself Alive' cropping up on a Hollywood Records compact disc that same year, it is evident that Queen recorded more material in this early period than they remember (or will admit to). There has always been specualtion about this particular prospect; what exists in the archive, what doesn't, and the extent and quality of any out-takes or alternative versions. Only the arrival of the proposed, but as yet unscheduled *Queen Anthology* sets will give up these secrets and provide the fans with the answers they so desperate want. Suffice to say that it is categorically *not* the case that the archive is devoid of early recordings worthy of release one day. There *are* interesting items therein, it's just that the Queen camp is playing its cards close to its chest until the right time.

In addition to live performances and studying, the band rehearse in the Imperial College lecture theatre three or four times a week. Brian is regarded as a trustworthy student by the college management, who permit him to use the facilities. It is during this period that Queen begin to assemble a modest but loyal team of helpers to assist with concert preparation, lighting and sound. John Harris is one of the first, and over the coming months and years will prove to be a pivotal member of the crew, providing, not least, vital stability to ever growing show. He remains with Queen for many years and witnesses innumerable concerts.

In 1975 Roger dedicates 'I'm In Love With My Car' (from *A Night At The Opera*) to John Harris. The *Jazz* album in 1978 is also dedicated to him.

Although the group's budget will eventually allow them to employ the services of Zandra Rhodes to design their stage attire, for the time being they utilise Freddie's design training by adapting clothes and jewellery from his and Roger's stall in Kensington Market.

On September 18, 1970, Freddie and Roger close the stall as a mark of respect to their hero Jimi Hendrix, who died that day. They are devastated. Freddie cries when he hears the news. That night Queen perform 'Voodoo Chile' in rehearsals as a further gesture of respect. Three weeks later the same song reaches number one in the British charts. It is the only time Hendrix reaches the top of the singles chart.

June 27
City Hall, Truro, Cornwall, England ①

This is the very first concert using the name Queen, despite the local Cornish papers billing them under their former name, Smile. This is due to the event having been arranged a good while earlier, by Roger Taylor's mother, when the foursome were still known as Smile – the Tim Staffell, Roger Taylor, Brian May group which had in fact disbanded some time earlier.

This show pre-dates the arrival of John Deacon by a full year.

July 12
Imperial College, London

Rather appropriately, since this venue is truly Queen's college *home*, this is the first gig where Freddie's suggestion for group name is used on the promotional flyers and modest press notices of the day. From here on, of course, that element never changes.

July 18
Imperial College, London

Freddie is already beginning to think about the band image and Queen *branding* at this time, for he designs the hand-drawn ticket for this show.

Significantly, it features the word 'Queen' in similar typeface to that which will later adorn the earliest record sleeves and press releases. The ticket he creates even includes a map showing the college's proximity to South Kensington tube station. It reads: *'Queen invite you to a private showing at Imperial College New Block, Imperial Institute Road, Level 5, Lecture Theatre A, on Sunday 18 July'.*

July 25
PJ's Club, Truro, Cornwall

August 23
Imperial College, London

September 4
Swiss Cottage Private School, London

October 16
College of Estates Management Hall, London

October 30
College of Technology, St Helens, Merseyside

October 31
Cavern Club, Liverpool

November 14
Balls Park College, Hertford, Hertfordshire

December 5
Shoreditch College, Egham, Surrey

December 18
College of Technology, St Helens, Merseyside

December 19
Congregational Church Hall, St Helens, Merseyside

The four members develop Queen through 1971, slowly honing their image and crafting the show and set repertoire, but all the while continuing college studies and rehearsals.

Queen's reputation begins to grow steadily, but even so, John and Brian, more so than Freddie and Roger, are as yet unwilling to commit themselves exclusively to the band. They rehearse only when all four members are available at the same time. Though Freddie and Roger have their hearts set on a rock and roll career, Brian and John still regard Queen as a venture to occupy free time between studies. It will take the *Queen II* album, in Brian's case, and *Sheer Heart Attack*, in John's, before all four men (and their parents) are convinced a rock band can be a full-time occupation, a 'proper job', from which a decent living can be earned.

In an attempt to attract more interest and additional bookings, in September Brian arranges another show at Imperial College. Though most of the invited agency-related audience attend, no bookings are forthcoming. A somewhat disillusioned Queen find themselves in need of a boost in morale.

The break comes when a friend of Brian's, working for Pye Studios, mentions that his company are seeking a group to test out the facilities of its new Wembley-based recording studio. Queen are exactly what they need.

Days later the band are at De Lane Lea Studios putting the equipment through its paces. In return for their time, they are permitted to record demonstration tapes with which they will subsequently approach record companies.

It is at De Lane Lea that the band are seen by producers John Anthony and Roy Thomas Baker, who subsequently recommend them to Trident Studios co-owners Barry and Norman Sheffield. Although Anthony remembers Brian and Roger from Smile's recording days, it is a slick rendition

of 'Keep Yourself Alive' that impresses him and his colleague.

From October 6 until the end of the year, Queen play mostly college gigs, utilising a repertoire that remains a combination of rock'n'roll cover versions and self-penned material. A typical set of the time includes 'Liar', 'Son & Daughter', 'Doing All Right', 'Jesus', 'Hangman', 'Stone Cold Crazy', 'Keep Yourself Alive' and 'Jailhouse Rock'. The covers are performed during the first encore, and 'See What A Fool I've Been' as a second encore, but only infrequently. 'The Night Comes Down' also features, but not regularly.

'Liar' occasionally changes position to conclude the show, and 'Son & Daughter' and 'Keep Yourself Alive' are both considerably accelerated renderings to those which later appear on the eponymously titled début album.

'Keep Yourself Alive', a concert favourite thoughout Queen's fifteen years as a touring band, will undergo many changes before it reaches the form that will eventually be recorded. Brian's song will become the LP's opening track and, most importantly, also the band's first single (released in July 1973).

Roger Taylor

A fascinating insight into one of these versions emerges in 1991, when the four-minute so-called 'Long Lost Re-Take' is added as a bonus track to Hollywood Records' 'Queen' compact disc. A short sleeve note from Brian reads: "*This is a complete remake of 'Keep Yourself Alive'. This version never surfaced anywhere. It contains many new ideas and quirks, as well as reproductions of some of the old ones.*"

These early live renditions of 'Keep Yourself Alive' gradually begin to incorporate examples of crowd participation, of which Freddie will become a master. As the concert repertoire grows, so too do opportunities for this aspiring showman to manipulate and converse with his audience.

By no means a frequent supplement to the set is the mysterious 'See What A Fool I've Been' which never appears on any studio album and for a long period only available as B-side to 'Seven Seas Of Rhye'. When it is performed live it features late in the set or else as an encore, and at no time does Freddie go into its origins. Brian May is credited as the composer, but in many years later he reveals that the song was inspired by an old blues number by Brownie McGhee & Sonny Terry that he saw performed live on television. Research will ultimately confirm the song to be 'That's How I Feel'.

If 'Liar' does not conclude the show, Queen close instead with 'Jailhouse Rock', 'Stupid Cupid' or 'Bama Lama Bama Loo'. A typical concert spans forty or fifty minutes. In contrast, the shows performed on the final tour, in 1986, run to three times that length.

January 8
Marquee Club, London

January 9
Technical College, Ewell, Surrey

Other bands playing at this venue include Genesis, Kevin Ayres & The Whole World Band and Flying Fortress.

Close band friend Ken Testi records this concert, on a Grundig reel-to-reel tape recorder, but due to a technical fault only the rock'n'roll medley survives. Everything else is lost. This tape is now said to reside in the personal collection of ex-Queen bass player Barry Mitchell.

February 19
Hornsey Town Hall, London

February 20
Kingston Polytechnic, London

July 2
Surrey College, Surrey

This is John Deacon's first concert as Queen's bassist. The evening is marred somewhat by a disagreement relating to stage attire between he and Freddie. Like those before him, Deacon John (as he will soon be christened) is a strictly jeans and t-shirt man, but Freddie has other, more grand ideas. He prefers smart dress (that's 'smart dress', not 'a' smart dress!) and thereafter gives the whole subject of band stage attire and image his serious consideration.

From this day on – to the very last Queen concert on August 9, 1986 – the band line-up remains the same. Neither of the four members misses one single live performance. The same may not be true of studio recording sessions!

July 11
Imperial College, London

Queen begin an 11-date tour of Cornwall, which Roger has arranged through his various contacts in the area - hence the band are frequently billed as 'Roger Taylor and Queen'.

The tour culminates at the Tregaye Festival of Contemporary Music, on August 21.

July 17
The Garden, Penzance, Cornwall

July 19
Rugby Club, Hayle, Cornwall

July 24
Young Farmers' Club, Wadebridge, Cornwall

July 29
The Garden, Penzance, Cornwall

July 31
City Hall, Truro, Cornwall

August 2
Rugby Club, Hayle, Cornwall

August 9
Driftwood Spars, St Agnes, Cornwall

August 12
Tregye Hotel, Truro, Cornwall

August 14
NCO's Mess, RAF Culdrose, Truro, Cornwall

August 17
City Hall, Truro, Cornwall

August 21
Carnon Downs Festival, Tregye, Cornwall
   Though they open this festival, Queen are second from bottom on the bill, with only Barracuda beneath them.
   Arthur Brown's Kingdom Come is the headline act, followed by Hawkwind, The Duster Bennett Band, Tea And Symphony, Brewer's Droop, Indian Summer and Graphite.

October 6
Imperial College, London

December 9
Swimming Baths, Epsom, Surrey

December 31
Rugby Club, Twickenham, London
1971 concludes with a New Year's Eve gig at the London Rugby Club.

1972

Queen perform only five shows in 1972. This is due to academic studies, personal commitments and lengthy negotiations with would-be managers, brothers Norman and Barry Sheffield. Ultimately the Sheffield's sign the band to their Trident Audio Productions Company later in the year. Untimately, this proves to be an unfortunate liaison for Queen that will result in great anguish in the future. On a positive note, however, the Sheffield 'situation' does later inspire Freddie to write an extraordinary song for *A Night At The Opera*, featuring a vituoso piano performance from him and giving the band a much loved composition for the live show.

   Prior to Trident's interest, Queen spend much of early 1972 approaching record companies with the demonstration tapes they recorded at De Lane Lea Studios. They have little success and become not a little disillusioned.

The tapes are produced by Louis Austin and contain versions of 'Keep Yourself Alive', 'Liar', 'Jesus', 'Great King Rat' and 'The Night Comes Down'. The quality of the last take is such that it is eventually used on the début album, hence the album's only production credit to Louis Austin.

   By the end of 1972 Queen will finish recording their self-titled début album. They use Trident Studios, in St Anne's Court, Soho, the facility owned by their management company. The drawback is that they cannot create their music in the regular way, but only only in 'downtime' periods - when the studio is not required by paying customers, or when a room becomes unexpectedly available. The irregular (cheap) nature of these tiresome sessions does little to inspire confidence between the band and the Sheffield's.

🗨 Brian May: "They would call us up and say David Bowie's finished a few hours early, so

John Deacon

you've got from 3.00 am to 7.00 am, when the cleaners come in, to do a bit – if you want to come in now boys. A lot of it was done that way. There were a few full days, but mainly bits and pieces."

Despite the frustration of working within the management-imposed limitations of downtime, Queen do manage to record some remarkable music, as the (late and very great) Mike Stone (Trident sound engineer) later recalled.

● "That first album was completely different to anything else I had been doing. The remixes took ages and ages, and the band all seemed such perfectionists that every little squeak had to be just right. It was quite nerve-racking working with a born superstar on the first major work I had engineered."

On November 1 the band sign a recording contract with Trident, committing all material recorded up to that point, and a number thereafter, to the company. In return Trident will negotiate the best available distribution deal on Queen's behalf. Eventually, in March 1973, a deal with EMI is secured. They had previously been

offered a deal by Chrysalis Records, but they decline it on the grounds that the advance is insufficient.

By late November, the often arduous recording sessions are at last at an end. Despite the unusual schedule, both band and record company are pleased with the final product. Queen waste no time in starting on plans for the second album, not realising that an incredible period of frustration will now follow before the first album reaches the shops.

January 28
Bedford College, London

The first show of the year at Bedford College is organised by John Deacon. Only six paying customers attend and John later cites it as one of the most embarrassing experiences of his life. The four remaining gigs are all London based.

March 10
King's College Hospital, London

■ *Son and Daughter / Great King Rat / Jesus / The Night Comes Down / Liar / Keep Yourself Alive / See What A Fool I've Been / Stone Cold Crazy / Hangman / Jailhouse Rock / Bama Lama Bama Loo*

This is the earliest Queen concert from which the original handwritten setlist survives to this day. Written by Freddie (on Trident internal memo paper), and no doubt discarded at the time like one might dispose of litter, this scrap of paper (which only emerged recently) is among the rarest and most precious of all Queen concert memorabilia. Not only does it offer definitive details of the songs performed, but significantly it confirms that both 'Jesus' and 'The Night Comes Down' were indeed played live, as was suspected, but could not be confirmed.

March 24
Forest Hill Hospital, London

This show is attended by Barry Sheffield, who until this point has only heard Queen's five-song demo tape and is taking up John Anthony's recommendation to see them live before

on stage get this showcase gig off to a poor start. John Deacon and the ever loyal John Harris desperately scramble to wire everything up in time, but technical problems blight this important show. It is probably just as well that not one of the invited record company A&R people actually turn up.

🗩 Queen Manager Norman Sheffield: "It was a disastrous gig. Four great players – the talent within the four was absolutely totally apparent to me. But as a unit, it was pretty scruffy."

December 20
The Marquee Club, London

A cassette of this show, though emerging late in 2001, makes this the earliest Queen concert bootleg yet to have surfaced. However, upon closer inspection, it is more likely to be a compilation of material taken from numerous other, later recordings, and not the significant find it first seemed. The tape contains no Freddie between-song banter, which is suspicious, and cuts, frustratingly, at the points when clues would be present.

committing his company to a deal. Sheffield realises Anthony's claims are not exaggerated, and Queen finally sign to Trident in November.

November 6
The Pheasantry Club, London

Problems resulting from the PA system arriving at the venue only an hour before Queen are due

1973

February 5
Langham 1 Studio, London
◀ *My Fairy King / Keep Yourself Alive / Doing All Right / Liar*

Queen attend Langham 1 Studio in London to record their first session for the BBC. It will be the first of six in all, and is organised by Trident. Bernie Andrews produces the session with John Etchells as engineer.

A proportion of the material committed to tape is significantly different to that already recorded for the début album – which won't be released for another five months.

Because of limited production time, which

would normally have seen additional layers of percussion, guitar and vocal harmonies added to the mix, 'My Fairy King' emerges somewhat less fussy than the album cut. The lead and backing vocals are much clearer and Freddie's subtle piano parts are more defined. While 'Keep Yourself Alive' and the Smile refugee 'Doing All Right' are reproduced almost note for note, 'Liar' contains vocal ad-libs from Freddie which are not on the album. As you might expect, the LP rendition is the better of the two.

For an entirely alternative approach to 'Liar', albeit not an authentic 1973 one, Hollywood Records *Queen* compact disc of 1991 offers the definitive example. Remixed by John Luongo and Gary Hellman, a six and a half minute interpretation offers a club/dance-type heavily guitar-oriented mix, and brings previously less dominant incidental instruments such as tambourine and maracas very much to the fore, as they are much higher up in the mix. The bongo drum accompaniment is a nice touch too. This is not the purists' cup of tea, for sure, but it is certainly *alternative*.

This BBC session was broadcast ten days after recording, on John Peel's Radio One show, as part of the *Sounds Of The Seventies* series.

Although originally booked for only one session, Queen return a further five times – the last ocassion being in 1977. To date only two of the sessions have emerged officially (numbers one and three), released as *Queen At The Beeb* in December 1989. Despite the album's sleevenote advice to the contrary, bootleg copies of most of the tracks *have* been easy to access for years.

Queen record 24 tracks in all for the BBC, between 1973 and 1977:

Session 1: My Fairy King, Keep Yourself Alive, Doing All Right, Liar / **Session 2**: See What A Fool I've Been, Liar, Son & Daughter, Keep Yourself Alive / **Session 3**: Ogre Battle, Great King Rat, Modern Times Rock'n'Roll, Son & Daughter / **Session 4**: Modern Times Rock'n'Roll, The March Of The Black Queen, Nevermore, White Queen / **Session 5**: Now I'm Here, Stone Cold Crazy, Flick Of The Wrist, Tenement Funster / **Session 6**: Spread Your Wings, It's Late, My Melancholy Blues, We Will Rock You.

There is some confusion as to which studio Queen used to record the first session, but it is definitely Langham 1 Studio, and not Maida Vale. Ken Norman's *The Complete BBC Sessions*, which details every session ever recorded for the BBC, provides conclusive evidence.

April 9
Marquee Club, Wardour Street, London
■ *Father To Son / Son & Daughter / Doing All Right / Hangman / Stone Cold Crazy / Keep Yourself Alive / Liar / Jailhouse Rock / Encore: Be Bop A Lula*
'Father To Son' now begins the show, and 'Liar' instead concludes it.

This show is set up as a showcase event for Elektra executive Jack Holtzman, who may sign the band, but first wants to see them perform live.

Queen's newly appointed publicist, Tony Brainsby, asks his assistant John Bagnall to attend this concert. He later recalls:
● "It really was the embryonic Queen stage act that night. I remember going backstage afterwards and seeing Freddie slumped in their dressing room, physically shattered by the act. What I remember most clearly is that as he was changing, I saw that his legs were absolutely black with bruises, and he explained that that was where he had been slapping his thighs with a tambourine during different numbers. I think that was the first time I ever had a real awareness of how much physical pain and effort could go into such a stage performance."

July 6
❖ Queen's début single 'Keep Yourself Alive' is issued in the UK - coupled with 'Son & Daughter'. Both are Brian May compositions. The same pairing is issued in Japan and America too, and each disc sports a picture sleeve (something curiously not offered at home) which will soon become greatly sought-after. Fanatical interest in collecting Queen memorabilia, particularly rare foreign singles, is born at this point. Little does anyone know; the band are about to become one of the most collected groups in the world.

When Queen are told that 'Keep Yourself Alive' failed to chart because it "takes too long to happen" (a reference to the intro), they decide the follow-up single will, if nothing else, feature an introduction that cannot be ignored.
● Brian: "We said, 'Right, in the next one we're gonna put everything into the first ten seconds'. So we did that. You can hear in 'Seven Seas Of Rhye' the piano thing, then you hear these monstrous guitar swoops come in, and then you get this big crunch and the beat starts. So everything has happened in the first eight seconds of the record. We said if this doesn't get them – nothing will."

July 13

Queen Mary College, Basingstoke, Hampshire

■ *Father To Son / Son & Daughter / Ogre Battle / Doing All Right / Hangman / Stone Cold Crazy / Keep Yourself Alive / Liar / Jailhouse Rock / Encore: Be Bop A Lula*

❖ Also on July 13, EMI release Queen's eponymously titled début album in the UK.

This body of work might easily have emerged instead as 'Top Fax, Pix and Info' or 'Deary Me', had it been left to Roger Taylor or Roy Baker, but thankfully Freddie fights hard for *Queen*, with Brian on side, and it is that which prevails.

Freddie tells the audience about the new single and album during the show. He also expresses irritation at the album's delay, part of which is due to minor printing errors on the sleeve notes which Queen insisted be rectified. A note on the LP reads: *'Representing at last something of what Queen music has been over the last three years.'*

The American LP release did not follow until September 4, where despite considerable promotional backing, it only reached number 83. It fared rather better at home, climbing to number 24.

As will become evident throughout this book, each new Queen album contains material which is never included in the live shows of the day. Although some of it would surely have converted well to the stage, had it been given the opportunity, in most cases it is never even tried once. Most of the forsaken material progresses no further than band rehearsals.

Several of these omissions are inexplicable, and the début album is no exception. Brian May's beautiful 'The Night Comes Down' should have been an obvious choice for concert repertoire, especially since Queen invariably took to the stage just before or after darkness had fallen. Many fans regard this track as one of the album high points, yet it was overlooked for the show.

Freddie's 'Seven Seas Of Rhye', though featuring on the first album, does so only in vocal-less form – at the end of side two. Simply, it was not finished in time for the début work, thus

explaining its concert absence during this period. When the song was finally completed, for *Queen II* in 1974, it was immediately featured in concert. Moreover, it became a single in February of that year and gave the band their first UK and international hit.

The most glaring absentees, however, are Freddie's 'My Fairy King' and the album's penultimate track 'Jesus', both of which epitomise the early Queen sound, with stunning guitar and piano work, and driving bass and drums. Both songs feature only rarely in the show.

Another song from this period curiously ignored (and yet another Freddie composition with a biblical theme) is 'Mad The Swine'. Though intended for the début album, and actually recorded, it is ultimately dropped when band and producer (Roy Thomas Baker) cannot agree on the mix (the percussion sound, evidently). Quite why the track could not be issued as a non-album B-side, like 'See What A Fool I've Been', is baffling to say the least. 'Mad' would have been a wonderful addition to the concert repertoire of this period, so why on earth it was ignored remains a total mystery.

These songs are just the first in a catalogue of some 50+ titles which never – for reasons known only to the band – feature in a Queen concert... or if they do, they do so only once.

While there will always be a proportion of material on every album that cannot possibly be recreated in the concert environment (in full at least), some of the band's selections over the years are certainly inexplicable. The other side of this coin, it has to be said, are some of the songs that *were* played – some inordinately unlikely contenders among them. Some of those are equally unfathomable.

July 24

'Keep Yourself Alive' is featured on the BBC's *Old Grey Whistle Test*.

Since producer Mike Appleton has only an anonymous white label test pressing of the début album in his office, he is unaware of the identity of the artist. Nevertheless, he commissions visual accompaniment from the BBC archive, and this comes in the form of an unusual piece of election campaign footage once used by President Franklin Roosevelt. Having seen the broadcast, staff at both Trident and EMI call the BBC to inform them it's Queen.

July 25
Langham 1 Studio, London
◄▮ *See What A Fool I've Been / Liar / Son & Daughter / Keep Yourself Alive*

Queen attend Langham 1 Studios again to record their second session for the BBC. It is produced by Jeff Griffin and Chris Lycett, and engineered by John Etchells.

The band record further versions of 'Liar' and 'Keep Yourself Alive', as they had in February, and a fresh rendering of 'Son & Daughter'. Though Brian's 'See What A Fool I've Been' is not included on the album, it does feature in the live set and is therefore a logical choice for this session.

Three of the tracks are transmitted on August 13, and 'Keep Yourself Alive' on September 24, on the Bob Harris show, again as part of the *Sounds Of The Seventies* series.

Langham 1 Studios, the venue for Queen's first four BBC sessions, was only ever intended to be a temporary recording location, while the Maida Vale studio underwent refurbishment. However, it remained in almost constant use right up until 1981.

August

The band return to Trident Studios to begin work on what will become *Queen II*. This time they record under proper conditions, not in downtime, and progress much more efficiently. They cover a great deal of ground and capture on tape faithful renditions of the material they have been playing live and experimenting with in rehearsals. They try many new techniques, most of which were too time-consuming to be attempted during the previous album sessions, and they learn in meticulous detail all about what a recording studio can offer an imaginative band and producer team. The entire album is recorded during August.

September 13 ♪
Golders Green Hippodrome, London
■ *Procession / Father To Son / Son & Daughter / Ogre Battle / Hangman / Stone Cold Crazy / Keep Yourself Alive / Liar / See What A Fool I've Been / Encore Medley: Jailhouse Rock; Stupid Cupid; Bama Lama Bama Loo; Jailhouse Rock (reprise)*

The show now opens with a pre-recorded passage of music just recorded for the new album. It is the very first time a tape features in a Queen concert, but certainly not be the last. The band will use this method many times over the coming years.

Brian's eerie, medieval-sounding 'Procession' begins as the house lights suddenly dim. The band make their way in darkness to their respective stage positions, in time for Freddie's opening words of the night: "A word in your ear... from father to son."

'Father To Son' contains guitar riffs and flights of fancy from Brian absent on the *Queen II* cut. This composition was *made* for the concert domain, and offords Freddie all that he needs to make a lasting impression on the audience. His delivery of the lyrics is menacing and his stage presence thrilling. This becomes a favourite of the fans, and later, a much loved album highlight too.

No time is wasted on introductions between

songs as Freddie moves straight into 'Son & Daughter', Brian's début album tale of teenage insurrection. Although the album version of this includes the line "The world expects a man to buckle down and shovel shit", in concert Freddie instead sings "A woman expects a man to buckle down and shovel it."

In order to give a song, *any* song, a fresh slant, Freddie often sings alternative lyrics, and likewise the guitar arrangements on certain tracks changes quite dramatically too over these formative years. It is for this reason that some of these early live recordings sound almost like demo versions at times. 'Son & Daughter', for example, clearly underwent significant changes along the way, and the version performed here, and in subsequent concerts, contains what is essentially the origins of the 'Brighton Rock' guitar solo.

Some bootlegs of this show contain 'See What A Fool I've Been' at this point in the set, but it is actually played much later in the show.

Next up is the somewhat frantic 'Ogre Battle', whose lyrics become at times indecipherable in concert. Even so, Freddie's inimitable handling of his own lyric, make this a notable recital.

'Liar' begins with a drum solo introduction from Roger, before Brian and John join him, and the song quickly builds to the opening vocals.

Unlike the studio version of 'Keep Yourself Alive', the live renditions during this period commence with a drum solo too, instead of guitar from Brian. It also features an occasional mid-song drum solo, in which Roger demonstrates that every part of his kit is there for a reason, and not just for ostentation.

The rock'n'roll medley here is a classic example of Queen's early delivery and style – not to mention camp and tongue-in-cheek qualities.

The show is recorded by the BBC for an *In Concert* broadcast, and a forty minute edit is transmitted the following month, on October 20, on Radio 1. The transmission yields many bootlegs, most notably *Queen On The Green*. Originally available on vinyl only, it now circulates in both audio cassette and CD formats.

Since so few first or second generation tapes exist, contemporary purchases are usually disappointing. New collectors are unwittingly buying copies of copies, of yet further copies (as is so often the case), hence the appalling sound quality. The chances of locating good quality copies now are remote. (Having said that, however, in 2004 I came across an original BBC transcription copy, in prestine condition, featuring the long forgotten Radio 1 announcer of the time, and snapped it up with all haste.)

📢 BBC Producer Jeff Griffin: "At Golders Green Hippodrome we recorded Queen's first live-ish concert session – compered by Alan Black. They didn't do the whole hour; I had Peter Skellern as the support. I must admit now that it seems a bit of a bizarre combination.

"Queen were good on that. What I do remember about it, is thinking that during rehearsals and during the concert, though I thought they were very good, Freddie himself showed some signs of nervousness - not altogether surprising, because I don't think at that stage they had done a lot of live work.

"That show went down very well and got a lot of interest."

October 13
The Underground Club, Bad Godesburg, Bonn, Germany ①

■ *Procession / Father To Son / Son & Daughter / Ogre Battle / Hangman / Stone Cold Crazy / Keep Yourself Alive / Liar / See What A Fool I've Been / Encore Medley: Jailhouse Rock; Stupid Cupid; Big Spender; Bama Lama Bama Loo; Jailhouse Rock (Reprise)*

Queen's very first concert outside the United Kingdom is a free show.

Again, as with much of Queen's early concert material, 'Liar' is performed rather differently from the version recorded for the début album issued three months earlier. There is no *typical* version as such. Instead the band play slight variations around the same theme, rather like Brian would later do during 'Brighton Rock'.

Early versions of 'Liar' are essentially a combination of whatever works best during rehearsals, and the ideas which evoke the best reaction in concert. No two live recordings of the song from this period are identical. In later concerts the track would retain a more rigid structure.

For 'Ogre Battle' Freddie invariably invites the audience to accompany him to the battlefield, and so begins the mythological tale of ogre men inside two-way mirror mountains, and the like. The song is one of Queen's busiest, and loudest, and strangest, on vinyl, and live recitals are equally boisterous and hard on the ears.

Only segments of this show seem to have survived on bootleg recordings. Two examples have the first three tracks missing. If the recording which currently circulates is indeed from this show – which is questionable – then it is worth acquiring. The medley sequence is outstanding, especially 'Big Spender' and 'Bama Lama'

October 14
Le Blow Up Club, Luxembourg ①
■ *Procession / Father To Son / Son & Daughter / Ogre Battle / Hangman / Stone Cold Crazy / Keep Yourself Alive / Liar / See What A Fool I've Been / Encore Medley: Jailhouse Rock; Stupid Cupid; Bama Lama Bama Loo; Jailhouse Rock (Reprise)*

This show was to be broadcast as a Radio Luxembourg *In Concert* special, but the recording equipment fails and nothing is recorded.

October 20
Paris Theatre, London

This show is rumoured to have been recorded by Radio 1 for an *In Concert* broadcast too – presumably because the first attempt, a week earlier, failed. But since no good quality bootlegs from it have ever appeared, as would certainly have been the case, it is unlikely that it was ever transmitted. The programme was supposedly aired at some point late in October '73.

A recording from this show does exist, but the poor sound quality suggests it was made by a member of the audience.

October 26
Imperial College, London
■ *Procession / Father To Son / Son & Daughter / Ogre Battle / Hangman / Stone Cold Crazy / Keep Yourself Alive / Liar / See What A Fool I've Been / Encore Medley: Jailhouse Rock; Shake Rattle And Roll; Stupid Cupid; Bama Lama Bama Loo; Jailhouse Rock (Reprise) / 2nd Encore: Big Spender*

🗭 This show is attended by EMI's Paul Watts who is anxious to see his company's latest signing. "It was simply amazing. Their stage performance was superb, as was their music, and the rapport they built up with the audience was fantastic."

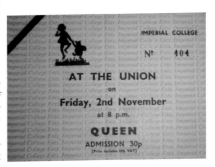

November 2
Imperial College, London
■ *Procession / Father To Son / Son & Daughter / Ogre Battle / Hangman / Stone Cold Crazy / Keep Yourself Alive / Liar / See What A Fool I've Been / Encore Medley: Jailhouse Rock; Stupid Cupid; Bama Lama Bama Loo; Jailhouse Rock (Reprise)*

Queen perform this concert as a last minute rehearsal for the tour due to begin in ten days time. The sell-out show is attended by a host of music journalists, one of whom, Rosemary Horride, later writes:

🡕 *'The atmosphere in the hall was electric, the kids*

were with Queen all the way. The group were musically very good, their stage presence was excellent and when you consider that the material was all their own, it was a remarkable performance. It was obvious how hard the band have worked at entertaining, by the tremendous rapport that was established.'

Such complimentary reviews prove to be the exception, rather than the rule, for Queen, because from this moment on most reviews highlight only the low points of the show and technical problems, and blatantly ignore the good points. While a less than satisfactory performance always guarantees a poor review, a faultless one rarely and curiously inspires the reverse.

In subsequent years, the British press in particular will take great exception to Queen's reluctance to give interviews, especially during the two to three years leading up to Freddie's death. This reluctance stems from the biased and loaded reviews they receive as far back as this era.

Misquote after misquote, seemingly endless exaggerated "darlings" and "dears", and tedious 'camping up' of everything Freddie says and does typically dominate each article. Ranging anywhere between generally grudging, to outright insulting, if not slanderous, Queen's bad press in England soon esculates to absurd proportions, and leads inevitably to the band concluding that enough is enough. With pieces such as the infamously headed, 'Is This Man A Prat?', ahead of him, Freddie will be the first to remove himself from the interview forum, but latterly all the members will do likewise.

1973 UK TOUR

Queen embark on a five-week, 25-date tour of England and Scotland, supporting Mott The Hoople. The tour opens in Leeds and concludes in Peterborough.

The performances at Cheltenham College, Liverpool University and Liverpool Top Rank are not part of the Mott tour, and feature Queen only, with no other act.

Mott are enjoying chart success with 'All The

Way From Memphis', and will later see their follow-up single 'Roll Away The Stone' peak at number eight. With big sellers like 'Honaloochie Boogie' and the David Bowie produced 'All The Young Dudes' already under their belt, they are a force to be reckoned with. Supporting them will be no easy task.

November 12
Town Hall, Leeds
■ *Procession / Father To Son / Son & Daughter / Ogre Battle / Hangman / Great King Rat / Medley: Jailhouse Rock; Shake Rattle And Roll / Keep Yourself Alive / Liar / Encore: Big Spender / Modern Times Rock'n'Roll*

'Stone Cold Crazy' is not performed on this tour.

Although the bootleg from this concert supposedly includes two tracks recorded at the pre-show soundcheck ('Hangman' and 'Liar'), there really is no way of confirming it. At one time there were only a handful of recordings in circulation with soundcheck material included, then suddenly, almost overnight, there emerged a whole series of them. It seems likely that the bootleggers simply found another way to tempt collectors into buying more spurious items.

November 13
St Georges, Blackburn, Lancashire

November 15
Gaumont, Worcester
■ *Procession / Father To Son / Son & Daughter / Ogre Battle / Great King Rat / Medley: Jailhouse Rock; Shake Rattle And Roll; Stupid Cupid; Jailhouse Rock*

(Reprise) / Keep Yourself Alive / Liar / Encore: Big Spender / Bama Lama Bama Loo

November 16
University, Lancaster
■ *Procession / Father To Son / Son & Daughter / Ogre Battle / Great King Rat / Medley: Jailhouse Rock; Shake Rattle And Roll; Stupid Cupid; Be Bop A Lula; Jailhouse Rock (Reprise) / Keep Yourself Alive / Liar / Encore: Big Spender / Modern Times Rock'n'Roll*

November 17
Stadium, Liverpool
■ *Procession / Father To Son / Son & Daughter / Hangman / Ogre Battle / Great King Rat / Medley: Jailhouse Rock; Tutti Frutti; Shake Rattle And Roll; Stupid Cupid; Jailhouse Rock (Reprise) / Keep Yourself Alive / Liar / Encore: Big Spender / Modern Times Rock'n'Roll*

November 18
Victoria Hall, Hanley, Staffordshire

November 19
Civic, Wolverhampton
Queen play a similar set to that of Lancaster University, but with 'See What A Fool I've Been' included. It is unclear exactly where in the set this song featues. Two collectors' lists from different sources offer conflicting advice on this; one has it after 'Ogre Battle', the other as the very last song – the encore.

November 20 ♪
New Theatre, Oxford
■ *Procession / Father To Son / Son & Daughter / Ogre Battle / Hangman / Great King Rat / Medley: Jailhouse Rock; Shake Rattle And Roll; Stupid Cupid; Be Bop A Lula; Jailhouse Rock (Reprise) / Keep Yourself Alive / Liar / Encore: Big Spender*
Again, some of the original vinyl bootleg recordings of this show include an extremely poor quality pre-show soundcheck. Likewise, subsequent cassettes contain even worse copies of it. On close examination, almost all can be

exposed as fraudulent. They actually consist of snippets of material edited together from numerous other *shows* (not soundchecks) of the period.
As a general rule, a typical Queen set of the time would rarely last longer than 45 minutes. Any recording which exceeds that running time is therefore clearly spurious. Bootlegs appearing to offer every conceivable song in the Queen repertoire, as well as half a dozen rock'n'roll medley numbers, should be regarded as dubious.

November 21
Guildhall, Preston, Lancashire
■ *Procession / Father To Son / Son & Daughter / Ogre Battle / Great King Rat / Medley: Jailhouse Rock; Shake Rattle And Roll; Stupid Cupid; Jailhouse Rock (Reprise) / Keep Yourself Alive / Liar / Encore: Big Spender / Bama Lama Bama Loo*

November 22
City Hall, Newcastle-Upon-Tyne

November 23
Apollo Theatre, Glasgow, Scotland ①
■ *Procession / Father To Son / Son & Daughter / Ogre Battle / Great King Rat / Medley: Jailhouse Rock; Shake Rattle And Roll; Stupid Cupid; Jailhouse Rock (Reprise) / Keep Yourself Alive / Liar / Encore: Big Spender / Bama Lama Bama Loo*
● John Bagnall recalling a conversation he had after this performance: "I remember talking to Roger that night and saying that it had gone so well that I had the feeling they were going to happen now, and him saying to me: 'I really feel we're going to make it now. I really feel it's going to happen'."

November 25
Caley Cinema, Edinburgh

November 26
Opera House, Manchester
■ *Procession / Father To Son / Son & Daughter / Ogre Battle / Hangman / Great King Rat / Medley: Jailhouse*

period is a good deal more subdued than most fans today would imagine. He isn't nearly so confident, and even sounds nervous at times.

"Good evening. We're called Queen. It's nice to be in Birmingham - there's so many of you. It's lovely. We'll do a number from our album now - it's called 'Son & Daughter'."

"As you've probably gathered, this is the first time we're playing Birmingham, and you're very nice – that's nice (nervous laugh). That's right. We're gonna do one from our second album, it's called... ("Can we have a bit more in the monitors?")... 'Ogre Battle'"

Freddie's request to John Harris, in the middle of introducing a song, as above, would soon become as frowned upon as a Sheffield brother on a Christmas card list. It would no more happen after this tour than it would in the much later Works and Magic shows. Here, though, Freddie thought nothing of it.

"Thank you... that's nice. I can just see people all round me, and there's a few out there… Oi! (he shouts). How you doin' out there? You seem a bit quiet (laughs again). Anyway we'd like to play a little snootchie woochie one. It's called 'Hangman' – that's right, you're enjoying yourself, so is everybody else, I see…"

Later: "Some time ago we had a single out, written by Brian here, I don't know if you've heard of it, I don't know if you bought it, it's called 'Keep Yourself Alive'."

Rock; Shake Rattle And Roll; Stupid Cupid; Jailhouse Rock (Reprise) / Keep Yourself Alive / Liar / Encore: Big Spender / Modern Times Rock'n'Roll

The rock'n'roll medley differs significantly from one evening to the next, depending on various factors – Freddie's rapport with the audience, the atmosphere inside the venue, and general mood within the band. Most frequently played were Elvis Presley's 'Jailhouse Rock', Little Richard's 'Bama Lama Bama Loo', Gene Vincent's 'Be Bop A Lula', Joe Turner's 'Shake Rattle And Roll' and less frequent renditions of 'Big Spender' and 'Stupid Cupid'.

November 27
Town Hall, Birmingham

■ *Procession / Father To Son / Son & Daughter / Ogre Battle / Hangman / See What A Fool I've Been / Great King Rat / Medley: Jailhouse Rock; Shake Rattle And Roll; Stupid Cupid; Jailhouse Rock (Reprise) / Keep Yourself Alive / Liar / Encore: Big Spender / Bama Lama Loo*

Freddie's between-song patter during this

November 28
Brangwyn Hall, Swansea, Wales ①

↗ A benevolent American critic of the time writes: *'A singular and lightly stylised pot-pourri of heavy metal, rococo and English vaudeville themes, soldered together with explosions, dry ice, strobes, spots and a workshop full of technological tricks.'*

November 29
Colston Hall, Bristol

■ *Procession / Father To Son / Son & Daughter / Ogre Battle / Hangman / Great King Rat / Medley: Jailhouse Rock; Shake Rattle And Roll; Stupid Cupid; Jailhouse*

Rock (Reprise) / Keep Yourself Alive / Liar / Encore: Big Spender / Bama Lama Bama Loo

During the show Freddie says: "Er, we feel pleased that you're a nice mild audience. Er, we'd like to carry on with a number now, it's from our first album, it's called 'Son & Daughter'."

Following a blistering 'Brighton Rock'-type guitar solo, complete with delays and echoes, and the usual addition of an extra "A woman expects a man to buckle down and shovel it", not present on the studio cut, but always added in concert, the band move on to the battlefield again, and the *Queen II* side two opening track 'Ogre Battle'. Roger brings it to an end with a scream to wake the dead, and Freddie remarks simply, "Wicked!"

Freddie hesitates for a moment and then initiates the next song. "Okay, this is gonna be one of our slow ones. It's a real hip-swinger, we do it from time to time. We thought we'd put it in especially for you – as you're a nice audience, yes. It's called 'Hangman'."

And so begins a song which sounds like a mish-mash of various Queen material from the time, all mixed together. While Freddie, as always, sings the main vocal, Roger and Brian combine to provide backing on the "hang that rope from the highest tree" part, and main chorus. This is a rare and exciting insight into a song which has never been released, or even recorded (in the studio).

"Now, a long time ago we had a little single out. I don't know whether you heard it? It's called 'Keep Yourself... Alive'." Towards the end of this, and in keeping with the studio version, Roger sings, "Do you think you're better ev'ry day?" "No, I just think I'm two steps nearer to my grave," Freddie retorts. John then plays a bass line bridge, and everyone unites for the conclusion.

During the main chorus of 'Liar', John adds some rare vocal backing. This is a technically complex composition, but still it converts well to the live situation, building into a powerful crescendo of driving drums, bass and lead guitar. This is a powerhouse concert favourite.

Having given Brian a barely audible cue, exactly as rehearsed, the band crash into a breathtaking rendition of 'Jailhouse Rock'. A few seconds of 'Shake Rattle' and 'Stupid Cupid' follow, before 'Jailhouse' is reprised and then Brian fingers the instantly recognisable opening chords of 'Big Spender'. Little Richard's 'Bama Lama Bama Loo' concludes the show with lyrics borrowed from 'Tutti Frutti'. This was the shape of things to come.

Some bootlegs purporting to represent this performance again boast the inclusion of the pre-show soundcheck. But, again, it is clear that a large audience is present which would not be the case at a soundcheck. The tapes are still worth locating, however, if only for a stunning recital of 'Father To Son' – even if Freddie's slightly amended words do not make complete sense. This version also features some wonderful bass guitar. On some bootlegs, John's faultless backing can easily be overlooked, but it's impossible to do so here.

November 30
Winter Gardens, Bournemouth

December 1
Kursaal, Southend, Essex

Having already performed their usual warm-up spot, three quarters of Queen return to the stage later on (minus John) to join Mott The Hoople, contributing backing vocals to 'All The Young Dudes'.

It has not been possible to track down a recording (in any format) of this show, from either Mott The Hoople or Queen collectors.

December 2
Central, Chatham, Kent

December 3
Langham 1 Studio, London
◀» *Ogre Battle / Great King Rat / Modern Times Rock'n'Roll / Son & Daughter*

Queen record their third BBC session. Bernie Andrews and Mike Franks produce, and Nick Griffiths engineers. Like all the sessions (except the final one), it is broadcast as part of the Radio One *Sounds Of The Seventies* series, three days later, on John Peel's programme.

Compared to the painstakingly refined album versions, Queen's beeb session material, generally speaking, had minimum production time, as is the whole point of them, and as a result have a totally different feel and charm about them. They are familiar songs, of course, but they take on an entirely alternative atmosphere. Playing the *Queen At The Beeb* CD back to back with *Queen* and *Queen II* throws up all kinds of interesting details.

Roger's 'Modern Times Rock'n'Roll' appears here in a greatly improved form from that on the album version. The quirky "It's not that I'm bright, just happy-go-lucky" line – not present on the album – adds to its appeal. Brian May recently attributed this strange phrase to Queen's good friend Ariel Bender (of Mott The Hoople). An explanation at last!

On the subject of the *Queen At The Beeb* album, this session features as half of that compilation. A sequel album looks likely to emerge at some point; perhaps even a double album comprising all remaining sixteen tracks. It may even make up part of the long awaited Queen rarities anthology, Part 1 – tentatively planned to cover the early years.

December 6
Cheltenham College, Cheltenham

December 7
Shaftesbury Hall, London
■ *Procession / Father To Son / Son & Daughter / Ogre Battle / Hangman / Great King Rat / Medley: Jailhouse Rock; Shake Rattle And Roll; Stupid Cupid; Jailhouse Rock (Reprise) / Keep Yourself Alive / Liar / Encore: Big Spender / Bama Lama Bama Loo*

December 8
University, Liverpool

December 14
Hammersmith Odeon, London

■ *Procession / Father To Son / Son & Daughter / Ogre Battle / Hangman / Great King Rat / Medley: Jailhouse Rock; Shake Rattle And Roll; Stupid Cupid / Keep Yourself Alive / Liar / Encore Medley: Big Spender / Bama Lama Bama Loo / 2nd Encore: Modern Times Rock'n'Roll*

Queen and Mott play two shows here today. When the first Hoople set overruns, Queen's show is shortened to compensate. They are not happy about it, but complain little.

In attendance for this, the last London (home town) gig of the year, and also Queen's biggest audience up to this point (3,500), are Brian May's parents.

🕭 Harold May: "We had seats down the front and we'd never been to a concert like that before. I suppose at our age we must have looked a little out of place. Anyway, there was a young man sitting in front of me who suddenly turned round and said 'Who's dad are you then?' He was an out-and-out Mott The Hoople fan, but when I explained that Brian was my son, he handed me his programme and asked me to sign it. 'Don't be silly, I'm just a humble civil servant', I said, but he insisted and then asked me to put 'Brian May's dad' in brackets, after it."

December 15
University, Leicester

December 21
County Hall, Taunton, Somerset

December 22
Town Hall, Peterborough
■ *Procession / Father To Son / Son & Daughter / Ogre Battle / Hangman / Great King Rat / Medley: Jailhouse Rock; Shake Rattle And Roll; Stupid Cupid; Jailhouse Rock (Reprise) / Keep Yourself Alive / Liar / Encore: Big Spender / Bama Lama Bama Loo*

This is the last show of the tour. Queen's support role to Mott The Hoople has provided invaluable concert experience. On the whole it has been a most productive and rewarding undertaking. The press, however, rather predictably, paint a different picture of events. While Mott's reviews are for the most part complimentary, Queen do not inspire such praise.

↗ *'A chilly, gutless sound that could not project itself on stage. No one number was distinctive, except perhaps 'Liar'.'*

December 28
Top Rank, Liverpool
■ *Procession / Father To Son / Son & Daughter / Ogre Battle / Hangman / Great King Rat / Medley: Jailhouse Rock; Shake Rattle And Roll; Stupid Cupid; Jailhouse Rock (Reprise) / Keep Yourself Alive / Liar / Encore: Big Spender / Bama Lama Bama Loo*

The band perform their final show of the year with a Christmas concert on the same bill as 10cc, who have already enjoyed their first number one in England ('Rubber Bullets'), and two other Top Ten hits. A local group called Great Day kick off the show, and Queen follow them.

The setlist differs little from the shows already outlined, but it does feature a lengthy rock'n'roll medley.

1974

January

The year gets off to a disastrous start when, following an injection in preparation for the Australian dates, Brian develops gangrene in his arm. So serious is the condition that for some time there is the real possibility that he may lose his arm.

January 28

Queen fly to Melbourne to perform at the annual three day Sunbury Music Festival. It is their first visit to Australia and their first performances in a continent other than Europe.

February 2
Sunbury Music Festival, Melbourne, Australia
①

■ *Procession / Father To Son / Son & Daughter / Ogre Battle / Hangman / Great King Rat / Medley: Jailhouse Rock; Shake Rattle And Roll; Stupid Cupid; Jailhouse Rock (Reprise) / Keep Yourself Alive / Liar / Encore: Big Spender / Modern Times Rock'n'Roll*

🐟 Queen's introduction to stage here is the most appalling they will ever endure. Brian will later recall that it went something along the lines of: "Well, we've got another load of limy bastards here tonight, and they're probably going to be useless, but let's give 'em something to think about."

The compère then pulls down his trousers and moons at the crowd, before describing Queen as "stuck up pommies". The same individual returns to the stage later in the show and cajoles the audience into not accepting an encore. During the show the lighting rig uncharacteristically breaks down. It is later discovered that it has been sabotaged. Queen are disenchanted with their first taste of Australia. They would return on only two more occasions.

Though Brian's arm causes him considerable discomfort, and Freddie has an ear infection and can hardly hear anything, the second show of the

43

day goes on regardless. It is not a memorable performance, but not a bad one either. Queen do not perform the second of their scheduled shows the next day.

When they arrive home after the festival, the band are bemused to find a hoard of journalists awaiting them at Heathrow. They quickly disperse (having taken not one single photograph) when they discover that Queen is not Her Majesty the Queen, as expected, but four long-haired, exhausted rockers.

February 20

When David Bowie pulls out of *Top Of The Pops*, Queen are hastily drafted in as a replacement. They record a backing tape and at Ramport Studios pre-record a film which will be used. The unscheduled performance of 'Seven Seas Of

Rhye', broadcast the next day, is the first of many appearances on the programme.

February 23

❖ Queen's second single 'Seven Seas Of Rhye' is released in the UK, paired with the non-album track 'See What A Fool I've Been'. Their first chart entry, it peaks at No.10 on March 9, helped largely by the *Top Of The Pops* coverage and the British tour dates two months earlier.

UK 1974 *Queen II* Tour

Following rehearsals at Ealing film studios, the band commence their first British headlining tour. The four week tour includes 22 performances in England, Scotland and Wales, and one gig on the Isle Of Man. The dates conclude with a show at Barbarella's in Birmingham that should have happened on March 16, but which is cancelled and rescheduled for April 2. Nutz are the support act for all but two of the shows.

March 1

Winter Gardens, Blackpool

■ *Procession / Father To Son / Ogre Battle / White*

Queen / Great King Rat / Hangman / Doing All Right / Son & Daughter / Keep Yourself Alive / Liar / Encore Medley: Jailhouse Rock; Shake Rattle And Roll; Stupid Cupid; Jailhouse Rock (Reprise) / 2nd Encore: Big Spender

On the way to the gig, the vehicle transporting the band's lighting rig equipment breaks down miles from the venue. Although jeopardised, the show eventually goes ahead, albeit delayed.

'White Queen' is new to this set on this tour, and 'Stone Cold Crazy' is absent.

There is speculation that Queen also perform 'The Night Comes Down' and 'The Fairy Feller's Masterstroke' at this show, but that remains unconfirmed. If either song did feature, it would have been the first and only time it did so – to my knowledge. I have never heard even a segment of either track on any official or bootleg recording.

March 2
Friars, Aylesbury, Buckinghamshire

This show is shorter than planned because Brian's arm becomes too painful for him to continue.

March 3
Guildhall, Plymouth
■ *Procession / Father To Son / Ogre Battle / White*

Queen / Great King Rat / Hangman / Doing All Right / Son & Daughter / Keep Yourself Alive / Liar / Encore Medley: Jailhouse Rock; Shake Rattle And Roll; Stupid Cupid; Jailhouse Rock (Reprise) / 2nd Encore: Big Spender

Local band Nutz are the support act here. They back-up Queen for all remaining shows on this tour.

At the end of the show the audience acknowledge a memorable performance by singing verses of 'God Save The Queen'. The gesture is much appreciated by the band, who eventually record an arrangement of it which will be used to conclude the show. It first does so on October 30, 1974. They record a definitive version during sessions for *A Night At The Opera* and use it to conclude the album.

March 4
Festival Hall, Paignton, Devon
■ *Procession / Father To Son / Ogre Battle / White Queen / Great King Rat / Hangman / Doing All Right / Son & Daughter / Keep Yourself Alive / Liar / Encore Medley: Jailhouse Rock; Shake Rattle And Roll; Stupid Cupid; Jailhouse Rock (Reprise) / 2nd Encore: Big Spender / Modern Times Rock'n'Roll*

'Son & Daughter' is performed somewhat differently now from previous years. It resembles more closely the album version, and features fewer improvised parts. This debut album classic remains in the set until 1978.

March 8
Locarno, Sunderland, Tyne & Wear

Queen play a similar set to March 4, but with additional medley material.

❖ Also on March 8, *Queen II* is released in the UK. It reaches number five, and a month later, number 49 in America. The 'Deacon John' mis-credit from the first album is corrected, as John dislikes it, but the 'Nobody played synthesizers' line proudly remains.

↗ Reviews are again mixed.

Sounds: *'This album captures them in their finest hours.'*

Record Mirror: *'As a whole it is dire. Freddie Mercury's voice is dressed up with multi-tracking.'*

As with its predecessor, and numerous successors, the album contains songs that are not featured in the live show. Both 'Someday One Day' and 'The Loser In The End' from Side 1 (White Side) are overlooked, and although Side 2 (Black Side) contains material regarded by many as the very heart of the album, half of it never receives a concert airing. 'The Fairy Feller's Masterstroke' is among the most intricate and technically complex compositions ever committed to vinyl by Queen. This probably explains why it is disregarded, although in subsequent shows the band *would* attempt versions of other equally complicated material on stage, such as 'The Prophet's Song', 'Rhapsody' and 'Somebody To Love'.

'The Fairy Feller' merges effortlessly with

Freddie's 'Nevermore', which in turn segues into the heaviness of 'The March Of The Black Queen'. Though the lavish 'Black Queen' did feature in the set many times (in much abridged form), the remaining two thirds of the medley never appear. The penultimate track, Freddie's reflective 'Funny How Love Is' is also never performed live.

March 9
Corn Exchange, Cambridge

■ *Procession / Father To Son / Ogre Battle / White Queen / Great King Rat / Hangman / Doing All Right / Son & Daughter / Keep Yourself Alive / Liar / Encore*

Medley: Jailhouse Rock; Shake Rattle And Roll; Stupid Cupid; Jailhouse Rock (Reprise) / 2nd Encore: Big Spender / Modern Times Rock'n'Roll

'Modern Times' resembles very closely the album cut, and also features Roger singing lead vocals.

March 10
Greyhound, Croydon

March 12
Roundhouse, Dagenham

March 14
Town Hall, Cheltenham
■ *Procession / Father To Son / Ogre Battle / White Queen / Great King Rat / Hangman / Doing All Right / Son & Daughter / Keep Yourself Alive / Liar / Encore Medley: Jailhouse Rock; Shake Rattle And Roll; Stupid*

Cupid; Jailhouse Rock (Reprise) / 2nd Encore: Big Spender / Modern Times Rock'n'Roll

After the show the lighting crew decide they no longer wish to endure the tedium of assembling and disassembling the Queen rig night after night, nor the general disharmony between themselves, and promptly quit. Trident arrange a replacement in the form of James Dann and others, thus beginning a long working relationship. Dann proves to be invaluable.

March 15
University, Glasgow
Set: as March 14

March 16
University, Stirling
■ *Procession / Father To Son / Ogre Battle / White Queen / Great King Rat / Hangman / Doing All Right / Son & Daughter / Keep Yourself Alive / Liar / Encore: See What A Fool I've Been / 2nd Encore: Jailhouse Rock / Stupid Cupid / 3rd Encore: Jailhouse Rock (Reprise)*

Despite having performed a full show and three encores, the audience refuse to let the band leave. The police interject and the situation quickly escalates into a riot and two people are stabbed. Two of the crew are also hurt. Meanwhile, the four band members are locked in the kitchen backstage.

Due to this upset, the following night's concert at Barbarella's in Birmingham is cancelled and rescheduled for April 2.

March 19

Winter Gardens, Cleethorpes, Humberside

■ *Procession / Father To Son / Ogre Battle / White Queen / Great King Rat / Hangman / Doing All Right / Son & Daughter / Keep Yourself Alive / Liar / Encore Medley: Jailhouse Rock; Shake Rattle And Roll; Stupid Cupid; Jailhouse Rock (Reprise) / 2nd Encore: Big Spender / Modern Times Rock'n'Roll*

March 20

University, Manchester

March 22

Civic Centre, Canvey Island, Essex

March 23

Links Pavilion, Cromer, Norfolk

March 24

Woods Leisure Centre, Colchester

March 26

Palace Lido, Douglas

■ *Procession / Father To Son / Ogre Battle / White Queen / Great King Rat / Hangman / Doing All Right / Son & Daughter / Keep Yourself Alive / Liar / Encore Medley: Jailhouse Rock; Shake Rattle And Roll; Stupid Cupid; Jailhouse Rock (Reprise) / 2nd Encore: Big Spender / Modern Times Rock'n'Roll*

March 28

University of Aberystwyth

Set: as March 26

March 29

The Gardens, Penzance

■ *Procession / Father To Son / Ogre Battle / White Queen / Great King Rat / Hangman / Doing All Right / Son & Daughter / Keep Yourself Alive / Liar / Encore Medley: Jailhouse Rock; Shake Rattle And Roll; Stupid Cupid; Jailhouse Rock (Reprise) / 2nd Encore: Big Spender / Modern Times Rock'n'Roll*

March 30

Century Ballroom, Taunton

March 31 ♪

Rainbow Theatre, London

■ *Procession / Father To Son / Ogre Battle / White Queen / Great King Rat / Hangman / Doing All Right / Son & Daughter / Keep Yourself Alive / Seven Seas Of Rhye / Liar / Encore Medley: Jailhouse Rock; Shake Rattle And Roll; Stupid Cupid; Jailhouse Rock (Reprise) / 2nd Encore: Big Spender / Modern Times Rock'n'Roll*

This would have been the final show of the tour had it not been for the following night's rescheduled concert.

During 'Liar' there is a complete power breakdown. The show grinds to an embarrassing halt, but resumes again a short while later, without further incident. The 3,500 capacity crowd are good humoured and await the restoration of power without resorting to jeering – or a riot.

Despite suggestions to the contary, this show is that which makes up the *Sheetkickers* bootleg (aka *Shitkickers*). Freddie's pre 'Seven Seas Of Rhye' comment about it being the current single, provides conclusive proof of this.

🖝 This venue will prove to be the source of great frustration to Brian over the years. "The Rainbow Theatre always gave me real problems. I suppose it was because the roof was so high, all the sound seemed to be dragged upwards and away from the amps."

April 2
Barbarella's, Birmingham
■ *Procession / Father To Son / Ogre Battle / White Queen / Great King Rat / Hangman / Doing All Right / Son & Daughter / Keep Yourself Alive / Seven Seas Of Rhye / Liar / Encore Medley: Jailhouse Rock; Shake Rattle And Roll; Stupid Cupid; Jailhouse Rock (Reprise) / 2nd Encore: Big Spender / Modern Times Rock'n'Roll*

In an end-of-tour display of high spirits, the support band's lead singer and members of the road crew run naked across the stage during the encore. Though the audience is surprised at the spectacle, Roger is not; he bet them a bottle of champagne that they would not do it.

April 3
Langham 1 Studio, London
◀» *Modern Times Rock'n'Roll / March Of The Black Queen / Nevermore / White Queen*

Queen return once more to Langham to record their fourth and final session at this venue for the BBC. The session is transmitted on the Bob Harris show on April 15th.

Three stand-out tracks from *Queen II* and one from the début album are recorded. While the session immediately prior to this saw a somewhat accelerated version of Roger's 'Modern Times Rock'n'Roll' recorded, this time the pace is a little slower. The only other significant difference between the two versions comes at halfway mark. On this session a whistle can be heard following the "And you know there's one thing every single body could use" line, but on the previous session it's the "not that I'm bright, just happy-go-lucky" thing.

Other material from *Queen II* would have been of more interest to fans than another rendition of Roger's song, already reinterpreted in the previous session. Freddie's 'Fairy Feller' is an obvious choice, though attempting to recreate such an elaborate piece in a relatively short time, would surely have proved troublesome.

USA 1974
Queen embark upon their very first North American tour, again supporting Mott The Hoople. The tour spans four weeks, and includes

↗ An unimpressed American critic of this time tediously observes: *'Queen's on-stage presence was an almost laughable bizarre mish-mash of every other more successful band of their genre.'*

Another adds:*'They are doing nothing special. There are moments when they sound influenced by The Who and moments when they are nearer Zeppelin.'*

No-one mentions that the band's record sales are soaring, in Europe *and* America, or that concert ticket sales are steadily increasing too.

April 19
Fairgrounds Appliance Building, Oklahoma City

April 20
Mid South Coliseum, Memphis, Tennessee
■ *Procession / Father To Son / Ogre Battle / White Queen / Hangman / Doing All Right / Son & Daughter / Keep Yourself Alive / Seven Seas Of Rhye / Liar / Encore Medley: Jailhouse Rock; Shake Rattle And Roll; Stupid Cupid; Be Bop A Lula; Jailhouse Rock (Reprise) / 2nd Encore: Big Spender / Modern Times Rock'n'Roll*

nineteen shows, six of which are consecutive gigs at the Uris Theater, in New York.

No-one imagines at this point that the tour is destined for a premature and dramatic demise.

April 9
❖ *Queen II* is released in the US, to coincide with the beginning of the tour. The shows help to push it to number 49.

April 16
Regis College, Denver, Colorado, USA ①
Set: as April 2, but without 'Great King Rat', which was absent on this tour.

This is Queen's first concert in America.

April 17
Memorial Hall, Kansas City, Missouri

April 18
Keil Auditorium, St. Louis, Missouri

April 21
St Bernard Civic Center, New Orleans, Louisiana

After this show, Brian suffers pain again. No specific cause can be found and the entourage continues onward. The full extent of the problem does not emerge until May 12.

April 26
Orpheum Theater, Boston, Massachusetts
■ *Procession / Father To Son / Ogre Battle / White Queen / Hangman / Doing All Right / Son & Daughter / Keep Yourself Alive / Seven Seas Of Rhye / Liar / Encore Medley: Jailhouse Rock; Shake Rattle And Roll; Stupid Cupid; Jailhouse Rock (Reprise) / 2nd Encore: Big Spender / Modern Times Rock'n'Roll*

April 27
Palace Theater, Providence, Rhode Island
The tour thus far is something of a triumph for Queen. Any pre-tour anxieties are soon forgotten and the band more than live up to their warm-up spot obligations. They are even considered to be as good as the headlining act by many who see them, including music journalists.
● Mott The Hoople band member Griffin: "Queen are not a sabotage band, and we have had

to work with some in the past - roadies who fall over leads, pulling them out by accident on purpose.

"The concert itself is excellent; one of the best I have seen in ages. Queen's peculiar equipment serves them well. Lead singer Freddie Mercury parodies everybody, but has style and gets away with it."

Queen were often accused of employing *peculiar* or *unorthodox* equipment combinations for their concerts, especially in these early days. Financial restrictions dictate largely what is or isn't used at this time, and if a particular piece of equipment is beyond the touring budget, then invariably John or Brian will design and build their own version – and use it until the cashflow improves.

April 28
Exposition Hall, Portland, Maine
■ *Procession / Father To Son / Ogre Battle / Son And Daughter / See What A Fool I've Been / Liar / Keep Yourself Alive / Modern Times Rock'n'Roll / Encore: Big Spender / Bama Lama Bama Loo*

May 1
Farm Arena, Harrisburg, Pennsylvania
■ *Procession / Father To Son / Ogre Battle / White Queen / Hangman / Doing All Right / Son & Daughter / Keep Yourself Alive / Seven Seas Of Rhye / Liar / Encore Medley: Jailhouse Rock; Shake Rattle And Roll; Stupid Cupid; Jailhouse Rock (Reprise) / 2nd Encore: Big Spender / Modern Times Rock'n'Roll*

May 2
Agricultural Hall, Allentown, Pennsylvania

May 3
King's College, Wilkes Barre, Pennsylvania

May 4
Palace Theater, Waterbury, Connecticut

Mott The Hoople On Broadway
Just for the Uris Theater shows.

May 7 / 8 / 9 / 10 / 11 / 12
Uris Theater, New York
■ *First night*: *Procession / Father To Son / Ogre Battle / White Queen / Hangman / Doing All Right / Son & Daughter / Keep Yourself Alive / Seven Seas Of Rhye / Liar / Encore Medley: Big Spender; Modern Times Rock'n'Roll*

Queen and Mott The Hoople play six consecutive nights at this venue. Other songs performed during the shows include 'Jailhouse Rock' and a brief recital of 'Good Rocking Tonight'.

■ *Final night*: *Procession / Father To Son / Ogre Battle / White Queen / Doing All Right / Son & Daughter / Keep Yourself Alive / Seven Seas Of Rhye / Liar / Encore Medley: Big Spender; Modern Times Rock'n'Roll*

Brian collapses after the show on May 12, and though his condition is at first thought to be a form of food poisoning, it is soon discovered he has hepatitis. The injection he had prior to the Australian shows, in January, is almost certainly responsible. Not only is the following night's show cancelled, but Queen's entire involvement in the tour is thwarted. The band head home.

Kansas are drafted in to take over as Mott's support. Their first show is two days later, in Boston.

Having managed to smuggle a decidedly unwell Brian aboard a London-bound flight, the dismayed (no pun intended) Queen fly home to re-evaluate their position. In subsequent interviews years later, Brian admits that he spends the first weeks of his recuperation worrying that the other three might find a replacement and continue without him. As far as the remainder of Queen are concerned, however, replacing Brian is never an option.

Meanwhile, staff at Queen's American record label Elektra contact everyone who came into contact with Brian, with the news that protective gamma globulin inoculations are necessary.

🗨 Brian: "Getting ill really turned my life upside-down. Before that I must say I had worried about things in the band and my life in general. There always seemed to be something that needed some worry. Today I don't worry nearly as much."

Throughout June and July Queen work on material for the third album, rehearsing at Rockfield Studios in Gwent. Brian's health is still poor but he continues as best he can, until August, when he is again rushed into hospital. This time a duodenal ulcer is detected and an emergency operation quickly follows. The North America tour scheduled for September is cancelled.

The band continue work on the album without

Brian, leaving spaces for him to add his guitar and vocal parts later. Although most sessions take place at Rockfield Studios, they record some of the early material at Trident.

Brian experiences bouts of depression during his recuperation, but spends his time at home as productively as possible. From his bed he writes 'Now I'm Here', the inspiration for which comes from the American tour dates with Mott The Hoople – hence the reference to the band in the lyrics.

It is during this period, while still recovering and frantically scribbling down song lyrics and humming guitar riffs into his bedside tape recorder, that Brian is approached by Ron and Russell Mael, of the group Sparks. Having heard that Queen's American tour has been cancelled on account of Brian, but unaware of the reasons, they ask if he will consider joining their band. He declines.

Brian's health steadily improves, allowing him to return to the sessions. He is extremely impressed by the material that's been recorded, and especially by Freddie's lyric writing. By September 1974 the sessions are complete and *Sheer Heart Attack*, released two months later, emerges as Queen's most accomplished work to date. Roger Taylor's album title track is written for the album, but is not finished in time to be included. The album retains the song's title, but the actual track finally emerges on the sixth album *News Of The World*, in October 1977.

❖ **October 11**

'Killer Queen' / 'Flick Of The Wrist' is released in the UK. It is the first track to be taken from *Sheer Heart Attack*, and is Queen's first double A-sided issue. The disc peaks at number two in the UK, kept off the top spot by David Essex. The same pairing is issued ten days later in America, and provides Queen with their first chart placing there - peaking at number 12.

October 16

Maida Vale 4 Studio, London

◁ *Now I'm Here / Stone Cold Crazy / Flick Of The Wrist / Tenement Funster*

Queen record their penultimate BBC session. It is broadcast on November 4, on Bob Harris' show.

Since the previous month had seen the conclusion of the *Heart Attack* album sessions, the band record slightly alternative versions of four tracks from it.

While 'Stone Cold Crazy' and 'Now I'm Here' are only marginally different to the album versions, Roger's vocal on 'Tenement Funster' is more aggressive and intense, as well as significantly louder. Also, the lead and bass guitar backing is so close to that of the original recording, that it appears as if Roger's voice has simply been recorded over the original backing track, which is not the case. Accustomed as one is to hearing the track segue into 'Flick Of The Wrist' on the album, when it instead fades to silence here, there is a sense of waiting for something that never arrives. The phased ending seems strange, but none the less interesting.

'Flick Of The Wrist' is equally impressive. It so close to the *Sheer Heart Attack* version that it is only around the two minute mark that it varies enough to make the distinction. Brian's lead guitar solo after the 'Don't look back, don't look back - it's a rip-off' line is dramatically different. Like 'Tenement Funster', 'Wrist' seems somehow incomplete with a phased conclusion. All in all though, the Queen / Jeff Griffin combination yields another memorable session, and one which is long overdue proper release on compact disc.

🔊 **Bob Harris' comments from the original broadcast;** "We have music to come on the programme tonight from Queen. Surely, I think, one of the most exciting British bands to have emerged for a long time. Four numbers from their new album *Sheer Heart Attack*, and here's the first...

"Ah that's great. Brian May wrote that. That's the first of four songs tonight from their new album. It was recorded especially for the Monday

programme. Queen. That was called 'Now I'm Here'...

"Well that's the best thing I've heard for a long time. Queen, and 'Stone Cold Crazy'...

"It's a pleasure to have them on the programme, it really is. Queen. That was called 'Flick Of The Wrist'...

"Well, the last number coming up on the programme tonight. If you're having a bonfire night party tomorrow, this is for you. Queen to close the programme, with 'Tenement Funster'...

"Great. Well it's rare to hear Queen without Freddie Mercury taking the lead vocal. That was the last number from them. If you can over the next few weeks, get to see them on tour, because they really are an amazing band."

UK 1974 - *Sheer Heart Attack* Tour

Nineteen concerts at eighteen different venues conclude Queen's British shows of the year, with Hustler as support. It is the band's second tour as the headlining act and the set list contains much of

Son / White Queen / Flick Of The Wrist / Medley: In The Lap Of The Gods; Killer Queen; The March Of The Black Queen; Bring Back That Leroy Brown / Son & Daughter / Keep Yourself Alive / Seven Seas Of Rhye / Stone Cold Crazy / Liar / In The Lap Of The Gods (Revisited) / Encore Medley: Big Spender; Modern Times Rock'n'Roll / God Save The Queen

Queen use a specially recorded version of the national anthem to conclude this show. It will go on to be used to finish almost every performance of the band's career; the band offer their goodbyes and leave the stage as the piece begins. To the fans, it will come to signify the all too soon end to the evening's entertainment.

'Flick Of The Wrist' and 'Now I'm Here' are new to the set on this tour. The latter is performed rather differently to the version that will appear on the *Sheer Heart Attack* album, and it too will become a regular of the Queen repertoire. It is performed it in a variety of ways over the years and will afford Freddie the perfect opportunity for some audience participation – as is nicely evident on *Live Killers*.

The band unveil a brand new lighting rig here.

October 31
Victoria Hall, Hanley, Staffordshire
Set: as October 30

Although 'White Queen' entails a very complex musical arrangement on the album, the band perform it with dramatic mood and tempo changes in concert, instead of taking the easy option with a simplified, condensed version. Brian's track establishes itself quickly to the set, and the fans embrace it fully.

November 1
Liverpool Empire, Liverpool
■ *Procession / Now I'm Here / Ogre Battle / Father To Son / White Queen / Flick Of The Wrist / Medley: In The Lap Of The Gods; Killer Queen; The March Of The Black Queen; Bring Back That Leroy Brown / Son & Daughter / Keep Yourself Alive / Seven Seas Of Rhye / Stone Cold Crazy / Liar / In The Lap Of The Gods (Revisited) / Encore Medley: Big Spender; Modern*

the new album material – 'Now I'm Here', 'Killer Queen', 'Leroy Brown', 'In The Lap Of The Gods Revisited', 'Flick Of The Wrist', 'Stone Cold Crazy'. 'Brighton Rock' will feature on following tour. 'White Queen' and 'Seven Seas Of Rhye' are also new.

The tour programme consists of four pages of biographical text and discography, and a wonderful black and white photograph of an extremely youthful looking Queen in the centre pages, all housed in an orange jacket, the front of which reads, 'This book is designed for your further enjoyment of the show.'

The typical cost of a ticket for this tour is £1.30.

October 30 ⌔
Palace, Manchester
■ *Procession / Now I'm Here / Ogre Battle / Father To*

Times Rock'n'Roll / 2nd Encore: Jailhouse Rock / God Save The Queen

As in London and Cornwall (two of the band's home towns), Queen enjoy huge popularity in Liverpool. From their very earliest concerts in 1970, they establish a loyal and ever increasing alliance of devotees. Many are in attendance here.

A responsive audience always inspires the very best performances from Queen, and this is no exception. Many fans cite the show as the best they've ever seen. A full page local newspaper review next day opens with a quote from Freddie:

🔎 "People think I'm an ogre at times. Some girls hissed at me in the street... 'You devil'. They think we're really nasty, but that's only on stage. Well I'm certainly not an ogre."

🔎 The same article notes that while Brian uses AC30 amplifiers on stage, as The Beatles had done in the Sixties, Queen's music is very much from the Aeventies. It goes on: *'It is cleverly arranged, carefully timed, and delivered with maximum effort to create the greatest impact. It works on a young and receptive audience like a bombshell. Forget eight year olds screaming at the Osmonds.'*

The reviewer also had a sense of humour: *'An atmosphere approaching bedlam is prevalent inside the Empire. Hustler have come and gone and now the audience are hungry for action. They whistle and chant and clap with all the precision of the football terraces. The ancient cry of "Wally" as is still heard in northern territories, echoes around the faded gilt décor. Jack Nelson (Queen's American manager) is intrigued by the cry and wonders if Wally are a local group and wants to sign them – until enlightened.*

'The only agro comes when Queen's entourage from London try to claim their seats near the front. 'Fuck Off' directs one youth, as PR Tony Brainsby pleads for his seat. 'All these seats are taken up by that gentleman there,' says Tony, pointing at me. Ribald laughter from the watching stalls and repeated cries of 'Ooh Gentleman!'. The seat pirates eventually relinquish their hold with dark mutterings of 'alright, but we'll see you outside'.

'Within seconds most of the audience were standing up to gaze desperately at the darkened empty stage, and there they were – shadowy figures bounding towards the waiting instruments. The lights blazed and there was evil Freddie, clad all in white, the archetypal demon jock singer, pointing and snarling: "Queen is back, what do you think of that?"'

🔎 **'Queen / Liverpool'**. NME. By Tony Stewart. November 9, 1974: *'It's only a year since Queen supported Mott the Hoople on tour, but if the turn out and response to their concert at the Liverpool Empire on Friday night is any guide, their fortunes have spiralled to such a degree they're now in the Big League themselves.*

'Nevertheless, encountering 3000 Liverpool looners going completely bonkers over a band is an occurrence which does rather unbalance and astound this writer. Frankly I hadn't expected it.

'Whether they deserve this acclaim is of course, a different matter entirely; however, after seeing the Liverpool gig, I think they do.

Queen Live '74

'Musically, the band pull off an act that is both enjoyable and entertaining, shifting through apparent disparities in style that encompass white heat energy rock, vaudeville knees-up, melodic sophistication and high camp (witness the first part of their encore, "Big Spender").

'They also demonstrate an excellent standard of musicianship. Guitarist Brian May has a style that can be unruly and dominating for the over-drive effect required on "Son and Daughter", but at other times diplomatically sensitive as on "Killer Queen".

'And to a large degree this subtle approach is also adopted by vocalist Freddie Mercury, whose considerable vocal range is often put to the test and usually proves to be as controlled as his contributions to "Sheer Heart Attack", had indicated.

'Somewhat unfortunately the sound system tended to highlight May's and Mercury's efforts to an unnecessary degree, with the predictable result that drummer Roger Taylor and bassist John Deacon were all but drowned in a jarring cacophony of sound.

'To a certain extent the poor balance also exaggerated the heavy metal qualities of the band; the delicate melodies being constructed underneath the abrasive roar of the song were all but inaudible.

'Not unexpectedly Stage Presence played quite an important part in the act (though it was never used to disguise musical inadequacies).

'I must confess the sight of Mercury hurling his all across the stage proved to be a visual bonus to complement the exciting dynamics of their numbers, pulled from all three albums, but with a preference for material on "II" and "Heart Attack".

'The gig could have been better I'm sure, but it was still a hotsie.'

November 2
University, Leeds

Following the show, hysteria uncannily similar to March's Stirling University gig erupts in the audience. Scuffles between fans and over-zealous bouncers break out. On this occasion however, Freddie manages to calm the situation down before anything too serious can develop.

During the set, Roger's on-stage monitor fails.

He attempts to signal to his roadie – but to no avail, and for the rest of the performance he is unable to hear anything he plays or sings. After the show, an irate Roger throws a tantrum in the dressing room which results in him having to be driven to the Leeds Infirmary with a severely bruised foot.

↗ 'The contents of Freddie Mercury's pants are his alone - They belong to him and to no-one else'. NME. November 2nd 1974; Julie Webb relentlessly probes the cut and contour of QUEEN'S Lead Trouser: 'One particular review from the US sticks out in Mercury's mind since it was, in a sense, on a personal level. "We played a theatre in New York with Mott and this particular chick (well, they notice everything down to the pimple on your arse, dear) wrote that she noticed that when I did a costume change I changed even my shoes and socks. She also added she was so close she could tell what religion I was, and that I wasn't wearing any knickers. She also pointed out that Ian Hunter had knickers on. Ian's going to die ...". Indeed.'

November 3
Theatre, Coventry

■ Procession / Now I'm Here / Ogre Battle / Father To Son / White Queen / Flick Of The Wrist / Medley: In The Lap Of The Gods; Killer Queen; The March Of The Black Queen / Bring Back That Leroy Brown / Son & Daughter / Keep Yourself Alive / Seven Seas Of Rhye / Stone Cold Crazy / Liar / In The Lap Of The Gods (Revisited) / Encore Medley: Big Spender; Modern Times Rock'n'Roll / 2nd Encore: Jailhouse Rock / God Save The Queen

'Jailhouse Rock' now concludes nearly every show.

November 5
City Hall, Sheffield

'Leroy Brown' is new to this tour. Although the music is performed in much the same way as on Sheer Heart Attack, Freddie sings hardly any words, seeming to use the opportunity to rest before the vocally demanding 'Son & Daughter', 'Keep Yourself Alive' and 'Liar'. Brian plays a

short ukulele solo towards the end of 'Leroy Brown'.

November 6
St George's Hall, Bradford
■ *Procession / Now I'm Here / Ogre Battle / Father To Son / White Queen / Flick Of The Wrist / Medley: In The Lap Of The Gods; Killer Queen; The March Of The Black Queen; Bring Back That Leroy Brown / Son & Daughter / Keep Yourself Alive / Seven Seas Of Rhye / Stone Cold Crazy / Liar / In The Lap Of The Gods (Revisited) / Encore Medley: Big Spender; Modern Times Rock'n'Roll / 2nd Encore: Jailhouse Rock / God Save The Queen*

' Big Spender' is now rarely out of the set.

November 7
City Hall, Newcastle-Upon-Tyne
As well as the *Sheer Heart Attack* material, Queen also incorporate a medley section into the set - setting a trend that will endure through all subsequent tours. On this tour the medley comprises excerpts from 'Killer Queen' and 'Black Queen', together with the largely lyricless 'Leroy Brown'.

Contrary to some collectors' lists, both versions of 'In The Lap Of The Gods' are performed live. The first features at the start of the medley and the 'revisited' one at the end of the show.

November 8
Apollo Theatre, Glasgow
■ *Procession / Now I'm Here / Ogre Battle / Father To Son / White Queen / Flick Of The Wrist / Medley: In The Lap Of The Gods; Killer Queen; The March Of The Black Queen; Bring Back That Leroy Brown / Son & Daughter / Keep Yourself Alive / Seven Seas Of Rhye / Stone Cold Crazy / Liar / In The Lap Of The Gods (Revisited) / Encore Medley: Big Spender; Modern Times Rock'n'Roll / 2nd Encore: Jailhouse Rock / God Save The Queen*

Towards the end of this show, Freddie is dragged into the audience, only to be dragged back out again by security men. He later recalls the incident as a rather undignified affair, but the experience teaches him to be more careful in future.
❖ Also on November 8, *Sheer Heart Attack* is released in the UK, and four days later in America. It reaches numbers 2 and 12 in the charts respectively. The cost of producing the album reputably falls between £28-30,000, a fraction of the cost of most contemporary albums, but a significant amount in 1974.

Material which never features in the live show, is Freddie's timeless 'Lily Of The Valley', Roger's self sung and much underrated 'Tenement Funster', Brian's 'Dear Friends' and 'She Makes Me' (bafflingly subtitled 'Stormtrooper In Stilettos') and John Deacon's first composition for Queen, 'Misfire'.

The omission of 'Funster', particularly, is a crying shame. Sung by Roger or Freddie, or both, it would have been a stunning addition to the medley, or even as an encore. This is quite simply one of the most staggering oversights in the entire catalogue.

● Brian: "For some strange reason we seemed to get a rather different feel on *Sheer Heart Attack* because of the way we were forced to record it (referring to his absence because of illness), and even allowing for all the problems we had, none of us were really displeased with the final result."

November 9
University, Lancaster
■ *Procession / Now I'm Here / Ogre Battle / Father To Son / White Queen / Flick Of The Wrist / Medley: In The Lap Of The Gods; Killer Queen; The March Of The Black Queen; Bring Back That Leroy Brown / Son & Daughter / Keep Yourself Alive / Seven Seas Of Rhye / Stone Cold Crazy / Liar / In The Lap Of The Gods (Revisited) / Encore Medley: Big Spender; Modern Times Rock'n'Roll / 2nd Encore: Jailhouse Rock / God Save The Queen*

↗ **'May time**. Melody Maker. November 16th 1974.

Brian May, guitarist and astronomer royal of Queen – No 1 in the singles chart – talks to Brian Harrigan.

'On Saturday Queen played Lancaster University and the next day, in a hotel on the outskirts of Preston, I spoke to Brian about the gig, himself and the band.

'First on the agenda was the pensive pose. "It's not really a planned thing," he said. "We're not really choreographed. It's just that Freddie is the natural extrovert and I suppose I'm a foil to that, in a way. And

when I'm on stage I'm not really conscious of where I'm standing in particular."

November 10
Guildhall, Preston

November 12
Colston Hall, Bristol

November 13
Winter Gardens, Bournemouth
  Set: as November 3

November 14
Gaumont, Southampton

November 15
Brangwyn Hall, Swansea
■ *Procession / Now I'm Here / Ogre Battle / Father To Son / White Queen / Flick Of The Wrist / Medley: In The Lap Of The Gods; Killer Queen; The March Of The Black Queen; Bring Back That Leroy Brown / Son & Daughter / Keep Yourself Alive / Seven Seas Of Rhye / Stone Cold Crazy / Liar / In The Lap Of The Gods (Revisited) / Encore Medley: Big Spender; Modern Times Rock'n'Roll / 2nd Encore: Jailhouse Rock / God Save The Queen*

TOWN HALL, BIRMINGHAM
MEL BUSH ORGANISATION presents
QUEEN and HUSTLER
SATURDAY, 16th NOVEMBER, 1974,
at 1930 hours
GROUND FLOOR   **£1.30**

PLEASE RETAIN
LATECOMERS will not be admitted until a convenient break in the programme. Tickets cannot be exchanged or money refunded.

November 16
Town Hall, Birmingham

November 18
New Theatre, Oxford
■ *Procession / Now I'm Here / Ogre Battle / Father To Son / White Queen / Flick Of The Wrist / Medley: In The Lap Of The Gods; Killer Queen; The March Of The Black Queen; Bring Back That Leroy Brown / Son &*

Daughter / Keep Yourself Alive / Seven Seas Of Rhye / Stone Cold Crazy / Liar / In The Lap Of The Gods (Revisited) / Encore Medley: Big Spender; Modern Times Rock'n'Roll / 2nd Encore: Jailhouse Rock / God Save The Queen

November 19/20 ⬈
Rainbow Theatre, London

■ ***Both Nights***: *Procession / Now I'm Here / Ogre Battle / Father To Son / White Queen / Flick Of The Wrist / Medley: In The Lap Of The Gods; Killer Queen; The March Of The Black Queen; Bring Back That Leroy Brown / Son & Daughter / Keep Yourself Alive / Seven Seas Of Rhye / Stone Cold Crazy / Liar / In The Lap Of The Gods (Revisited) / Encore Medley: Big Spender; Modern Times Rock'n'Roll / 2nd Encore: Jailhouse Rock / God Save The Queen*

Queen are originally scheduled to play only the one show here, but when it sells out in just two days, promoter Mel Bush adds a further one. For purposes of promotion, the second performance is sound recorded and filmed, the first time Queen have been professionally filmed live in concert. For once, the recording equipment functions properly and a great concert is captured forever.

The footage is later edited down to thirty minutes and screened at selected British cinemas as an opener for the Led Zeppelin film *The Song Remains The Same.* After a limited run, the film is stored away in the Queen archives, not to see the light of day until almost twenty years later.

In 1991 the original master tapes are discovered, still in pristine condition. The missing sections are edited back into the cinema cut, and a 53-minute video is issued as part of the *Box Of Tricks* package, in May the following year. Both versions of the film have featured at Queen fan club conventions.

The sound recording is considered for release as Queen's first live album, but when they eventually change their minds, the project is abandoned. It would be a further five years before Queen get around to issuing their first live album.

Both shows see Queen performing before a capacity crowd of 3,500. In keeping with their image of the time, their stage costumes are exclusively black and white. Freddie wears white from head to toe but changes during the show into all black. John wears a typically seventies style velvet jacket and flared trousers, while Brian wears his famous white caped outfit - which is frequently copied thereafter. Roger is dressed in rather less flamboyant attire.

On the second night Freddie's first words are: "The nasty Queenies are back – what do you think of that? Thank you very much. It really is nice to be back home. It's been so long, we've missed you all – we really have. Have you missed us?"

⬈ **'The Scourge of Europe? … being an instrument or manifestation of divine wrath'.** Brian talks to Martin Thorpe in *Record & Popswop Mirror*, December 7 1974: *"We didn't enjoy the first Rainbow gig, though we'd had a hard day and we started changing things on stage, and there were the lights for the video to set up - It was like Bertram Mills' Circus, there were so many things going on we didn't feel too easy.*

"London is very inhibited, you feel as though you're in a theatre, and since people seem to be tightening up on bouncers, you don't feel as though you can run

around. We'd like to see a more subtle attitude from bouncers, it's not our wish that they should be heavy. The presence of bouncers probably provokes more violence anyway."'

Europe 1974

Queen's first proper European tour consists of ten shows in six countries, performed over a two and a half week period. The tour would have been longer had it not been for the truck transporting their equipment being involved in an accident, and being unable to reach the remaining scheduled venues.

November 23
Konserthuset, Gothenburg, Sweden ①
■ *Procession / Now I'm Here / Ogre Battle / Father To Son / White Queen / Flick Of The Wrist / Medley: In The Lap Of The Gods; Killer Queen; The March Of The Black Queen; Bring Back That Leroy Brown / Son & Daughter / Keep Yourself Alive / Seven Seas Of Rhye / Stone Cold Crazy / Liar / In The Lap Of The Gods (Revisited) / Encore Medley: Big Spender; Modern Times Rock'n'Roll / 2nd Encore: Jailhouse Rock / God Save The Queen*

November 25
Helsingin Kulttuuritalo, Helsinki, Finland ①
■ *Procession / Now I'm Here / Ogre Battle / Father To Son / White Queen / Flick Of The Wrist / Medley: In The Lap Of The Gods; Killer Queen; The March Of The Black Queen; Bring Back That Leroy Brown / Son & Daughter / Keep Yourself Alive / Seven Seas Of Rhye / Stone Cold Crazy / Liar / In The Lap Of The Gods (Revisited) / Encore: Modern Times Rock'n'Roll / 2nd Encore: Jailhouse Rock / God Save The Queen*

November 27
Olympan, Lund

November 28
Tivoli, Copenhagen

December 1
140 Theatre, Brussels, Belgium ①
■ *Procession / Now I'm Here / Ogre Battle / Father To Son / White Queen / Flick Of The Wrist / Medley: In The Lap Of The Gods; Killer Queen; The March Of The Black Queen; Bring Back That Leroy Brown / Son & Daughter / Keep Yourself Alive / Seven Seas Of Rhye / Stone Cold Crazy / Liar / In The Lap Of The Gods (Revisited) / Encore Medley: Big Spender; Modern Times Rock'n'Roll / 2nd Encore: Jailhouse Rock / God Save The Queen*

December 2
Brienner Theatre, Munich
Set: as previous night

With their equipment truck repaired only two days previously, on the way to this gig the driver attempts to negotiate a low bridge. It is *too* low, and the equipment gets stuck. Another company come to the rescue and the show goes ahead as planned. An appreciative Queen employ the services of Edwin Shirley Trucking for every tour hereafter.

December 4
Frankfurt
↗ **'Killing Them Softly In Frankfurt'**. By Peter Harvey, Record & Popswop Mirror, December 14, 1974: 'It was, said the tall and studious Brian May, like playing to a vacuum cleaner. *"We were just pouring it out and they (the audience) were sucking it in, with nothing coming back. I tell you, for the first time in many months I felt like I'd done a hard day's work when I came off stage."*

'The fact is, support band Lynyrd Skynyrd, were *exactly what stoned-out Frankfurt wanted. As In England with Golden Earring, so in Germany with Queen, Lynyrd Skynyrd make an over-poweringly successful support band. Here in Frankfurt there were even more difficulties for the English band. Most of the audience are American GI's, looking like inmates from the local borstal with their cropped hair and rippling muscles.*

'*As you enter the 1,100 capacity hall, the air is stuffed with the stench of dope - an intermingling of hash and grass and the sweat of a crowd at least 300 over the top. It's a strange place, a former stock-*

exchange for farmers, complete with balcony, and surrounded by tropical plants.

'Up on the balcony above the stage a group of Queen supporters self-consciously tap their feet to Skynyrd's rhythmic weave. Roger Taylor ever grinning, appears to check on the band, notes the wild applause and disappears, no doubt to plan strategy.

'There's a long break between sets leading to the dissipation of part of the crowd. Heidi, the whizz-kid of EMI Germany, explains the local GI's problem: "Zey have to report back to camp by 11.00 pm". So when Queen's little rock 'n' roll drama explodes, there are considerably fewer people and even less enthusiasm.

'Mercury, the self-styled rock supremo, looks unabashed as Queen open with as much presence as a band can muster. Lights, tapes, and screaming dynamics combine to counter the audience apathy. It's a highly professional first assault..

'Procession, Now I'm Here, and Ogre Battle make a promising start which draws warm applause. But unlike many gigs, this one did not cook to boiling point. If anything the crowd were almost undecided when Queen departed after an energetic stab. It took fully two minutes before muted applause turned to a good old stamp and chant, bringing the boys back on stage for a stirring finale.

'Freddie stalks the stage with controlled aggression as they bash into Big Spender and you realise that here's a rock artist who can sing, cavort, and write songs with an almost contemptuous level of excellence. He is a classic rock star — complete with costume changes and bare hairy chest. Seems his only real need is to develop that outrageous off-stage campery into the act. He's very much the mincing Queen, yet on stage this seemingly natural personality is overtaken with a host of: "Right now we'd like to do" type announcements. Roger Taylor, a veritable demon on the drums and a very fine musician, has more idea when he tells the crowd to get off their arses. Nevertheless there were those in the company who felt Queen showed too much aggression in the face of audience apathy.

'Anyway, by all account there's a huge row in the dressing room afterwards which sends the EMI rep scurrying away with cries of: "Don't let them break the windows."

December 5
Musikhalle, Hamburg

December 6
Sporthalle, Cologne
■ Procession / Now I'm Here / Ogre Battle / Father To Son / White Queen / Flick Of The Wrist / Medley: In The Lap Of The Gods; Killer Queen; The March Of The Black Queen; Bring Back That Leroy Brown / Son & Daughter / Keep Yourself Alive / Seven Seas Of Rhye / Stone Cold Crazy / Liar / In The Lap Of The Gods (Revisited) / Encore Medley: Big Spender; Jailhouse Rock; Stupid Cupid; Be Bop A Lula; Jailhouse Rock (Reprise) / God Save The Queen

December 7
Siegen
   Set: as December 6, but with different rock'n'roll medley
   ↗ **'Queen Lose Gear'**. NME, December 7, 1974:'Queen were forced to cancel the last two gigs in their Scandinavian tour last weekend, after their equipment lorry had been involved in an accident. The lorry overturned, spewing the gear over a wide area and causing extensive damage. The band hurriedly returned to London to collect replacement equipment, and were resuming in Germany this week.'

December 8
Congress Gebouw, The Hague, Holland ①
   Set: as December 6

December 10
Palacio De Los Deportes, Barcelona, Spain ①
■ Procession / Now I'm Here / Ogre Battle / Father To Son / White Queen / Flick Of The Wrist / Medley: In The Lap Of The Gods; Killer Queen; The March Of The Black Queen; Bring Back That Leroy Brown / Son & Daughter / Keep Yourself Alive / Seven Seas Of Rhye / Stone Cold Crazy / Liar / In The Lap Of The Gods (Revisited) / Encore: Modern Times Rock'n'Roll / 2nd Encore Medley: Big Spender; Jailhouse Rock; Stupid Cupid; Be Bop A Lula; Jailhouse Rock (Reprise) / God Save The Queen
   This is the final show of the tour.

❖ **January 17**

N ow I'm Here' / 'Lily Of The Valley' is released as the second single from 'Sheer Heart Attack'. Though the same song is also issued in Japan (coupled with 'Keep Yourself Alive'), curiously it is not issued in America, despite a tour looming in that territory. Though unaided by a promotional video – a tool that would really only kick off with 'Bo Rhap', the following year, the single still reaches No.11 in England.

January 18

The band members attend the wedding of John Deacon, to school teacher Veronica Tetzlaff, in London.

USA 1975
January 31

Queen fly to New York to spend seven days rehearsing at the Beacon Theater, ahead of the 38-show, 30-venue American tour. Further shows in late February and April will be cancelled when Freddie develops problems with his throat.

Indeed, the proposed sell-out end of tour show, in Portland, April 7, is one of them.

The tour is promoted by Mel Bush, with sound mixing as usual by John Harris. Lighting is organised by James Dann, and the tour manager is Iain Brown.

The support acts are Kansas, who replaced Queen in America the previous May, and Mahogany Rush. Some of the shows on the tour feature Styx as support, instead of Kansas.

February 5
Agora, Columbus, Ohio
■ *Procession / Now I'm Here / Ogre Battle / Father To Son / White Queen / Flick Of The Wrist / Medley: In The Lap Of The Gods; Killer Queen; The March Of The Black Queen; Bring Back That Leroy Brown / Son & Daughter; Guitar Solo / Keep Yourself Alive; Drum Solo / Seven Seas Of Rhye / Stone Cold Crazy / Liar / In The Lap Of The Gods (Revisited) / Encore Medley: Big Spender; Modern Times Rock'n'Roll / 2nd Encore: Jailhouse Rock / God Save The Queen*

February 7
Palace Theatre, Dayton, Ohio

February 8
Music Hall, Cleveland, Ohio (Two shows)
■ *Procession / Now I'm Here / Ogre Battle / Father To Son / White Queen / Flick Of The Wrist / Medley: In The Lap Of The Gods; Killer Queen; The March Of The*

Times Rock'n'Roll / Jailhouse Rock / God Save The Queen

February 15
Orpheum Theatre, Boston (2 shows)

February 16
Avery Fisher Hall, New York (2 shows)
■ *Procession / Now I'm Here / Ogre Battle / Father To Son / White Queen / Flick Of The Wrist / Medley: In The Lap Of The Gods; Killer Queen; The March Of The Black Queen; Bring Back That Leroy Brown / Son & Daughter; Guitar Solo / Keep Yourself Alive; Drum Solo / Seven Seas Of Rhye / Stone Cold Crazy / Liar / In The Lap Of The Gods (Revisited) / Encore: Modern Times Rock'n'Roll / 2nd Encore: Big Spender / Jailhouse Rock / God Save The Queen*

Freddie's first words here are familiar ones: "The nasty Queenies are back." He particularly likes this expression.

When he reaches the front of the stage, he is handed a bouquet of white roses. He accepts them, and as a result this too occurs many times hereafter. Queen fans the world over will become accustomed to seeing Freddie receiving flowers, or else casting them out into the audience.

● Freddie is interviewed after the show by Lisa Robinson for Circus magazine. Among other things, she asks whose idea it was to perform "Big Spender":

"Oh (laughs) it was my idea entirely. I like that approach to entertainment. I like that cabaretish sort of thing. I adore Liza Minnelli - I think she's a *wow*. It does appeal to me, the thought of doing more lavish stage type things, but somehow I would like to combine it with the group, not divorce from it. That's a difficult thing, because you've got to approach the others with it and convince them that it's going to work."

February 17
War Memorial, Trenton, New Jersey

February 19
Armory, Lewiston, New York

Black Queen; Bring Back That Leroy Brown / Son & Daughter; Guitar Solo / Keep Yourself Alive; Drum Solo / Seven Seas Of Rhye / Stone Cold Crazy / Liar / In The Lap Of The Gods (Revisited) / Encore Medley: Big Spender; Modern Times Rock'n'Roll / 2nd Encore: Jailhouse Rock / God Save The Queen

February 9
Morris Civic Auditorium, South Bend, Indiana

February 10
Ford Auditorium, Detroit, Michigan

February 11
Student Union Auditorium, Toledo, Ohio

February 14
Palace Theater, Waterbury, Connecticut
■ *Procession / Now I'm Here / Ogre Battle / Father To Son / White Queen / Flick Of The Wrist / Medley: In The Lap Of The Gods; Killer Queen; The March Of The Black Queen; Bring Back That Leroy Brown / Son & Daughter; Guitar Solo / Keep Yourself Alive; Drum Solo / Seven Seas Of Rhye / Stone Cold Crazy / Liar / In The Lap Of The Gods (Revisited) / Encore Medley: Big Spender; Be Bop A Lula / 2nd Encore: Modern*

chance. They have already left for Washington, the venue of the next show.

Not wanting to disappoint the fans, especially at such short notice, and despite strict advice to the contrary Freddie decides he will perform one more show. His problems do not end here, however, as he still has to get to Washington for the gig, and time is running out.

Dave Thomas (of Trident) and Jack Nelson, who have remained behind with Freddie, board a train to Washington, but get no further than Baltimore before they encounter a derailed train blocking their path. As every taxi and hire car has already been booked, an alternative is required, and quickly. By this time it is five o'clock, and Queen are due on stage in three hours.

Eventually another train is found, a sleeper without seats. The three men book it and spend the duration of the journey on their backs in bunk beds. They eventually arrive at the JFK Center at 7.15 pm. John, Roger and Brian are told that the show will be Queen's last for at least three months. The band go on stage only slightly later

February 21
Capitol Theater, Passaic, New Jersey
■ *Procession / Now I'm Here / Ogre Battle / Father To Son / White Queen / Flick Of The Wrist / Medley: In The Lap Of The Gods; Killer Queen; The March Of The Black Queen; Bring Back That Leroy Brown / Son & Daughter; Guitar Solo / Keep Yourself Alive; Drum Solo / Seven Seas Of Rhye / Stone Cold Crazy / Liar / In The Lap Of The Gods (Revisited) / Encore Medley: Jailhouse Rock; Big Spender; Be Bop A Lula; Stupid Cupid; Modern Times Rock'n'Roll; Jailhouse Rock (Reprise) / God Save The Queen*

February 22
Farm Arena, Harrisburg, Pennsylvania

February 23
Erlinger Theater, Philadelphia, Pennsylvania (2 shows)

February 24
Kennedy Center, Washington, Pennsylvania
   Set: Same as February 16
   Having performed the two shows at Erlinger Theater with increasing voice problems, Freddie is taken to see a throat specialist at the Philadelphia University Hospital. The diagnosis is two suspected throat nodes, and the specialist recommends Freddie refrains from singing or speaking for three months. His initial reaction is "the band will kill me", but they do not get the

than scheduled and perform an extraordinary show - despite Freddie having missed the soundcheck.

🖝 Dave Thomas: "They went on stage and did the most amazing gig that I have ever seen them do in my life. It was an amazing show because they seemed to have so much energy, and to our astonishment there was Freddie hitting all the high notes again."

After the show it is suggested Freddie seek a second opinion on his throat condition. He sees a specialist in Washington and is told that nodules are not the cause, but that he has rather severe swelling. He is told to rest his voice, and that three months is excessive. One or two weeks will suffice. To be completely sure, a third consultation in New Orleans, by a specialist who has also treated Tom Jones and Barbra Streisand, confirms the swelling diagnosis, and antibiotics are prescribed.

Six concerts are cancelled: Pittsburgh, Kuzton, Buffalo, Toronto, London (Ontario) and Davenport. The tour recommences on March 5.

March 5
Mary E. Sawyer Auditorium, La Crosse, Wisconsin

In an attempt to save his voice, Freddie keeps his usually considerable between-song banter and vocal improvisations to a minimum now. Even so, further dates have to be cancelled when similar

problems recur. Rather than cancel a number of consecutive shows, however, Queen instead perform some of them, leaving a greater period of time between each one.

March 6
Madison, Wisconsin

■ *Procession / Now I'm Here / Ogre Battle / Father To Son / White Queen / Flick Of The Wrist / Medley: In The Lap Of The Gods; Killer Queen; The March Of The Black Queen; Bring Back That Leroy Brown / Son & Daughter; Guitar Solo / Keep Yourself Alive; Drum Solo / Seven Seas Of Rhye / Stone Cold Crazy / Liar / In The Lap Of The Gods (Revisited) / Encore Medley: Jailhouse Rock; Big Spender; Modern Times Rock'n'Roll; Jailhouse Rock (Reprise) / God Save The Queen*

March 7
Uptown Theater, Milwaukee, Wisconsin

March 8
Aragon Ballroom, Chicago, Illinois

March 9
Keil Auditorium, St Louis, Missouri

The three 'Queens' - 'White', 'Killer' and 'Black', now all feature in the set. This marks an even more exciting period of Queen shows for the fans who have been around from day one. The songs will appear together only during 1975 and 1976, but there will be extensive bootleg coverage.

March 10
Coliseum, Fort Wayne, Indiana

March 12
Municipal Auditorium, Atlanta, Georgia

■ *Procession / Now I'm Here / Ogre Battle / Father To Son / White Queen / Flick Of The Wrist / Medley: In The Lap Of The Gods; Killer Queen; The March Of The Black Queen; Bring Back That Leroy Brown / Son & Daughter; Guitar Solo / Keep Yourself Alive; Drum Solo / Seven Seas Of Rhye / Stone Cold Crazy / Liar / In The Lap Of The Gods (Revisited) / Encore Medley:*

Big Spender; Modern Times Rock'n'Roll / 2nd Encore: Jailhouse Rock / God Save The Queen

March 13
Civic Auditorium, Charleston, South Carolina

March 15
Marina, Miami, Florida

March 18
St Bernard Civic Auditorium, New Orleans, Louisiana

March 20
Municipal Hall, San Antonio, Texas

■ *Procession / Now I'm Here / Ogre Battle / Father To Son / White Queen / Flick Of The Wrist / Medley: In The Lap Of The Gods; Killer Queen; The March Of The Black Queen; Bring Back That Leroy Brown / Son & Daughter; Guitar Solo / Keep Yourself Alive; Drum Solo / Seven Seas Of Rhye / Stone Cold Crazy / Liar / In The Lap Of The Gods (Revisited) / Encore Medley: Jailhouse Rock; Be Bop A Lula; Big Spender; Modern Times Rock'n'Roll; Jailhouse Rock (Reprise) / God Save The Queen*

March 23
McFarlin Auditorium, Dallas, Texas

March 25
Municipal Theater, Tulsa, Oklahoma

March 29♫
Santa Monica Civic Auditorium, Los Angeles (2 Shows)

■ *Procession / Now I'm Here / Ogre Battle / Father To Son / White Queen / Flick Of The Wrist / Hangman / Medley: In The Lap Of The Gods; Killer Queen; The March Of The Black Queen; Bring Back That Leroy Brown / Son & Daughter; Guitar Solo / Keep Yourself Alive; Drum Solo / Seven Seas Of Rhye / Stone Cold Crazy / Liar / In The Lap Of The Gods (Revisited) / Encore Medley: Big Spender; Modern Times Rock'n'Roll / 2nd Encore: Jailhouse Rock / God Save The Queen*

March 30
Winterland, San Francisco, California
Set: as March 29, with longer rock'n'roll medley
➚ **'Killer Queen Slay America'**. *Melody Maker*, April 26, 1975; special report from Beverley Hills California. Justin Pierce & Harvey Kubernik: *'It was mid-afternoon in Beverly-Hills as Freddie Mercury peered over the spacious swimming pool of the Hilton hotel and reflected on Queen's latest tour of the States.*

'"The tour has been going just great. The only drawback has been the problems with my voice, which I've been overtaxing. But since I've been taking care of it and resting more, it's been fine. The problem is that when you do a tour, you try to schedule the concerts as close as possible.

'"Therefore, it's like a constant workout. However,

at the moment it's raring to go and at the conclusion of this tour, we're going to take a rest in Hawaii, which we really deserve. From there it'll be on to Japan and Australia."'

April 2

Kindmens Fieldhouse, Edmonton, Alberta, Canada ①

■ *Procession / Now I'm Here / Ogre Battle / Father To Son / White Queen / Flick Of The Wrist / Hangman / Medley: In The Lap Of The Gods; Killer Queen; The March Of The Black Queen; Bring Back That Leroy Brown / Son & Daughter; Guitar Solo / Keep Yourself Alive; Drum Solo / Seven Seas Of Rhye / Stone Cold Crazy / Liar / In The Lap Of The Gods (Revisited) / Encore Medley: Jailhouse Rock; Be Bop A Lula / 2nd Encore: Big Spender; Modern Times Rock'n'Roll; Jailhouse Rock (Reprise) / God Save The Queen*

This is Queen's first concert in Canada. They are joined on stage for the encore by the support band Kansas.

April 3

Calgary, Alberta

Set: as April 2, but with different medley (unknown)

April 6

Seattle, Washington

■ *Procession / Now I'm Here / Ogre Battle / Father To Son / White Queen / Flick Of The Wrist / Hangman / Medley: In The Lap Of The Gods; Killer Queen; The March Of The Black Queen; Bring Back That Leroy Brown / Son & Daughter; Guitar Solo / Keep Yourself Alive; Drum Solo / Seven Seas Of Rhye / Stone Cold Crazy / Liar / In The Lap Of The Gods (Revisited) / Encore Medley: Big Spender; Modern Times Rock'n'Roll / 2nd Encore: Jailhouse Rock / God Save The Queen*

An additional tour of North America – comprising eighteen concerts, is pencilled in for the summer of 1975, but ultimately cancelled, despite tickets having been sold for many venues. This time it is due to problems with Trident.

In December 1974 the band recruit the services

of music lawyer Jim Beach to free them from their Trident obligations. This is both a tricky and greatly significant undertaking. Ties with the Sheffield brothers will eventually be severed in August 1975.

1975 JAPANESE TOUR
April 18

The band arrive in Tokyo to begin their first tour of Japan. All four members are overwhelmed to discover over 3,000 screaming fans gathered to welcome them. They cover every available vantage point. The phenomenon is christened 'Queen Mania', and will recur at every Japanese tour hereafter. Freddie will later cite Japan as his very favourite country, and his shopping expeditions there will become legendary.

There exists some quite wonderful footage in the *Magic Years* videos of this astonished, bemused and young looking Queen arriving at the airport. Each band member stepping out of the aircraft is clearly shocked at the scene. Banners proclaiming 'Japan Welcomes Queen' and 'We

Love You Brian' are totally unexpected.

The tour opens and concludes at the same venue, the vast Budokan Hall, in Tokyo, which is most commonly used to stage martial art events and Sumo wrestling competitions. Although the tour entails only eight shows, between them they yield many bootlegs – and very good ones at that.

April 19
Budokan Hall, Tokyo, Japan ①

■ *Procession / Now I'm Here / Ogre Battle / Father To Son / White Queen / Flick Of The Wrist / Hangman / Great King Rat / Medley: In The Lap Of The Gods; Killer Queen; The March Of The Black Queen; Bring Back That Leroy Brown / Son & Daughter / Doing All Right / Stone Cold Crazy / Keep Yourself Alive / Seven Seas Of Rhye / Liar / In The Lap Of The Gods (Revisited) / Encore: Jailhouse Rock / 2nd Encore: See What A Fool I've Been / God Save The Queen*

This concert is filmed for a Japanese documentary on the band. Although it is not broadcast as a purely live programme, and only a small amount of material is transmitted, numerous bootleg recordings of various types subsequently appear.

Queen perform this, and the concluding show here, before a capacity audience of 10,000 people. Sumo wrestlers are employed to keep over-zealous fans off the stage. However, when the band appear, there is a huge surge forward which turns into a potentially dangerous situation. Freddie halts the show momentarily and appeals for calm. This achieves the desired effect and she show continues without further drama.

April 22
Aichi-ken Taiikukan, Nagoya

John Deacon commented during this tour that the collective audience noise was so deafening, that it seemed to him as if the whole arena was shaking.

April 23
Kokusai Taikan, Kobe

■ *Procession / Now I'm Here / Ogre Battle / Father To Son / White Queen / Flick Of The Wrist / Hangman / Great King Rat / Medley: In The Lap Of The Gods; Killer Queen; The March Of The Black Queen; Bring Back That Leroy Brown / Son & Daughter / Doing All Right / Stone Cold Crazy / Keep Yourself Alive / Seven Seas Of Rhye / Liar / In The Lap Of The Gods (Revisited) / Encore Medley: Big Spender; Modern Times Rock'n'Roll / 2nd Encore: Jailhouse Rock / See What A Fool I've Been / God Save The Queen*

April 25
Kyuden Taiikukan, Fukuoka

● Brian May, on performing in Japan: "It's such an amazing novelty. It's so different to everywhere else, because in addition to the immediate feeling you get from the people you're playing to, you have all the real magic of the traditional part of Japanese life which affects you very much while you're there."

It quickly becomes impossible for any member of the band to go anywhere and not be recognised.

● Roger Taylor: "I went into a shop to buy a tape recorder and suddenly the shop keeper stared at me. 'Ah so... you Queen', and proceeded to drag a camera from underneath the counter. He just kept taking pictures all the time, for about ten minutes. I couldn't get another word out of him."

April 28
Okayama-ken Taiikukan, Okayama

■ Procession / Now I'm Here / Ogre Battle / Father To Son / White Queen / Flick Of The Wrist / Hangman / Great King Rat / Medley: In The Lap Of The Gods; Killer Queen; The March Of The Black Queen; Bring Back That Leroy Brown / Son & Daughter / Doing All Right / Stone Cold Crazy / Keep Yourself Alive / Seven Seas Of Rhye / Liar / In The Lap Of The Gods (Revisited) / Encore Medley: Big Spender; Modern Times Rock'n'Roll / 2nd Encore: Jailhouse Rock / See What A Fool I've Been / God Save The Queen

April 29
Yamaha Tsumagoi Hall, Shizuoka

As the main lights dim and a single spotlight picks out Brian for the start of his guitar solo, the other members disappear to the back of the stage, in darkness. Roger bends to sit on a box for the duration of the solo, but unbeknown to him it is overhanging the back of the stage. The box disappears off the edge, and takes Roger with it. Despite somersaulting backwards and landing heavily on his back, he sustains no serious injuries and continues the show. The audience are unaware of the incident.

April 30
Bunka Taiikukan, Yokohama

The band return to the stage after the encore dressed in traditional Japanese kimonos. The gesture is greatly appreciated by the audience and the band repeat it many times, in Japan, and elsewhere.

May 1 ⬀
Budokan Hall, Tokyo

■ Procession / Now I'm Here / Ogre Battle / Father To Son / White Queen / Flick Of The Wrist / Hangman / Great King Rat / Medley: In The Lap Of The Gods; Killer Queen; The March Of The Black Queen; Bring Back That Leroy Brown / Son & Daughter / Doing All Right / Stone Cold Crazy / Keep Yourself Alive / Seven Seas Of Rhye / Liar / In The Lap Of The Gods (Revisited) / Encore Medley: Big Spender; Modern Times Rock'n'Roll / 2nd Encore: Jailhouse Rock / See What A Fool I've Been / God Save The Queen

This show is filmed and later broadcast on Japanese television.

↗ **'Kimono my Place'**. Melody Maker, May 24, 1975: 'Ah so - its Fleddie Mercury! Queen Elizabeth II is not the only British Queen to wow Japan. The band has just returned from an amazing tour there, and Freddie tells CHRIS WELCH all about their adventures ...

'PANT NUEDE! " roared Tokyo fans as Queen swaggered across the stage 'midst flashing lights, smoke and dry ice.

'A curious cry but roughly translated into English, it means "Get your knickers off," and such debasement of the language was a direct result of coaching from one Freddie Mercury, and his trusty interpreter.

'Freddie was inspired to introduce his Japanese fans to the art of coarse shouting when he attended a strip club one night during Queen's recent highly successful tour of the land of the rising steel production.

'To his surprise the buxom Nipponese wenches were shedding kimonos to the swelling rhythms of "Killer Queen". the hit song that has sent hearts pulsing throughout decadent Western style society. "We were shouting 'Get 'em off and our interpreter asked what it meant. When we explained they fell about laughing, and translated it into Japanese.

'Soon Queen audiences found themselves encouraged to shout, not only "Yeah, yeah," and expressions to the effect that they felt "all right," but such diverse variations as "Shag out!"

'Freddie chuckled at the memory as he sipped tea

from a ceremonial bowl. He was clad in a dazzling kimono, and sat crossed legged on the floor of his abode, decorated with Samurai swords and hand-made parasols, just down the road from Shepherd's Bush.

'Rather like the Victorian explorers, he had brought home the lifestyle and artifacts of a foreign culture, and seemed anxious not to lose the magic of a country that had obviously made a considerable impression,"I loved it there, the life style, the art ... I'd go back tomorrow if I could," insisted Freddie shooing his cats Tom and Jerry off a Led Zeppelin album that had been carelessly left exposed.'

May 22

Freddie receives an Ivor Novello award for 'Killer Queen'. It is the first such recognition of his songwriting talent.

August

Queen work upon new material for their fourth album *A Night At The Opera*. The sessions eventually conclude in November.

❖ October 31

EMI 2375 is issued as the fifth UK single. 'Bohemian Rhapsody', coupled with 'I'm In Love With My Car', provides Queen with their first number one single. The same pairing is issued on December 2 in America, and peaks at number nine. The two tracks are a universal pairing.

UK 1975 - A Night At The Opera Tour

Following rehearsals at Elstree Studios, the location of the 'Rhapsody' video shoot, the band kick off their third headlining tour. It begins in familiar Queen territory with two shows at the Liverpool Empire, and concludes on Christmas Eve at the renowned Hammersmith Odeon show. The support act is Oxford-based Mr Big.

The set takes on a very different feel for this tour, now accommodating 'The Prophet's Song' and 'Sweet Lady' from *A Night At The Opera*. Other material from the album would follow later - 'Death On Two Legs', 'Lazing On A Sunday Afternoon', 'You're My Best Friend' and '39'. The

album is released during the tour, on November 21.

The tour programme cover reads simply, 'Queen Invite You To A Night At The Opera'.

November 14
Empire, Liverpool

■ *Bohemian Rhapsody (Taped Intro) / Ogre Battle / Sweet Lady / White Queen / Flick Of The Wrist / Medley: Bohemian Rhapsody; Killer Queen; The March Of The Black Queen; Bohemian Rhapsody (Reprise); Bring Back That Leroy Brown / Son & Daughter / The Prophet's Song / Stone Cold Crazy / Doing All Right / Keep Yourself Alive / Seven Seas Of Rhye / Liar / In The Lap Of The Gods (Revisited) / Encore: Now I'm Here / 2nd Encore Medley: Jailhouse Rock; Stupid Cupid; Be Bop A Lula; Jailhouse Rock Reprise) / God Save The Queen*

The set now opens with a pre-recorded introduction put together by Queen champion Kenny Everett, but not before a small drama unfolds.

In somewhat of a panic, Freddie calls Kenny the day before the tour is to commence and begs suggestions for a way to begin the show. Kenny obliges with a typically unorthodox approach, which he gets to them just in time for the first show: "Ladies and Gentlemen... 'A Night At The Opera' / 20 second pause / snippet of 'Ogre Battle' / the opera section from 'Bo Rhap', up to the point of "Beelzebub, has the devil put aside for me?" and the band bound onto the stage. This is performed in more or less the same way as most fans today will recall it in latter Queen concerts, from the *Works* and *Magic* shows. Queen leave the stage at the appropriate point and allow the light-show extravaganza to take over for the opera section which cannot be recreated live, before they return for the heavy section and tranquil conclusion. The final verse ("Nothing really matters") is excised. Queen instead segue straight into 'Ogre Battle' which now includes a dramatic false ending. Roger has added a gong to his drum kit for the conclusion of 'Rhapsody'.

Because 'Now I'm Here' no longer opens the show, it is performed instead as the first encore. Freddie concludes each concert by throwing red roses into the audience. Queen's staff have already painstakingly removed the thorns to save Freddie's fingers. He also discard his tambourine in similar fashion, having used it first for 'Liar'.

This is the period which sees Freddie painting the finger nails on one hand black. Many fans will subsequently copy the trend.

November 15
Empire, Liverpool

Set: as preceding night, but with 'Modern Times' after 'Keep Yourself Alive'

Brian's 'The Prophet's Song' is new to the set. It is far too complex to recreate on stage exactly as it is on recordon, but Queen manage a startlingly close rendition. For the multi-tracked vocal parts, Freddie sings essentially improvised lines based on the real lyrics, with a delayed echo on his voice. The fans adore this song, and it always go down a storm.

🕮 Brian (on 'The Prophet's Song'): "I had a dream about what seemed like revenge on people, and I couldn't really work out in the dream what it was that people had done wrong. It was something like a flood. Things had gone much too far and as a kind of reparation, the whole thing had to start again.

"In the dream, people were walking on the streets trying to touch each other's hands, desperate to try and make some sign that they were caring about other people. I felt that the

trouble must be – and this is one of my obsessions anyway – that people don't make enough contact with each other.

"A feeling that runs through a lot of the songs I write is that if there is a direction to mankind, it ought to be a coming together, and at the moment it doesn't seem to be happening very well. I worry about it a lot. I worry about not doing anything about it. Things seem to be getting worse.

"But I wasn't trying to preach in the song at all. I was just trying to put across the questions which are in my mind rather than the answers, which I don't believe I have. The only answer I can see, is to be aware of things like that and to sort of try and put yourself to rights. There is an overseer in the song though, whose cry to the multitudes is to 'Listen to the warning of the Seer'.

"In the song is this guy who also appeared in the dream. I don't really know whether he was a prophet or an impostor, but anyway, he's standing up there and saying: 'Look, you've got to mend your ways.' I still don't know whether he's the man who thinks he's sent from God or whether he isn't. The song asks questions rather than gives answers."

November 16
Coventry Theatre, Coventry
■ *Bohemian Rhapsody (Taped Intro) / Ogre Battle / Sweet Lady / White Queen / Flick Of The Wrist / Medley: Bohemian Rhapsody; Killer Queen; The March Of The Black Queen; Bohemian Rhapsody (Reprise); Bring Back That Leroy Brown / Son & Daughter / The Prophet's Song / Stone Cold Crazy / Doing All Right / Keep Yourself Alive / Seven Seas Of Rhye / Liar / In The Lap Of The Gods (Revisited) / Encore: Now I'm Here / 2nd Encore Medley: Big Spender; Jailhouse Rock / God Save The Queen*

In a repeat of the final Budokan show, in May, Freddie emerges for the encore dressed in a kimono. He later discards it and finishes the show in shorts.

November 17/18
Colston Hall, Bristol
Set: as November 16

↗ **'The SUFFERING of QUEEN FREDDIE'.** (Last of the Big Spenders)... I mean, you try scoring a silk sash in downtown Bristol... Among other things – most of them unrelated to the concert.' *NME*, November 29, 1975.

Queen
Invite You To
A Night At The Opera

● Interviewer Julie Webb is intrigued by Freddie's Japanese kimono, which is now lacking its sash, following the preceding night's show. *'Well, you saw it last night. Came on for 'Big Spender' in the kimono (which is apparently worth £2-300) and did the impromptu strip. I took the belt off and thought 'I'll dangle the sash'."* He pauses... *"I dropped it. Then I thought 'Can I get it back?' Of course I couldn't. Then I spotted this girl obviously after my kimono. I thought: 'No way dearie'. I flung it to safety offstage."'*

November 19
Capitol, Cardiff
■ *Bohemian Rhapsody (Taped Intro) / Ogre Battle / Sweet Lady / White Queen / Flick Of The Wrist / Medley: Bohemian Rhapsody; Killer Queen; The March Of The Black Queen; Bohemian Rhapsody (Reprise); Bring Back That Leroy Brown / Son & Daughter / The Prophet's Song / Stone Cold Crazy / Doing All Right / Keep Yourself Alive / Seven Seas Of Rhye / Liar / In The Lap Of The Gods (Revisited) / Encore: Now I'm Here / 2nd Encore Medley: Big Spender; Be Bop A Lula; Jailhouse Rock / God Save The Queen*

November 20
The promotional video for 'Bohemian Rhapsody' is shown on *Top Of The Pops* for the first time. It is directed by Bruce Gowers who previously directed the Rainbow concert footage, a year earlier.

November 21
Odeon, Taunton
❖ Also on November 21, the album that Brian May later refers to as Queen's *Sgt Pepper*, is released in the UK. *A Night At The Opera* is their fourth album, and provides the band with their first number one, on December 13. Elektra release it two weeks later in America. Only two tracks on the album are not incorporated into the live show.

While Brian's charming 'Good Company' is not an entirely surprising absentee, Freddie's vaudeville inspired 'Seaside Rendezvous' certainly is. Featuring as it does vocal impressions

of various brass and woodwind instruments from Roger and Freddie, its visual concert potential is sadly overlooked. Queen do eventually get to vocally emulate these instruments on stage, however, during the song "39'. The European tour of '79 will proffer probably the most notable examples of this.

November 23
Winter Gardens, Bournemouth
🎤 Trevor Cooper (roadie for Queen's support group on this tour, Mr Big): "Queen really were good guys. They demanded perfection and Freddie would sometimes throw tantrums, but it was because he always wanted things to be right.

"You could tell Freddie was gay by his effeminate gestures but he could swear like the best of them. He'd be 'fuck this' and 'fuck that' and the next minute he was calling everyone 'darling' and having a laugh.

"I once saw him literally shrink this six foot bloke down to an inch. Queen had just taken the stage and this bloke shouted to Freddie, 'You fucking poof', or something like that. Freddie demanded that the crew turn the spotlight on the crowd and find this fella. He then said to him, 'Say that again, darling', and the bloke didn't know what to do. Everyone was laughing. Freddie just

had this ability to cream an audience - milk it. If he'd have said take your clothes off, they would have done. He was a showman - one of only a very few in the world."

November 24
Gaumont, Southampton

November 26 🎵
Free Trade Hall, Manchester (2 Shows)
■ **First show:** *Bohemian Rhapsody (Taped Intro) / Ogre Battle / Sweet Lady / White Queen / Flick Of The Wrist / Medley: Bohemian Rhapsody; Killer Queen; The March Of The Black Queen; Bohemian Rhapsody (Reprise); Bring Back That Leroy Brown / Son & Daughter / The Prophet's Song / Stone Cold Crazy / Doing All Right / Keep Yourself Alive / Seven Seas Of Rhye / Liar / In The Lap Of The Gods (Revisited) / Encore: Now I'm Here / 2nd Encore: Jailhouse Rock / God Save The Queen*
Second show: Same as first show, but with 'Big Spender' after 'Jailhouse Rock'.
Brian encounters problems here while attempting to set up his guitar before the soundcheck. For inexplicable reasons horrible feedback noise is created, but only at certain areas of the stage. After a thorough examination of the stage, the fault is discovered: a hidden electric cable to the generator system. The entire stage earthing is re-wired. The soundcheck goes ahead somewhat delayed, but the show begins on time.

The mood on stage for this show is even more jovial than usual. 'Bo Rhap' has provided Queen with their first number one the previous day. Spirits are high. The band is on a roll.

Freddie, after 'Ogre Battle': "Good evening everybody. You feeling fine? We're just feeling great, so there's gonna be some good fun here tonight."

After 'Sweet Lady': "By the way, I forgot to say, how nice it is to be here in Manchester. And it's really nice to do two shows. Right now I'd like to drink a toast to all you lovely people here. Cheers! We'll carry on with a number called 'White Queen'."

Brian then introduces 'Flick Of The Wrist'. Freddie opens the song on piano but it is noticeably shorter than the album version. He cuts it dead after the line: "He's taken an arm, taken a leg, all this time honey." Brian sustains a guitar note, and Freddie concludes, "Baby you've been had." This is great song and a much loved concert favourite – though it did not stay for long.

"I'll tell you what. We'd like right now, to do a special little medley for you, about four songs all rolled up into one, and we're gonna start with a segment from a number called 'Bohemian Rhapsody'." The medley runs through two other tracks, and concludes with the poignant "Any way the wind blows" line, from the song which began it.

Roger then counts the band in for 'Leroy Brown'. Again, few of the words present on the album rendering are sung here by Freddie, but still it is very nice, and a little ukulele solo from Brian is an unexpected touch which the audience love.

When numerous fans shout out suggestions as to what song should be next, Freddie explains that the request bit comes later, and 'Brighton Rock' begins. The guitar solo has come a long way since the days of 'Son & Daughter' where its origins lie. Even so, it is still a part of that song. Only later is 'Brighton' played in its own right.

Freddie: "It's now time to do another number from this little album here. Let me see... I think we'll do a number called 'The Prophet's Song'." A breathtaking version of Brian's dream-inspired track then follows. Using a delayed echo on his voice, Freddie is able to mimic, quite incredibly, the multi-tracked harmonies in the song's mid section. It does, however, end rather strangely, with a speeded up guitar passage, which enables the band to segue into the frenzied mayhem of 'Stone Cold Crazy'.

Freddie then asks for requests. The audience duly respond with 'Seven Seas Of Rhye', 'Liar', 'In The Lap Of The Gods' and the like. "We'll do the lot of 'em" is Freddie's retort: "and this one's called 'Doing All Right'." Once more, he is seated at the piano for the opening section, but is soon on his feet again.

This starts out as a melancholy ballad but then, almost without warning, turns into one of the heaviest rock numbers in the Queen repertoire. John and Roger really go to town here.

After that, Freddie incites the audience to clap along to the rhythm. When they begin to clap too fast he tells them to slow down. "Stay with us," he implores. 'Keep Yourself Alive' starts and Freddie begins his now customary string of one-liners: "Join in with all the choruses! Are you with us? You in the balcony, sing up!"

"You might recall this one!" says Brian, later. "It's called the 'Seven Seas Of Rhye'."

The concert is nearing its end. And the audience knows it.

'Liar' is up next. This gives each member of the band an opportunity to show off their respective talent. The ever demure John Deacon really *shines* here, while Roger pounds his way around the entire drum kit at an identical pace to that of the album version. Freddie comments that it's "sounding good", and after another fine rendion the band exit the stage.

Just when the audience think there is no more, Queen return with 'Now I'm Here' and pretty well bring the house down. Brian's guitar parts, as ever, are faultless. Before the song fades completely away, Brian begins the next song, that which closes the show. Freddie misses the first

76

cue, but it is hardly noticed, and 'Jailhouse Rock' kicks off.

November 29/30
Hammersmith Odeon, London
■ *First night*: Bohemian Rhapsody (Taped Intro) / Ogre Battle / Sweet Lady / White Queen / Flick Of The Wrist / Medley: Bohemian Rhapsody; Killer Queen; The March Of The Black Queen; Bohemian Rhapsody (Reprise); Bring Back That Leroy Brown / Son & Daughter / The Prophet's Song / Stone Cold Crazy / Doing All Right / Keep Yourself Alive / Modern Times Rock'n'Roll / Seven Seas Of Rhye / Liar / In The Lap Of The Gods (Revisited) / Encore: Now I'm Here / 2nd Encore Medley: Jailhouse Rock ; Be Bop A Lula; Jailhouse Rock (Reprise) / God Save The Queen

'Brighton Rock' is also new to the set on this tour. Featuring a lengthy guitar work-out for Brian, it enables Freddie, John and Roger to leave the stage for five minutes before returning for the conclusion.

🕊 While in London Freddie and Roger are invited to participate in a Capital Radio phone-in. Actually, Freddie ends up appearing on Kenny Everett's programme and Roger on Maggie Norden's. Both answer Queen trivia questions, such as how many drum sticks did Roger get through during the Japanese tour. "Fourteen in ten days," he responds, "I was going wild, chucking them into the audience."

■ *Second night*: Bohemian Rhapsody (Intro) / Ogre

Battle / Sweet Lady / White Queen / Flick Of The Wrist / Medley: Bohemian Rhapsody / Killer Queen / The March Of The Black Queen / Bring Back That Leroy Brown / Bohemian Rhapsody (Reprise) / Brighton Rock / Son & Daughter / The Prophet's Song / Stone Cold Crazy / Doing All Right / Keep Yourself Alive / Modern Times Rock'n'Roll / Seven Seas Of Rhye / Liar / Now I'm Here / Jailhouse Rock / Be Bop A Lula / Jailhouse Rock (Reprise) / God Save The Queen

December 1/2
Hammersmith Odeon, London
↗ 'Queen Explode', by Ray Fox-Cumming. *Record Mirror & Disc*, December 13, 1975:
'Queen perfected the presentation of their show for this British tour very early, so there was little difference between the concert I saw at Bristol near the start of the tour and this fourth night at Hammersmith at around the halfway mark.

'They didn't quite manage to defeat the notorious Odeon echo, which wreaked minor havoc with 'The Prophet Song' and 'Son And Daughter'.

'Visually it has the most exciting start of any show I've seen with a silhouette of Freddie gracing a darkened stage before the show explodes into life with magnesium flares popping off all over the place. After that kind of beginning one wonders how they can possibly maintain the impact, but it only flags slightly for a couple of numbers about two-thirds the way through before they run into a succession of hit singles climaxing towards the end,

'Everyone makes mention of Freddie's fine singing, but on this particular night his piano playing was equally excellent, adding a great deal to a number of songs, especially White Queen, which for me is one of the major highlights of the show.

'It's certainly already a great show and, by the time they've had a chance to include one or more extra numbers from the new album (there are only three in the set at the moment), it should be even better…'

December 7
Civic Hall, Wolverhampton

December 8
Guildhall, Preston
■ Bohemian Rhapsody (Taped Intro) / Ogre Battle / Sweet Lady / White Queen / Flick Of The Wrist / Medley: Bohemian Rhapsody; Killer Queen; The March Of The Black Queen; Bohemian Rhapsody (Reprise); Bring Back That Leroy Brown / Son & Daughter / The Prophet's Song / Stone Cold Crazy / Doing All Right / Keep Yourself Alive / Modern Times Rock'n'Roll / Seven Seas Of Rhye / Liar / In The Lap

Of The Gods (Revisited) / Encore: Now I'm Here / 2nd Encore: Jailhouse Rock / God Save The Queen

December 9/10
Odeon, Birmingham

December 11
City Hall, Newcastle-Upon-Tyne
🗩 After this concert the entourage moves on towards Dundee, but after only two miles they encounter a road block. Plain clothes policemen then escort everyone to the local station, on suspicion of being in possession of drugs. The group, crew and tour coach are all searched, before being allowed to continue on their way. Freddie is asked if he has any drugs: "Don't be so impertinent, you stupid little man!" is his retort.

"The strongest drug anyone imbibed was the odd bottle of Southern Comfort or two," Dicken (lead singer of Mr Big) later explained.

December 13
Caird Hall, Dundee
■ Bohemian Rhapsody (Taped Intro) / Ogre Battle / Sweet Lady / White Queen / Flick Of The Wrist / Medley: Bohemian Rhapsody; Killer Queen; The March Of The Black Queen; Bohemian Rhapsody (Reprise); Bring Back That Leroy Brown / Son & Daughter / The Prophet's Song / Stone Cold Crazy / Doing All Right / Keep Yourself Alive / Modern Times Rock'n'Roll / Seven Seas Of Rhye / Liar / In The Lap Of The Gods (Revisited) / Encore: Now I'm Here / 2nd Encore Medley: Big Spender; Jailhouse Rock; Shake Rattle And Roll; Jailhouse Rock (Reprise) / God Save The Queen

"Shake Rattle And Roll" is included in the set for a short spell. It was always an infrequent visitor to the Queen show.

December 14
Capitol, Aberdeen

December 15/16
Glasgow Apollo, Glasgow
■ **Both nights**: Bohemian Rhapsody (Taped Intro) / Ogre Battle / Sweet Lady / White Queen / Flick Of The

Queen Live '75

Wrist / Medley: Bohemian Rhapsody; Killer Queen; The March Of The Black Queen; Bohemian Rhapsody (Reprise); Bring Back That Leroy Brown / Son & Daughter / The Prophet's Song / Stone Cold Crazy / Doing All Right / Keep Yourself Alive / Modern Times Rock'n'Roll / Seven Seas Of Rhye / Liar / In The Lap Of The Gods (Revisited) / Encore: Now I'm Here / 2nd Encore Medley: Big Spender; Jailhouse Rock; Be Bop A Lula; Jailhouse Rock (Reprise) / God Save The Queen

'Be Bop A Lula' and the reprised 'Jailhouse Rock' were omitted on the second night.

↗ *Record Mirror & Disc*, December 13, 1975: 'QUEEN ARE to play a special concert at Hammersmith Odeon on Christmas Eve.

'*It will be broadcast live on BBC 2's* Old Grey Whistle Test. *The band will be doing a different stage presentation for this concert.*

'*The event is something of a triumph for their manager John Reid, who organised a similar show last Christmas Eve, with a TV tie up, starring Elton John. The BBC will be rescreening the Elton Christmas show on December 27th. On December 19th, the Russell Harty show will feature the Rocket Records trip to the states, which happened in October.*

'*Next year, Queen are preparing for their visit to Australia, Japan and the States.*'

↗ **'QUEEN, Hammersmith Odeon'.** Melody Maker, December 1975: 'Queen hit London at what is probably the most successful point in their career to date. Their new album, *A Night At The Opera* has met with critical acclaim and the single 'Bohemian Rhapsody' sells in huge numbers despite its bizarre structure. The band should be well into their set by the time the London shows open. A few of the tracks from the new album are featured plus old greats, 'Liar' and 'Keep Yourself Alive'. Queen are well on their way to becoming one of Britain's biggest bands and Kenny Everett is playing them to death on his Capitol Radio Sunday afternoon show. What more could you want? Britain's most regal band awaits your presence.'

December 24✍
Hammersmith Odeon, London

■ *Now I'm Here / Ogre Battle / White Queen / Medley: Bohemian Rhapsody; Killer Queen; The March Of The Black Queen; Bohemian Rhapsody (Reprise); Bring Back That Leroy Brown / Brighton Rock / Son & Daughter / Keep Yourself Alive / Liar / In The Lap Of The Gods (Revisited) / Encore Medley: Big Spender; Jailhouse Rock; Stupid Cupid; Be Bop A Lula; Shake Rattle And Roll; Jailhouse Rock (Reprise) / Seven Seas Of Rhye / See What A Fool I've Been / God Save The Queen* (Unusual track sequence, but correct)

This show is broadcast live on both *Radio One* and *The Old Grey Whistle Test*, whose host Bob Harris introduces the band on stage. Due to the television and radio coverage (including numerous brutally edited repeats), this performance will go on to become the most heavily bootlegged of the band's career.

Although at one point only three vinyl albums were in circulation – *Command Performance, Christmas At The Beeb* and the curiously titled *Halfpence* – since the advent of compact disc, innumerable alternatives have flooded the market: *Eve Of Christmas, London 1975, Rhapsody In Red, Command Performance, X'Mas 1975, Live Dates Vol.17, Christmas At The Beeb, Unauthorised*, and most recently *High Voltage*.

Due to public demand, the radio broadcast will be repeated the following year, on December 28.

Freddie looks fantastic in a white silk Dickensian style outfit, with a custom designed mini-jacket, exaggerated flared trousers and white boots. He also wears numerous rings and bangles, and has the finger nails of his left hand painted black. His hair is long, thick, wavy and jet black. John wears white trousers and waistcoat, and a black shirt. Brian too, is clad entirely in white; sporting his beloved Zandra Rhodes cape, and reminiscent of a white Batman. Both he and Freddie look decidedly God-like!

Following 'White Queen' Freddie speaks: "Now then, we're gonna do a nice tasty little medley for you... just like the one we did the other day, yes, and we're gonna start off with a little segment from a numberrrr, called 'Bohemian Rhapsody'."

A Concert Documentary

After just two minutes Freddie is fingering the opening chords of 'Killer Queen' which replace the finger clicking of the album cut. The crowd assist with accompanying handclaps and the band perform the song up to the point where the line "To avoid complications she never kept the same address" is due, then the direction changes again and the band are into 'Black Queen' which in turn goes into the 'Bo Rhap' reprise: "Ooh yeah - ooh yeah, nothing really matters, anyone can see, nothing really matters, nothing really matters to me." There the medley ends.

Later. "Now then, we're now gonna feature Brian - Brian May on guitar. This number's entitled 'Brighton Rock'." Nearly eleven minutes later and an exhausted Brian (with help from Roger and John) abruptly ends the song.

Roger opens the next song before Brian's familiar guitar intro identifies 'Keep Yourself Alive'. By now Freddie has changed into a tight fitting frontless black satin jump-suit. Even by today's standards, it is provocative apparel.

Freddie: "Now it's time to join in everybody... and you can sing along in all the choruses, give us a helping hand. You can take all your clothes off. What about you in the balcony... are you with us? Everybody at home, let's go." 'Keep Yourself Alive' begins. Roger takes a fifty-second drum solo mid-way through and Freddie seems as impressed as the audience.

"And now, a special rendition of a little number called 'Liar'." Roger pounds his way around his drum kit again and Freddie quips: "Sock it to 'em Rog."

Brian introduces the next one: "It's been like a party here tonight. Thanks for making it really something for us, it's felt a lot different. Thanks for giving us a good year. We'd like to leave you in the lap of the gods." Following 'Gods', during which Freddie is obscured by an over-active dry ice machine, Brian owns up to a band oversight: "This is where we start, I think", he says, realising that a song has been overlooked in the set.

Freddie: "Right, a number we forgot to do in the set... it's called 'Seven Seas Of Rhye'."

For the encore, Freddie returns to the stage in a Japanese kimono once more, discarding it to reveal tight white shorts and T-shirt. The show ends with hundreds of festively decorated balloons dropping from nets above the hall. Curiously, a number of fully inflated blow-up ladies also descend.

🔹 Although this show is widely regarded by fans as one of Queen's finest, the band feel differently. Brian: "Freddie and I, though me particularly, had dreadful flu and could hardly walk, let alone play - so it wasn't one of our greatest performances. But it was still all very exciting. It was the adrenaline that kept us going."

Jeff Griffin (BBC producer of this broadcast): "I next worked with Queen on the Christmas Eve concert of 1975. By that time I had started to do Christmas Eve simulcasts for BBC 2 with my colleague Mike Appleton, who was also producing the Whistle Test. We'd done Elton John at the Hammersmith Odeon the previous year and it so happened in 1975 that Queen were having a run just up to Christmas. We had a chat with their management and they said 'Yeah, okay, fine. We'd be happy with that'. So that's what we did.

"That show went marvellously well. By that time - this is now about a year and a half after I'd done the in-house concert, as it were, up at the Hippodrome (September 13, 1973) - the band were well in form, and there were no problems with Freddie's voice or pitch, or anything else.

"It was a great show and as well as being broadcast live as a simulcast on Christmas Eve 1975 on Radio One and BBC 2 TV, I put part of it out in sound only on Radio One - on the 28th February 1976."

Brian and Freddie's parents meet for the first time at this show. It transpires they had lived close to one another for over sixteen years, yet somehow have never actually encountered one another.

USA 1976
January 20

Queen fly to New York for rehearsals ahead of their third American tour – and their second as a headlining act. The 33-date tour begins in Connecticut and concludes six weeks later with five shows in Los Angeles and one in San Diego, on March 13.

January 27
Palace Theater, Waterbury, Connecticut
■ *Bohemian Rhapsody (Taped Intro) / Ogre Battle / Sweet Lady / White Queen / Flick Of The Wrist / Medley: Bohemian Rhapsody; Killer Queen; The March Of The Black Queen; Bohemian Rhapsody (Reprise); Bring Back That Leroy Brown / Brighton Rock / Son & Daughter / The Prophet's Song / Stone Cold Crazy / Doing All Right / Lazing On A Sunday Afternoon / Keep Yourself Alive / Seven Seas Of Rhye / Liar / In The Lap Of The Gods (Revisited) / Encore: Now I'm Here / God Save The Queen*

The band introduce a new and unexpected angle to 'Now I'm Here' on this tour. The audience briefly glimpses a spotlit Freddie on one

side of the dark stage, singing 'Now I'm Here', and then apparently see him again an instant later, on the opposite side of the stage, repeating the line. One of the Freddies is in reality the band's personal assistant Pete Brown, dressed in an identical costume – "In one of Fred's frocks," as he later recalls. Sadly, Pete Brown died in 1993.

January 29
Music Hall, Boston, Massachusetts
■ *Bohemian Rhapsody (Taped Intro) / Ogre Battle / Sweet Lady / White Queen / Flick Of The Wrist / Medley: Bohemian Rhapsody; Killer Queen; The March Of The Black Queen; Bohemian Rhapsody (Reprise); Bring Back That Leroy Brown / Brighton Rock / Son & Daughter / The Prophet's Song / Stone Cold Crazy / Doing All Right / Lazing On A Sunday Afternoon / Keep Yourself Alive / Seven Seas Of Rhye / Liar / In The Lap Of The Gods (Revisited) / Encore Medley: Big Spender; Jailhouse Rock / God Save The Queen*

Freddie's quirky 'Sunday Afternoon' from the *Opera* album is new to the set on this tour too, but it does not remain for long as the band think it doesn't work well enough.

January 30
Music Hall, Boston, Massachusetts

January 31/February 1
Tower Theater, Philadelphia, Pennsylvania
■ *Second night*: Bohemian Rhapsody (Taped Intro) /
Ogre Battle / Sweet Lady / White Queen / Flick Of The
Wrist / Medley: Bohemian Rhapsody; Killer Queen;
The March Of The Black Queen; Bohemian Rhapsody
(Reprise); Bring Back That Leroy Brown / Brighton
Rock / Son & Daughter / The Prophet's Song / Stone
Cold Crazy / Doing All Right / Lazing On A Sunday
Afternoon / Keep Yourself Alive / Seven Seas Of Rhye
/ Liar / In The Lap Of The Gods (Revisited) / Encore
Medley: Jailhouse Rock; Big Spender; Be Bop A Lula;
Jailhouse Rock (Reprise) / God Save The Queen

February 5/6/7/8
Beacon Theater, New York
■ *Second night*: Bohemian Rhapsody (Taped Intro) /
Ogre Battle / Sweet Lady / White Queen / Flick Of The
Wrist / Medley: Bohemian Rhapsody; Killer Queen;
The March Of The Black Queen; Bohemian Rhapsody
(Reprise); Bring Back That Leroy Brown / Brighton
Rock / Son & Daughter / The Prophet's Song / Stone
Cold Crazy / Doing All Right / Lazing On A Sunday
Afternoon / Keep Yourself Alive / Seven Seas Of Rhye
/ Liar / In The Lap Of The Gods (Revisited) / Encore:
Now I'm Here / God Save The Queen

February 11/12
Masonic Temple, Detroit, Michigan

February 13
Riverfront Coliseum, Cincinnati, Ohio

February 14
Public Hall, Cleveland, Ohio

Back in the UK, *Record Mirror & Disc* magazine
publish their annual poll results which feature
Queen in several categories: World's Best Group
(1st) / Best Single: 'Bohemian Rhapsody' (1st) /
World's Best Singer: Freddie (6th) / Best British
Singer: Freddie (5th) / Best British Songwriter:
Freddie (4th) / Best British Group (1st) / World's
Best Songwriter: Freddie (5th) / Best British
Musician: Brian May (4th) / World's Best
Musician: Brian May (4th) / Best Album: *A Night
At The Opera* (6th).

Queen Live '76

February 15
Sports Arena, Toledo, Ohio
■ *Bohemian Rhapsody (Taped Intro) / Ogre Battle / Sweet Lady / White Queen / Flick Of The Wrist / Medley: Bohemian Rhapsody; Killer Queen; The March Of The Black Queen; Bohemian Rhapsody (Reprise); Bring Back That Leroy Brown / Brighton Rock / Son & Daughter / The Prophet's Song / Stone Cold Crazy / Doing All Right / Lazing On A Sunday Afternoon / Keep Yourself Alive / Seven Seas Of Rhye / Liar / In The Lap Of The Gods (Revisited) / God Save The Queen*

February 18
Civic Center, Saginaw, Michigan

February 19
Veterans' Memorial Auditorium, Columbus, Ohio

February 20
Syrian Mosque, Pittsburgh, Pennsylvania

February 22
Auditorium Theater, Chicago, Illinois
■ *Bohemian Rhapsody (Intro) / Ogre Battle / Sweet Lady / White Queen / Flick Of The Wrist / Medley: Bohemian Rhapsody; Killer Queen; The March Of The Black Queen; Bohemian Rhapsody (Reprise); Bring Back That Leroy Brown / Brighton Rock / Son & Daughter / The Prophet's Song / Stone Cold Crazy / Doing All Right / Lazing On A Sunday Afternoon / Keep Yourself Alive / Seven Seas Of Rhye / Liar / In*

The Lap Of The Gods (Revisited) / Big Spender / Jailhouse Rock / God Save The Queen

February 23
Auditorium Theater, Chicago, Illinois

February 26
Keil Auditorium, St Louis, Missouri

February 27
Convention Center, Indianapolis, Indiana

February 28
Dane County Coliseum, Wisconsin

February 29
Fort Wayne Coliseum, Indiana State
■ *Bohemian Rhapsody (Intro) / Ogre Battle / Sweet Lady / White Queen / Flick Of The Wrist / Hangman / Medley: Bohemian Rhapsody; Killer Queen; The March Of The Black Queen; Bohemian Rhapsody (Reprise); Bring Back That Leroy Brown / Brighton Rock / Son & Daughter / The Prophet's Song / Stone Cold Crazy / Doing All Right / Lazing On A Sunday Afternoon / Keep Yourself Alive / Seven Seas Of Rhye / Liar / In The Lap Of The Gods (Revisited) / Jailhouse Rock / Big Spender / Be Bop A Lula / Jailhouse Rock (Reprise) / God Save The Queen*

March 1
Milwaukee Auditorium, Milwaukee, Wisconsin

March 3
St Pauls Auditorium, Minneapolis, Minnesota

March 7
Berkeley Community Hall, Berkeley
Set: as February 29, but with 'Saturday Night's Alright For Fighting' in the encore medley, after 'Big Spender'.

March 9 (2 shows) ♪ /10/11/12
Santa Monica Civic Auditorium, Los Angeles, California
■ *Bohemian Rhapsody (Taped Intro) / Ogre Battle / Sweet Lady / White Queen / Flick Of The Wrist / Medley: Bohemian Rhapsody; Killer Queen; The March Of The Black Queen; Bohemian Rhapsody (Reprise); Bring Back That Leroy Brown / Brighton Rock / Son & Daughter / The Prophet's Song / Stone Cold Crazy / Doing All Right / Lazing On A Sunday Afternoon / Keep Yourself Alive / Seven Seas Of Rhye / Liar / In The Lap Of The Gods (Revisited) / Jailhouse Rock / God Save The Queen*

March 13
Sports Arena, San Diego, California

JAPAN 1976

Queen arrive in Japan to begin their second tour there: eleven shows at seven different venues, again kicking off in the capital's main stadium. It concludes a week and a half later at the Nichidai Kodo, also in Tokyo.

March 22
Budokan Hall, Tokyo
■ *Bohemian Rhapsody (Taped Intro) / Ogre Battle / Sweet Lady / White Queen / Flick Of The Wrist / Hangman / Medley: Bohemian Rhapsody; Killer Queen; The March Of The Black Queen; Bohemian Rhapsody (Reprise); Bring Back That Leroy Brown / Brighton Rock / Son & Daughter / The Prophet's Song: incorporating Death On Two Legs / Stone Cold Crazy / Doing All Right / Lazing On A Sunday Afternoon / Father To Son / Keep Yourself Alive / Seven Seas Of Rhye / Liar / In The Lap Of The Gods (Revisited) / Encore: Now I'm Here / 2nd Encore Medley: Big Spender; See What A Fool I've Been / God Save The Queen*

Freddie, after 'Flick Of The Wrist': "Thank you. Thank you very much. That song was about a very nasty man. Now we're going to do a song about two nasty men - about two murderers... a song that we did last year. It's a song called 'Hangman'."

Later, after 'Brighton Rock', Freddie: "On the guitar... Brian May. And on the drums... Roger Taylor. And on the bass... John Deacon. Thank you. Thank you my cherubs."

'Death On Two Legs' is incorporated into 'The

A Concert Documentary

Prophet's Song' still, though it is eventually performed in its own right.

🐾 Freddie: 'Death On Two Legs' was the most vicious lyric I ever wrote. It's so vindictive that Brian felt bad singing it. I don't like to explain what I was thinking when I wrote the song."

March 23
Aichi-ken Taiikukan, Nagoya
■ *Bohemian Rhapsody (Taped Intro) / Ogre Battle / Sweet Lady / White Queen / Flick Of The Wrist / Medley: Bohemian Rhapsody; Killer Queen; The March Of The Black Queen; Bohemian Rhapsody (Reprise); Bring Back That Leroy Brown / Brighton Rock / Son & Daughter / The Prophet's Song: incorporating Death On Two Legs / Stone Cold Crazy / Doing All Right / Lazing On A Sunday Afternoon / Keep Yourself Alive / Seven Seas Of Rhye / Liar / In The Lap Of The Gods (Revisited) / Encore: Now I'm Here / God Save The Queen*

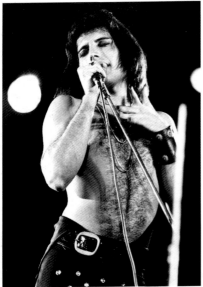

March 24
Kosei Nenkin Kaikan, Himeji
■ *Bohemian Rhapsody (Taped Intro) / Ogre Battle / Sweet Lady / White Queen / Flick Of The Wrist / Medley: Bohemian Rhapsody; Killer Queen; The March Of The Black Queen; Bohemian Rhapsody (Reprise); Bring Back That Leroy Brown / Brighton Rock / Son & Daughter / The Prophet's Song: incorporating Death On Two Legs / Stone Cold Crazy / Doing All Right / Lazing On A Sunday Afternoon / Keep Yourself Alive / Liar / In The Lap Of The Gods (Revisited) / Encore: Now I'm Here / God Save The Queen*

March 26
Kyuden Taiikukan, Fukuoka (2 shows)
■ *Bohemian Rhapsody (Taped Intro) / Ogre Battle / Sweet Lady / White Queen / Flick Of The Wrist / Medley: Bohemian Rhapsody; Killer Queen; The March Of The Black Queen; Bohemian Rhapsody (Reprise); Bring Back That Leroy Brown; Brighton Rock / Son & Daughter / The Prophet's Song; Stone Cold Crazy / Doing All Right / Lazing On A Sunday Afternoon / Keep Yourself Alive / Liar / In The Lap Of*

The Gods (Revisited) / Encore: Now I'm Here / 2nd Encore Medley: Big Spender; Jailhouse Rock; Shake Rattle And Roll; Stupid Cupid; Be Bop A Lula; Jailhouse Rock (Reprise) / God Save The Queen

March 29 ♫
Kosei Nenkin Kaikan, Osaka (2 shows)
■ *Bohemian Rhapsody (Taped Intro) / Ogre Battle / Sweet Lady / White Queen / Flick Of The Wrist / Medley: Bohemian Rhapsody; Killer Queen; The March Of The Black Queen; Bohemian Rhapsody (Reprise); Bring Back That Leroy Brown / Brighton Rock / Son & Daughter / The Prophet's Song / Stone Cold Crazy / Doing All Right / Lazing On A Sunday Afternoon / Keep Yourself Alive / Liar / In The Lap Of The Gods (Revisited) / Encore: Now I'm Here / 2nd Encore: Jailhouse Rock / God Save The Queen*

Quite what the Japanese audience made of the Kenny Everett taped introduction is anybody's guess but if the bootleg from this show is anything to go by, they loved it. The audience goes berserk at the 'Bo Rhap' opera part, even before the band have taken to the stage. Listening to bootleg recordings of this show is like watching old newsreel of a Beatles concert, such is the din emanating from the crowd. It is a colossal wall of sound which totally obliterates the music.

Freddie's opening words of the show, following 'Ogre Battle', are offered in the native tongue: "Konnichi-wa", he shouts (Japanese for "Good afternoon / Hello") and the fans love this detail.

After proposing a toast to the crowd, Freddie then introduces 'White Queen' but its quiet introduction is completely lost in the deafening roar. He continues regardless, and is bewildered at the relentless noise.

Later, Brian also addresses the audience partly in their own language when he introduces the next song as "something a little heavier, written by Freddie". 'Flick Of The Wrist' is received exceptionally well. The crowd joins in on the main chorus and Osaka embraces Queen like the best London audience.

There is a polite and welcomed silence while Freddie explains the medley sequence, but the crowd roars at the mention of 'Bohemian Rhapsody' and the tumult starts up all over again.

After 'Brighton Rock' and a brilliant rendering of 'The Prophet's Song', Freddie dedicates 'Stone Cold Crazy' to all the crazy rock'n'roll people present – not that the message is widely understood. Next up is 'Doing All Right' from the début album.

"Okay," Freddie continues, "we'd like you all to join in with this next number. It's called 'Lazing On A Sunday Afternoon'." By any standard this is one of Freddie's most self indulgent moments from *Opera*, or from *any* album, for that matter, but it is also one of the greatest. Thankfully, the song is performed almost note for note to the studio cut. The Japanese appreciate the fun side of

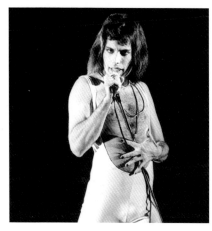

March 31/April 1
Budokan Hall, Tokyo
■ *Second night*: Bohemian Rhapsody (Taped Intro) / gre Battle / Sweet Lady / White Queen / Flick Of The Wrist / Hangman / Medley: Bohemian Rhapsody; Killer Queen; The March Of The Black Queen; Bohemian Rhapsody (Reprise); Bring Back That Leroy Brown / Brighton Rock / Son & Daughter / The Prophet's Song / Stone Cold Crazy / Doing All Right / Lazing On A Sunday Afternoon / Keep Yourself Alive / Liar / In The Lap Of The Gods (Revisited) / Encore: Now I'm Here / 2nd Encore Medley: Big Spender; Jailhouse Rock; Stupid Cupid; Be Bop A Lula; Jailhouse Rock (Reprise) / 3rd Encore: See What A Fool I've Been / God Save The Queen

Bootleg representation of this show is extensive. *Year Of The Opera* is perhaps the most notable disc and offers unusually good clarity of sound. 'Keep Yourself Alive' is wonderful, not least because Freddie incorporates parts of 'I've Got The Music In Me' into it.

April 2
Miyagi-ken Sports Centre, Sendai
■ Bohemian Rhapsody (Taped Intro) / Ogre Battle / Sweet Lady / White Queen / Flick Of The Wrist /

Queen more than most, and Freddie seems pleased that they 'get it'.

'Keep Yourself Alive' follows, along much the same lines as usual, but with different vocal ad-libs from Freddie. An exceptionally enthusiastic drum solo adds something special too. The Japanese fans scream even louder when Roger comes in with his 'Do you think you're better ev'ry day?'

Later, after 'Liar', Brian addresses the crowd again: "To finish off we'd like to do something from *Sheer Heart Attack*. Thank you for being really nice. This is 'In The Lap Of The Gods'." Freddie's opening piano chords are once again lost in the commotion, but when he reaches the "Wo wo la la la wo" part, the mighty wall of voices shadow every word he sings. Queen leave the stage, but return a minute later for 'Now I'm Here'.

Again, the show concludes with 'Jailhouse Rock'. Though Freddie's voice is starting to show signs of stress, he still plays improvised word games with the audience during the mid section. "Thank you – Arigato – Sayonara – Goodbye." The national anthem begins, Queen bow and leave the stage, waving.

Medley: Bohemian Rhapsody; Killer Queen; The March Of The Black Queen; Bohemian Rhapsody (Reprise); Bring Back That Leroy Brown / Brighton Rock / Son And Daughter / The Prophet's Song / Stone Cold Crazy / Father To Son / Doing All Right / Lazing On A Sunday Afternoon / Keep Yourself Alive / Liar / In The Lap Of The Gods (Revisited) / Encore: Now I'm Here / 2nd Encore Medley: Big Spender; Jailhouse Rock; Shake Rattle And Roll; Stupid Cupid; Jailhouse Rock (Reprise) / God Save The Queen

Similar set as previous night, but with 'Shake Rattle' added, and no 'Hangman'.

April 4 ⏎

Nichidai Kodo, Tokyo

■ *Bohemian Rhapsody (Taped Intro) / Ogre Battle / Sweet Lady / White Queen / Flick Of The Wrist / Medley: Bohemian Rhapsody; Killer Queen; The March Of The Black Queen; Bohemian Rhapsody (Reprise) / Bring Back That Leroy Brown / Brighton Rock / Son & Daughter / The Prophet's Song / Stone Cold Crazy / Father To Son / Doing All Right / Lazing On A Sunday Afternoon / Keep Yourself Alive / Liar / In The Lap Of The Gods (Revisited) / Encore: Now I'm Here / 2nd Encore: Big Spender / God Save The Queen*

'Sweet Lady' here features Roger's voice more prominently than usual. During the middle section of the song, Brian seems to go off into what sounds like an unrehearsed improvised solo, with Freddie and Roger ad-libbing accordingly. The overall sound is incredible, and vastly different from the album cut.

'White Queen' finds Freddie in stunning voice. A lively bass line from John is complemented by haunting guitar solos and subtle piano work, to make this version one of the best I've heard. The band are in perfect musical harmony for this performance and Freddie is acutely aware of it.

"Listen, listen, listen, listen, please listen to this next medley," Freddie implores. "It comprises four songs, and we're gonna start it with our current single released here, called 'Bohemian Rhapsody'."

↗ Following Queen's second Japanese tour, Jon Tiven, in the New York magazine *Back Pages*,

writes: '*In the Forties, Japanese pilots occasionally dove aeroplanes into passing Allied warships. Today, Japanese teenagers have taken up a more innocent occupation: diving into the four British rockers known as Queen. When Queen landed in Tokyo recently for an extensive tour of the Land of the Rising Sun, the rhapsodic quartet found their plane surrounded by 5,000 frantic fans. But limousines were driven through the throng to the jet's landing steps and the group was rushed down the stairs, flung into the black Cadillacs, and delivered safely to the hotel.*

'*All in all, Queen's tour of Japan was a triumphant one. The nation's top radio stations had just voted them the world's number-one rock band, and their 12-day, eight concert tour included three nights at Tokyo's Budokan, the country's largest arena. From there three nights they went to Australia for another eight dates and then to vacation at an unspecified locale. Preparations three nights for a fifth album began immediately afterwards. All this followed the group's*

row about everything, even the air we breathe. We're the bitchiest band on earth, darling. We're always at each others throats.

"One night Roger was in a foul mood and he threw his entire bloody drum set across the stage. The thing only just missed me - I might have been killed. Yes, we're all very highly strung.

"Once, Roger squirted Brian in the face with hair spray in a tiny, steaming dressing room. They nearly came to blows. We've all got massive egos, my dear.

"The others don't like my interviews. And frankly, I don't care much for theirs. I'm very emotional. I think I may go mad in several years time."

AUSTRALIA 1976

Queen embark upon their first proper tour of Australia; an eleven day visit with eight concerts at five different venues. The band had performed there only once before (at the Sunbury Music Festival in Melbourne two years earlier), and that unhappy experience leaves them apprehensive about this return trip.

All eight concerts are sold out, however, and there is no need to worry. The shows are attended by extremely appreciative and knowledgable audiences, and this time around the band are permitted to perform their encores.

most successful US tour to date. Arriving on the heels of their Night At The Opera *album, the group was greeted with almost universal acclaim. The normally staid* Boston Globe *said the group was so sensational as to make people forget about such other recent sensations as Bruce Springsteen and Patti Smith, and newspapers across the country continually compared them with The Beatles. And luckily, the group made it through the entire thirty-one date twenty-one city schedule without a cancellation – another first. Queen's first American tour had to be cut short because of guitarist Brian's hepatitis, and their second was interrupted when Freddie Mercury developed throat problems. But this time, despite a 'flu attack which threatened to level Brian, their trip continued unabated.'*

🗨 Meanwhile, elsewhere, Freddie has this to say: "The lavish presentation appeals to me, and I've got to convince the others. You don't know how I had to fight for Big Spender on the last tour. We

April 11
Entertainments Centre, Perth
■ *Bohemian Rhapsody (Taped Intro) / Ogre Battle / Sweet Lady / White Queen / Flick Of The Wrist / Hangman / Medley: Bohemian Rhapsody; Killer Queen; The March Of The Black Queen; Bohemian Rhapsody (Reprise); Bring Back That Leroy Brown / Brighton Rock / Son & Daughter / The Prophet's Song / Stone Cold Crazy / Doing All Right / Lazing On A Sunday Afternoon / Keep Yourself Alive / Liar / In The Lap Of The Gods (Revisited) / Encore: Now I'm Here / 2nd Encore Medley: Jailhouse Rock; Big Spender; Be Bop A Lula; Jailhouse Rock (Reprise) / God Save The Queen*

April 14/15
Apollo Stadium, Adelaide

April 17/18
Horden Pavillion, Sydney
■ *Second night: Bohemian Rhapsody (Taped Intro) / Ogre Battle / Sweet Lady / White Queen / Flick Of The Wrist / Medley: Bohemian Rhapsody; Killer Queen; The March Of The Black Queen; Bohemian Rhapsody (Reprise); Bring Back That Leroy Brown / Brighton Rock / Son & Daughter / The Prophet's Song / Stone Cold Crazy / Father To Son / Doing All Right / Lazing On A Sunday Afternoon / Keep Yourself Alive / Liar / In The Lap Of The Gods (Revisited) / Encore: Now I'm Here / 2nd Encore: Big Spender / God Save The Queen*

April 19/20
Festival Hall, Melbourne

April 22
Festival Hall, Brisbane
↗ **'A Brief Introduction to Queen'**, by Kris Nicholson, *The Gig* magazine, April 1976:
   'You can imagine whatever you want to - about Queen's image - because beneath their satin sheen, not glitter, there lies a sincere and firm commitment to playing metal rock injected with an intelligent strategy. Guitarist Brian May and lead singer Freddie Mercury are the band's upfront ideas men. Separately they write the majority of the groups material.

'Like all heavy rock'n'roll, feeling is essential to their music. With Queen, feeling is lubricated by conscious thought to create ornate textures that are at once dynamic and subtle. John Deacon and Roger Meddows-Taylor are the group's spinal column. Simple and direct, their energies connect with Freddie's and Brian's. As a rhythm section their simplicity is crucial to Queen's entire effect. If they offered anything more than basics, their sound would not be directly focused. By combining and contrasting different levels of input, Queen has developed a flamboyant sound that creates an impact in numerous ways.'

❖ **June 18**
   John Deacon's only composition for *A Night At The Opera* is released as a single in Europe, America and Japan. 'You're My Best Friend' is paired with Brian May's (also) dream inspired ''39', and goes on to give the band number seven and 16 chart placings, in the UK and America.
   ● Brian (on 'You're My Best Friend'): "I think his (John) song on the album is amazing. He went out completely on a limb to do that. It's not the kind of thing we'd done before, but he knew exactly what he wanted."

July
   Queen begin work on *A Day At The Races*. The sessions will eventually conclude four months later, in November.

August
   In preparation for three British shows, the band book rehearsal time at Shepperton Studios. They work mainly on material from the new album but also on an acoustic version of ''39' from *A Night At The Opera*.
   The set now includes 'Tie Your Mother Down' and 'You Take My Breath Away' from *Races*, though the album itself will not actually be released until December 10.
   Other material from the album will feature in the set throughout the US tour which begins ● the following January: 'White Man', 'Good Old Fashioned Lover Boy', 'Somebody To Love' and

'Millionaire Waltz'. 'Teo Torriatte' will figure too, but only in Japan, beginning in April 1979.

September 1/2 ⌐⌐
Playhouse Theatre, Edinburgh
■ *First night*: Bohemian Rhapsody (Taped Intro) / Ogre Battle / Sweet Lady / White Queen / Flick Of The Wrist / Medley: You're My Best Friend; Bohemian Rhapsody; Killer Queen; The March Of The Black Queen; Bohemian Rhapsody (Reprise); Bring Back That Leroy Brown / Brighton Rock / Son & Daughter / '39 / You Take My Breath Away / The Prophet's Song / Stone Cold Crazy / Doing All Right / Lazing On A Sunday Afternoon / Tie Your Mother Down / Keep Yourself Alive / Liar / In The Lap Of The Gods (Revisited) / Now I'm Here / Big Spender / Jailhouse Rock / God Save The Queen

Queen perform these two shows as part of the Scottish Festival of Popular Music. The venue has just reopened after extensive refurbishment and they appear alongside Elton John, John Miles, Rainbow and comedian Billy Connelly.

'Tie Your Mother Down' is new to the set and from here on will feature in almost every concert Queen perform – including the last one. Brian later cites it as one of the compositions of which he is most proud, adding that it always seemed to sound right, even if other material in the set did not.

John Deacon's 'Best Friend' (the new single) is also featured for the first time, replacing 'Bo Rhap' as the opening song in the medley.

An acoustic segment in the set featured 'Breath Away' and "39" for the very first time here. Roger emerges from behind the drum kit with a tambourine and accompanies Freddie, John and Brian centre stage. Brian plays an acoustic guitar.

Freddie throws his maracas into the audience afterwards, repeating the gesture every night thereafter.

There is speculation that 'Good Company' is performed at this show, but I am unable to confirm it. I have never heard any live recital of the song, nor even seen mention of it on any bootleg.

■ *Second night*: Bohemian Rhapsody (Taped Intro) / Ogre Battle / Sweet Lady / White Queen / Flick Of The Wrist / Medley: You're My Best Friend; Bohemian Rhapsody; Killer Queen; The March Of The Black Queen; Bohemian Rhapsody (Reprise): Bring Back That Leroy Brown / Brighton Rock / Son & Daughter / '39 / You Take My Breath Away / The Prophet's Song / Stone Cold Crazy / Doing All Right / Lazing On A Sunday Afternoon / Tie Your Mother Down / Keep Yourself Alive / Liar / In The Lap Of The Gods (Revisited) / Encore: Now I'm Here / 2nd Encore: Big Spender / Jailhouse Rock / God Save The Queen

↗ Ta, Queen
Dear Mailman,

After seeing Queen at the Edinburgh Playhouse on September 2, I had to let others know what they missed. I've never seen such a polished performance - and it lasted two hours. It was sheer perfection and worth the small fortune I spent getting there. Thank you Queen. S. Peacock, Hull.

↗ 'Queen At The Castle'. Record Mirror, August 28, 1976: *'Queen are to play an open - air concert, at Cardiff Castle on Friday, September 10, and a free concert in London's Hyde Park on September 18. Tickets for Cardiff are £3.50. The concert starts at 4 pm and capacity will be limited to 15,000. Other names for the show will be announced next week.'*

September 10
Cardiff Castle, Cardiff
■ Bohemian Rhapsody (Taped Intro) / Ogre Battle / Sweet Lady / White Queen / Flick Of The Wrist / Medley: You're My Best Friend; Bohemian Rhapsody / Killer Queen; The March Of The Black Queen; Bohemian Rhapsody (Reprise); Bring Back That Leroy Brown / Brighton Rock / Son & Daughter / '39 / You Take My Breath Away / The Prophet's Song / Stone Cold Crazy / Doing All Right / Lazing On A Sunday Afternoon / Tie Your Mother Down / Keep Yourself Alive / Liar / In The Lap Of The Gods (Revisited) / Encore: Now I'm Here / Jailhouse Rock / God Save The Queen

Queen headline a one-day event that also

Music Centre in Association with John Reid presents

Queen at Cardiff Castle

Friday 10th September 1976
Gates open 4.00 p.m.

Queen
daybyday

with Special Guests
**RITCHIE BLACKMORE'S RAINBOW
ANDY FAIRWEATHER LOW
FRANKIE MILLER'S FULL HOUSE**

Tickets:
£3.50

Compere:
BOB HARRIS

features Manfred Mann, Andy Fairweather-Low and Frankie Miller's Full House. Bob Harris is the compère.

A much sought-after Queen bootleg entitled *Queen At The Castle* emerges from this show.

↗ **'Killer Queen'**. *Melody Maker*, September 18, 1976: 'BRIAN MAY remembers Queen's first-ever free gig well. It was in London, five years ago, when the band invited 120 people along to a lecture theatre in Imperial College to hear them play. Orange juice and popcorn were served to the 80 or so who bothered to show their faces and lend an ear.

'Since that unremarkable debut, the capital has hosted many landmarks in Queen's well-planned climb to the top: The Imperial College gig in September '75; the Rainbow in March. '74 (promoter Mel Bush convinced the band that they were big enough to sell out a concert there); two sell-out gigs at The Rainbow during November '75; and, last year, four shows at Hammersmith Odeon. The icing on the cake, to confirm that Queen have well and truly arrived, is on Saturday, when the band play in front of perhaps 200,000 at Hyde Park. They insist, however, that the gig should not be interpreted as a "we're a big band now" gesture. "I really hope it's not taken in that way," May said sincerely. "There must be other ways of doing that. You can play Wembley Stadium. I really hope that it's taken in the spirit that we're thinking of — just a nice thing to do. It's a dream to be able to do a free gig in Hyde Park, like the old days. It's as romantic as that.'

September 18 ↗
Hyde Park, London
■ *Bohemian Rhapsody (Taped Intro) / Ogre Battle / Sweet Lady / White Queen / Flick Of The Wrist / Medley: You're My Best Friend; Bohemian Rhapsody; Killer Queen; The March Of The Black Queen; Bohemian Rhapsody (Reprise); Bring Back That Leroy Brown / Brighton Rock / Son & Daughter / '39 / You Take My Breath Away / The Prophet's Song / Stone Cold Crazy / Keep Yourself Alive / Liar / In The Lap Of The Gods (Revisited) / No encore*

In a repeat of an event staged by The Rolling Stones in 1969, Queen perform their first free concert.

Due to the drought of 1976 and the poor condition of the park as a result, the show comes perilously close to being cancelled. It does get the go-ahead, however, and between 150,000 and 200,000 are estimated to be in attendance at one of Queen's best ever concerts.

The event is conceived by Freddie and Brian as both a thank you to the British fans for their

John Reid in association with Virgin Records presents

Queen
at Hyde Park

5

he is soon heard again with: "So you think you can love me and leave me to die."

'Ogre Battle' follows without a break, with Freddie exaggerating the lyrics and emphasising certain lines with body language. The audience love it, and the show is off to a classy start.

"Thank you very much, good evening everybody. Welcome to our picnic by the Serpentine. You all look very beautiful, I must say. We should like to carry on now with a song called... 'Sweet Lady'." The 'picnic' is now in full swing.

'White Queen' follows, then an ominous sounding 'Flick Of The Wrist' which Brian introduces as "a song slightly more in the vicious vein, written by Freddie in one of his more passionate moments, of which he has many."

Later. Freddie: "Now then my darlings – listen. I have been requested by the constabulary, for you not to throw those things around... tin cans or whatever. Make this a peaceful event, okay. Now sit on your arses and listen. This is a medley, and this is a special little one coz we've increased it in length this time round. To start off with, a song called 'You're My Best Friend'."

The medley moves through 'Best Friend' and on to 'Bo Rhap', 'Killer' and 'Black Queen', and concludes with Roger striking the gong on the 'Rhapsody' reprise. 'Black Queen' would never again feature in the set after this show.

After a sprightly rendition of 'Leroy Brown', including Brian's ukulele solo, Freddie announces that it was a slow version. 'Brighton Rock' follows, and this in turn segues into 'Son & Daughter', as usual.

Brian introduces the next song: "From one piece of nonsense to another, I've said it before, this is something which we were gonna do with the London Philharmonic, but they didn't turn up, so we will do the ethnic version... of a song called "39"." All four members of the band assemble at the front of the stage, Roger with a tambourine, but also operating a bass drum with his foot, and Brian swapping his electric guitar for an acoustic one. John assists with minimal bass.

continued support, and to commemorate the sixth anniversary of the death of Jimi Hendrix. Support acts are Steve Hillage, Kiki Dee and Liverpudlian band Supercharge.

Supercharge singer/saxophonist Albie Donnelly is dressed in a blatantly Mercury-esque white leotard. He struts and prances around the stage like Freddie too, but it is all in good fun, and no one takes offence. One of their songs is a cover of the Bay City Rollers' 'Bye Bye Baby'.

Having enjoyed a number one hit in July with 'Don't Go Breaking My Heart', with Elton John, Kiki Dee had invited her co-star to join her on stage at this show. Elton is unable to attend, so Kiki shares the stage with a life size cardboard cut-out of Elton for the encore.

After the lights dim, the introduction to 'Tie Your Mother Down' from *A Day At The Races* fills the air. Then, abruptly, it ends and cuts into Kenny Everett's tape, this time with the opening "Ladies and Gentlemen" and *Opera* elements excised. Following the pre-recorded "Has the devil put aside for me" line, Queen bound on to the huge stage. Due to what sounds like a problem at the mixing desk, Freddie's first words of 'Bohemian Rhapsody' go unheard by most, but

95

Freddie: "Right now I'm gonna do a very special song. This is a new song from our forthcoming album. It hasn't quite been recorded yet. Anyway, it's a song called 'You Take My Breath Away'."

This fine ballad features Freddie alone, accompanying himself at the piano. The audience remains silent throughout, for which Freddie is much relieved.

"Something heavy, aye?" he says afterwards, and 'The Prophet's Song' follows with an opening section almost identical to the album version and a similar operatic middle section. This is a version the fans will talk about for years to come.

'Stone Cold Crazy' follows at its usual furious pace, and is followed by the contrasting mellowness of the 'Sheer Heart Attack' closing track, which Brian always introduced: "Thank you for making this a great day and a great evening for us. I hope you come again. We're gonna finish in the manner in which we are accustomed. This is 'In The Lap Of The Gods' - or something like that." The rock ballad is performed as usual, and closes with Freddie bidding farewell to his 'darlings', following which Roger bashes the gong a dozen times and the band exit the stage.

Despite cries of "We want Queen", the band does not reappear because the police forbid them to. Instead, compere Bob Harris walks on to offer an explanation no-one wants to hear: "What a fantastic day today has been. That is the end of the day [laughs nervously]. The band are off and gone, that's the end of the evening, but it's been amazing, thanks to you. Thank you very much indeed, we'll see you soon."

The show was transmitted live on Capital Radio. DJ's Kenny Everett and Nicky Horne provide the commentary. It is also filmed for inclusion in a proposed documentary, put together by Bob Harris.

The absence of the usual encore was due to Queen's set overrunning by half an hour, and the police warning Freddie that he would be arrested if he attempts to go back on stage. He grudgingly abandons the idea, and the band are unable finish as planned. Then the police, in their wisdom, pull the power to the stage equipment, not realising that the same power source is also feeding the lighting to the many exit points and surrounding car parks. As a result, thousands of fans are left to find their way out in pitch darkness.

➚ *'As the masses emanated towards Marble Arch and Queensway, people still threw up, fell down and hit each other. But that was the aftermath. The Picnic by the Serpentine was just fine.'* (Tim Lott)

Brian: "I think Hyde Park was one of the most significant gigs in our career. There was a great affection because we'd kind of made it in a lot of countries by that time, but England was still, you know, we weren't really sure if we were

96

acceptable here. So it was a wonderful feeling to come back and see that crowd and get that response."

A variety of bootlegs emerge from Queen's performance. Some include the radio presenter's commentary and others offer only edited accounts without it. Predictably, the sound quality of many of the recordings has declined drastically over the years. Most of the tapes currently exchanging hands are sixth or seventh generation copies with dreadful background hiss.

One of the organisers of the concert is Virgin boss Richard Branson. During the show preparations, Roger Taylor is introduced to his French personal assistant Dominique Beyrand. They begin dating soon afterwards and eventually marry.

❖ **November 12**

'Somebody To Love' / 'White Man' is released as the first single from *A Day At The Races*. It is issued almost a month later in America where it peaks at number 13. At home it reaches number two.

The accompanying promotional video contains moody snippets recorded at the Hyde Park concert.

December 1

At the last minute Queen pull out of appearing on the *Bill Grundy Today* television programme. EMI are asked to provide a replacement, which they do – in the form of The Sex Pistols. What follows is a watershed in British rock. The Pistols, provoked by the wretched Grundy, shock the nation with their language and, proving the maxim that all publicity is good publicity, become the hottest property in British rock almost overnight. Grundy is sacked.

Rather strangely, the catalogue number for 'Somebody To Love' is EMI 2565. The next single in the sequence is 'Anarchy In The UK', by the Pistols (EMI 2566).

❖ **December 10**

Queen release their second album with a title inspired by a Marx Brothers' film. *A Day At The Races* quickly climbs the British album charts to reach number one on Christmas Day. The American issue comes on December 18 and reached number five.

Three songs from the album are bypassed for the live show, though all would seem to be ideal candidates. 'Long Away', Brian's subtle, rather reflective tale of becoming wealthy and famous too quickly, John's 'You And I' – to which Freddie lends another breathtaking vocal - and Roger's underrated 'Drowse'.

Though 'Drowse' is not deemed strong enough to be considered as a single (it is sung by Roger, and therefore lacks the instantly recognisable Queen sound), it is issued as the B-side to the American and Japanese 'Tie Your Mother Down' singles.

USA 1977

Queen fly to Boston for ten days of rehearsals before commencing a two-month, 41-show tour of North America. The tour also includes seven shows in Canada. Thin Lizzy are the support act, fronted by Phil Lynott. The tour is aptly nicknamed the Queen Lizzy Tour. It is, after all, Queen Elizabeth II's Silver Jubilee year.

The set now looks very different. While 'Black Queen' has been dropped, 'White Man', 'Somebody To Love' and 'The Millionaire Waltz' (from *Races*) are all new additions. 'Tie Your Mother Down' now opens the show and 'Bo Rhap' is now performed virtually in its entirety. Queen do not attempt to re-create the opera section, but leave the stage and let the light show take over.

January 13
Auditorium, Milwaukee, Wisconsin
■ *Intro / Tie Your Mother Down / Ogre Battle / White*

Queen / Somebody To Love / Medley: Killer Queen; The Millionaire Waltz; You're My Best Friend; Bring Back That Leroy Brown / Sweet Lady / Brighton Rock / Guitar Solo / '39 / You Take My Breath Away / White Man / The Prophet's Song: incorporating Death On Two Legs / Bohemian Rhapsody / Stone Cold Crazy / Keep Yourself Alive / Liar / In The Lap Of The Gods (Revisited) / Encore: Big Spender / Jailhouse Rock / God Save The Queen

Queen's first impressions of Milwaukee are not great. They arrive on the coldest night for over a hundred years, and count their blessings the venue is not outdoors.

The show opens with the studio recording of 'Tie Your Mother Down' guitar-led introduction, before the band take the stage and perform the track proper.

For 'Bohemian Rhapsody' Queen leave the stage during the operatic sequence while the recording plays. Dry ice and a dazzling array of lighting trickery distract the crowd until the band reappear amid an explosion, at which point Brian begins his blistering guitar solo and Freddie reclaims his vocal mike for the song's hard rock conclusion.

The support acts for the first few shows are Cheap Trick and Head East. Thin Lizzy take over for most gigs thereafter.

January 14
Dane County Coliseum, Madison, Wisconsin
   'Killer Queen' now opens the medley, but 'Best Friend' still features in it.

January 15
Columbus Gardens, Columbus, Indiana

January 16
Convention Center, Indianapolis, Indiana

January 18
Cobo Hall, Detroit, Michigan

January 20
Civic Center, Saginaw, Michigan
■ *Intro / Tie Your Mother Down / Ogre Battle / White Queen / Somebody To Love / Medley: Killer Queen; The Millionaire Waltz; You're My Best Friend; Bring Back That Leroy Brown / Sweet Lady / Brighton Rock / Guitar Solo / '39 / You Take My Breath Away / White Man / The Prophet's Song: incorporating Death On Two Legs / Bohemian Rhapsody / Stone Cold Crazy / Keep Yourself Alive / Liar / In The Lap Of The Gods (Revisited) / Encore: Big Spender; Jailhouse Rock / 2nd Encore: Now I'm Here / God Save The Queen*

   'Sweet Lady' has now moved down the setlist somewhat. Instead of featuring very early in the set, it now follows the medley tracks.

January 21
Elliot Hall Of Music, Louisville, Kentucky

January 22
Wings Stadium, Kalamazoo, Michigan

January 23
Richfield Coliseum, Cleveland, Ohio
■ *Intro / Tie Your Mother Down / Ogre Battle / White Queen / Somebody To Love / Medley: Killer Queen; The Millionaire Waltz; You're My Best Friend; Bring Back That Leroy Brown / Sweet Lady / Brighton Rock / Guitar Solo / '39 / You Take My Breath Away / White Man / The Prophet's Song: incorporating Death On Two Legs / Bohemian Rhapsody / Stone Cold Crazy / Keep Yourself Alive / Liar / In The Lap Of The Gods (Revisited) / Encore: Big Spender; Jailhouse Rock / God Save The Queen*

   Queen perform a wonderful version of 'Millionaire Waltz' at this show, with Freddie coping effortlessly with the constant changes in pitch and tempo.

January 25
Central Canadian Exhibition, Ottawa, Ontario
■ *Intro / Tie Your Mother Down / Ogre Battle / White Queen / Somebody To Love / Medley: Killer Queen; The Millionaire Waltz; You're My Best Friend; Bring Back That Leroy Brown / Sweet Lady / Brighton Rock / Guitar Solo / '39 / You Take My Breath Away / White Man / The Prophet's Song: incorporating Death On Two Legs / Bohemian Rhapsody / Stone Cold Crazy / Keep Yourself Alive / Liar / In The Lap Of The Gods (Revisited) / Encore Medley: Jailhouse Rock; Big Spender; Be Bop A Lula; Jailhouse Rock (Reprise) / 2nd Encore: Now I'm Here / God Save The Queen*

Like the previous night's 'Millionaire Waltz', 'Somebody To Love' here finds the band in dazzling form with a sympathetic audience

singing along in perfect harmony and with great enthusiasm. It is one of those rare occasions when no-one spoils the mood by shouting out during the quieter passages. All too often songs like 'Love Of My Life', 'Breath Away' and 'Doing All Right' are spoilt by attention-seeking individuals bent on making themselves heard over the more poignant moments.

January 26
The Forum, Montreal, Quebec
The band meet up with Roy Thomas Baker and Ian Hunter of Mott The Hoople before this show. The two have just finished work on Hunter's new album and are in attendance to see Queen's show.

'The Prophet's Song' now incorporates segments of 'Death On Two Legs' which is still not yet performed in its own right.

January 28
Chicago Stadium, Chicago, Illinois

from guitarist Brian May, bassist John Deacon and drummer Roger Taylor have stayed at the same level since they departed the States last year. It's one of the best integrated, most fully developed power trio sounds remaining today, and without a lot of noise to mimic the real music. Deacon and Taylor remain visually unobtrusive, but run together with May like finely lubed cogs; and May's royal leads constantly tug the show to new levels. That's where Lizzy can take a lesson from the royalty: Queen know their own dynamics and their audiences' interdynamics well. Their pacing has become exquisite.'

So appalling is the weather that on the way to this show, en route from Montreal, the trucks transporting the equipment are blown off the road. Another PA system is hastily arranged and flown in for the Chicago show.

Queen were to play a show the following evening, at the Hara Arena in Dayton, but because of freezing conditions, tanker lorries transporting

■ Intro / Tie Your Mother Down / Ogre Battle / White Queen / Somebody To Love / Medley: Killer Queen; The Millionaire Waltz; You're My Best Friend; Bring Back That Leroy Brown / Sweet Lady / Brighton Rock / Guitar Solo / '39 / You Take My Breath Away / White Man / The Prophet's Song: incorporating Death On Two Legs / Bohemian Rhapsody / Stone Cold Crazy / Keep Yourself Alive / Liar / In The Lap Of The Gods (Revisited) / Encore Medley: Big Spender; Jailhouse Rock / 2nd Encore: Now I'm Here / God Save The Queen

↗ Ted Joseph, New York Times: 'It should, by all means and stretches of the imagination, have been the hot show to end the winter freeze-out that finds rock and roll barrenness haunting this windy city in a post-Christmas hangover. But, Thin Lizzy's challenge to Queen's throne turned out to be a rather luke-warm battle...

'The superb lighting, pyrotechnics and musical pulse

the fuel needed to heat the arena, are stranded at harbours with frozen diesel tanks. Despite the band offering to go ahead with the show regardless, the local council refuse permission and it is cancelled.

January 29
Hara Arena, Dayton, Ohio (cancelled)

January 30
St. John's Arena, Toledo, Ohio
■ *Intro / Tie Your Mother Down / Ogre Battle / White Queen / Somebody To Love / Medley: Killer Queen; The Millionaire Waltz; You're My Best Friend; Bring Back That Leroy Brown / Sweet Lady / Brighton Rock / Guitar Solo / '39 / You Take My Breath Away / White Man / The Prophet's Song: incorporating Death On Two Legs / Bohemian Rhapsody / Stone Cold Crazy / Keep Yourself Alive / Liar / In The Lap Of The Gods (Revisited) / Encore: Jailhouse Rock / 2nd Encore: Now I'm Here / God Save The Queen*

During the customary post-medley champagne toast, Freddie calls the American audience a load of tarts. They seem confused at the remark, but cheer anyway. Freddie moves on and introduces a Brian May number – 'Sweet Lady'.

February 1
Maple Leaf Gardens, Toronto, Ontario

February 3
Civic Center, Springfield, Massachusetts

February 4 ♪
College Park, University Of Maryland, Maryland State
■ *Intro / Tie Your Mother Down / Ogre Battle / White Queen / Somebody To Love / Medley: Killer Queen; The Millionaire Waltz; You're My Best Friend; Bring Back That Leroy Brown / Sweet Lady / Brighton Rock / Guitar Solo / '39 / You Take My Breath Away / White Man / The Prophet's Song: incorporating Death On Two Legs / Bohemian Rhapsody / Stone Cold Crazy / Keep Yourself Alive / Liar / In The Lap Of The Gods (Revisited) / Encore: Jailhouse Rock / 2nd Encore: Now I'm Here / God Save The Queen*

Following 'Ogre Battle' Freddie addresses the audience for the first time: "Thank you. Good

evening everybody. Are you ready for a fun night tonight? Okay then, we're gonna give it to you. It's very nice to be here in Maryland. We'd like to thank you for a very good welcome."

Later: "I think we're gonna go straight into something brand new. This was our last released single, it's called 'Somebody To Love'."

This song will remain a concert favourite of both the band and its audiences for many years to come. Following the line "I've just got to get out of this prison cell, one day I'm gonna be free", Roger commences a rhythmic, almost anthem-like drum backing which the audience mimic with deafening hand claps. Then Freddie begins the chorus of "Find - me - somebody - to - love." Having hit the infamous high note of the song, Freddie makes his way back down the scale again for the climax, while John and Brian await their cue from Roger to get into the big finish - a barely audible click of the drumsticks. The audience do not hear this, but the band do, and they come in together in perfect time for an impressive conclusion.

"Thanks a lot for making that a hit here," Brian remarks afterwards.

February 5
Madison Square Garden, New York

After the show Elektra throw a party for the band in a restaurant in New York's Soho. Guests include Peter Frampton and Monty Python star Eric Idle.

February 6
Nassau Coliseum, Nassau, The Bahamas

February 8
War Memorial Auditorium, Syracuse, New York

February 9
Boston Garden, Boston, Massachusetts

February 10
Civic Center, Providence, Rhode Island

February 11
Civic Center, Philadelphia, Pennsylvania
Brian's 'Brighton Rock' guitar solo here is absolutely stunning. The acoustics within the venue are ideal. Bootleg recordings from this show are marred only by irritating shouts from the audience, which inevitably come during the quieter moments.

by inappropriate shouts from members of the crowd at all the wrong moments. Most people respect Freddie's wishes to "listen carefully", but there are always those who will try to make it onto the mix-desk recording (or live video) they assume the band will be making.

February 24
Kiel Auditorium, St. Louis, Missouri

February 25
Lloyd Noble Center, Norman, Oklahoma

February 26
Moody Coliseum, Dallas, Texas
   Freddie: "Changing the mood now again ladies and gentlemen. This is for all you heavy people out there okay. This song seems to get better every time we do it. This is 'White Man'."
   Freddie is not exaggerating; what follows is a dazzling rendition of the 'Somebody To Love' B-side which surely must leave Roger exhausted.

February 27
Sam Houston, Houston, Texas

March 1
Phoenix Coliseum, Phoenix, Arizona
■ *Tie Your Mother Down / Ogre Battle / White Queen / Somebody To Love / Medley: Killer Queen; The Millionaire Waltz; You're My Best Friend; Bring Back That Leroy Brown / Sweet Lady / Brighton Rock / '39 / You Take My Breath Away / White Man / The Prophet's Song / Bohemian Rhapsody / Stone Cold Crazy / Keep Yourself Alive / Liar / In The Lap Of The Gods (Revisited) / Encore: Now I'm Here / 2nd Encore Medley: Big Spender; Jailhouse Rock / God Save The Queen*

March 3/4
Inglewood Forum, Los Angeles, California
■ *First night*: *Tie Your Mother Down / Ogre Battle / White Queen / Somebody To Love / Medley: Killer Queen; Millionaire Waltz; You're My Best Friend; Bring Back That Leroy Brown / Sweet Lady / Brighton*

February 19
Sportatorium, Miami, Florida

February 20
Civic Center, Lakeland, Florida
■ *Intro / Tie Your Mother Down / Ogre Battle / White Queen / Somebody To Love / Medley: Killer Queen; The Millionaire Waltz; You're My Best Friend; Bring Back That Leroy Brown / Sweet Lady / Brighton Rock / Guitar Solo / '39 / You Take My Breath Away / White Man / The Prophet's Song: incorporating Death On Two Legs / Bohemian Rhapsody / Stone Cold Crazy / Keep Yourself Alive / Liar / In The Lap Of The Gods (Revisited) / Encore Medley: Jailhouse Rock; Big Spender; Be Bop A Lula; Jailhouse Rock (Reprise) / God Save The Queen*

February 21
Fox Theater, Atlanta, Georgia

February 22
Auditorium, Birmingham, Alabama
   Freddie offers a lovely recital of 'You Take My Breath Away' here which, once again, is marred

Queen Live '77

Rock / '39 / You Take My Breath Away / White Man / The Prophet's Song / Bohemian Rhapsody / Stone Cold Crazy / Keep Yourself Alive / Liar / In The Lap Of The Gods (Revisited) / Encore: Jailhouse Rock / 2nd Encore: Saturday Night / Stupid Cupid / God Save The Queen
Here 'Somebody To Love' is amazingly similar to the album version, but has the added appeal of Roger and Brian's harmonies being more audible than usual, which is not always the case. The audience participation also helps make this a memorable show.

Brian: "The next song, we were gonna do with an orchestra. Do you think that's a good idea?"

"I might play drums," quips Freddie. "You're not supposed to say yes!" adds Brian, and ''39' begins.

Queen also perform a superb version of 'Jailhouse Rock'. Freddie's vocal ad-libs are many and varied, if a little nonsensical, but are all the better for that: "Give it a little swing, eh. Keep on moving. Yeah. I like it! It's getting to me! Can you feel it, ah baby? Can I take you home tonight?" and so on.

Then, almost without a break, the band are off into a cover of Elton John's 'Saturday Night'. Roger's backing vocals are just as loud as Freddie's lead. Brian plays some manic guitar, while Freddie repeats "rock and roll tonight". John takes over where Brian leaves off, and Freddie addresses the masses again. "Thank you for being such a beautiful audience tonight. Thank you very much. We've really had a good time, I just hope you have."

March 5
Sports Arena, San Diego

March 6
Winterland, San Francisco

March 11 ⌐
PNE Coliseum, Vancouver, Canada
■ *Tie Your Mother Down / Ogre Battle / White Queen / Somebody To Love / Medley: Killer Queen; The Millionaire Waltz; You're My Best Friend; Bring Back That Leroy Brown / Sweet Lady/ Brighton Rock / '39 / You Take My Breath Away / White Man / The Prophet's Song / Bohemian Rhapsody / Stone Cold Crazy / Keep Yourself Alive / Liar / In The Lap Of The Gods...Revisited / Encore: Now I'm Here / 2nd Encore: Big Spender / Jailhouse Rock / Stupid Cupid / Be Bop A Lula / Jailhouse Rock (reprise) / God Save The Queen*

March 12
Paramount, Portland

styles," he says. "This is one of them. It's from our latest release, you might even recognise it if you bought *A Day At The Races*. It's called 'You Take My Breath Away'."

Later, Brian's introduces the medley: "Okay then, we have some more goodies for you I think. These are some of the old things we used to do. We've put them all together in a medley which we hope you'll like. We hope you recognise this." 'Killer Queen' begins.

March 17
Jubilee Auditorium, Calgary, Alberta
↗ **'Queen's Freddie Mercury: The Circus Magazine Tapes'**. *Circus* magazine, by Don Rush, March 17, 1977: *'We've been slagged in the press for our flamboyant stage show. We think a show should be a spectacle. A concert is not a live rendition of our album. It's a theatrical event.*

'In the early days, we just wore black onstage. Very bold, my dear. Then we introduced white, for variety, and it simply grew and grew. "Stone Cold Crazy" was the first song Queen ever performed onstage.

'I have fun with my clothes onstage; it's not a concert you're seeing, it's a fashion show. I dress to kill, but tastefully. My nail polish? I used to use Biba, now I use Miners. One coat goes on really smooth.

'If we're weird onstage, I don't know what you'd call the Tubes. We're a bit flashy, but the music's not one big noise. I think we're sophisticated. I like the cabaretish sort of thing. In fact, one of my early inspirations came from Cabaret. I absolutely adore Liza Minnelli, she's a total wow. The way she delivers her songs -the sheer energy. The way the lights enhance every movement of the show. I think you can see similarities in the excitement and energy of a Queen show. It's not glamrock, you see; we're in the showbusiness tradition.'

March 13 ♫
Seattle Arena, Seattle, Washington

Two different bootleg recordings originate from this show, *Mania* and *Duck Soup*, and both offer alternative track listings. Neither features the complete show, and there are ruthless edits with nearly every bit of between-song patter excised. *Duck Soup* takes its name from another Marx Brothers film. One of the discs on the *Mercury Is Rising* CD (1993) also features material from this show.

March 16
Jubilee Auditorium, Calgary, Alberta

Following ''39', which is every bit as good as the *Live Killers* version, Freddie announces that just as Queen have done right throughout the tour so far, they would like to continue on a somewhat experimental note.

"We are trying out lots of new and different

March 18
Northlands Arena, Edmonton, Alberta
❖ **March 25**

Elektra issue 'Teo Torriatte' / 'Good Old Fashioned Lover Boy' (P-157E) as an exclusively Japanese single. Predictably, it quickly becomes a hugely collectable disc. Like all Queen's Japanese discs, it features a unique full colour picture sleeve, and lyric sheet insert.

April

Sometime during this month John Deacon, whose turn it is to write the quarterly fan club magazine newsletter, recalled details of the recently completed 41-date America / Canada tour: *"We left for America soon after Christmas on January 4. We flew to Boston, Massachusetts (of Boston Tea Party fame), for ten days' rehearsal before the first show in Milwaukee, Wisconsin. We covered the whole of the US this time and did quite a few shows in Canada too. It was the first time we had played in the very large auditoriums like Los Angeles Forum and Madison Square Garden, New York, so it was very exciting for us to play to 20,000 people in one concert. Our show went over really well in those auditoriums, and the American crowds wouldn't let us go until we had done two or even three encores.*

"As you probably know by now, we are doing a UK and European tour soon, which we're really looking forward to, as we haven't done a concert tour of England since November '75 and we haven't played in Europe for over two years. We hope to include material from our forthcoming album, if we have time to rehearse it well enough before we hit the road."

May 8♪
Ice Stadium, Stockholm

■ *Tie Your Mother Down / Ogre Battle / White Queen / Somebody To Love /Medley: Killer Queen; Good Old-Fashioned Lover Boy; The Millionaire Waltz; You're My Best Friend / Bring Back That Leroy Brown / Death On Two Legs / Brighton Rock / 39 / You Take My Breath Away / White Man / The Prophet's Song / Bohemian Rhapsody /Keep Yourself Alive / Stone Cold Crazy / Now I'm Here / Liar / Big Spender / Jailhouse Rock / God Save The Queen*

'Good Old Fashioned Lover Boy' is incorporated into the medley, not quite as it appears on the album, but as a slightly accelerated, short sample.

May 10
Scandinavium, Gothenburg

MAY 12♪
Broendby Hall, Copenhagen, Denmark ①
From this show emerged one of the very best known bootlegs, *Queen Invite You To A Night At The Warehouse*. It represents what was by all accounts one of the band's most memorable performances.

May 13
Congress Centrum, Hamburg

■ *Tie Your Mother Down / Ogre Battle / White Queen / Somebody To Love / Medley: Killer Queen; Good Old Fashioned Lover Boy; The Millionaire Waltz; You're My Best Friend; Bring Back That Leroy Brown / Death On Two Legs / Sweet Lady / Brighton Rock / '39 / You Take My Breath Away / White Man / The Prophet's Song / Bohemian Rhapsody / Stone Cold Crazy / Keep Yourself Alive / In The Lap Of The Gods (Revisited) /*

Encore: Now I'm Here / Liar / 2nd Encore: Jailhouse Rock / God Save The Queen

Slade, who are also in Germany at this time, come to see this show.

↗ **'A Blinder in the Night'**. *Record Mirror*, May 21, 1977: *'It's been three years since Queen played Hamburg, but it's a near sell-out in a hall which looks like a giant lecture theatre with rows and rows of cushioned, spotless white seats. The stage is tiny but somehow the roadies have managed to squeeze on the batteries of lights…*

'… Band and audience are helping one another along — corny, but true. One girl is so moved that she kisses a security guard. He gently helps her down from her seat at the end of the concert. After just over two hours it's all over and the audience goes home without leaving a speck of dirt or a damaged seat.

'Judging by the reaction in Europe, Queen will play blinders on home ground. Many people delight in

knocking big established bands, but Queen constantly show what thorough professionals they are.'

May 14
Jahrhunderthalle, Frankfurt

May 16
Philipshalle, Dusseldorf

When the band pause briefly during 'The Millionaire Waltz', the audience think the song has ended and begin to applaud. In fact, the song is far from over and Freddie continues. The same thing occurred at most shows. Only fans familiar with *A Day At The Races* remain silent.

May 17
Ahoy Hall, Rotterdam

■ *Tie Your Mother Down / Ogre Battle / White Queen / Somebody To Love / Medley: Killer Queen; Good Old Fashioned Lover Boy; The Millionaire Waltz; You're My Best Friend; Bring Back That Leroy Brown / Death On Two Legs / Sweet Lady / Brighton Rock / '39 / You Take My Breath Away / White Man / The Prophet's Song / Bohemian Rhapsody / Stone Cold Crazy / Keep Yourself Alive / In The Lap Of The Gods (Revisited) / Encore: Now I'm Here / Liar / 2nd Encore: I'm A Man / Jailhouse Rock / God Save The Queen*

Despite this show being only the second Queen performance in Holland, all tickets are sold within an hour of going on sale. After the show, a riot ensues at the front of the hall. No-one is seriously hurt.

Later, at an EMI reception for the band, held aboard a boat, Queen are presented with no less than 38 silver, gold and platinum discs for sales of singles and albums in Holland.

May 19
Sporthalle, Basle, Switzerland ①

■ *Tie Your Mother Down / Ogre Battle / White Queen / Somebody To Love / Medley: Killer Queen; Good Old Fashioned Lover Boy; The Millionaire Waltz; You're My Best Friend; Bring Back That Leroy Brown / Death On Two Legs / Sweet Lady / Brighton Rock / '39 / You Take My Breath Away / White Man / The Prophet's*

A Concert Documentary

Song / Bohemian Rhapsody / Stone Cold Crazy / Keep Yourself Alive / In The Lap Of The Gods (Revisited) / Encore: Now I'm Here / Liar / 2nd Encore: Jailhouse Rock / God Save The Queen

This is the last of the European dates. The band fly back home the following day.

❖ **May 20**

Queen issue their first and only Extended Play single 'Good Old Fashioned Lover Boy' / 'Death On Two Legs' / 'Tenement Funster' / 'White Queen'.

Featuring material from the second, third, fourth and fifth albums, the disc peaks at number 17 at home, and was not issued in Japan or the USA. The band insist the disc be sold at the same price as a traditional two track single.

May 23/24
Hippodrome, Bristol
■ *First night*: Tie Your Mother Down / Ogre Battle / White Queen / Somebody To Love / Medley: Killer Queen; Good Old Fashioned Lover Boy; The Millionaire Waltz; You're My Best Friend; Bring Back That Leroy Brown / Death On Two Legs / Sweet Lady / Brighton Rock / '39 / You Take My Breath Away / White Man / The Prophets Song / Bohemian Rhapsody / Stone Cold Crazy / Keep Yourself Alive / In The Lap Of The Gods (Revisited) / Encore: Now I'm Here / Liar / 2nd Encore: I'm A Man / Jailhouse Rock / God Save The Queen

'I'm A Man', the Spencer Davis Group hit, makes an extremely rare appearance here.

■ *Second night*: Tie Your Mother Down / Ogre Battle / White Queen / Somebody To Love / Medley: Killer Queen; Good Old Fashioned Lover Boy; The Millionaire Waltz; You're My Best Friend; Bring Back That Leroy Brown / Death On Two Legs / Brighton Rock / '39 / You Take My Breath Away / White Man / The Prophet's Song / Bohemian Rhapsody / Stone Cold Crazy / Sweet Lady / Keep Yourself Alive / In The Lap Of The Gods (Revisited) / Encore: Now I'm Here / Liar / 2nd Encore: Jailhouse Rock / God Save The Queen

'Brighton Rock' on this tour sees Brian's guitar solo extended to the longest it would ever be. Like

the show's finale, this would remain a part of the Queen live show right through to the last tour.

May 26/27
Gaumont, Southampton

Freddie (on 'White Man' / 'The Prophet's Song'): "Let me tell you about these next two songs. They're two songs rolled into one, both written by Brian. Every night we do this sort of segue thing, and every night it seems to be getting a little better. It depends on the audience really. It starts with a song called 'White Man'."

The band then perform one of the best recitals of the pairing to have been captured on tape, albeit unsanctioned tape. The bootleg recording of this show is definitely worth searching for, although it offers only approximately two thirds of the performance.

During 'The Millionaire Waltz' and 'You're My Best Friend' on the second night here, there are slight problems with Freddie's microphone. Although it's nothing serious, it does mar an otherwise faultless performance.

May 29

Bingley Hall, Stafford

No seats are available for this show and the entire audience has to stand. There is a rush towards the stage when Queen appear, but no one is hurt.

May 30♪/31♪

Apollo, Glasgow

■ *First night*: Tie Your Mother Down / Ogre Battle / White Queen / Somebody To Love / Medley: Killer Queen; Good Old Fashioned Lover Boy; The Millionaire Waltz; You're My Best Friend; Bring Back That Leroy Brown / Death On Two Legs / Sweet Lady / Brighton Rock / Guitar Solo / '39 / You Take My Breath Away / White Man / The Prophet's Song / Bohemian Rhapsody / Keep Yourself Alive / Stone Cold Crazy / In The Lap Of The Gods (Revisited) / Encore: Now I'm Here / Liar / I'm A Man / 2nd Encore: Jailhouse Rock / God Save The Queen

Freddie's intro: "Good evening everybody. Are you all ready for a rock and roll night? We're gonna give it to you. It's really nice to be back here in Glasgow, and thanks for such a lovely welcome. We have a lot of music to play for you tonight, of various kinds... a lot of the heavy stuff... a lot of the quieter stuff. I think straight away we'd like to do a song entitled 'White Queen'."

The medley section here is truly exceptional. Each song segues effortlessly into the next, especially the two *Races* tracks, which at first glance seem to be a strange coupling to put back to back. Not so. The two work together well, as bootleg recordings ably confirm. The audience clearly know every single word, better than Freddie sometimes, and join in every verse. They do that for the duration of the show, in fact.

Freddie: "Okay, we're gonna do something heavy. This is a song that we only just recently included in the set. It's a song called 'Death On Two Legs'."

No four letter expletives are used to intro 'Death' yet, but that will soon evolve. It is curious that Freddie's outrage about the acrimony with

the Sheffield brothers only makes its way into the stage in 1978/79 – nearly four years after the fall-out.

"I know we do this every time we come here, but every time we come here you give us a little present – a little statuette for getting a full house. But we'd like to drink a toast to you. Queen would like to drink a toast to everybody here tonight... Cheers Glasgow!" Freddie then goes on to inform the crowd that Brian is featured next, and 'Brighton Rock' begins.

Queen performed 'I'm A Man' at both shows here. One bootleg recording purporting to come from the first night, includes 'Manish Boy' too, but this was only played on the second night.

■ *Second night*: Tie Your Mother Down / Ogre Battle / White Queen / Somebody To Love / Medley: Killer Queen; Good Old Fashioned Lover Boy; The Millionaire Waltz; You're My Best Friend; Bring Back That Leroy Brown / Death On Two Legs / Sweet Lady

/ Brighton Rock / Guitar Solo / '39 / You Take My Breath Away / White Man / The Prophet's Song / Bohemian Rhapsody / Keep Yourself Alive / Stone Cold Crazy / In The Lap Of The Gods (Revisited) / Encore: Now I'm Here / Liar / I'm A Man / 2nd Encore: Manish Boy / Jailhouse Rock / God Save The Queen

June 2/3

Empire Theatre, Liverpool

■ **First night:** Tie Your Mother Down / Ogre Battle / White Queen / Somebody To Love / Medley: Killer Queen; Good Old Fashioned Lover Boy; The Millionaire Waltz; You're My Best Friend; Bring Back That Leroy Brown / Death On Two Legs / Sweet Lady / Brighton Rock / '39 / You Take My Breath Away / White Man / The Prophet's Song / Bohemian Rhapsody / Stone Cold Crazy / Keep Yourself Alive / In The Lap Of The Gods (Revisited) / Encore: Now I'm Here / Liar / I'm A Man / 2nd Encore: Jailhouse Rock / God Save The Queen

Second night: Same as first night but with 'Doing All Right' instead of 'Sweet Lady', and 'Lucille' after 'Now I'm Here.'

The band play a small segment of Paul McCartney's 'Mull Of Kintyre' after 'Keep Yourself Alive'. This is a rare occurance indeed, but again no good recording survives.

'Doing All Right' rejoins the set here. It remained only briefly, however.

June 6/7

Earls Court, London

■ **First night:** Procession / Tie Your Mother Down / Ogre Battle / White Queen / Somebody To Love /

SUMMER TOUR 1977

Queen

BACKSTAGE

Medley: Killer Queen; Good Old Fashioned Lover Boy; Millionaire Waltz; You're My Best Friend; Bring Back That Leroy Brown / Death On Two Legs / Doing All Right / Brighton Rock / '39 / You Take My Breath Away / White Man / The Prophet's Song / Bohemian Rhapsody / Keep Yourself Alive / Stone Cold Crazy / In The Lap Of The Gods (Revisited) / Encore: Now I'm Here / Liar / 2nd Encore Medley: Lucille; Jailhouse Rock; Saturday Night's Alright For Fighting; Stupid Cupid; Be Bop A Lula; Jailhouse Rock (Reprise) / God Save The Queen

Surprised audience members are greeted by bagpipers and a display of frisbee expertise in the foyer as they enter the auditorium for these concerts.

Front row tickets for both shows are reserved for fan club members.

The pre-show music is chosen by Freddie, and features passages by Chopin, one of his great favourites.

Both shows here are recorded because like the Rainbow gigs of 1974, the band are considering another live album. No such project ever materialises.

Queen use a brand new £50,000 lighting rig for the first time here. It consists of a huge silver framework covered in black sheets, with copious lights situated at its base. It weighs almost nine and a half tons, is twenty feet high, forty-five feet

EARLS COURT, LONDON
(Opposite Warwick Road Exit, Earls Court Tube Station)

Harvey Goldsmith and John Reid cordially invite you to a night with

Queen

TUESDAY, 7th JUNE, 1977
at 8.00 p.m.

2nd Floor Gallery £2.00

For Conditions of Sale see over

BLOCK
87

C24

To be retained

deep and fifty-four feet wide, and is referred to as The Crown.

As the house lights slowly dim, the classical music fades and is replaced by the pre-recorded guitar introduction to 'Tie Your Mother Down'. The Crown begins its gradual forty foot ascent to illuminate a smoke-filled stage. As the smoke clears, the taped introduction suddenly ends and the band become visible as they bound onto stage.

Later in the show: "Before we please you with some heavier rock'n'roll towards the end, I'd like you to listen carefully to a simple little song, with me on piano - it's called 'You Take My Breath Away'.

Freddie treats the audience to a recital of his ballad which many consider to be the finest ever recorded. It is moving, utterly emotive, and executed with real class. As requested, 17,000 fans listen intently to Freddie, in absolute silence. They seem almost mesmerised by his voice.

This concert is regularly shown at Queen fan club conventions, but is also unofficially available on video – and now DVD. Like audio cassette bootlegs, however, most of the tapes currently in

circulation are third or fourth generation copies, and offer poor sound quality and ropey pictures.

The band are dressed in classic Queen apparel. Freddie wears the famous green, white and orange diamond-patterned cat suit, with white ballet slippers, Brian wears the Dickensian style white pleated cape, and John has on a white T-shirt with black waistcoat.

As this is the last show of the tour, and it's in Queen's home town, they perform an extended rock'n'roll medley, including 'Lucille'.

■ *Second night: Processions / Tie Your Mother Down / Ogre Battle / White Queen / Somebody To Love / Medley: Killer Queen / Good Old Fashioned Lover Boy / Millionaire Waltz / You're My Best Friend / Bring Back That Leroy Brown / Death On Two Legs / Doing All Right / Brighton Rock / '39 / You Take My Breath Away / White Man / The Prophet's Song / Bohemian Rhapsody / Stone Cold Crazy / Sweet Lady / Keep Yourself Alive / In The Lap Of The Gods (Revisited) / Encore: Now I'm Here / Liar / 2nd Encore Medley: Lucille; Jailhouse Rock; Stupid Cupid; Be Bop A Lula; Jailhouse Rock (Reprise) / God Save The Queen*

This period sees Freddie dressed in some of his most famous costumes. For the first part of the show, he invariably wears a harlequin leotard, an exact replica of that worn by the dancer Nijinsky, before changing into either red striped shorts beneath a Japanese kimono, or the infamous, much photographed lurex outfit.

After the show, numerous celebrities join Queen at a party held in a marquee in London's Holland Park. Among them are Olivia Newton-John, Elton John and Bob Harris.

The band donate the proceeds of this show to the Queen's Silver Jubilee Fund.

↗ 'QUEEN – London'. By Nigel Morton, *Record Mirror*, June 18, 1977.
'The stage lights dim, eighteen thousand people stomp their feet on the floor as thunder flashes explode blinding everyone for a split second and the song 'Tie Your Mother Down' comes screaming out of the speakers.

'Queen are back with vengeance.

A Concert Documentary

'Freddie Mercury struts around thrusting his chest out of a tight black jump suit and Brian May stands stage right, his brow furrowed with concentration as he churns out power chords. The lyrics of the song are sunk well down in a muddy mix but it is obvious the tune is as hot as molten steel.

'The guitar runs sear across your eardrums as you watch Mercury acting it up, his left hand flapping like a broken wing and his right clutching tightly at the oh so phallic microphone. Freddie we love ya…'

↗ **'Does Queen Deserve Rock's Crown?'** *Circus* magazine, 1977; Freddie Mercury and Brian May Hawk Their 'News of the World'

'Queen have just finished a special tour of the states. Not the longest they've ever undertaken, by any means, but special nevertheless.

"It was the first tour we've ever done without the support band," Freddie explained. "There was so much going on on stage that I doubt there would have been room for another band anyway. We have so much material we want to play for people now that it would have been far too long a concert. It's hard enough anyway to know what to leave out: we'd like to play all the new material, but there are some things we just would not dare leave out or I think the fans would lynch us."

❖ **June 7**

Elektra in America release 'Long Away' as the third single from *A Day At The Races*. It is paired with John Deacon's 'You And I'. The track is not issued in Europe or Japan, and neither song is performed in the live set.

July

The band spend July, August and September at Basing Street and Wessex Studios working on new material for their next album. They are assisted by Mike Stone, who engineered all five previous albums, but essentially they produce the album themselves. *News Of The World* is eventually released in the UK on the same day as Queen record their sixth and final session for the BBC, October 28 1977.

October 6
New London Theatre Centre, London
■ *Tie Your Mother Down / Keep Yourself Alive / Somebody To Love / White Man / The Prophet's Song / Liar / Bohemian Rhapsody / Now I'm Here / Jailhouse Rock / Encore: See What A Fool I've Been*

For the purposes of promoting the new single 'We Are The Champions', five thousand British fan club members are invited to attend the filming of the video. With only four days notice, however, many receive their invitations too late and are unable to get to London in time.

As the fans enter the Drury Lane venue, each one is given a copy of the single. The track is played three or four times for the audience to familiarise themselves, and then the filming commences. The band perform the song several times as it is necessary to shoot it from numerous angles. This footage later appears on *Top Of The Pops*. A second, seldom seen version is destined to emerge as and when *Queen Rarities* appears.

stacks of promotional material very few people have ever seen). In fact, I'm off to America next week to finish off the remainder of the concert footage (from the gigs in Texas, as well as filming the major interview with all the band). Then we have to edit it all, fit it all together and get it ready for the television by mid-way through January. (I say that knowing that these things always take much longer than everybody expects) but keep a look out for it on Whistle Test towards the end of this series."

Unfortunately, the BBC never air this documentary. Indeed, it seems that Harris never got to finish it, which explains why. However, snippets of the footage can be seen on *The Magic Years* videos.

❖ October 7

'We Are The Champions' / 'We Will Rock You' is released in the UK. It provides the band with their sixth Top Ten chart placing. The same pairing is issued universally. The American release is delayed until October 25, to coincide with the beginning of the tour there.

October 28
Maida Vale Studio, London
🔊 *Spread Your Wings / It's Late / My Melancholy Blues / We Will Rock You*

Following a break after filming, the band return to the stage to play an impromptu performance by way of a thank you. They perform ten of their best known tracks. As radio presenter Bob Harris is present to film additional material for a documentary he is putting together, he introduces Queen to the stage.

● In the Winter 1977 fan club magazine, a handwritten letter from Bob Harris is printed. He refers not only to the 'We Are The Champions' video filming, but also to the documentary that he and Queen are involved in putting together: "*All this brings me on to the film that the band and I are currently making together. It's a one hour documentary, tracing their history (through films from The Rainbow, Hyde Park, Earls Court concerts and*

A Concert Documentary

115

Returning to Maida Vale for the second time, Queen record their final session for the BBC. On this occasion four tracks from the brand new album, released this day too, are reworked. The session is produced by Jeff Griffin and engineered by Mike Robinson, and is eventually broadcast two weeks later, on November 14.

Some of the tapes in circulation from this session ('No News Is Good News') perhaps being the best known.) are infuriatingly 'enhanced' by overdubbed audience cheering, whistling and clapping, added in an attempt to simulate a concert environment - an exercise that fails miserably and ruins an otherwise faultless performance.

The noise level of the audience remains unrealistically consistent throughout, and does not even quieten when a song concludes. While Brian May's 'It's Late' and 'We Will Rock You' are not entirely destroyed by the din, the sentiment of 'Spread Your Wings' and 'My Melancholy Blues' are destroyed. Such sacrilege has only ever been paralleled (in Queen's case) by the 1974 American 'Liar' single edit.

Another odd aspect of this session is the inclusion of a curious narrative passage, preceding 'We Will Rock You'. Immediately following an explosion, an effect which is later employed to kick off the live shows of 1978/79/80, and just prior to the familiar opening chords of 'Rock You' (fast version), a female voice cuts in briefly with a tale of a Buddha and Brahmanism. The band discover this when they

assemble in the control room to play back the material just recorded.

The tape contains remnants of a Radio 4 programme - including extracts of a reading of Herman Hesse's *Siddartha* - recorded in the same studio a few days earlier, though it had not yet been broadcast. The band like what they hear and incorporate a small segment of it into their own work.

'It's Late' contains a unique improvised section absent from the album version. There are many similarities with 'Get Down Make Love' (from the same album) which is largely due to a custom made tape delay machine which the band bring with them to the studio. Because no commercially available device exists to provide the desired length of delay, the band design their own.

This session take of 'It's Late' offers the only recorded version in that form. Even the many live versions do not feature the song performed in this experimental manner.

● BBC Producer Jeff Griffin: "This time we had a much longer time booked, I actually booked from 2.30 in the afternoon right through 'til 2 o'clock the following morning, so that it would give them plenty of time. But I should point out that we were still only recording on 8-track machines at that time, and I did make it very clear to Brian when he came in. I said, 'I don't want this to get out of hand because given 8-tracks, 16-tracks or 32-tracks, or probably 48-tracks, you'd probably use every bloody one to overdub your guitars, and that's not what this is about. I know we've got a bit more time and slightly more sophisticated equipment than we used to have (for previous Queen BBC sessions), but we still have to be disciplined about this because we want to get the four tracks done and out and mixed by the end of session.' He said, 'Yeah, okay, no problem. I'd like to do a few overdubs, but nothing out of hand.' And that's what we stuck to.

"And then there was 'We Will Rock You'. Now that was fun - particularly for me and my engineer Mark Robinson, because the band said, 'Look, we need as many voices on this as possible, so we

is scheduled for November, so Queen have to finish the album in nearly half the time they would normally take. This accounts for certain songs emerging with a decidedly under-produced sound – by Queen standards at least. Even so, the album does well in the charts and also contains the classic pairing of 'We Will Rock You' and 'We Are The Champions'. Other stand-out tracks include 'Get Down Make Love', 'It's Late', 'Spread Your Wings' and 'My Melancholy Blues' – all of which will eventually feature in the live show.

Brian May's exquisite 'All Dead All Dead', John Deacon's 'Who Needs You' and Roger's 'Fight From The Inside' are discounted for the stage show, while 'Sleeping On The Sidewalk', also a May composition, is at least tried once, on November 11, before being dropped because it does not work as well as expected.

USA 1977 - US Tour (2nd Leg)

On November 4, Queen fly to America for final rehearsals. Three days later they move on to the Metro Coliseum in New Haven to make last minute adjustments to the show. The band now tour with over 60 tons of equipment, including a specially modified Crown lighting rig - unveiled at the Earls Court gigs in London, in June.

It is necessary for the lighting rig to be more mobile than it is, and to be more easily adapted to whichever arena it has to function in. A Boston-based sail making company are given the task of redesigning it, and The Crown emerges more impressive than ever.

The actual stage consists of three catwalks and a further two raised platforms, which are constructed above the PA system, giving the band access to all areas of the stage, and the ability to see the entire audience, including those seated behind the stage.

There is no support act for this tour, which allows Queen to play a two and a quarter hour set.

The show includes new material from *News Of The World* - 'We Will Rock You' (fast and slow versions), 'Get Down Make Love', 'Sheer Heart Attack', 'Spread Your Wings', 'We Are The

want you two to come in and sing in the studio.'

"Mike and I were a bit reluctant at first, but that's what we did; we built up, layered the vocal tracks to make it sound a bit more stadium-ish - at least that's what we thought at the time. If I listen to it now it probably sounds not quite like that, but there we are. It was a great session and certainly the two Johns (Peel and Walters) were very pleased with it when they heard it and it went out. I think it caused quite a bit of a stir at the time because people were a bit surprised that it would be going out on the *John Peel Show*, amongst all the other things of that time."

❖ Also on October 28, the sixth album *News Of The World* is released in the UK.

Though the band took three months and five months respectively to record *A Night At The Opera* and *A Day At The Races*, barely ten weeks is allocated to *News Of The World*. An American tour

Queen Live '77

Champions' and 'My Melancholy Blues'. 'It's Late' will feature later in the tour. 'Sweet Lady', 'Ogre Battle', 'White Queen' and 'Liar' are all dropped to make way for the new songs.

Although 'Get Down Make Love' differs from one night to the next, depending upon the atmosphere at a given venue, it generally contains a set amount of improvised material. A good example of this is contained on *Live Killers*.

● Brian: "It's just an exercise in using guitar harmonizer effects together with noises from Freddie... a sort of erotic interlude."

John Deacon sports severely cropped hair during this tour. This makes photographs originating from this period easy to date.

November 11
Cumberland County Civic Center, Portland, Maine

■ We Will Rock You (Slow) / We Will Rock You (Fast version) / Brighton Rock / Somebody To Love / Medley: Death On Two Legs; Killer Queen; Good Old Fashioned Lover Boy; I'm In Love With My Car / Get Down Make Love; The Millionaire Waltz; You're My Best Friend / Spread Your Wings / It's Late / Sleeping On The Sidewalk / Now I'm Here / Love Of My Life / '39 / My Melancholy Blues / White Man / Improvisation / The Prophet's Song / Liar / Keep Yourself Alive / Bohemian Rhapsody / Tie Your Mother Down / Encore: We Will Rock You / We Are The Champions / 2nd Encore: Sheer Heart Attack / Jailhouse Rock / God Save The Queen

The stage is very impressive and features the immense custom-built lighting rig suspended over it. As the show commences and the music starts, the Crown rises slowly, amid an eerie cloud of smoke billowing across the stage from hidden machines.

'We Will Rock You' kicks thing off; first the pounding drum slow version, for which Roger and John are not yet visible, and then, when Brian has concluded the track with his familiar solo, the pair are revealed when a curtain in front of the drum kit suddenly parts. An explosion creates plumes of smoke, and a much accelerated 'We Will Rock You' begins. The crowd is shaken into action and the night's work is under way. A great example of this fast, live version is contained on the *Greatest Flix* video compilation of 1981.

For the first time on stage, Roger sings his *Opera* song, 'I'm In Love With My Car'. Another first is the addition of Freddie's beautiful 'Love Of My Life', also from *Opera*. This is performed in a very different form from that of the album version. John and Roger leave the stage to Freddie and Brian, who perform it acoustically, seated on stools.

When Freddie stops singing half way through the song, to let the already word-perfect audience continue without him, they willingly do so. It sets a precedent that Freddie continues from that show on – to the very last. This does not remain exclusive to English speaking audiences, for in subsequent years the band are pleasantly surprised to discover European, Japanese and South American audiences singing along in perfect English too.

'Tie Your Mother Down' is no longer the opening track of the show. It is never completely dropped from the set, only politely moved around a little.

Much later on, it will be 'Rock You' and 'Champions' that provide the finale to the show, and so it will remain for virtually every concert thereafter. For now though, it is 'Sheer Heart Attack' and 'Jailhouse Rock' that close the show. Freddie returns to stage, for this second and last encore, adorned in the famous lurex suit.

November 12
Boston Garden, Boston, Massachusetts

November 13
Civic Center, Springfield, Massachusetts

November 15
Civic Center, Providence, Rhode Island
■ *We Will Rock You (Slow/Fast) / Brighton Rock / Somebody To Love / Medley: Death On Two Legs; Killer Queen; Good Old Fashioned Lover Boy; I'm In Love With My Car; Get Down Make Love; The Millionaire Waltz; You're My Best Friend / Spread Your Wings / Liar / Love Of My Life / '39 / My Melancholy Blues / White Man / Improvisation / The Prophet's Song / Keep Yourself Alive / Stone Cold Crazy / Bohemian Rhapsody / Tie Your Mother Down / Encore: We Will Rock You / We Are The Champions / 2nd Encore: Sheer Heart Attack / Jailhouse Rock / God Save The Queen*

November 16
Memorial Coliseum, New Haven, Connecticut

November 18/19
Cobo Hall, Detroit, Michigan

November 21
Maple Leaf Garden, Toronto, Ontario
After this show the band fly to Philadelphia in their own aeroplane. Previously they had resisted hiring their own air transport as they considered commercial flights a safer option.

November 23/24
The Spectrum, Philadelphia, Pennsylvania
■ *First night: We Will Rock You (Slow/Fast) / Brighton Rock / Somebody To Love / Medley: Death On Two Legs; Killer Queen; Good Old Fashioned Lover Boy; I'm In Love With My Car; Get Down Make Love / The Millionaire Waltz; Spread Your Wings / Liar / Love Of My Life / '39 / My Melancholy Blues / White Man / Improvisation / The Prophet's Song / Keep Yourself Alive / Stone Cold Crazy / Bohemian Rhapsody / Tie Your Mother Down / Encore: We Will Rock You / We Are The Champions / 2nd Encore: Sheer Heart Attack / Jailhouse Rock / God Save The Queen*

Following the two shows here, Queen fly to Norfolk, Virginia, to meet Frank Kelly Freas, the artist they had commissioned earlier in the year to paint the cover artwork for their *News Of The World* album. Freas' spectacular painting of a robot with a dead human in its hand, had been adapted to show instead the four Queen band members at the mercy of the giant. They band meet him at the Chrysler Museum of Art, where he is exhibiting his work, including the original robot painting. The event is covered by local press and TV.

November 25
Scope Arena, Norfolk, Virginia

November 27
Richfield Coliseum, Cleveland, Ohio
Before this show Queen are visited backstage by ELO drummer Bev Bevan, who is in town on a promotional tour.

November 29
Capitol Center, Washington DC
While at this venue, the band stay at the famous Watergate Hotel, which Freddie finds most agreeable.

December 1/2
Madison Square Garden, New York
When Freddie appears for the first encore, he is dressed in a jacket and hat sporting the New York Yankees logo. The baseball team have just won the World Series and have adopted 'We Are The Champions' as their theme tune. Freddie appreciates the gesture.
■ *First night: We Will Rock You (Slow/Fast) / Brighton Rock / Somebody To Love / It's Late / Medley: Death On Two Legs; Killer Queen; Good Old Fashioned Lover Boy; I'm In Love With My Car; Get Down Make Love; The Millionaire Waltz; You're My Best Friend / Spread Your Wings / Liar / Love Of My Life / '39 / My Melancholy Blues / White Man / Vocal Improvisation / The Prophet's Song / Now I'm Here / Stone Cold Crazy / Bohemian Rhapsody / Tie Your*

Mother Down / Encore: We Will Rock You / We Are The Champions / 2nd Encore: Sheer Heart Attack / Jailhouse Rock / God Save The Queen
Second night: 'Saturday Night's Alright For Fighting' makes an appearance in the encore after 'Jailhouse Rock'.

While in New York, the band take time out to see various shows. Freddie attends Liza Minnelli's *The Act*, and together all four members see Daryl Hall & John Oates in concert.

Only hours before Queen are scheduled to leave New York, Freddie goes shopping and purchases a Japanese style grand piano, which he has shipped home. He will subsequently write many songs on it.

December 4
University Arena, Dayton, Ohio

December 5
Chicago Stadium, Chicago, Illinois
■ *We Will Rock You (Slow/Fast) / Brighton Rock / Somebody To Love / Medley: Death On Two Legs; Killer Queen; Good Old Fashioned Lover Boy; I'm In Love With My Car; Get Down Make Love; The Millionaire Waltz; You're My Best Friend / Spread Your Wings / Liar / Love Of My Life / '39 / My Melancholy Blues / White Man / Vocal Improvisation / The Prophet's Song / Now I'm Here / Stone Cold Crazy / Bohemian Rhapsody / Tie Your Mother Down / Encore: We Will Rock You / We Are The Champions / 2nd Encore: Sheer Heart Attack / Jailhouse Rock / God Save The Queen*

December 8
The Omni, Atlanta, Georgia
Also on December 8, Bob Harris arrives with a film crew to cover two Queen shows for his proposed documentary. They begin with the Fort Worth gig on December 10, and conclude with the wonderful performance in Houston the night after. This is the show that features at fan club conventions and which appears on the *Rare Live* video collection – though too fleetingly, as with everything on that tape!

Though the film crew fly home, Bob remains and travels with the band to the next venue, in Las Vegas, where additional interview material is recorded.

December 10
Tarrant County Convention Center, Fort Worth, Texas

Parts of this show are filmed for the Bob Harris documentary (which never materialises).

December 11 ♫
The Summit, Houston, Texas

■ *We Will Rock You (Slow/Fast) / Brighton Rock / Somebody To Love / Medley: Death On Two Legs; Killer Queen; Good Old Fashioned Lover Boy; I'm In Love With My Car; Get Down Make Love; The Millionaire Waltz; You're My Best Friend / Spread Your Wings / Liar / Love Of My Life / '39 / My Melancholy Blues / White Man / Vocal Improvisation / The Prophet's Song / Now I'm Here / Stone Cold Crazy / Bohemian Rhapsody / Tie Your Mother Down / Encore: We Will Rock You / We Are The Champions / 2nd Encore: Sheer Heart Attack / Jailhouse Rock / God Save The Queen*

This winter evening in Texas finds the band in truly dazzling form and this is without doubt one of the greatest Queen concerts ever to have been filmed – albeit not in full.

'My Melancholy Blues' sees Freddie once again seated at the piano: "Okay, we'd like to try something very different right now. This is from the new album *News Of The World*. Have you got it yet? The album, that is. You might just about recognise this... this is 'My Melancholy Blues'."

Having sung the opening line, he then counts Roger in by clicking his fingers. Roger and John (who is seated on a stool) provide only subtle accompaniment while Brian does not feature at all. This is as perfect a recital of 'Blues' as you will ever hear. It later appeared as a bonus track on the 12" and CD single formats of 'The Miracle' single in November, 1989.

While Queen are in Houston, Roger Taylor takes the opportunity to attend a Rod Stewart show in Los Angeles, as he too is in the middle of an American tour.

December 15
Aladdin Center, Las Vegas, Nevada

December 16
Sports Arena, San Diego, California

Bootleg recordings of this show are worth locating if only for the wonderful version of 'Spread Your Wings'. The song remains in the set, on and off, until late 1979.

December 17
County Coliseum, Oakland, California

With only four shows of the tour left, John manages to put his hand through a plate glass window. The injury requires nineteen stitches to his arm and hand, but the tour continues with him playing with a bandaged right arm.

December 20/21
Long Beach Arena, Long Beach, California

While here, the band are the subject of a fifteen minute NBC six o'clock news slot, which includes a rare insight into the stage being set up, and interviews with them.

■ *Second night*: *We Will Rock You (Slow/Fast) / Brighton Rock / Somebody To Love / Medley: Death On Two Legs; Killer Queen; Good Old Fashioned Lover Boy; I'm In Love With My Car; Get Down Make Love / The Millionaire Waltz; You're My Best Friend /*

Spread Your Wings / Liar / Love Of My Life / '39 / My Melancholy Blues / White Man / Vocal Improvisation / The Prophet's Song / Now I'm Here / Stone Cold Crazy / Bohemian Rhapsody / Tie Your Mother Down / Encore: We Will Rock You / We Are The Champions / 2nd Encore: Sheer Heart Attack / Jailhouse Rock / God Save The Queen

December 22
Inglewood Forum, Los Angeles, California
We Will Rock You (Slow/Fast) / Brighton Rock / Somebody To Love / It's Late / Medley: Death On Two Legs; Killer Queen; Good Old Fashioned Lover Boy; I'm In Love With My Car; Get Down Make Love / The Millionaire Waltz; You're My Best Friend / Spread Your Wings / Liar / Love Of My Life / White Christmas / '39 / My Melancholy Blues / White Man / Vocal Improvisation / The Prophet's Song / Now I'm Here / Stone Cold Crazy / Bohemian Rhapsody / Keep Yourself Alive / Tie Your Mother Down / Encore: We Will Rock You / We Are The Champions / 2nd Encore: Sheer Heart Attack / Jailhouse Rock / God Save The Queen

Freddie: "Your just terrific, do you know we've been listening to you from the dressing room and you're the best already. Thank you for giving us such a beautiful welcome tonight. Tonight we have a lot of music for you. We're just going to play til we drop, and we'd like you to be with us all the way – okay?"

Brian: "Thank you. I hope it feels as good to be down there as it feels to be here. I tell you it feels good. We're going to enjoy ourselves tonight if it kills us. Okay, this is the last night of the tour as you probably know, a special night. We'd like to remind you of last year, at the same time, we did a song called 'Somebody To Love' - and this is it."

Later. Freddie: "Okay, on with the show. Tonight's really going to be a fun night as it's very near Christmas. I mean it's *almost* Christmas anyway, so we'd really like you to join in and just do what you like. We're going to do our bit, you do yours. Okay. This is… 'Ogre Battle'… we might do that. But right now we'd like to do a song from a very new album of ours called The News Of The

World, this is a song written by Brian May, entitled 'It's Late'"

Freddie: "Okay let me see you. We've come to the point in the show where we have a so called medley that we do every time we do a show. Tonight is… Do you remember it from last time? Okay, only this time it's slightly different and we've added a few more songs to it. I think we could call it something nice and pretentious - just for all the critics. Any way and to start off, this is ' Death On Two Legs'."

Freddie: "Thank you. It's just like a Christmas party I can tell. Okay, the last number in that sort of segment was a song called 'You're My Best Friend', written by John Deacon… yes he's writing some good songs lately, in fact they're pretty good - very good. We'd like to do another one of his numbers from the new album News Of The World, this is a song entitled 'Spread Your Wings'."

Brian: "Thank you. Okay, right. Something completely different now. We're going to do a little interlude now and we have some stuff which I hope you haven't heard before. We did one acoustic song last time I think, we're going to a few more this time, just to make it better. We have all the time in the world, don't we? Okay."

After 'Love Of My Life', Brian: "Thank You. We enjoy doing that one. Right, we have a little surprise for you now…"

Freddie: "I think the surprise is going to be for us. Okay. We've kind of cooked up something in the dressing room we've never ever done before, as it's Christmas. People are saying 'You've gotta do something', you've gotta do something Christmassy'.

"Okay, so we're going to try something tonight which we've never done before. We really need your help so we'd like you all to sing along - now don't be shy. I think Brian's going to start it off, It goes something like this…"

Freddie and Brian perform a specially rehearsed acoustic rendition of 'White Christmas', during which 5,000 balloons are released into the audience, and mock snow and glitter is shot across the stage, to add to the festive atmosphere.

Freddie: "If only my mother could see me now!"

Brian: "She's in the first row! You'll never see the likes of that again, I tell you. Okay, this isn't a Christmas carol but we'd like you to join in anyway, this is '39."

Later, after 'Melancholy Blues'. Freddie: "Thank you. I really enjoyed that, I really did. Okay we're going to do something in total contrast now get you in a bit more... This is a real bitch of a song, I must tell you. I've been really suffering from these bloody vocal chords, and this is the song that really hurts, but we're going to do it for you tonight. It's a song written by Brian - the heavy merchant over there. A song entitled 'White Man'."

Freddie: "Thank you. Okay, this is a compliment to a rock'n'roll band called Mott The Hoople. Do you remember those guys? I'd like to pay them a compliment with a song entitled 'Now I'm Here'."

For the final encore, the band's six and a half foot bodyguard takes to the stage, dressed as Father Christmas, carrying a huge sack on his back from which Freddie emerges. An assortment of people then join the band on stage, also attired in festive costumes. Included in the unlikely line-up is the director of EMI dressed as a gingerbread man, John Reid (Queen's manager) dressed as an elf, and members of the road crew assuming the roles of reindeers, clowns and walking Christmas trees.

Freddie: "Goodnight. God bless you. Merry Christmas."

Following a party after the show, John Harris (sound engineer) is taken seriously ill and rushed to hospital. He spends almost a year in hospital, before making a full recovery.

Queen fly back to the UK on Christmas Eve. On the same day, the first half of a two-part two-hour documentary on the band is broadcast on Radio One – presented by Tom Browne. It concludes on Boxing Day.

1978

❖ **February 10**

'Spread Your Wings' is released as Queen's eleventh UK single. The choice of B-side is Roger Taylor's manic 'Sheer Heart Attack', a track originally written for the album of the same name. 'Wings' is not issued in America as Brian May's epic 'It's Late' is considered a better alternative.

EUROPE 1978

In April, the band embark on a four-week European tour of 20 shows in nine countries at 13 different venues. The final three shows are consecutive nights at the Wembley Empire Pool, in London.

Fitting the huge Crown lighting rig into some of the theatres will prove to be troublesome. For the rig to lift properly, a minimum height is necessary above the stage, but the theatres at Copenhagen and Hamburg prove too small to accommodate it. In such venues, just the base lights are used.

"Good evening everybody. We're gonna have a good rock'n'roll night tonight. Okay?" says Freddie, greeting the audience for the first time.

"It's really nice to see you guys here. We have a lot of music for you tonight, that's why we don't have a support (act). I just wish there were a few more of you."

April 14
Ernst Merck Halle, Hamburg

April 16/17
Forêst Nationale, Brussels

Problems with the lighting rig at the beginning of the set threatens to jeopardise this show.

The immense weight of the Crown means it has to be lifted hydraulically, in a controlled sequence using four switches. But, the sequence fails and only one side rises, causing the other side to be dragged downward. There is much confusion on and off stage, before it is decided that the show should restart, which it does. It begins again without further interruption.

April 12
Ice Stadium, Stockholm, Norway ①

■ We Will Rock You (Slow/Fast) / Brighton Rock / Somebody To Love / Medley: Death On Two Legs; Killer Queen; Good Old Fashioned Lover Boy; I'm In Love With My Car; Get Down Make Love; The Millionaire Waltz; You're My Best Friend / Spread Your Wings / It's Late / Now I'm Here / Love Of My Life / '39 / My Melancholy Blues / White Man / Instrumental Improvisation / The Prophet's Song / Stone Cold Crazy / Bohemian Rhapsody / Keep Yourself Alive / Tie Your Mother Down / Encore: We Will Rock You / We Are The Champions / 2nd Encore: Sheer Heart Attack / Jailhouse Rock / God Save The Queen

April 13
Falkoner Theatre, Copenhagen

■ We Will Rock You (Slow/Fast) / Brighton Rock / Somebody To Love / Medley: Death On Two Legs; Killer Queen; Good Old Fashioned Lover Boy; I'm In Love With My Car; Get Down Make Love; The Millionaire Waltz; You're My Best Friend / Spread Your Wings / It's Late / Now I'm Here / Love Of My Life / '39 / My Melancholy Blues / Medley: White Man; The Prophet's Song: incorporating You Take My Breath Away; Guitar Solo; The Prophet's Song (Reprise) / Stone Cold Crazy / Bohemian Rhapsody / Keep Yourself Alive / Tie Your Mother Down / Encore: We Will Rock You / We Are The Champions / 2nd Encore: Sheer Heart Attack / Jailhouse Rock / God Save The Queen

As part of the promotion for these shows, a large mock-up of the *News Of The World* album sleeve robot is driven around Brussels before each show. It had originally been constructed on the back of a car by local Queen fans, for the Mardi Gras carnival in Antwerp, but is borrowed by the concert promoters who spot it at the carnival and transfer it to the back of a trailer. By the end of the second day, however, little is left of the robot – courtesy of Belgium's over-zealous Queen fans.

April 19⁄20
Ahoy Hall, Rotterdam

■ **First night**: We Will Rock You (Slow/Fast) / Brighton Rock / Somebody To Love / Medley: Death On Two Legs; Killer Queen; Good Old Fashioned Lover Boy; I'm In Love With My Car; Get Down Make Love; The Millionaire Waltz; You're My Best Friend / Spread Your Wings / It's Late / Now I'm Here / Love Of My Life / '39 / My Melancholy Blues / Medley: White Man; The Prophet's Song; Guitar Solo; The Prophet's Song (Reprise) / Stone Cold Crazy /

Bohemian Rhapsody / Keep Yourself Alive / Tie Your Mother Down / Encore: We Will Rock You / We Are The Champions / 2nd Encore: Sheer Heart Attack / Jailhouse Rock / God Save The Queen

As a welcome, EMI arrange for a small aeroplane to circle the band's hotel with a trailing banner that reads 'EMI Welcome Queen'. The gesture is appreciated by Queen, but this reveals the band's whereabouts and local fans descend on the hotel in their hundreds.

■ **Second night**: We Will Rock You (Slow/Fast) / Brighton Rock / Somebody To Love / Medley: Death On Two Legs; Killer Queen; Good Old Fashioned Lover Boy; I'm In Love With My Car; Get Down Make Love; The Millionaire Waltz; You're My Best Friend / Spread Your Wings / Liar / It's Late / Now I'm Here / Love Of My Life / '39 / My Melancholy Blues / Medley: White Man; The Prophet's Song; Instrumental Improvisation; The Prophet's Song (Reprise) / Stone Cold Crazy / Bohemian Rhapsody / Keep Yourself Alive / Tie Your Mother Down / Encore: We Will Rock You / We Are The Champions / 2nd Encore: Sheer Heart Attack / Jailhouse Rock / Stupid Cupid / Be Bop A Lula / Jailhouse Rock (Reprise) / God Save The Queen

April 21
Forêst Nationale, Brussels

the odd "bub bub bubba" line instead. This is something he did openly on the rare occassions where a lyric suddenly escaped him.

'We Will Rock You', though always a concert favourite, whatever the tour and territory, goes down especially well here. This is because the song had spent 12 weeks at number one in France the previous year, only to be replaced by 'We Are The Champions'. Given that France is a notoriously difficult market for rock'n'roll artists to penetrate, this is no small feat.

Due to problems at previous concerts at the Pavillion, local police enforce a limit on the number of people allowed into the hall. For these Queen's shows, however, a number of tickets above that limit have already been sold. The restriction is lifted only for the second show, as no trouble occurs during the first.

↗ Tim Lott, Record Mirror: *'At 8.21 Freddie makes his entrance – a predictable but dramatic spectacle as he taunts and postures to the thud of 'We Will Rock You'. His dress sense is as gauche as always, a harlequin leotard with neckline sweeping to his waist, and a small leather belt round his hips. The lights go up to reveal Queen units B, C and D.*

'Brian May in benign intensity stands on a

This show (the third at this venue) is added because demand for tickets for the first two shows is so great. Queen are the first band to sell out three nights at the Forêst Nationale, the largest concert hall in Belgium.

April 23 ↗/24
Pavillion De Paris, Paris, France ①

■ *We Will Rock You (Slow/Fast) / Brighton Rock / Somebody To Love / Medley: Death On Two Legs; Killer Queen; Good Old Fashioned Lover Boy; I'm In Love With My Car; Get Down Make Love; The Millionaire Waltz; You're My Best Friend / Spread Your Wings / It's Late / Now I'm Here / Love Of My Life / '39 / My Melancholy Blues / Medley: White Man; Instrumental Inferno; The Prophet's Song / Stone Cold Crazy / Bohemian Rhapsody / Keep Yourself Alive / Tie Your Mother Down / Encore: We Will Rock You / We Are The Champions / 2nd Encore: Sheer Heart Attack / Jailhouse Rock / God Save The Queen*

Roger's rendition of 'I'm In Love With My Car' is superb, here. Singing lead vocals and drumming simultaneously cannot be a simple undertaking, yet Roger makes it seem precisely that.

Freddie forgets a few of the words to 'Lover Boy', in the medley section, and improvises with

protruding plinth on the opposite side of the stage to Freddie. John Deacon looks monumentally uninterested, as always. There go Freddie's cheeks again right between his back teeth. Bonjour madames et messieurs, comment ça va? A cliché is a cliché even in Gallic...'

April 26
Westfallenhalle, Dortmund

April 28
Deutschlandhalle, Berlin
■ *We Will Rock You (Slow/Fast) / Brighton Rock / Somebody To Love / Medley: Death On Two Legs; Killer Queen; Good Old Fashioned Lover Boy; I'm In Love With My Car; Get Down Make Love; The Millionaire Waltz; You're My Best Friend / Spread Your Wings / It's Late / Now I'm Here / Love Of My Life / '39 / My Melancholy Blues / Medley: White Man; The Prophet's Song; Instrumental Inferno; The Prophet's Song (Reprise) / Stone Cold Crazy / Bohemian Rhapsody / Keep Yourself Alive / Tie Your Mother Down / We Will Rock You / We Are The Champions / Encore: Big Spender / Sheer Heart Attack / 2nd Encore: Jailhouse Rock / God Save The Queen*
   This is Queen's first-ever show in Berlin.

April 30
Hallenstadion, Zurich
■ *We Will Rock You (Slow/Fast) / Brighton Rock / Somebody To Love / Medley: Death On Two Legs;Killer Queen; Good Old Fashioned Lover Boy; I'm In Love With My Car; Get Down Make Love; The Millionaire Waltz; You're My Best Friend / Spread Your Wings / It's Late / Now I'm Here / Love Of My Life / '39 / My Melancholy Blues / Medley: White Man; Instrumental Inferno; The Prophet's Song / Stone Cold Crazy / Bohemian Rhapsody / Keep Yourself Alive / Tie Your Mother Down / Encore: We Will Rock You / We Are The Champions / 2nd Encore: Sheer Heart Attack / 3rd Encore: Jailhouse Rock / God Save The Queen*
   Queen perform a stunning version of the encore track 'Sheer Heart Attack'. Although it is as fast and furious as ever, every word is clearly audible.

May 2 ♪
Stadthalle, Vienna, Austria ①
■ *We Will Rock You (Slow/Fast) / Brighton Rock / Somebody To Love / Medley: Death On Two Legs ; Killer Queen; Good Old Fashioned Lover Boy; I'm In Love With My Car; Get Down Make Love; The Millionaire Waltz; You're My Best Friend / Spread Your Wings / It's Late / Now I'm Here / Love Of My Life / '39 / My Melancholy Blues / Medley: White Man; The Prophet's Song; Instrumental Inferno; The Prophet's Song (Reprise) / Stone Cold Crazy / Bohemian Rhapsody / Keep Yourself Alive / Tie Your Mother Down / Encore: We Will Rock You / We Are*

QUEEN U.S. TOUR 1978

Of My Life / '39 / My Melancholy Blues / Medley: White Man; The Prophet's Song; Instrumental Inferno; The Prophet's Song (Reprise) / Stone Cold Crazy / Bohemian Rhapsody / Keep Yourself Alive / Tie Your Mother Down / We Will Rock You / We Are The Champions / Encore: Sheer Heart Attack / 2nd Encore: Jailhouse Rock / God Save The Queen

During 'Love Of My Life' Freddie decides to stop singing again and let the crowd take over. They do so with great vigour and the band are extremely touched. From this show on, the audience/Freddie duet becomes a tradition, and a high point of the show.

May 11/12/13
Empire Pool, London
■ **First night**: We Will Rock You (Slow/Fast) / Brighton Rock / Somebody To Love / Medley: Death On Two Legs; Killer Queen; Good Old Fashioned Lover Boy; I'm In Love With My Car; Get Down Make Love; The Millionaire Waltz; You're My Best Friend / Spread Your Wings / It's Late / Now I'm Here / Love Of My Life / '39 / My Melancholy Blues / Medley: White Man; The Prophet's Song; Instrumental Inferno; The Prophet's Song (Reprise) / Stone Cold Crazy / Bohemian Rhapsody / Keep Yourself Alive / Tie Your Mother Down / Encore: We Will Rock You / We Are The Champions / 2nd Encore: Sheer Heart Attack / 3rd Encore: Jailhouse Rock / God Save The Queen

The Champions / 2nd Encore: Sheer Heart Attack / 3rd Encore: Jailhouse Rock / God Save The Queen

This is Queen's début show in Vienna. It is attended by the winners of a competition organised by the *Daily Mirror* newspaper in Britain. The winners are flown out specially for the show, and later meet with the band.

May 3
Olympiahalle, Munich
Before the show commences, the catwalk at the front of the stage collapses under the pressure of the audience. No one is seriously hurt, and following a slight delay the show goes ahead as planned.

The last twenty minutes of this show are filmed for a German television programme called *Szene 78*.

May 6♩/7
Bingley Hall, Stafford
■ **First night**: We Will Rock You (Slow/Fast) / Brighton Rock / Somebody To Love / Medley: Death On Two Legs; Killer Queen; Good Old Fashioned Lover Boy; I'm In Love With My Car; Get Down Make Love; The Millionaire Waltz; You're My Best Friend / Spread Your Wings / It's Late / Now I'm Here / Love

QUEEN

GUEST PASS
No Stage
Access

■ *Final night*: *We Will Rock You (Slow/Fast) / Brighton Rock / Somebody To Love / White Queen / Medley: Death On Two Legs; Killer Queen; Good Old Fashioned Lover Boy; I'm In Love With My Car; Get Down Make Love; Millionaire Waltz; You're My Best Friend / Spread Your Wings / It's Late / Now I'm Here / Love Of My Life / '39 / My Melancholy Blues / Medley: White Man; The Prophet's Song; Instrumental Inferno; The Prophet's Song (Reprise) / Stone Cold Crazy / Bohemian Rhapsody / Keep Yourself Alive / Tie Your Mother Down / Encore: Sheer Heart Attack / 2nd Encore: We Will Rock You / We Are The Champions / God Save The Queen*

For this, the last show of the European leg of the tour, Queen re-arrange the encore to conclude with 'Rock You' / 'Champions'.

July

Queen work on material for their seventh album *Jazz*. The sessions are recorded at Mountain Studios, in Switzerland, and Superbear Studios in Southern France. The recording is finished by October.

❖ October 13

'Fat Bottomed Girls' / 'Bicycle Race', the first single from *Jazz*, is released in the UK. Though promotional videos for both tracks are filmed, the 'Bicycle Race' footage is deemed unsuitable for

television broadcast in its original form. The famous footage of sixty-five female models cycling naked around Wimbledon Stadium (as depicted in the LP's triple-spread poster) has to be obscured with special effects for its few television screenings. Regardless of the censorship, the disc peaks at No.11.

❖ October 24

Four days prior to the beginning of American tour dates, 'Bicycle Race' / 'Fat Bottomed Girls' is issued in the US. It reaches number 24.

USA 1978 - North American Tour

In late October Queen fly to Dallas to prepare for a 35- show, seven week tour of North America. Five concerts in Canada are also included. The tour concludes with three consecutive shows at the Inglewood Forum, in Los Angeles.

A new hydraulic operated lighting rig is unveiled on this tour. It weighs five tons and utilises six hundred lights. The bulbs generate so much heat that the rig earns the nickname The Pizza Oven.

The brand new set now features material from the *Jazz* album – due for British release on November 10 – 'Let Me Entertain You', 'Bicycle Race', 'If You Can't Beat Them', 'Dreamers Ball'

and 'Fat Bottomed Girls'. 'Don't Stop Me Now' and 'Mustapha' will also feature in the set, but not yet. 'Lover Boy', 'Stone Cold Crazy', 'My Melancholy Blues', 'White Man' and 'The Millionaire Waltz' are all dropped from the set to make way for the new arrivals. The medley is now comprised of the same tracks and in the same sequence as the one featured on *Live Killers* – though of course the actual recordings on that album do not come from this tour.

This tour sees the first time Queen close a show with their own material rather than a cover version.

October 28
Convention Center, Dallas, Texas
■ *We Will Rock You / Let Me Entertain You / Somebody To Love / If You Can't Beat Them / Medley: Death On Two Legs; Killer Queen; Bicycle Race; I'm In Love With My Car; Get Down Make Love; You're My Best Friend / Now I'm Here / Spread Your Wings / Dreamers Ball / Love Of My Life / '39 / It's Late / Brighton Rock / Fat Bottomed Girls / Keep Yourself Alive / Bohemian Rhapsody / Tie Your Mother Down / Encore: Sheer Heart Attack / 2nd Encore: We Will Rock You / We Are The Champions / God Save The Queen*

Like its predecessor, the new rig moves above the stage throughout the show, and ultimately comes to rest facing out towards the audience – a spectacular and dazzling sight, which few photographs capture properly.

October 29
Mid South Coliseum, Memphis, Tennesse
■ *We Will Rock You / Let Me Entertain You / Somebody To Love / If You Can't Beat Them / Medley: Death On Two Legs; Killer Queen; Bicycle Race; I'm In Love With My Car; Get Down Make Love; You're My Best Friend / Now I'm Here / Spread Your Wings / Dreamers Ball / Love Of My Life / '39 / It's Late / Brighton Rock / Fat Bottomed Girls / Keep Yourself Alive / Bohemian Rhapsody / Tie Your Mother Down / Encore: Sheer Heart Attack / Jailhouse Rock / 2nd Encore: We Will Rock You / We Are The Champions / God Save The Queen*

Although 'Jailhouse Rock' is dropped from the set during this tour, the band perform it here as a tribute to Elvis Presley – who had died earlier in the year. This is the first opportunity Queen have had to offer an appropriate tribute to him, being as it is his home town.

October 31
Civic Auditorium, New Orleans
Following the show, a huge party takes place for the world premier of the *Jazz* album. It is the very first event jointly organised by EMI and Elektra, and it includes an elaborate assortment of entertainment: fire-eaters, African dancers, unicyclists, strippers, drag artists and local jazz bands. The event is such a success that the album is never actually played. The group have wisely scheduled two days off before the next show.

November 3
Sportorium, Miami

November 4
Civic Center, Lakeland, Florida

November 6
Capitol Center, Washington DC

November 7
New Haven Coliseum, Connecticut

November 9/10
Cobo Arena, Detroit

QUEEN QUEEN QUEEN QUEEN QUEEN

❖ Also on November 10, Queen's seventh album, *Jazz*, is released in the UK. It reaches number two in the UK and number six in America. It is the first Queen LP to have been recorded in a studio outside the UK.

As with every album, a proportion of the material is not used in the live show. Though most or all of *Jazz* might *seem* to be adaptable for stage, there are still tracks that never feature. The most glaring omission has to be Brian May's 'Dead On Time', which, with its frantic pace, exceptional lyrics and 'Courtesy of God' thunderclap (taped by Brian during a power failure at a recording session), really would have made a wonderful addition to the set.

Likewise, John Deacon's 'In Only Seven Days' is evidently deemed unsuitable, as is Brian's emotive 'Leaving Home Ain't Easy', Freddie's 'Jealousy' and Roger's 'More Of That Jazz'. These are curious omissions indeed.

Roger's 'Fun It', does eventually feature in the show, but only fleetingly, as part of 'Keep Yourself Alive".

The running order of *Jazz* seems disjointed. 'Jealousy' is entirely misplaced between 'Fat Bottomed Girls' and 'Bicycle Race', two songs which really ought to have appeared back to back. Though 'Let Me Entertain You' is an obvious album opener, instead it concludes Side 1, and 'Dead On Time' does not segue well into 'Seven Days'. It is fortunate indeed, and essential in this case, that CD players offer the facility to hear discs in alternatives running orders.

November 11
Wings Stadium, Kalamazoo, Michigan

Also on November 11, the very first Queen Fan Club Convention is held, at the Empire Ballroom in London's Leicester Square. A general invitation is issued in the Autumn fan club magazine and hundreds of eager fans from all around the UK assemble outside the Leicester Square venue.

Alan Freeman hosts the event, which unlike subsequent conventions, is only a half day affair, held on a Saturday afternoon. It kicks off with Freeman explaining the programme for the afternoon and continues with him playing various tracks from the albums. The music is accompanied by a slide show of pictures of the band.

The promotional videos for 'Rhapsody', 'Best Friend', 'Somebody To Love', 'Tie Your Mother Down', 'Rock You', 'Champions' and 'Spread Your Wings' are also shown.

The afternoon concludes with a complete play-through of the brand new album *Jazz*, before a telegram sent by the band from America, is read out.

By comparison, the UK convention now spans three days.

November 13
Boston Gardens, Boston, Massachusetts

November 14
Civic Center, Providence, Rhode Island

November 16/17 ♫
Madison Square Garden, New York
■ *First night*: We Will Rock You / Let Me Entertain You / Somebody To Love / If You Can't Beat Them / Medley: Death On Two Legs; Killer Queen; Bicycle Race; I'm In Love With My Car; Get Down Make Love; You're My Best Friend / Now I'm Here / Spread Your Wings / Dreamers Ball / Love Of My Life / '39 / It's Late / Brighton Rock / Fat Bottomed Girls / Keep Yourself Alive / Bohemian Rhapsody / Tie Your Mother Down / Encore: Sheer Heart Attack / 2nd Encore: We Will Rock You / We Are The Champions / God Save The Queen

The band perform a blistering set here. 'Somebody To Love', 'Dreamers Ball', ''39', 'It's Late' and 'Tie Your Mother Down' in particular, are exceptional. Freddie has much to say and takes full advantage of an enthusiastic and compliant audience.

■ *Second night*: We Will Rock You / Let Me Entertain You / Somebody To Love / If You Can't Beat Them / Medley: Death On Two Legs; Killer Queen; Bicycle Race; I'm In Love With My Car; Get Down Make Love; You're My Best Friend / Now I'm Here / Spread Your Wings / Dreamers Ball / Love Of My Life / '39 / It's Late / Brighton Rock / Fat Bottomed Girls (*not Bad Bottom Girl* - *see below*) / Keep Yourself Alive / Bohemian Rhapsody / Tie Your Mother Down / Encore: Sheer Heart Attack / 2nd Encore: We Will Rock You / We Are The Champions / God Save The Queen

Queen are joined on stage during 'Bicycle Race' by five girls on bicycles, wearing only G-strings. Since the notorious nude ladies poster has not been included in the American album package, the band offer this lucky audience the real thing instead.

November 19
Nassau Coliseum, Uniondale, Long Island, New York

November 20
Spectrum, Philadelphia, Pennsylvania

November 22
Nashville Auditorium, Nashville, Tennessee

November 23
Checkerdome, St Louis, Missouri

November 25
Richfield Coliseum, Cleveland, Ohio

November 26
Riverfront Coliseum, Cincinnati, Ohio

November 28
War Memorial Auditorium, Buffalo, New York
Brian composes a letter for the Winter fan club magazine. In it he explains: *"We're almost exactly half-way through our two and a half month tour of America and it is going spectacularly well. Every city has given us a great welcome. Many of the radio stations are transmitting 'mini-Queen concerts' on the nights of the shows.*

"We were very happy to be presented with a special plaque from Madison Square Garden, for being one of the very few groups to sell over 100,000 tickets in New York City. Our album Jazz entered the US charts at 30 – our previous highest being 65 – so everything looks great. As you probably know, our touring schedule takes us to Europe in January and to Japan after that..."

November 30
Central Canadian Exhibition Center, Ottawa, Ontario

December 1
The Forum, Montreal, Quebec

■ *We Will Rock You / Let Me Entertain You / Somebody To Love / If You Can't Beat Them / Medley: Death On Two Legs; Killer Queen; Bicycle Race; I'm In Love With My Car; Get Down Make Love; You're My Best Friend / Now I'm Here / Spread Your Wings / Dreamers Ball / Love Of My Life / '39 / It's Late / Brighton Rock / Fat Bottomed Girls / Keep YourselfAlive / Bohemian Rhapsody / Tie Your Mother Down / Encore: Sheer Heart Attack / 2nd Encore: We Will Rock You / We Are The Champions / God Save The Queen*

This is another show mirroring almost exactly the *Live Killers* album set. The six medley songs ('Death' – 'Best Friend') appear here in the same order as they do on the album, and Freddie and Brian's introductions to certain songs are similar. Only four of the songs performed at this show are not represented on *Killers* – 'Somebody To Love', 'If You Can't Beat Them', 'It's Late' and Fat Bottomed Girls'. All are curious, inexcusable omissions.

December 3/4
Maple Leaf Garden, Toronto, Ontario

■ **First night**: *We Will Rock You / Let Me Entertain You / Somebody To Love / If You Can't Beat Them / Medley: Death On Two Legs; Killer Queen; Bicycle Race; I'm In Love With My Car; Get Down Make Love; You're My Best Friend / Now I'm Here / Spread Your Wings / Dreamers Ball / Love Of My Life / '39 / It's Late / Brighton Rock / Fat Bottomed Girls / Keep Yourself Alive / Bohemian Rhapsody / Tie Your Mother Down / Encore: Sheer Heart Attack / 2nd Encore: We Will Rock You / We Are The Champions / God Save The Queen*

December 6
Dane County Coliseum, Madison, Wisconsin

December 7
Chicago Stadium, Chicago

■ *We Will Rock You / Let Me Entertain You / Somebody To Love / If You Can't Beat Them / Medley: Death On Two Legs; Killer Queen; Bicycle Race; I'm In Love With My Car; Get Down Make Love; You're My Best Friend / Now I'm Here / Spread Your Wings / Dreamers Ball / Love Of My Life / '39 / It's Late / Brighton Rock / Fat Bottomed Girls / Keep Yourself Alive / Bohemian Rhapsody / Tie Your Mother Down / Encore: Sheer Heart Attack / 2nd Encore: We Will Rock You / We Are The Champions / God Save The Queen*

December 8
Kemper Arena, Kansas City, Missouri

↗ **'Regal Queen At The Garden'**, by Richard Torregrossa, December 8, 1978:

'THEIR Highnesses deigned to give audience to their adoring subjects thirty-five minutes late. But what's that to the converted thousands, many of whom have been queuing since the previous day?

'Their arrival, accompanied by majestic music of the spheres and a fair representation of a spaceship take-off, transforms what should be a pop concert into more of a rock mass. The barn-like hall takes on the atmosphere of a cathedral.

'The regal quartet have style and swagger – and the skill to accompany it, as they pulsate their way through their rhythmic hymnal. The show is ostentatious, exciting, and the only lull as they skip from heavy, to light and fantastic, is during indulgent guitar and vocal solos which are electronic exercises rather than music.

'Quicksilver Freddie Mercury, in black plastic trousers and red braces makes 'Bohemian Rhapsody' into something of a revelation.

'They also treated their listeners to songs off the new album, Jazz.

'Bad Bottom Girl' [sic] was performed as five girls, adequately described by the song's title, rode across the stage in outfits quite risqué, as the male populace seated in the upper promenades frantically reached for the binoculars...

'Mercury bowed and gestured to the audience as he

emphasised the lyrics in 'We Are The Champions': *You've brought me fame and fortune and everything that goes with it - I Thank You All...*

'...As the final notes from Brian May's self-made guitar echoed throughout the Garden after the band's third and final encore, fearless Freddie sauntered to the front of the stage, bowed graciously and said brashly: "I thank you for your time and I thank you for your money!'

December 12
Seattle Coliseum, Seattle

December 13
Portland Coliseum, Portland, Oregon

December 14
Pne Coliseum, Vancouver, British Columbia

December 16
Oakland Coliseum, Oakland, California

■ *We Will Rock You / Let Me Entertain You / Somebody To Love / If You Can't Beat Them / Medley: Death On Two Legs; Killer Queen; Bicycle Race; I'm In Love With My Car; Get Down Make Love; You're My Best Friend / Now I'm Here / Spread Your Wings / Dreamers Ball / Love Of My Life / '39 / It's Late / Brighton Rock / Fat Bottomed Girls / Keep Yourself Alive / Bohemian Rhapsody / Tie Your Mother Down / Encore: Sheer Heart Attack / 2nd Encore: We Will Rock You / We Are The Champions / God Save The Queen*

Before 'Love Of My Life' Freddie announces, quite casually, that "John and Roger have gone backstage for their blowjobs. We get ours after the show."

December 18/19/20
Inglewood Forum, Los Angeles

The third night here was the last show of the tour, and indeed the year. The band play 'Jailhouse Rock' and 'Big Spender' to conclude the set.

December 23

When the band arrive back in London they announce their intention to perform a concert on the Centre Court at Wimbledon. This application is eventually rejected by the Club's management.

Queen spend Christmas at home, which in Roger's case is a beautiful newly acquired house set in 20 acres of ground on the outskirts of Guildford, Surrey. The house apparently once belonged to Dr Crippen's lawyer.

EUROPE 1979 - European Tour

After spending Christmas in England, the band travel to Germany to start their biggest European tour to date. The tour comprises 28 shows in seven countries over a six week period, and includes the first gigs in Yugoslavia. The tour will spawn the band's first (and best) live album. It will also come to be regarded as Queen's finest ever tour, in the mind's of many who are there. The concerts will collectively come to be known as *Live Killers* or *Crazy* shows, even though some of them actually come after the album is issued.

January 17
Ernst Merckhalle, Hamburg
■ *We Will Rock You / Let Me Entertain You / Somebody To Love / If You Can't Beat Them / Medley: Death On Two Legs; Killer Queen; Bicycle Race; I'm In Love With My Car; Get Down Make Love; You're My Best Friend / Now I'm Here / Don't Stop Me Now / Spread Your Wings / Dreamers Ball / Love Of My Life / '39 / It's Late / Brighton Rock / Guitar Solo / Keep Yourself Alive / Bohemian Rhapsody / Tie Your Mother Down / Encore: Sheer Heart Attack / 2nd Encore: We Will Rock You / We Are The Champions / God Save The Queen*

January 18
Ostee Hall, Kiel

January 20
Stadthalle, Bremen
■ *We Will Rock You / Let Me Entertain You / Somebody To Love / If You Can't Beat Them / Medley: Death On Two Legs; Killer Queen; Bicycle Race; I'm In Love With My Car; Get Down Make Love; You're My Best Friend / Now I'm Here / Don't Stop Me Now / Spread Your Wings / Dreamers Ball / Love Of My Life / '39 / It's Late / Brighton Rock / Guitar Solo / Keep Yourself Alive / Bohemian Rhapsody / Tie Your Mother Down / Encore: Sheer Heart Attack / 2nd*

Encore: We Will Rock You / We Are The Champions / God Save The Queen

'Don't Stop Me Now' is now featured in the set. It is a slightly accelerated account to that contained on *Jazz*, and is also one of the most exciting tracks to have appeared in any Queen set - due largely to an immensely powerful drumming accompaniment and backing vocal from Roger. The live renderings of the song seem to have a vibrancy and edge not present on the studio cut. This will be amply demonstrated on the *Killers* album, later in the year. Indeed, Side 3 of that album ('Don't Stop Me Now', 'Spread Your Wings', 'Brighton Rock') is arguably the finest 23 minutes of live material available from this period.

'Fun It', with shared vocals by Fredie and Roger, is also a new addition to the set, but only fleetingly. It features at the beginning of 'Keep Yourself Alive', but not every night.

January 21
Westfallenhalle, Dortmund
Both 'Bicycle Race' and 'Fat Bottomed Girls' make chart appearances while the band are in Germany.

January 23
Messesportspalace, Hanover

January 24♪
Deutschlandhalle, Berlin

■ *We Will Rock You / Let Me Entertain You / Somebody To Love / Medley: Death On Two Legs; Killer Queen; Bicycle Race; I'm In Love With My Car; Get Down Make Love; You're My Best Friend / Now I'm Here / Don't Stop Me Now / Spread Your Wings / Dreamers Ball / Love Of My Life / '39 / It's Late / Brighton Rock / Guitar Solo / Fat Bottomed Girls / Keep Yourself Alive / Bohemian Rhapsody / Tie Your Mother Down / Encore: Sheer Heart Attack / 2nd Encore: We Will Rock You / We Are The Champions / God Save The Queen*

January 26
Forêst Nationale, Brussels

■ *We Will Rock You / Let Me Entertain You / Somebody To Love / Medley: Death On Two Legs; Killer Queen; Bicycle Race; I'm In Love With My Car; Get Down Make Love; You're My Best Friend / Now I'm Here / Don't Stop Me Now / Spread Your Wings / Dreamers Ball / Love Of My Life / '39 / It's Late / Brighton Rock / Guitar Solo / Fat Bottomed Girls / Keep Yourself Alive / Bohemian Rhapsody / Tie Your Mother Down / Encore: Sheer Heart Attack / 2nd Encore: We Will Rock You / We Are The Champions / God Save The Queen*

This concert is the first of nineteen that sound engineer John Etchells records for what will emerge as the *Live Killers* album, in June.

❖ Also on January 26, EMI release the band's thirteenth single, 'Don't Stop Me Now' - coupled with 'In Only Seven Days'. It goes on to attain a number nine chart position in the UK. The American and Japanese issues feature instead Roger's 'More Of That Jazz' as the flipside.

January 27
Forêst Nationale, Brussels

January 29♪
Ahoy Hall, Rotterdam

■ *We Will Rock You (fast) / Let Me Entertain You / Somebody To Love / If You Can't Beat Them / Medley: Death On Two Legs; Killer Queen; Bicycle Race; I'm In Love With My Car; Get Down Make Love; You're My Best Friend / Now I'm Here / Don't Stop Me Now / Spread Your Wings / Dreamers Ball / Love Of My Life / '39 / It's Late / Brighton Rock / Guitar Solo / Keep Yourself Alive / Bohemian Rhapsody / Tie Your Mother Down / 1st Encore: Sheer Heart Attack / 2nd Encore: We Will Rock You / We Are The Champions / God Save The Queen*

● Part/s of this show feature on the *Live Killers* double album.

Freddie: "Alright. We have a lot of music for you tonight from all the various albums. This next song is from an album called *A Night At The Opera*. The song in question is dedicated to a manager we used to have a long long time back. Do you know

A Concert Documentary

137

his name? You can call him anything you want, we call him 'Death On Two Legs'."

Later on. "This next song is going to need some participation from you guys... and you're gonna sing like fuck - like crazy. This is a duet between Brian and myself, a song called 'Love Of My Life'."

January 30

Ahoy Hall, Rotterdam

Similar setlist to previous night, but with 'Fat Bottomed Girls' replacing 'Somebody To Love', 'Mustapha' replacing 'Keep Yourself Alive' and 'If You Can't Beat Them' moved to later in the set, following 'Brighton Rock'.

● Part/s of this show may well feature on the *Live Killers* double album.

Freddie: "Hello Holland. How you feeling tonight?

"We're gonna give you something you'll never forget! Are you ready to rock? Are you ready to roll? Well let's do it!"

Brian: "Thank you. Good evening. We're gonna make some noise tonight! Okay? This is a little song from Mr Mercury, entitled 'Somebody To Love'."

Later on. Freddie (to the ever loyal Royal Family in the front row): "Have you all got your bicycle bells? Let me hear them. Okay. Alright. Maybe we'll use them later? This next song is dedicated to all you ladies with great big tits, or great big bazookas - or whatever you call them. This is a song called 'Fat Bottomed Girls'."

Freddie: "I think we're gonna need a choir for the next song. Sing your balls out. This is a quiet little song entitled 'Love Of My Life'."

With a wonderful recital of this much admired ballad still resonating around the hall, Freddie is pleased. "Nice work fellas; John, Roger and Brian, everybody…"

Later on. Freddie: "Oh yes. I think it's about time we did something totally new from a very new album. This happens to be our latest album anyway, called *Jazz*. Have you got it yet? This is a John Deacon composition... 'If You Can't Beat 'Em - Join 'Em!'"

February 1

Sportshalle, Cologne

■ *We Will Rock You / Let Me Entertain You / Somebody To Love / If You Can't Beat Them / Medley: Death On Two Legs; Killer Queen; Bicycle Race; I'm In Love With My Car; Get Down Make Love / You're My Best Friend / Now I'm Here / Band Intro / Don't Stop Me Now / Spread Your Wings / Dreamers Ball / Love Of My Life / '39 / It's Late / Brighton Rock / Guitar Solo / Keep Yourself Alive / Bohemian Rhapsody / Tie Your Mother Down / Encore: Sheer Heart Attack / 2nd Encore: We Will Rock You / We Are The Champions / God Save The Queen*

- Part/s of this show feature on *Live Killers*.

Freddie's introduction to 'Death On Two Legs' here, sheds interesting light on what is frustratingly bleeped out of the *Live Killers* version: "This next song comes from *A Night At The Opera*. It was conceived and written during the time we were having a lot of problems with our managers... you understand what I mean! He was a real motherfucker of a gentleman! I don't know what you would call him over here... Schweinhund, or whatever, but we also call him 'Death On Two Legs'."

When 'Death' appeared on the *Opera* album credits, four years earlier, with a "Dedicated To..." subtitle, EMI are believed to have paid an aggrieved Norman Sheffield a substantial sum of money not to delay its pre-Christmas release date with court proceedings. Though never mentioned by name, Sheffield concluded it was obviously aimed at him. No chances are taken with *Live Killers* and the offending words are removed and replaced by three bleeps.

📣 As is evident from the lyric, Queen's split from Trident and the Sheffield's in 1975 was acrimonious to say the very least. Freddie would later liken the experience to a lavatorial visit: "As far as Queen are concerned, our old management is deceased. They cease to exist in any capacity with us whatsoever. We feel so relieved. One leaves them behind like one leaves excreta."

Back to this show again... After 'Love Of My Life', for which Roger and John are both absent, Brian reintroduces the band as follows: "I would like to welcome back to the stage, the rest of the band. On drums and percussion... Mr Roger Meddows-Taylor, and on bass... Mr John Deacon. And on wondrous vocals... Mr Freddie Mercury." This is close to the version later used on the live LP, but not the same.

February 2 🖉
Festhalle, Frankfurt
■ *We Will Rock You (fast) / Let Me Entertain You / Somebody To Love / Fat Bottomed Girls / Medley: Death On Two Legs; Killer Queen; Bicycle Race; I'm In*

Love With My Car; Get Down Make Love; You're My Best Friend / Now I'm Here / Don't Stop Me Now / Spread Your Wings / Dreamers Ball / Love Of My Life / '39 / It's Late / Brighton Rock / Guitar Solo / Keep Yourself Alive / Mustapha / Bohemian Rhapsody / Tie Your Mother Down / 1st Encore: Sheer Heart Attack / 2nd Encore: We Will Rock You / We Are The Champions / God Save The Queen

- Part/s of this show feature on *Live Killers*.
'Fat Bottomed Girls' replaces 'If You Can't Beat Them' here, and 'Mustapha' is in the set.

Freddie: "Hello Frankfurt! How are you feeling tonight - good? Ready to rock? Are you ready to roll? Okay lets do it!"

Brian: "Thank you. It's good to see you again after two years. I want to say a special thank you to you people in the Festhalle. This is the biggest crowd we've ever played to in Europe, so thank you. Okay."

Freddie: "We're gonna have a fine night tonight – do you hear? You bet! We have a song now that's dedicated to you all you ladies with big tits and great big asses. This is a song called 'Fat Bottomed Girls'."

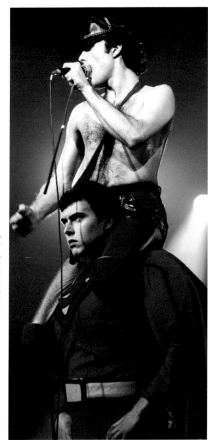

Hoople? Alright. We did a tour with those guys a long long time back and Brian wrote a song in dedication to them. This is from the *Sheer Heart Attack* album - it goes like this..."

Later on, Freddie (reacting to an exceptionally enthusiastic audience): "You're too much! Terrific! This is called 'Don't Stop Me Now'."

Brian: "Thanks a lot. How are you doing - alright? I tell you, we've been looking forward to this for a long time; coming back to Frankfurt. It feels really good. Thank you. Okay, a bit of fun now..." ('Dreamers Ball')

Brian: "I'd like to welcome back to the stage the rest of the Queen group. On drums and tiger skin trousers... Mr Roger Meddows-Taylor. On dazzling tie and bass guitar... Mr John Deacon. And on maracas and sometimes vocals... Mr Freddie Mercury... How 'bout that!" ('Meddows' was omitted from the LP at Roger's request.)

Freddie: "We're gonna have to come back again here soon. This is from the *News Of The World*, a song written by Brian, called 'It's Late'."

Later on. Freddie: "Thank you very much. You want 'Mustapha', yeah... We'll think about it. We'll think about this. Right now we have a song that features John, Roger and Brian. They're gonna to do a little bit of improvisation tonight. The song is called 'Brighton Rock'."

'Keep Yourself Alive' features a short vocal pre-amble from Freddie before he and Roger break into what sounds to be a spontaneous segment from 'Fun It', but actually is a rehearsed piece. They repeat this several times during this leg of the tour. The *Live Killers* version does not feature this rare departure.

February 4
Hallenstadium, Zurich

■ *We Will Rock You (fast) / Let Me Entertain You / Somebody To Love / Fat Bottomed Girls / Medley: Death On Two Legs; Killer Queen; Bicycle Race; I'm In Love With My Car; Get Down Make Love; You're My Best Friend / Now I'm Here / Mustapha / Don't Stop Me Now / Spread Your Wings / Dreamers Ball / Love Of My Life / '39 / It's Late / Brighton Rock / Guitar*

Later: "We're gonna take you to an album called *A Night At The Opera*. This next song was written about a real dirty old man... I mean a nasty, creepy motherfucker as you call him. We call him that! He's also called 'Death On Two Legs'."

Freddie (intro to 'Now I'm Here'): "Thank you. Okay! Do you remember a group called Mott The

Solo / Keep Yourself Alive / Bohemian Rhapsody / Tie Your Mother Down / Encore: We Will Rock You / We Are The Champions / God Save The Queen

● Part/s of this show may well feature on the *Live Killers* double album.

Once again 'Fat Bottomed Girls' replaces 'If You Can't Beat Them', and 'Mustapha' features in the show. 'Sheer Heart Attack' is not performed.

Brian: "Thank you and good evening people of Zurich. We're going to give you a concentrated dose of Queen music tonight. We'd like to start with an old song called 'Somebody To Love'."

Freddie (after 'Dreamers Ball'): "We had fun doing that one then - do you like that one? We've got a couple more acoustic songs to do. This next song really requires a very good singing choir. Do you think you can do it? Okay lets see. This is from *A Night At The Opera* - a song called 'Love Of My Life'."

February 6
Dom Sportova, Zagreb, Yugoslavia ①

■ *We Will Rock You (fast) / Let Me Entertain You / Somebody To Love / Fat Bottomed Girls / Medley: Death On Two Legs; Killer Queen; Bicycle Race; I'm In Love With My Car; Get Down Make Love; You're My Best Friend / Now I'm Here / Mustapha / Don't Stop Me Now / Spread Your Wings / Dreamers Ball / Love Of My Life / '39 / It's Late / Brighton Rock / Guitar Solo / Keep Yourself Alive / Bohemian Rhapsody / Tie Your Mother Down / 1st Encore: Sheer Heart Attack / 2nd Encore: We Will Rock You / We Are The Champions / God Save The Queen*

Freddie: "Feelin' Okay? Alright? "I must say it's really nice to be here in Yugoslavia. Thank you for giving us such a nice welcome. We have a lot of music to play for you tonight. This next song happens to be the latest single, right here - this is called 'Fat Bottomed Girls'."

During 'Now I'm Here', Freddie, as usual at this point of the evening, tries to entice the Yugoslavian audience to do what all the other European fans do at this point; mimic everything he sings or speaks. The locals are baffled by it, however, and remain silent. Freddie summons them to repeat him, but they don't; they just look up at him, bemused.

"This ain't gonna work, but I'm gonna try."

The response is minimal but Freddie does not give up - it isn't in his nature. Eventually, inevitably, he has them repeating a lyric or two. Then, instead of going into the "I think I'll stay around" part of the song, Freddie coaxes them into an unscheduled part of 'Mustapha', and this they *do* repeat. When he's finished, Brian resumes 'Now I'm Here' and Queen are back on track again.

Later on. Freddie: "It's just the two of us for this next song; Roger and John are going to get their Yugoslavian blow jobs. I have to say it. Now... this is a song called 'Love Of My Life'."

Unlike their German, Dutch and Swiss counterparts, the Yugoslavian fans are unfamiliar with the words, and this is a relatively tame affair. Freddie helps them through and they soon get the idea. They will be ready for Freddie next time.

Later. Brian: "Thank you. You're great! Now, we'd like to welcome back the rest of the Queen group. On drums... Mr Roger Taylor. On bass guitar... Mr John Deacon. And on virtuoso maracas and vocals... Mr Freddie Mercury."

February 7
Tivoli Halle, Ljubljana

February 10
Basketball Halle, Munich

■ *We Will Rock You (fast) / Let Me Entertain You / Somebody To Love / If You Can't Beat Them / Medley: Death On Two Legs; Killer Queen; Bicycle Race; I'm In Love With My Car; Get Down Make Love; You're My Best Friend / Now I'm Here / Don't Stop Me Now / Spread Your Wings / Dreamers Ball / Love Of My Life / '39 / It's Late / Brighton Rock / Guitar Solo / Keep Yourself Alive / Mustapha / Bohemian Rhapsody / Tie Your Mother Down / 1st Encore: Sheer Heart Attack / 2nd Encore: We Will Rock You / We Are The Champions / God Save The Queen*

Freddie: "Hello Munchen. Are you ready to rock? Are you ready to roll? Okay lets do it."

Later on, Freddie: "Would you guys like to sing? Okay. This next song we'd like everybody to participate in. This is a song that might make you remember a group called Mott The Hoople. Some of you do... C'mon! A long time back we did a tour with the guys, and Brian wrote a song in dedication to them. This is from the *Sheer Heart Attack* album, it goes like this…"

Later, Brian: "Okay, seeing as you're in the mood, a sentimental number now." ('Dreamers Ball')

Freddie: "We know you want to sing, 'cos we tried you out earlier on, but this next song requires a very good choir. So if you all have a seat, this is a song called 'Love Of My Life'.

Later, Freddie: "Munich are a good audience. Thank you. Fantastiche! Okay, we're going to go on to do something with the electric guitar right now; This is from an album called *The News Of The World*. It's called 'It's Late'."

Towards the end of the show Freddie asks, "What do you want?" The audience demands 'Mustapha'. Freddie ponders this a moment.

"I tell you what we're gonna do... You want 'Mustapha', yeah... We might try that later on - what do you say girls? (to the band). This next song features John, Roger and Brian, and they're going to do a little bit of improvisation tonight. This is a song called 'Brighton Rock'."

Not for the first time, Freddie refers to Roger, John and Brian as *girls*. Later on in the tour, in Paris, he will address the road crew in the same way. This amusing exchange would have been great to feature on *Live Killers*, but it is overlooked.

Bootleg recordings of this show (and others from this part of the tour) present the setlist in the wrong sequence. This is probably down to the *Live Killers* running order, which is also inexact. The LP has 'Don't Stop Me Now' and 'Spread Your Wings' on Side 3 (with 'Brighton Rock'), *after* Side 2's 'Dreamers Ball', 'Love Of My Life', '39' and 'Keep Yourself Alive', when in fact those two tracks were actually ahead of the later four. 'Brighton Rock' should have been the penultimate song on Side 2, not the final song of the next side.

As stated earlier, four other audience favourites ('Somebody To Love', 'It's Late', 'If You Can't Beat Them' and 'Fat Bottomed Girls') should also have featured on *Killers*, but didn't! I hope to see the day, sooner rather than later, when a revised *Killers* album is released with the correct running order, no bleeps, the four AWOL's, an unabridged 'Mustapha', the alternative 'Keep Yourself Alive' featuring Roger and Freddie's 'Fun It' routine, and Freddie's references to 'the girls'. I will be the first to fight for it!

February 11 ⌀
Basketball Hall, Munich

Similar set to previous show but with no 'If You Can't Beat Them' and with 'Fat Bottomed Girls' in after Brian's solo.

Brian: "Good evening. I want to give you a special thank you for giving us the opportunity to play two nights in this place. Thank you. We appreciate that. Okay, for the people of Munich we would like to say... find us 'Somebody To Love'."

Freddie: "Alright? Okay? Okay, on with the show… I think we're going to do a song from an album called *A Night At The Opera*... What do you think? Okay, this song was dedicated to a sort of management we had a long long time back - I'm sure you know about that. You can call him anything you want you can call him... yes you can call him anything you like. We call him 'Death On Two Legs'."

After a lovely rendition of 'Best Friend', the masses demand 'Mustapha' *again*. This became a peculiar aspect of gigs on this tour, and sometimes a minor irritation to Freddie. Here, he deals with it in typical fashion.

"I've never heard of the bloody song. Quiet! Quiet! We might do that a bit later on... we gotta practice it first." A few people boo. "Aah! Boo, your ass!"

Later, Freddie: "Did anybody here come to see us last night? Some of you did... okay. Last night the audience were very good; They sang a lot. Tonight we want you to do a better job - okay?

Following a decidedly mellow, bluesy recital of 'Dreamers', Freddie addresses the crowd again and, perhaps under orders from the chaps, quashes any speculation that might have arisen from his comments in Zagreb, a week earlier.

"Okay... Roger and John are going to take a rest. They're NOT going to get their blowjobs tonight." He goes on, "This has transformed into a duet, from the album *A Night At The Opera*. If you want to sing along we'd like that very much - this is called 'Love Of My Life'."

Brian: "Thank you. That was very nice. Thank you for listening to that. We could hear a pin drop up here. Okay, we'd like to welcome back the rest of the Queen group for this. On drums... Mr Roger Meddows-Taylor. And on luminous tie and bass... Mr John Deacon. On vinyl and maracas... Mr Freddie Mercury." [Freddie's outfit was almost exclusively black leather-look vinyl]

Then it's back to the business of rocking again.

Freddie: "Are all you tarts gonna sing?"

They do sing. Queen perform a blistering rendition of ''39' after which Freddie has more to say – or *half* say! "We have a... this next song features John, Roger and Brian. They're gonna do a bit of improv... improvising tonight... a bit of improvisation – I never get that fucking word right. This is called 'Brighton Rock'."

Half starting sentences and not finishing them, changing tack in mid- audience address (just as he did in most of his interviews) is normal for Freddie. He seems to get bored with whatever it is he has started, or distracted, and wants to get onto the next thing on his mind, without finishing what he is already saying. Freddie Mercury is a one off!

Later: "Thank you. Thanks very much. We have a song that's dedicated to all you young ladies with great big tits... you like that? And a great big ass! This is a Brian May composition from *Jazz*, and it's called 'Fat Bottomed Girls'."

Freddie seems obsessed with girls with large busts and backsides on this tour, and, following a raunchy rendition of the song here, he jokes about after post-show *activity*. "Hey... Thank you girls. The road crew will look out for you later on!"

Alright, we'll see what you can do. This is a song from the *Sheer Heart Attack* album, it goes like this..."

Following the abrupt ending to 'Now I'm Here', the audience begins to chant 'Mustapha' yet again, despite Freddie's comments only a few minutes earlier. Here, as happened at least a dozen other times in Europe, the audience seems somehow programmed like automatons to chant 'Mustapha' at regular intervals, regardless of whether it is mentioned or even actually performed! It is a very strange, and curiously exclusive to 'Mustapha'.

Brian (before 'Dreamers Ball'): "Right, we're gonna have a little fun now. Alright... a little experiment here. How do you feel - okay? I hope you're getting all this? This is a little blues song which we've adapted for stages like this..."

February 13
Sporthalle Boeblingen, Stuttgart

■ *We Will Rock You (fast) / Let Me Entertain You / Somebody To Love / Fat Bottomed Girls / Medley: Death On Two Legs; Killer Queen; Bicycle Race; I'm In Love With My Car; Get Down Make Love; You're My Best Friend / Now I'm Here / Don't Stop Me Now / Spread Your Wings / Dreamers Ball (aka Stuttgart Blues) / Love Of My Life / '39 / It's Late / Brighton Rock / Guitar Solo / Keep Yourself Alive / Mustapha / Bohemian Rhapsody / Tie Your Mother Down / 1st Encore: Sheer Heart Attack / 2nd Encore: We Will Rock You / We Are The Champions / God Save The Queen*

● Part/s of this show feature on *Live Killers*.

Brian: "Thank you and welcome to the concert – the Queen show for 1979. It took us a long time to see you. We're glad we came, I can tell you. Thank you. This is a song from some years ago called 'Somebody To Love'."

Later. Brian (referring to 'Dreamers Ball'): "Thank you very much... a little Stutgart blues there."

Freddie: "We'll have to do a little rock'n'roll version of that one of these days. I'll speed it up."

Brian: "If you can take that, you can take anything!"

Freddie: "Okay, for those of you who know the words to this next song, we'd like you all to sing along. This is called 'Love Of My Life'."

Brian: "You're good singers - that's nice. You wanna sing some more? Okay, from the depths of backstage come the rest of the Queen group. Featuring on drums, Mr Roger Taylor... there he is. And on bass... Mr John Deacon. And on virtuoso maracas... Mr Freddie Mercury."

Freddie (after 'Champions'): "Thank you everybody. You've been a tremendous audience."

Part of Brian's "You're good singers" comment and Freddie's final audience address is used on *Live Killers* – though the latter lacks its "See you soon" conclusion.

February 15
Saalandhalle, Saarbrucken

■ *We Will Rock You (fast) / Let Me Entertain You /*
Somebody To Love / Fat Bottomed Girls / Medley: Death On Two Legs; Killer Queen; Bicycle Race; I'm In Love With My Car; Get Down Make Love; You're My Best Friend / Now I'm Here / Don't Stop Me Now / Spread Your Wings / Dreamers Ball / Love Of My Life / '39 / It's Late / Brighton Rock / Guitar Solo / Keep Yourself Alive / Mustapha / Bohemian Rhapsody / Tie Your Mother Down / 1st Encore: Sheer Heart Attack / 2nd Encore: We Will Rock You / We Are The Champions / God Save The Queen

● Part/s of this show may well feature on the *Live Killers* double album.

Brian: "Thank you. Good evening. You look like a nice rowdy crowd tonight! How do you feel? Okay, we have a lot of different music for you tonight, of all different kinds, from different albums. We'd like to start off with something from *A Day At The Races* and this is called 'Somebody To Love'."

Never one to sit on the stage fence, if Freddie becomes frustrated with overzealous fans, he lets it be known. "Hey hey hey! Hey hey hey. Alriiiiiight! We'd like everyone to sing in this next song, so get your lungs together. This is a song we dedicate... (a fan interrupts). Oh shut up listen to me! This is from an album called *Sheer Heart Attack* - a dedication to Mott The Hoople. It goes like this..."

"I wonder if you feel as exhausted as we are?" asks Brian, after a particularly heavy rendition of 'Now I'm Here'. The crowd is far from spent yet and a collective cheer provides the answer. Even so, Queen are ready for something softer. Brian: "Okay, a little easy song now..."

Freddie: "We're gonna try a few acoustic songs - I think it's time we kind of cooled you down a bit. What do you think? We're gonna give you the heavy rock'n'roll at the end of the show, don't you worry. But right now we need a bit of assistance. That means something like this... yeah." The fans begin to clap in perfect time.

Later, following Roger's rather delicate and perfectly executed falsetto harmony during the start of 'Dreamers Ball', Freddie comments simply, "You big show off!" When the song ends,

Brian declares, "I bet you didn't think we did anything as silly as that!" and then Roger and John leave the stage, as is usual at this point of the show.

Freddie: "I must say, you've been a really tremendous audience up to now and if this keeps on we're really gonna like you. Right now we'd like you to put your voices to this next song This is called 'Love Of My Life'."

After another stirring account of Freddie's *Opera* ballad, Brian has more to say. "Some of you may know it's the last night of the German tour. I want to say, it's been amazing in Germany this time. Thank you very much." Much cheering from the crowd follows, and muttering from the stage.

"I'd like to re-introduce the rest of the band... On drums, we have Mr Roger Taylor. On bass guitar... Mr John Deacon. And on pure sweat and vocals, Mr Freddie Mercury.... Okay, now you sing."

Freddie: "Alright, we're gonna do some rock'n'roll right now - we're going to switch back to the electric guitar for a nice little number entitled 'It's Late'."

February 17
Palais De Sport, Lyon

■ *We Will Rock You (fast) / Let Me Entertain You / Somebody To Love / Fat Bottomed Girls / Medley: Death On Two Legs; Killer Queen; Bicycle Race; I'm In Love With My Car; Get Down Make Love; You're My Best Friend / Now I'm Here / Don't Stop Me Now / Spread Your Wings / Dreamers Ball / Love Of My Life / '39 / It's Late / Brighton Rock / Guitar Solo / Keep Yourself Alive / Bohemian Rhapsody / Tie Your Mother Down / 1st Encore: Sheer Heart Attack / 2nd Encore: We Will Rock You / We Are The Champions / God Save The Queen*

● Part/s of this show feature on *Live Killers*.

Freddie: "Bonsoir Lyon! Alright! Are you ready to rock? Are you ready to roll? Okay let's do it!"

Brian: "Thank you. Good evening. Beaucoup, beaucoup. I would like to introduce you to our young pianist, Mr Freddie Mercury. This is 'Somebody To Love'."

Freddie: "Feeling okay? We have a lot of music for you tonight from all the various albums. This next song is from an album called *Jaaaaaaazz*. This is dedicated to all you girls with great big tits and great big asses. Alright this is called 'Fat Bottomed Girls'."

Freddie's comments may seem spontaneous to those in attendance, but as the reader will have determined by now, he actually varies his mental script very little from night to night. The 'great big tits and big arses' quip, is as good an example as any.

Brian (before 'Dreamers Ball'): "We're gonna do some little relaxing songs now. As you know this is our very first time in Lyon, and we want to say a special thank you for filling this place. Thank you. We appreciate it. It's a great welcome and we

145

appreciate it... Well, a little bit of a nonsense now..."

Later, Freddie: "Roger and John are going to take a rest, and in the meantime Brian and myself are going to do a song - a duet. This is from *A Night At The Opera*... I *think* it's from *A Night At The Opera*? The song is called 'Love Of My Life'."

Freddie thinks right. It *is* from *Opera*. This too is an endearing aspect of the great man: that he does not always remember (in interviews mainly, less so in concert) which tracks come from which albums. This perhaps explains his need of a mental script. He does, however, ALWAYS know exactly who wrote or collaborated in writing any given song - this information seems never to escape him.

Later, Freddie: "Oh yeah. We're gonna feature John, Roger and Brian in this next song. They're going to do something special tonight - do you know what I mean? Something different. This is called 'Brighton Rock'."

'Keep Yourself Alive' is rather different here. It contains the 'Fun It' digression at the beginning, but also some unusual guitar riffs and ideas from Brian. It further contains the drum solo that will feature several more times throughout this tour.

Freddie: " Merci beaucoup - thank you. Goodnight Lyon."

February 19♪/20♪/21♪
Palacio de los Deportes, Barcelona
■ **First night**: *We Will Rock You (fast) / Let Me Entertain You / Somebody To Love / Medley: Death On Two Legs; Killer Queen; Bicycle Race; I'm In Love With My Car; Get Down Make Love; You're My Best Friend / Now I'm Here / Don't Stop Me Now / Spread Your Wings / Dreamers Ball / Love Of My Life / '39 / It's Late / Brighton Rock / Guitar Solo / Keep Yourself Alive / Bohemian Rhapsody / Tie Your Mother Down / 1st Encore: Sheer Heart Attack / 2nd Encore: We Will Rock You / We Are The Champions / God Save The Queen*
● Part/s of this show may well feature on the *Live Killers* double album.

'Fat Bottomed Girls', 'If You Can't Beat Them'

and 'Mustapha' are all absent from this show.

Brian's introduction: "At this stage we'd like to welcome back the rest of the group. To feature on tiger skin trousers and drums, Mr Roger Taylor. And now, on bass guitar, Mr John Deacon. And on silken vocals, Mr Freddie Mercury."

Freddie: "Alright, lets get on with it..."

Second night: Setlist same as first night.
● Part/s of this show feature on *Live Killers*.
Brian: "Thank you. Welcome to a night of Queen music."

Later, Freddie: "You feeling good? Alright. We're gonna do a song from an album called *Jazz*."

This news evokes no response from the audience at all. Freddie turns to Brian. "Now that went down well, didn't it?"

He smiles, and the show goes on. "This is a John Deacon composition called 'If You Can't Beat 'Em - Join 'Em!"

After this, Freddie walks to the front of the stage and offers a toast: "Salute, Barcelona! And take *that*." He throws his drink over the audience and laughs to himself.

Later, Freddie: "Gracias. Would you like to sing? Because you can't sit there being turkeys all night. No... In this next song we'd like you all to join in - everybody to sing along... if not, I'll murder you."

In the middle of 'Now I'm Here', during the usual audience participation interlude, Freddie realises the Spanish fans are not only repeating the adlibbed lyrics he offers them, but copying every word he *speaks*, too. "Mama Mia!" he exclaims. "I can get them to do *anything*!"

Then he slips spontaneously into 'Mustapha' and the people mimic that too. Freddie truly is a Master Showman. Rarely is it more evident than here.

Later still, Freddie: "Muchos Gracias. Hey hey hey hey hey... Are you still there? We'll do another song now. We would like everybody to sing along to this next song – it's called 'Spread Your Wings'."

Midway through the show. Freddie: "We are going to do a few acoustic songs and then after that we'll do some heavy rock'n'roll. The beat goes like this..."

Brian: "Give us a hand - c'mon."

Freddie: "The next song is called 'Titties Grandes'... They don't believe me... I said big tits."

This amuses Freddie, but the audience look at one another in bewildered silence.

February 22/23
Pabellon Del Real Madrid

■ *First night*: *We Will Rock You (fast) / Let Me Entertain You / Somebody To Love / Medley: Death On Two Legs; Killer Queen; Bicycle Race; I'm In Love With My Car; Get Down Make Love; You're My Best Friend / Now I'm Here / Don't Stop Me Now / Spread Your Wings / Dreamers Ball / Love Of My Life / '39 / It's Late / Brighton Rock / Guitar Solo / Keep Yourself Alive / Bohemian Rhapsody / Tie Your Mother Down / 1st Encore: Sheer Heart Attack / 2nd Encore: We Will Rock You / We Are The Champions / God Save The Queen*

This was an unscheduled extra night of the tour.

Freddie performs a short, but great piano preamble to 'Death On Two Legs', to kick off the medley. Few people (beyond the die-hard fans) recognize it and only when the familiar opening chords ring out do the audience do likewise. This is something Freddie will introduce many times on this tour, with this song, and, later, with other songs on subsequent tours. Two good examples from future tours are 'Somebody To Love' and 'Play The Game'. The duration of these adlibbed piano moments varies from night to night, according to Freddie's mood. From as early as 1974-75, he can be heard, and seen, experimenting on stage with these charming piano pre-ambles. 'Death On Two Legs' affords Freddie the perfect opportunity to 'tinker', and this evening's tinker is particularly wonderful.

Freddie (after 'Best Friend'): "Hey hey hey, yeah – alriiiiiiiiight. Okay. Would you like to sing? In tune – I hope... 'March Of The Black Queen', did you hear that? We might do that, we might do that later (Freddie knows they won't be doing it later). This next song comes from an album called *Sheer Heart Attack*, it goes something like this..."

Later. Freddie (during the start of 'Dreamers Ball'): "Get the beat together - c'mon everybody. It feels just like Madison Square Gardens... don't you think?"

Following a slight error during 'Dreamers', Brian afterwards comments, "Truly dreadful!" Freddie's retort is immediate: "Bullshit! I thought that was wonderful. Didn't you think that? Yeah."

■ *Second night*: *We Will Rock You (fast) / Let Me Entertain You / Somebody To Love / Fat Bottomed Girls / Medley: Death On Two Legs; Killer Queen; Bicycle Race; I'm In Love With My Car; Get Down Make Love; You're My Best Friend / Now I'm Here / Don't Stop Me Now / If You Can't Beat Them / Dreamers Ball / Love Of My Life / '39 / It's Late / Brighton Rock / Guitar Solo / Keep Yourself Alive / Mustapha / Bohemian Rhapsody / Tie Your Mother Down / 1st Encore: Sheer Heart Attack / 2nd Encore: We Will Rock You / We Are The Champions / God Save The Queen*

A similar set to first night but featuring 'If You Can't Beat Them' later than usual and 'Fat Bottomed Girls'. 'Mustapha' is back again.

Brian's band introduction after 'Love Of My Life': "On the drums... Mr Roger Taylor. And on the bass guitar... Mr John Deacon. And at enormous expense... Mr Freddie Mercury."

Later on, there is no escaping the Mustaphaians. Again they demand the song, and again Freddie seems less than enthused. "Okay - I can hear you. We have a few 'Mustapha' fanatics down here. What's your name - Ibrahim?"

Queen are ahead of the fans, for they have reintroduced 'Mustapha' and it *will* feature tonight – just as soon as the predictable and inevitable demands come in for it.

February 25

Les Arenas, Poitiers

■ *We Will Rock You (fast) / Let Me Entertain You / Somebody To Love / Fat Bottomed Girls / Death On Two Legs / Killer Queen / Bicycle Race / I'm In Love With My Car / Get Down Make Love / You're My Best Friend / Now I'm Here / Don't Stop Me Now / Spread Your Wings / Dreamers Ball / Love Of My Life / '39 / It's Late / Brighton Rock / Keep Yourself Alive / Mustapha / Bohemian Rhapsody / Tie Your Mother Down / Sheer Heart Attack / We Will Rock You / We Are The Champions / God Save The Queen*

● Part/s of this show may well feature on the *Live Killers* double album.

"Bonsoir Poitiers. Are you ready to Rock? Are you ready to roll? Okay let's do it... We'll wake them up."

Some way into the evening, facing the latest wave of requests for *that Jazz* track again, Freddie tries a different approach. "Who is this guy Mustapha? Well stick around, we'll do 'Mustapha' later, maybe." Later, following a particularly fine rendition of 'Somebody To Love', certain individuals are still asking for the track.

"I can hear you darling - don't worry... alright, alright. Well save it for later." This satisfies them for a while and true to his word the song does feature later in the evening.

The show moves on at breakneck speed, until, once again, just as he and Brian take centre stage to offer their famous acoustic duet, Freddie is back on the subject of sex again. This time he tells the French fans that John and Roger are going off for a rest and their "Poitiers blowjobs", but this evokes little reaction so Freddie quips, "You'll understand me one day."

This is a stunning concert, finding Queen on top form and an with an audience to match.

Freddie; "Goodnight, sweet dreams. Auvoir Poitiers!"

February 27/28/March 1

Pavillion De Paris, Paris

■ *First night*: *We Will Rock You (fast) / Let Me Entertain You / Somebody To Love / Fat Bottomed Girls / Medley: Death On Two Legs; Killer Queen; Bicycle Race; I'm In Love With My Car; Get Down Make Love; You're My Best Friend / Now I'm Here / Don't Stop Me Now / Spread Your Wings / Dreamers Ball / Love Of My Life / '39 / It's Late / Brighton Rock / Keep Yourself Alive (feat Fun It / Mustapha / Bohemian Rhapsody / Tie Your Mother Down / Sheer Heart Attack / We Will Rock You / We Are The Champions / God Save The Queen*

● Part/s of this show feature on *Live Killers*.

All three shows at this venue are filmed for possible use in a documentary that ultimately never materialises. One of the shows, however, does feature at the annual Queen fan club conventions, but its general quality is clearly not worthy of a proper home video release. Unlike the familiar live video issues, the shows are filmed from only one or two vantage points, without the usual elaborate camera set-ups. There is concert footage from Paris in the archive still to be investigated, however, so one day we will know definitively whether we can expect a Live At Paris DVD.

At the beginning of 'Dreamers Ball' Roger offers his falsetto harmony again, and once more it is executed to perfection. "I'm gonna murder you one of these days," jokes Freddie, adding, "The things you have to do for money!" This remark makes it onto the *Live Killers* LP.

Later, Freddie introduces the *Opera* love song once more and this too will ultimately find its way onto the first live album. "This is now... this next song has turned into a duet because that's the way we like it I think. We'd like everybody to join in, this is a song called 'Love Of My Life'."

Two hours later... "Merci beaucoup Paris. Thank you, God bless you... Au revoir."

Second night: Setlist as above but with 'If You Can't Beat Them' instead of 'Fat Bottomed Girls', and no 'Mustapha'.

● Part/s of this show (and the third night) may well feature on *Live Killers*.

■ ***Third night***: *We Will Rock You (fast) / Let Me Entertain You / Somebody To Love / Fat Bottomed Girls / Death On Two Legs / Killer Queen / Bicycle*

Race / I'm In Love With My Car / Get Down Make Love / You're My Best Friend / Now I'm Here / Don't Stop Me Now / Mustapha / If You Can't Beat Them / Spread Your Wings / Dreamers Ball / Love Of My Life / '39 / It's Late / Brighton Rock / Keep Yourself Alive / Bohemian Rhapsody / Tie Your Mother Down / Sheer Heart Attack / Jailhouse Rock / We Will Rock You / We Are The Champions / God Save The Queen

Brian: "Good evening. Bonsoir... This is the last concert, and we're going to have some fun."

Freddie: "We have a hell of a lot of music for you tonight. I don't know which order they're gonna come in - we'll see."

As part of the 'Now I'm Here' audience play-around spot, Freddie slips momentarily into an adlibbed "all day long, all day long" segment from 'Liar', from the first album. This appears to be a spontaneous tangent, as the rest of the band seem unaware what Freddie's going to do next. It works well and is much appreciated by the knowledgable Queenies in the front rows.

When Freddie notices that the same faces are again present in the front two rows of the audience, he acknowledges them by remarking that the Royal Family is here again. The name sticks, and Freddie makes numerous further references to them at subsequent concerts.

The Family consists mostly of British fans who have travelled all around Europe with them since the tour began, and who have begged, borrowed, remortgaged and borrowed some more to be there. They also make a point of delivering a bouquet of flowers backstage to the band at every show, and, on one ocassion, in a letter, demand with menaces that Queen performs a certain song for them.

Each member of The Family attending this concert does so with one additional item – a bicycle bell. At the appropriate point in the set they unite in a chorus of bell-ringing, much to the surprise of the band and the French audience - who copy the idea the following night. By March 1, hundreds of bells ring out all around the arena. They can even be heard on the *Live Killers* album,

and a bell can be seen on top of the piano of the album's back cover photograph, which was taken in Paris.

Before one of these French shows, members of the RF approach a roadie and hand him a bicycle bell. "Give this to Freddie," they say, "for the show." The confused roadie accepts the bell and disappears with it. Sure enough, during the concert, Freddie walks over to the grinning faces in the front row – by now familiar to him, produces the bell and rings it.

On another occasion, having discovered John Deacon is fond of dry roasted peanuts, the Family hands out packets of nuts to fans as they enter the theatre. Then, at a set point in the show, as Freddie introduces 'Best Friend' (a Deacon song), the band is showered with nuts from all directions. Although their immediate reaction is one of shock, they laugh when they realise the significance. None of them, thereafter, expresses a fondness for nuts, or anything else, within earshot of the lunatic fans.

Back to this concert again... Freddie: "Hey... Are you going to repeat everything I say? Okay, this next song is for the road crew. They've been fucking good on this tour, but don't let it go to your heads girls. This is called 'Don't Stop Me Now'."

Later, Brian's band introduction: "You know this is the last night of the tour, so you get a few little silly things... I would like to welcome back the rest of the Queen group. Especially, unusually NOT in snake-skin trousers, but a stunning top, Monsier Roger Taylor. And now, in extremely black... Mr John Deacon. And... somewhere... on virtuoso maracas, Mr Freddie Mercury."

A manic rendition of 'Jailhouse Rock' followed by the old faithfuls 'Rock You' and 'Champions' signifies the end of another show and tour. The national anthem rings out, the lights blaze, Queen wave and the audience roars.

"Thank you. Goodnight. See you soon. Auvoir Paris. Merci."

Queen leave the stage.

Japan 1979

Queen embarks on what will prove to be their biggest ever tour of Japan – though by American and European standards, it is relatively small. Three weeks of performances open with two shows at the Budokan Hall in Tokyo, and move through a further seven cities. The tour ends with two shows in Sapporo.

April 13/14
Budokan Hall, Tokyo

■ *First night*: We Will Rock You / Let Me Entertain You / Somebody To Love / Fat Bottomed Girls / Medley: Death On Two Legs; Killer Queen; Bicycle Race; I'm In Love With My Car; Get Down Make Love; You're My Best Friend / Now I'm Here / Teo Torriatte / Don't Stop Me Now / Dreamers Ball / Love Of My Life / '39 / It's Late / Brighton Rock / Keep Yourself Alive / Bohemian Rhapsody / Tie Your Mother Down / Encore: Sheer Heart Attack / 2nd Encore: We Will Rock You / We Are The Champions / God Save The Queen

'Teo Torriatte' ('Let Us Cling Together') is performed during this tour. Queen only ever include it in the set for Japanese shows because a signiciant part, including the main chorus, features Freddie singing Brian's Japanese lyrics – a point he later writes about in his own song 'Let Me Entertain You'.

April 19/20
Festival Hall, Osaka

■ *First night*: We Will Rock You (fast) / Let Me Entertain You / Somebody To Love / Fat Bottomed Girls / Medley: Death On Two Legs; Killer Queen; Bicycle Race; I'm In Love With My Car; Get Down Make Love ; You're My Best Friend / Now I'm Here / Don't Stop Me Now / Spread Your Wings / Dreamer's Ball / Love Of My Life / '39 / It's Late / Brighton Rock / Keep Yourself Alive / Bohemian Rhapsody / Tie Your Mother Down / 1st Encore: Sheer Heart Attack / 2nd Encore: We Will Rock You / We Are The Champions / God Save The Queen

■ *Second night*: We Will Rock You (slow) / We Will Rock You (fast) / Let Me Entertain You / Somebody To Love / If You Can't Beat Them / Medley: Death On Two Legs; Killer Queen; Bicycle Race ; I'm In Love With My Car; 10. Get Down Make Love; You're My Best Friend / Now I'm Here / Teo Torriatte / Don't Stop Me Now / Dreamer's Ball / Love Of My Life / '39 / It's Late / Brighton Rock / Keep Yourself Alive / Bohemian Rhapsody / Tie Your Mother Down / 1st Encore: Sheer Heart Attack / 2nd Encore: We Will Rock You (slow) / We Are The Champions / God Save The Queen

Freddie forgets about 'If You Can't Beat Them' and instead introduces 'Death On Two Legs' too soon. He realises his mistake, the audience teases him and Freddie exclaims "Fuck Off" as the song begins.

April 21
Jissen Rinri Kinen Kaikan, Kanazawa

April 23/24♪/25
Budokan Hall, Tokyo

■ *Second night*: We Will Rock You / Let Me Entertain You / Somebody To Love / Fat Bottomed Girls / Medley: Death On Two Legs; Killer Queen; Bicycle Race; I'm In Love With My Car; Get Down Make Love; You're My Best Friend / Now I'm Here / Teo Torriatte / Don't Stop Me Now / Dreamers Ball / Love Of My Life / '39 / It's Late / Brighton Rock / Keep Yourself Alive / Bohemian Rhapsody / Tie Your

Mother Down / Encore: Sheer Heart Attack / Jailhouse Rock / 2nd Encore: We Will Rock You / We Are The Champions / God Save The Queen

This concert is filmed and later broadcast on Japanese television.

April 27
Chuo Taiikukan, Kobe

❖ Also on April 27, 'Jealousy' / 'Fun It' is released as an exclusively American single. Both tracks are taken from 'Jazz'.

April 28
Kokusai Tenjijo, Nagoya

April 30/May 1
Kyuden Taiikukan, Fukuoka

May 2
Yamaguchi-ken Taiikukan, Yamaguchi

May 5/6
Makomani Ice Arena, Sapporo

■ *First night*: We Will Rock You (slow) / We Will Rock You (fast) / Let Me Entertain You / Somebody To Love / Medley: Death On Two Legs ; Killer Queen; Bicycle Race; I'm In Love With My Car; Get Down Make Love; You're My Best Friend / Now I'm Here / Teo Torriatte / Don't Stop Me Now / Dreamer's Ball / Love Of My Life / '39 / It's Late / Brighton Rock / Keep Yourself Alive / Bohemian Rhapsody / Tie Your Mother Down / 1st Encore: Sheer Heart Attack / 2nd Encore: We Will Rock You (slow) / We Are The Champions / God Save The Queen

■ *Second night*: We Will Rock You (slow) / We Will Rock You (fast) / Let Me Entertain You / Somebody To Love / If You Can't Beat Them / Medley: Death On Two Legs; Killer Queen; Bicycle Race; I'm In Love With My Car; Get Down Make Love; You're My Best Friend / Now I'm Here / Teo Torriatte / Don't Stop Me Now / Dreamer's Ball / Love Of My Life / '39 / Fat Bottomed Girls / Brighton Rock / Keep Yourself Alive / Bohemian Rhapsody / Tie Your Mother Down / 1st Encore: Sheer Heart Attack / Jailhouse Rock/ 2nd

Encore: We Will Rock You (slow) / We Are The Champions / God Save The Queen

❖ June 22

Queen release their first live album, the long awaited *Live Killers*. A double album, it comprises 22 tracks recorded at various locations on the European tour, between January 29 and February 28 (I can be precise about this now).

Killers is issued four days later in America, on June 26. In Japan it is also released as a fabulous red and green coloured vinyl set.

Though the album offers four sides of great material, there are some conspicuous absentees too. 'Somebody To Love', 'If You Can't Beat Them', 'Fat Bottomed Girls' and 'It's Late' are all on the missing list. EMI would have been better advised issuing a triple set.

While Queen do not actually really want to issue a live abum at this point, one of reasons for doing so is to try to halt the growth of bootlegs. In reality, though, this sensible thinking comes too late. Fans were crying out for concert recordings as far back as 1974, and by now a whole host of illegal recordings have began to surface.

● Brian: "Live albums are inescapable, really. Everyone tells you you have to do them, and when you do, you find that they're very often not of mass appeal, and in the absence of a fluke condition you sell your live album to the converted – the people who already know your stuff, and who come to the concerts.

"I think *Live Killers* was a kind of evidence of what we were doing live late in the Seventies. In some way, I'm unsatisfied. We had to work hard in every concert and there were serious sound problems. There were concerts that we had sounded great but then when we listened to the tapes they sounded awful. We recorded ten or fifteen shows, but we could only use three or four of them to work on. Anyway, live albums never sound good because there are noises and shouts that affect it. As it shows, *Live Killers* isn't my favorite album."

Several tracks from *Live Killers* are used as single B-sides, and two ('Rock You' and 'Love Of My Life') are actually put out as main A-sides.

❖ **June 29**

The first and only UK Queen single to feature two tracks recorded in concert is issued. 'Love Of My Life' / 'Now I'm Here' are lifted from the *Killers* album released a week earlier. Packaged in a dull plain black sleeve, and given little promotion, the single stalls at number 63.

The same pairing is issued in Japan, though its unique colour picture cover and lyric sheet makes it far more attractive than the UK equivalent. 'Love Of My Life (Live)' is not released in America. Instead Elektra opt for an entirely different coupling from the live album - the two opening tracks. 'We Will Rock You' / 'Let Me Entertain You' is released on August 24. While Japanese fans receive the same pairing in a different sleeve, UK fans are denied it. The UK is given the opportunity to purchase the same two tracks later, however, when they are issued as B-sides to the 'Crazy Little Thing Called Love' and 'Save Me' singles.

July

Queen purchase Mountain Studios in Montreux, Switzerland. The band first used the studios in 1978 to record parts of the 'Jazz' album, and they mixed 'Live Killers' there. David Richards is the resident engineer and he will become good friends with Queen.

August 18 ⟡
Ludwigsparkstadion, Saarbrucken

■ *We Will Rock You / Let Me Entertain You / If You Can't Beat Them / Medley: Mustapha; Death On Two Legs; Killer Queen; I'm In Love With My Car; Get Down Make Love; You're My Best Friend / Now I'm Here / Somebody To Love / Don't Stop Me Now / Spread Your Wings / Love Of My Life / '39 / It's Late / Keep Yourself Alive / Brighton Rock / Fat Bottomed Girls / Bohemian Rhapsody / Tie Your Mother Down / Encore: Sheer Heart Attack / Jailhouse Rock / 2nd Encore: We Will Rock You / We Are The Champions / God Save The Queen*

Queen are the headline act at this one day outdoor festival. Other artists on the bill are Rory Gallagher, Red Baron, Molly Hatchet, Alvin Lee & Ten Years After, Lake, Voyager, and The Commodores. 30,000 people attend the show. Although the capacity crowd is not the largest to have attended a Queen show, the band are aware

❖ October 5

Freddie Mercury's 'Crazy Little Thing Called Love' is released in the UK as the first single from *The Game* album. The *Live Killers* opening track 'We Will Rock You' is selected as B-side.

Unlike subsequent changes in the band's musical direction, this one is extremely well received by most fans. Some view the rockabilly Elvis-tinged song as a 'sell out', but the majority regard it as a notable landmark in Queen history. The motorbike and leather image of the accompanying video is considered by some as decidedly *Un-Queen*.

At home, the track climbs the charts and peaks (yet again) at number two (Queen endured half a dozen frustrating chart-topping number two near misses), but in America it gives the band their long awaited first number one. It is a smash hit. The B-side is different to the UK, with the *Live Killers* cut of John Deacon's 'Spread Your Wings' chosen instead, as it is for Japanese release.

'Crazy Little Thing' also reaches number one in Canada, Mexico, Holland, Australia and New Zealand.

October 7
London Coliseum, London

Freddie takes part in a charity gala ballet. The event is organised to benefit the City of Westminster Society for Mentally Handicapped Children, and many of the world's most respected ballet companies offer their services, including Margot Fonteyn, Peter Schaufuss, Wayne Sleep and Anthony Dowell.

Having rehearsed his routine several times at the London Dance Centre earlier in the week, assisted by Derek Dene and Wayne Eagling (both principal dancers with the Royal Ballet), Freddie stars in the finale to the show, dancing and singing 'Bohemian Rhapsody' and 'Crazy Little Thing Called Love', with orchestral accompaniment.

Freddie invites the audience to sing along to 'Crazy', forgetting the song was released only two days earlier, and only the few Queen fans in

that for a German venue, the turn out is significant, and a great compliment.

After a disastrous attempt at dying his hair earlier in the day, Roger plays this show with bright green hair. He later recalls the experience as one of the most embarrassing of his life, not least because Freddie seizes every opportunity to ridicule him during the set. He manages to restore it to normal colour immediately after the show.

Roger is rumoured to have demolished his drum kit after this show – believing that a whole series of technical problems had spoilt his performance. It has nothing to do with the teasing about his hair!

(I have seen no photographs from this show – thus, both of these rare incidents seem to have slipped through the 'recorded for posterity net'.)

attendance (and Roger Taylor) are able to comply. The event is a huge success which Freddie enjoys immensely. He later reveals it is one of the events in his life of which he is most proud.

● Roger: "I was more nervous than he was. I mean, I wouldn't do it. That's just not my scene. I'd like to see anyone else have the courage to do that – and carry it off as well as he did. He had a lot of balls to go on that stage. He loves all that stuff."

UK 1979 - The Crazy Tour

Queen begin a 20-date, four-week tour visiting mostly small venues, in stark contrast to the huge stadiums that have for so long been the norm. Although the band enjoy performing at large venues and to the huge audiences such places attract, they are also aware that the personal contact is sacrificed in doing so. They now decide to revert to the type of venue more typical of their early concerts.

Tour organiser Gerry Stickells is given the task of locating suitably appropriate sites. Among those he comes up with are: Tiffany's in Purley, The Lewisham Odeon and The Mayfair in Tottenham. The dates are christened the 'Crazy Tour'.

The lighting rig is a modified version of the so called Pizza Oven.

The tour gets under way in Dublin and concludes at the Alexandra Palace, in London. The show on Boxing Day at the Hammersmith Odeon is performed as a charity event.

The Royal Family are in attendance once again – for EVERY show.

November 22
Royal Dublin Society Hall, Dublin, Eire ①

■ *Let Me Entertain You / Somebody To Love / If You Can't Beat Them / Medley: Mustapha; Death On Two Legs; Killer Queen; I'm In Love With My Car; Get Down Make Love; You're My Best Friend / Save Me / Now I'm Here / Don't Stop Me Now / Love Of My Life / '39 / Fat Bottomed Girls / Brighton Rock / Keep Yourself Alive / Bohemian Rhapsody / Tie Your Mother Down / Encore: Danny Boy / Crazy Little Thing Called Love / 2nd Encore: Sheer Heart Attack / We Will Rock You / We Are The Champions*

'Save Me' is performed for the very first time here. Freddie introduces it as a song written by Brian which will soon be released as the new single. Brian plays the piano intro, and is handed his guitar just in time for the solo, and Freddie, as ever, pours his heart and soul into the words. The song becomes a great favourite with the fans during the concert on this tour.

'Mustapha' from the *Jazz* album now commence the medley. 'Fat Bottomed Girls', 'Bicycle Race' and 'Dreamers Ball' are all dropped.

This is Queen's first show in Ireland, hence they perform a specially rehearsed version of 'Danny Boy' (the one and only time they do so) and they do not play 'God Save The Queen'.

November 24
National Exhibition Centre, Birmingham

■ *We Will Rock You / Let Me Entertain You / Somebody To Love / If You Can't Beat Them / Medley: Mustapha; Death On Two Legs; Killer Queen; I'm In Love With My Car; Get Down Make Love; You're My Best Friend / Save Me / Now I'm Here / Don't Stop Me Now / Love Of My Life / '39 / Brighton Rock / Keep Yourself Alive / Bohemian Rhapsody / Tie Your Mother Down / Crazy Little Thing Called Love /*

Encore: Sheer Heart Attack / 2nd Encore: We Will Rock You / We Are The Champions / God Save The Queen

During 'Don't Stop Me Now' member's of the 'Royal Family' do a Conga at the back of the hall. The venue's security staff also partake.

↗ **'Cold And Dirty'**, by Stafford Hildred, Birmingham Evening Mail, November 26, 1979: *'QUEEN got a right royal reception from 14,000 loyal subjects in the giant hall at the NEC. It's a pity the setting was so unsuitable. Cold, dirty and acoustically appalling, at £4 a ticket the fans deserved more, much more. Still the stars of the show were in impressive form. The range and versatility that have elevated Queen to supergroup status was all there.*

'But the outfit were forced to pump out such volume to fill the hall that the distortion of the sound ruined the effect, unless you joined the Twickenham-style maul in front of the stage.

'After battling to be with the seething mass of real enthusiasts, the performance sounded much better. I didn't think the intricate recordings that Queen delight in would be possible to recreate live.

'And they weren't quite, but they came so close you couldn't complain. NEC organisers have tried to improve the concert sound quality, but they certainly haven't got it right yet.'

November 26/27
Apollo Theatre, Manchester
■ *First night: We Will Rock You (fast) / Let Me Entertain You Somebody To Love / Medley: Mustapha; Death On Two Legs; Killer Queen; I'm In Love With My Car; Get Down Make Love; You're My Best Friend / Save Me / Now I'm Here / Don't Stop Me Now / Spread Your Wings / Love Of My Life / '39 / Fat Bottomed Girls / Keep Yourself Alive / Brighton Rock / Crazy Little Thing Called Love / Bohemian Rhapsody / Tie Your Mother Down / 1st Encore: Sheer Heart Attack / 2nd Encore: We Will Rock You (slow) / We Are The Champions*

Some way into the show, Freddie: "We're gonna do a new song now, but before that I'd really like to say that it's nice... I know I did all this crap last night... but it's really nice to be back here

after such a long time - even though it's such a measley little theatre. We ALWAYS come back. Okay this is a new song entitled 'Save Me'."

Members of the Royal Family are again in attendance here – but this time with a cunning plan! Using a recording of the previous night's show, a fan transcribes the lyrics to the not yet available 'Save Me'. He photocopies the sheet and then, here, members of The Family hand them out to fellow fans as they enter the theatre. Later, in the actual concert, when Freddie introduces the brand new song as the next single, he is unprepared for the fans knowing every single word and joining in with him from start to end. The crowd is word-perfect, and this baffles him. It is only when Freddie spots fans reading and singing from their prompt sheets that the plot is revealed. Freddie laughs and mutters something to himself, then walks off to think about the next recital.

■ *Second night: We Will Rock You (fast) / Let Me Entertain You Somebody To Love / Medley: Mustapha; Death On Two Legs; Killer Queen; I'm In Love With My Car; Get Down Make Love; You're My Best Friend / Save Me / Now I'm Here / Don't Stop Me Now / Spread Your Wings / Love Of My Life / '39 / Keep Yourself Alive / Liar / Brighton Rock / Crazy Little Thing Called Love / Bohemian Rhapsody / Tie Your Mother Down / 1st Encore: Sheer Heart Attack / 2nd Encore: We Will Rock You (slow) / We Are The Champions*

Some way into the show. Brian: "Thank You. I hope you're all sitting comfortably. Are you alright? Good, good, good. You sound pretty good to me, I must say. A short while ago we had a live album out which I'm sure you've all bought... so thank you very much. It's well worth it, I'm sure you'll agree. And if you've heard that live album you'll know what happens in this one - if the night goes well. This is called 'Love Of My Life', so we hope you're going to sing along."

They do indeed sing along; for this is 'their time'. The fans love this song (a different arrangement to that of the album cut) and as usual they give it their all – conducted from the stage by Freddie, who is happy for them to take over and give his voice a break.

Brian: "Very good, very good"

Freddie, tongue firmly in cheek: "Do you like the way I sang that?"

Brian: "I tell you... it's alright for the singers in this business - you don't get *any* work to do!"

Freddie: "That's the easiest song I've ever sung, I tell you. Your session fees will be posted to you some time next week."

Prior to the show on the second night, the Royal Family send a card to the band. Because 'Liar' had been absent from the previous night's show the card reads:

"If you want to get to Glasgow alive, you'd better play 'Liar' tonight."

Wisely, they play it.

↗ **'More Than OK, Fred'**, by Mick Middles, *Sounds*, November 27, 1979:

'THE ULTIMATE rock show. Glittering and glorious. A music form that has long since reached its peak. I hate good/bad old rock music, but I can even enjoy cricket when it's played properly. The music of Queen pours from the sky and unless you are equipped with suitable weatherwear, you are going to get wet. I was drenched.

'I have never felt the slightest desire to listen to a Queen album since the heady days of 'Night At The Opera'. A string of awful (albeit cleverly awful) singles have succeeded only in transforming my lack of desire into a snobbish lack of respect. Do you catch my drift? You are anticipating another hatchet job, right? You are wrong. Y'see, I really hated Queen until... 8.45 Monday evening, when the rock band Queen ceremoniously exploded into life on the Manchester Apollo stage.

'Queen's Freddie Mercury bobbed charismatically into the centre of the crowd's attention, a confusing mass of flashing lights and pounding opening chords turned the initial tenseness into a staggering spectacle. Queen played with courage and, to my utter surprise, total conviction. I never imagined for one moment that they could be THIS good. The show (for it was a show

rather than a gig) continued to impress me with its professional ferocity. Dozens of familiar and totally meaningless songs seemed to change into enjoyable tunes packed with satirical humour. A humour that was never apparent to me before...

'I left the Apollo in a state of absolute amazement. The realisation that I'd actually enjoyed every second of a credibility-blowing Queen gig was beginning to burn away at my confused mind. There is no hope for me now.'

November 30/December 1
Apollo Theatre, Glasgow

■ *First night*: Let Me Entertain You / Tie Your Mother Down / Somebody To Love / If You Can't Beat Them / Medley: Mustapha; Death On Two Legs; Killer Queen; I'm In Love With My Car; Get Down Make Love; You're My Best Friend / Save Me / Now I'm Here / Don't Stop Me Now / Spread Your Wings / Love Of My Life / '39 / Fat Bottomed Girls / Keep Yourself Alive / Brighton Rock / Bohemian Rhapsody / Sheer Heart Attack / Crazy Little Thing Called Love / Encore: We Will Rock You / We Are The Champions / God Save The Queen

"Hello Glasgow - we're back! Are you all crazy? Okay let's 'Tie Your Mother Down'."

Later, Freddie: "Oh that sounds nice, we like a rowdy bunch... It's only champagne. Hey, I tell you what we're gonna do - a song from the album *Jazz* right now. This is a song written by John, it's called If 'You Can't Beat Em' - join 'em."

Later again: "Alright. I must tell you... I really can't hit those high notes; some nights I can, some nights I can't, so I mean, you've got higher voices than I have anyway, so let's see what you can do to this one..."

After 'Love Of My Life', Brian: "Okay, we'd like to welcome back to the stage at this point the sonic volcanoes that used to be known. On drums and various other things, Mr Roger Taylor."

Roger: "Thank you – ta."

Brian: "And on bass guitar, Mr John Deacon. And our new young singer... Mr Freddie Mercury."

Having sung the opening lines of 'I'm In Love

With My Car', Roger has a mental block and forgets the lyrics. He continues with an occasional word or two, until Freddie eventually drops in with some improvised vocals. The bootleg copy of this show is worth getting hold of, if only to hear this rare moment.

Freddie: "It seems a long time since we came back to the Apollo, but every time we come back you give us such a good time. Thank you kindly. We're going to do a brand new song now. This is gonna be our next single release. It's called… 'Save Me'."

Freddie: "Oh yes this is really good tonight. Let's do some more. I feel shagged!"

Then, after chants of 'Freddie… Freddie… Freddie': "What a lovely bunch of people… and they're all Scottish, as well! It's because you drink so much (laughs)… a lot of boozers!"

Brian: "We want to say a special thank you to you once agin for filling this place to the seams. It really feels lively. Thank you. And next time we'll do about 16 nights here, alright?… Okay, this is something to stretch all Glaswegian lungs this is called "39". Thank you."

'Crazy Little Thing' entails Brian swapping his Red Special guitar for a Fender Telecaster, while Freddie assists on acoustic. The track features constantly throughout the Crazy Tour, and in all subsequent tours (even though it will be left off the 1986 *Live Magic* album).

Freddie's intro to the song: "Alright, I'd like to give you a very big thank you for making this a gold record – thanks."

A while later, "Thank you Glasgow. You've been a tremendous audience. Thank you, good night."

December 3⚐/4⚐
City Hall, Newcastle-Upon-Tyne
■ *First night*: *Let Me Entertain You / Tie Your Mother Down / Somebody To Love / If You Can't Beat Them / Medley: Mustapha; Death On Two Legs; Killer Queen; I'm In Love With My Car; Get Down Make Love; You're My Best Friend / Save Me / Now I'm Here / Don't Stop Me Now / Spread Your Wings / Love Of My Life / '39 / Fat Bottomed Girls / Keep Yourself*

Alive / Bohemian Rhapsody/ Encore: Sheer Heart Attack / Crazy Little Thing Called Love / 2nd Encore: We Will Rock You (slow) / We Are The Champions / God Save The Queen

■ *Second night*: *Jailhouse Rock / We Will Rock You (fast) / Let Me Entertain You / Somebody To Love / Medley: Mustapha; Death On Two Legs; Killer Queen; I'm In Love With My Car; Get Down Make Love; You're My Best Friend / Don't Stop Me Now / Spread Your Wings / Love Of My Life / '39 / Keep Yourself Alive / Guitar Solo / Liar / Crazy Little Thing Called Love / Bohemian Rhapsody / Tie Your Mother Down / Encore: Sheer Heart Attack / 2nd Encore: We Will Rock You / We Are The Champions / God Save The Queen*
"Hello rock'n'rollers. Hey, are you feeling good? Okay, we're going to entertain you."

Later, Freddie: "It's bloody hot up here. I don't know what it's like down there - I mean you're not exactly miles away are you? It's just like my front room."

"Good old Newcastle… they're a bunch of boozers."

When the crowd breaks into a spontaneous, unprompted chorus of 'Crazy Little Thing Called Love', Freddie joins in. "Yeah mama – alright. Alriiiiiiiight!" Then Brian and Roger join in too, but subtly.

Freddie concludes the show with, "Thank you. Goodnight Newcastle. It's been beautiful. See you soon."

December 6/7
Empire Theatre, Liverpool
■ *Second night*: *Jailhouse Rock / We Will Rock You (fast) / Somebody To Love / If You Can't Beat Them / Medley: Mustapha; Death On Two Legs; Killer Queen; I'm In Love With My Car; Get Down Make Love; You're My Best Friend / Now I'm Here / Don't Stop Me Now / Spread Your Wings / Love Of My Life / '39 / Keep Yourself Alive / Guitar Solo / Liar / Crazy Little Thing Called Love / Bohemian Rhapsody / Tie Your Mother Down / Encore: Sheer Heart Attack / 2nd Encore: We Will Rock You / We Are The Champions / God Save The Queen*

Freddie: "I know I probably said all this crap to you last night, but it seems every time we come to Liverpool you give us a really good welcome. Thank you. Okay, that's enough of the seriousness... Lets fool around a little, hey? Okay, let's hear you pour your voices into this one."

Later, Freddie: "Thank you. Doesn't that feel good? Alright, you Liverpudlians... 'Don't Stop Me Now'!"

After 'Liar', Freddie: "I don't know why I'm wearing this... I guess I like to break strings. It's a nice sort of masochistic pleasure. Anyway, here's a crazy song..."

Once again the crowd burst into their own recital of 'Crazy Little Thing', and again Freddie helps them out. "You can keep going for as long as you like."

December 9
Hippodrome, Bristol
The soundcheck here is filmed for use in the British television programme *The South Bank Show*. It is the first time Freddie is seen playing guitar on television.

December 10/11
Brighton Centre, Brighton
■ *First night*: *Jailhouse Rock / We Will Rock You (fast) / Let Me Entertain You / Somebody To Love / Medley*: *Mustapha; Death On Two Legs; Killer Queen; I'm In Love With My Car; Get Down Make Love; You're My Best Friend / Save Me / Now I'm Here / Don't Stop Me Now / Spread Your Wings / Love Of My Life / '39 / Keep Yourself Alive / Guitar Solo / Liar / Crazy Little Thing Called Love / Bohemian Rhapsody / Tie Your Mother Down / Encore: Sheer Heart Attack / 2nd Encore: We Will Rock You / We Are The Champions / God Save The Queen*

Freddie: "Hello Brighton! Are you feeling crazy? Are you ready to rock? Are you ready to roll?"

Later, Freddie is baffled by the uncommonly calm audience. "What a funny crowd! There are so many of you but, you don't make a noise. Let me hear you. Alright, you ARE there. Can you sing in Arabic? You can... okay, lets see..." ('Mustapha' begins).

Freddie: "You're nice and cross down there aren't you - you people at the front? Alright? Okay? I must say it's really nice to finally play Brighton. Oh yes. We have a special song for you a little bit later... I'm sure you know what it is. Right now we'd like to do a very new song. This is going to be our next single release - it's called 'Save Me'."

Later, Brian: "Good evening. I hope you're all feeling okay. I hope you can hear alright, around the sides. You okay? I hope so. It's a bit of a strange building this. Is it loud enough? Half yes and half no, I think. Okay, we'll turn it up a bit after this."

Freddie: "They want their brains bashed in I think!"

■ *Second night*: *Jailhouse Rock / We Will Rock You (fast) / Let Me Entertain You / Somebody To Love / If You Can't Beat Them / Medley*: *Mustapha; Death On Two Legs; Killer Queen; I'm In Love With My Car; Get Down Make Love; You're My Best Friend / Save Me / Now I'm Here / Don't Stop Me Now / Spread Your Wings / Love Of My Life / '39 / Keep Yourself Alive / Guitar Solo / Liar / Crazy Little Thing Called Love / Bohemian Rhapsody / Tie Your Mother Down / Encore: Sheer Heart Attack / 2nd Encore: We Will Rock You / We Are The Champions / God Save The Queen*
"Okay you Brighton Belles, how you doing?"

December 13
Lyceum Ballroom, London

December 14
Rainbow Theatre, London

December 17
Tiffany's, Purley

December 19
Tottenham Mayfair, London
The band perform this show with no lighting rig as the venue is too small to accommodate it.

Freddie is very talkative during the show and discusses the presents he is buying for Christmas. Having said this, it is very noticeable that on this leg of the tour there is a good deal less chat from Freddie and Brian than was the case in Europe earlier in the year. The shows which make up *Live Killers* feature probably fifty percent more communication with the audience.

December 20
Lewisham Odeon, London

December 22
Alexandra Palace, London

■ *First night*: *Jailhouse Rock / We Will Rock You (fast) / Let Me Entertain You / Somebody To Love / Medley: Mustapha; Death On Two Legs; Killer Queen; I'm In Love With My Car; Get Down Make Love; You're My Best Friend / Save Me / Now I'm Here / Don't Stop Me Now / Spread Your Wings / Love Of My Life / '39 / Fat Bottomed Girls / Keep Yourself Alive / Liar / Crazy Little Thing Called Love / Bohemian Rhapsody / Tie Your Mother Down / Encore: Sheer Heart Attack / 2nd Encore: We Will Rock You / We Are The Champions / God Save The Queen* Most of the 'Save Me' promotional video footage is recorded at this show. The finished film, including animated sections conceived by Brian, later features on popular British television programmes of the time like *Swap Shop* and *Tiswas*.

Brian: "Did you know this magnificent place was built in 1863, and burned down 16 days later, and was rebuilt - especially for Queen in 1979?

Thank you. I should tell you I'm not an acoustic guitar player really (yeah, right!). Thank you for singing - we want you to sing this one if you will. This is something that was arranged for piano some time ago – it's a song by Freddie and nowdays we do it with this acoustic thing... this is called 'Love Of My Life'."

Freddie concludes the show in unusual fashion here. "Goodnight everybody, merry Christmas. It's a pleasure doing business with you. Thank you."

December 26 ♪
Hammersmith Odeon, London

■ *Jailhouse Rock / We Will Rock You / Let Me Entertain You / Somebody To Love / If You Can't Beat Them / Medley: Mustapha; Death On Two Legs; Killer Queen; I'm In Love With My Car; Get Down Make Love; You're My Best Friend / Save Me / Now I'm Here / Don't Stop Me Now / Spread Your Wings / Love Of My Life / '39 / Keep Yourself Alive / Silent Night (part) / Crazy Little Thing Called Love: Crazy Reprise / Bohemian Rhapsody / Tie Your Mother Down / Encore: Sheer Heart Attack / 2nd Encore: We Will Rock You / We Are The Champions / God Save The Queen*

Queen are approached by Paul McCartney to perform this show, conceived, organised and promoted by Harvey Goldsmith on behalf of the High Commission For Refugees and UNICEF, to raise funds for the people of Kampuchea (now Cambodia).

Apart from Wings, McCartney and Goldsmith have secured performances from Ian Dury & The Blockheads, The Clash, The Specials, Rockpile, The Who, The Pretenders, Billy Connolly and Elvis Costello & The Attractions.

Four separate shows are planned, with Queen the only group to appear on the first night. Unlike most other artists, they play a full set.

The concerts are filmed and later edited for television broadcast - eventually screening in the UK in March 1980. Peter Ustinov introduces Queen's material ('Now I'm Here' and 'Crazy Little Thing Called Love') and this is later used in the *Magic Years* documentary, but in an entirely different context. It is also given an American television airing at some point. Some of the other Queen material is later (and still today) shown at fan club conventions and provides irrefutable evidence that this is concert footage worthy of a proper home video release. It is truly exceptional.

"Hello rock and rollers. Having a good Christmas? Do you feel crazy? Okay let's do some more..."

Freddie walks around the stage and then throws a cup of water over the audience. "I'll keep the lager for myself. Listen... I know it seems like a Cecil B DeMille production of the *Ten Commandments* here tonight, but don't worry about the camera men, they're getting paid. Right now we'd like to do a song... My god it's quiet in here. It's always like this at Hammersmith - I don't know why? Are you supposed to be a sophisticated crowd? I suppose you are. Okay, this is a song called 'If You Can't Beat 'Em, Join 'Em'."

Later, Freddie: "For those of you who don't know, tonight brings us to the end of our tour." Collective sighs ring out. "We're gonna be here all the time anyway (in London), so don't worry about it. Don't worry your dear little hearts."

1980

❖ January 25

Brian May's 'Save Me' is issued in the UK as the second single from *The Game*. It is backed with 'Let Me Entertain You' from the double live set, and reaches number 11 in the charts. Though the song is also released in Japan, backed with the live rendering of 'Spread Your Wings', it remains unissued in America.

❖ May 30

'Play The Game' is released in the UK as the third single from *The Game*, even though the album itself is not yet available. Roger Taylor's non-album track 'A Human Body' is the B-side. In America the same pairing (released a week later to coincide with American and Canadian dates) peaks at number 42, while at home it fares better and reaches number 14.

USA 1980 - The Game Tour

Queen fly to Los Angeles on June 19 for seven days of rehearsals ahead of the impending tour. It entails 46 shows over a three-month period, the biggest tour Queen will ever undertake. Every

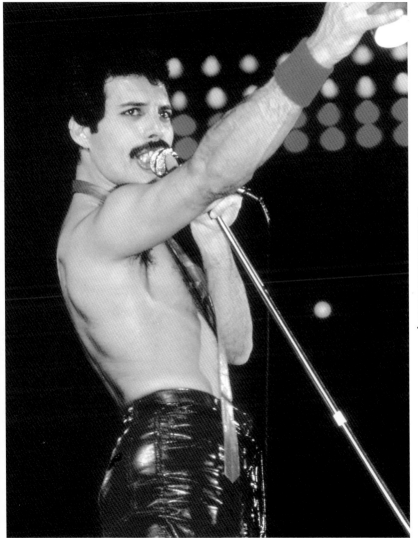

161

Queen Live '80

new album – 'Play The Game', 'Need Your Loving Tonight' and 'Dragon Attack'. 'Save Me' and 'Crazy' had already been incorporated into the set the previous November. 'Rock It' will feature in the set later.

'Fat Bottomed Girls' is back in the set again on a fairly regular basis, while 'You're My Best Friend' is dropped.

June 30
PNE Coliseum, Vancouver, British Columbia
■ *Jailhouse Rock / We Will Rock You / Let Me Entertain You / Need Your Loving Tonight / Play The Game / Medley: Mustapha; Death On Two Legs; Killer Queen; I'm In Love With My Car; Get Down Make Love / Somebody To Love / Save Me / Now I'm Here / Dragon Attack / Fat Bottomed Girls / Love Of My Life / Keep Yourself Alive / Brighton Rock / Guitar Solo / Crazy Little Thing Called Love / Bohemian Rhapsody / Tie Your Mother Down / Encore: Another One Bites The Dust / Sheer Heart Attack / 2nd Encore: We Will Rock You / We Are The Champions / God Save The Queen*

one of the 46 shows will be performed before a capacity audience. The itinerary includes four consecutive nights at the LA Forum and four at Madison Square Garden in New York.

The new lighting rig is called Fly Swatters and is made up of a number of moving arms (operated by a hidden roadie) covered in banks of lights, that rises up and down during the show. The crew refer to the individual pieces as G2 Razors. When the numerous sections work together in unison they are an awesome sight. The rig will also be used for the 1980 winter European tour (including the UK dates), the five Japanese Budokan shows in February 1981, and for two Canadian (Montreal Forum) shows in November 1981 - which are both filmed

As well as ocassionally opening with 'Jailhouse Rock', the set now includes new material from the

❖ June 30

The Game album is released worldwide and reaches number one all over Europe. It is also Queen's first chart-topping album in North America. Although the original album title is *Play The Game*, it is shortened when Roger objects to the conformity implications.

Though seven tracks from the album *are* included in the live set (at various times), three are not. Roger's provocatively titled 'Coming Soon' is perhaps an inevitable omission, but Brian's 'Sail Away Sweet Sister' would have been perfect for the acoustic part of the show, but is also dismissed. Ironically, though Queen overlook it for their show, Guns'n'Roses do not. In 1990, Brian makes one of his guest appearances and joins the band on stage for this song. He also performs it a few times himself during his solo tours of 1992/93.

Freddie's equally provocative 'Don't Try Suicide' is the other concert absentee. This is curious too, for the song will be issued as the American single B-side to 'Another One Bites The Dust' at exactly the time the Queen show is in that territory.

July 1
Seattle Coliseum, Seattle

July 2
Portland Coliseum, Portland, Oregon

July 5
Sports Arena, San Diego

During 'Crazy Little Thing' Freddie breaks yet another guitar string. He makes a joke of it by explaining to the audience that in twenty years he only ever managed to master two chords.

Little does he realise he will still be saying the same thing in 1986!

July 6
Compton Terrace, Phoenix

July 8/9/11/12♪
The Forum, Los Angeles

■ *Third night*: *Jailhouse Rock / We Will Rock You / Let Me Entertain You / Need Your Loving Tonight / Play The Game / Medley: Mustapha; Death On Two Legs; Killer Queen; I'm In Love With My Car; Get Down Make Love / Somebody To Love / Save Me / Now I'm Here / Dragon Attack / Fat Bottomed Girls / Love Of My Life / Keep Yourself Alive / Brighton Rock / Guitar Solo / Crazy Little Thing Called Love / Bohemian Rhapsody / Tie Your Mother Down / Encore: Another One Bites The Dust / Sheer Heart Attack / 2nd Encore: We Will Rock You / We Are The Champions / God Save The Queen*

Queen Live '80

■ *Final night*: *We Will Rock You / Let Me Entertain You / Need Your Loving Tonight / Play The Game / Medley: Mustapha; Death On Two Legs; Killer Queen; I'm In Love With My Car; Get Down Make Love / Somebody To Love / Save Me / Now I'm Here / Dragon Attack / Fat Bottomed Girls / Love Of My Life / Keep Yourself Alive / Brighton Rock / Guitar Solo / Crazy Little Thing Called Love / Bohemian Rhapsody / Tie Your Mother Down / Encore: Another One Bites The Dust / Sheer Heart Attack / 2nd Encore: Jailhouse Rock / We Will Rock You / We Are The Champions / God Save The Queen*

July 13/14 ♪
Oakland Coliseum, Oakland, California
■ *Second night*: *We Will Rock You / Let Me Entertain You / Need Your Loving Tonight / Play The Game / Medley: Mustapha; Death On Two Legs; Killer Queen; I'm In Love With My Car; Get Down Make Love / Somebody To Love / Save Me / Now I'm Here / Dragon Attack / Fat Bottomed Girls / Love Of My Life / Keep Yourself Alive / Brighton Rock / Guitar Solo / Crazy Little Thing Called Love / Bohemian Rhapsody / Tie Your Mother Down / Encore: Another One Bites The Dust / Sheer Heart Attack / 2nd Encore: Jailhouse Rock / We Will Rock You / We Are The Champions / God Save The Queen*

August 5
Mid South Coliseum, Memphis, Tennessee

August 6
Riverside Centroplex, Baton Rouge, Louisiana

August 8
City Myriad, Oklahoma, Oklahoma City

August 9
Reunion, Dallas, Texas

August 10
Summit, Houston, Texas

August 12
The Omni, Atlanta, Georgia

❖ Also on August 12, 'Another One Bites The Dust' is released in the US, as the third single from *The Game*. It is coupled with Freddie's 'Don't Try Suicide', and provides Queen with their second American number one. Still 'Suicide' does not receive its debut on stage.

At home, Brian May's 'Dragon Attack' is chosen as the B-side to 'Dust'. The Japanese issue, featuring the same two songs as the US, is held back until September 25.

August 13
Charlotte Coliseum, Charlotte, North Carolina

August 14
Greensboro Coliseum, Greensboro, North Carolina

August 16
Civic Center, Charleston, South Carolina

August 17
Riverton Coliseum, Cincinnati, Ohio

August 20
Civic Center, Hartford, Connecticut
Freddie becomes irritated by the echo machine during 'Now I'm Here'. He barks his disapproval to the back of the stage and immediately an unseen technician negates the annoyance. The audience knows nothing of this.

August 22
Spectrum, Philadelphia, Pennsylvania
❖ Also on August 22, the UK's fourth and last single from *The Game* is released. Backed with 'Dragon Attack', John Deacon's 'Another One Bites The Dust' reaches number seven, but is a spectacular success in America, where it storms into the charts at number one and remains there for over a month. The disc sells over three million copies. It is Elektra's first single to do so.

August 23
Civic Center, Baltimore, Maryland

August 24
Civic Center, Pittsburgh, Pennsylvania

August 26 ♪
Civic Center, Providence, Rhode Island
■ *Jailhouse Rock / We Will Rock You (fast) / Let Me Entertain You / Play The Game / Medley: Mustapha: Death On Two Legs; Killer Queen; I'm In Love With My Car; Get Down Make Love; You're My Best Friend / Save Me / Another One Bites The Dust / Now I'm Here / Dragon Attack / Now I'm Here (reprise) / Fat Bottomed Girls / Love Of My Life / Keep Yourself Alive / Brighton Rock / Crazy Little Thing Called Love / Bohemian Rhapsody / Tie Your Mother Down / Encore: Sheer Heart Attack / 2nd Encore: We Will Rock You (slow) / We Are The Champions / God Save The Queen*

August 27
Spectrum, Portland, Maine

August 29
The Forum, Montreal, Quebec

August 30

CNE Grandstand, Toronto

■ *Jailhouse Rock / We Will Rock You (fast) / Let Me Entertain You / Play The Game / Medley: Mustapha; Death On Two Legs; Killer Queen; I'm In Love With My Car; Get Down, Make Love; You're My Best Friend / Save Me / Now I'm Here / Dragon Attack / Now I'm Here (reprise) / Fat Bottomed Girls / Love Of My Life / Keep Yourself Alive / Brighton Rock / Crazy Little Thing Called Love / Bohemian Rhapsody / Tie Your Mother Down / Encore: Another One Bites The Dust / Sheer Heart Attack / 2nd Encore: We Will Rock You / We Are The Champions / God Save The Queen*

August 31

Convention Centre, Rochester, New York

After this show the band fly home for a nine-day break before resuming the tour again in Milwaukee.

September 10⌀

Mecca, Milwaukee, Wisconsin

■ *Jailhouse Rock / We Will Rock You / Let Me Entertain You / Play The Game / Medley: Mustapha; Death On Two Legs; Killer Queen; I'm In Love With My Car; Get Down Make Love / Somebody To Love / Save Me / Now I'm Here / Dragon Attack / Fat Bottomed Girls / Love Of My Life / Keep Yourself Alive / Brighton Rock / Guitar Solo / Crazy Little Thing Called Love / Bohemian Rhapsody / Tie Your Mother Down / Encore: Another One Bites The Dust / Sheer Heart Attack / 2nd Encore: We Will Rock You / We Are The Champions / God Save The Queen*

September 11

Market Square Arena, Indianapolis, Indiana

September 12

Kemper Arena, Kansas City, Missouri

September 13

Civic Center, Omaha, Nebraska

September 14

St Paul Civic Center, Minneapolis, Minnesota

September 16

Hilton Coliseum, Kansas City, Missouri

September 17

Checkerdome, St Louis, Missouri

September 19⌀

Horizon, Chicago, Illinois

■ *Jailhouse Rock / We Will Rock You / Let Me Entertain You / Play The Game / Medley: Mustapha; Death On Two Legs; Killer Queen; I'm In Love With My Car; Get Down Make Love / Somebody To Love / Save Me / Now I'm Here / Dragon Attack / Fat Bottomed Girls / Love Of My Life / Keep Yourself Alive / Brighton Rock / Guitar Solo / Crazy Little Thing Called Love / Bohemian Rhapsody / Tie Your Mother Down / Encore: Another One Bites The Dust / Sheer Heart Attack / 2nd Encore: We Will Rock You / We Are The Champions / God Save The Queen*

Freddie's opening lines here: "Do you realise that this is the first time we've come here when there's no snow on the ground... fucking good job too, I'll tell ya!"

Later on: "Do you think I should keep this moustache?"

The reaction is mixed. "Did you say no?... Fuck off! Actually a lot of people really hated it in San Francisco... they told me to shave it off... and I told *them* to fuck off - I really did.

"We're gonna detour for a dirty song right now. We're gonna dedicate this next song to anybody here with a huge pair of tits - BIG PAIR OF TITS - and a BIG arse. Do you know what I'm talking about?... 'Fat Bottomed Girls'."

The acoustics at this venue are not good. This irritates Brian in particular as he encounters problems during extended guitar parts. "There seems to be just a little bit of echo in this place. We used to play in a place called The Stadium... isn't that right? They told us this place was better, is that right too? I really don't know. In this age of computer acoustic design, how they can design a place this bad, I do not understand... it's very strange. There's only one reason for coming to this place, and that's one of the best rock and roll audiences in the country – you really are. I'd better stop talking."

Someone shouts: "Yeah... play that guitar!" Brian complies. "This is a song we used to do some time ago, and we've just revived it. It's called 'Love Of My Life'."

September 20
Joe Louis Arena, Detroit

September 21
Cleveland Coliseum, Cleveland, Ohio

September 23
Veterans' Memorial Coliseum, New Haven, Connecticut

September 24
War Memorial, Syracuse, New York
Set: Same as September 19

September 26
Boston Gardens, Boston, Massachusetts
Once again members of the audience make known their feelings for Freddie's new acquired moustache here, and once again he tells them to fuck off.

September 28/29/30/October 1
Madison Square Garden, New York

Following a holiday, the band work upon the 'Flash Gordon' soundtrack album. The sessions conclude in November.

November 20

Queen leave London and head for Zurich for two days of rehearsal before the European Tour begins.

EUROPEAN TOUR 1980

'Flash's Theme', 'Battle Theme', 'Vultan's Theme' and 'The Hero' from the *Flash Gordon* soundtrack are all performed during this tour. The band have a synthesizer on stage with them for the first time, in order to play this material.

'Need Your Loving' Tonight' also begins to make a regular appearance in the set.

November 23
Hallenstadion, Zurich

■ *Jailhouse Rock / We Will Rock You / Let Me Entertain You / Play The Game / Medley: Mustapha; Death On Two Legs; Killer Queen; I'm In Love With My Car; Get Down Make Love / Need Your Loving Tonight / Save Me / Now I'm Here; Dragon Attack; Now I'm Here (Reprise) / Fat Bottomed Girls / Love Of My Life / Keep Yourself Alive / Instrumental Inferno / Battle Theme / The Hero / Brighton Rock / Guitar Solo / Crazy Little Thing Called Love / Bohemian Rhapsody / Tie Your Mother Down / Encore: Another One Bites The Dust / Sheer Heart Attack / 2nd Encore: We Will Rock You / We Are The Champions / God Save The Queen*

Freddie is carried on stage for the first encore on the shoulders of the Darth Vader character from *Star Wars*, in reality band bodyguard Wally Verson. This will be repeated in Birmingham on December 6. It is not a new idea, for during the 1979 UK tour Freddie was carried by his good friend Superman.

The Support band here are fellow Brits Straight Eight.

❖ November 24

The only single to be issued from *Flash Gordon* is released in the UK. Backed with 'Football Fight', the film's main theme 'Flash' reaches number 10. The same pairing is issued universally, but in most cases not until the New Year.

November 25
Le Bourget La Retonde, Paris

■ *Jailhouse Rock / We Will Rock You / Let Me Entertain You / Play The Game / Medley: Mustapha; Death On Two Legs; Killer Queen; I'm In Love With My Car; Get Down Make Love / Need Your Loving Tonight / Save Me / Now I'm Here; Dragon Attack; Now I'm Here (Reprise) / Fat Bottomed Girls / Love Of My Life / Keep Yourself Alive / Instrumental Inferno / Battle Theme / The Hero / Brighton Rock / Guitar Solo / Crazy Little Thing Called Love / Bohemian Rhapsody / Tie Your Mother Down / Encore: Another One Bites The Dust / Sheer Heart Attack / 2nd Encore: We Will Rock You / We Are The Champions / God Save The Queen*

November 26
Sportshalle, Cologne

Set: same as previous night

November 27 ⌀
Groenoordhalle, Leiden

Set: also the same as November 25

November 29 ⌀
Grundhalle, Essen

■ *Jailhouse Rock / We Will Rock You / Let Me Entertain You / Play The Game / Medley: Mustapha; Death On Two Legs; Killer Queen; I'm In Love With My Car; Get Down Make Love / Need Your Loving Tonight / Save Me / Now I'm Here; Dragon Attack; Now I'm Here (Reprise) / Fat Bottomed Girls / Love Of My Life / Keep Yourself Alive / Instrumental Inferno / Battle Theme / The Hero / Brighton Rock / Guitar Solo / Crazy Little Thing Called Love / Bohemian Rhapsody / Tie Your Mother Down / Encore: Another One Bites The Dust / Sheer Heart Attack / 2nd Encore: We Will Rock You / We Are The Champions / God Save The Queen*

November 30 ↗
Deutschlandhalle, Berlin
   Set: same as previous night

December 1
Stadthalle, Bremen

December 5 ↗**/6** ↗
NEC, Birmingham
■ *First night*: Jailhouse Rock / We Will Rock You / Let Me Entertain You / Play The Game / Medley: Mustapha; Death On Two Legs; Killer Queen; I'm In Love With My Car; Get Down Make Love / Need Your Loving Tonight / Save Me / Now I'm Here; Dragon Attack; Now I'm Here (Reprise) / Fat Bottomed Girls / Love Of My Life / Keep Yourself Alive / Battle Theme / The Hero / Brighton Rock / Guitar Solo / Crazy Little Thing Called Love / Bohemian Rhapsody / Tie Your Mother Down / Encore: Another One Bites The Dust / Sheer Heart Attack / 2nd Encore: We Will Rock You / We Are The Champions / God Save The Queen

   Queen are the first band to play at this all seat venue.

↗ Patrick Humphries, in Melody Maker, December 6: *'If you want to be absolutely accurate, Queen are not the first band to play Birmingham's National Exhibition Centre. That honour fell to Straight Eight, who have been the opening act for Queen on their current European tour. They delivered a crisp, fast-paced set, but which tended to get lost in the vast auditorium.*

'But the capacity 10,500 people had not come to see Straight Eight, they were there to pay yearly homage to the visiting monarch. The Arena is a perfect venue for a rock show, everything under one roof, from trains to fish and chips. Acoustically, from where I was sitting, Queen sounded fine.

'...The cheers escalate to a crescendo as the band hit the stage and crash straight into 'Jailhouse Rock'. A tacit acknowledgement from Mercury greets the hysteria which followed the first number, and it's off into 'We Will Rock You'. Well no quibbles about the beginning, straight, no-nonsense down the line rock'n'roll. That was the real eye-opener of the evening as far as I was concerned. Wrenched away from the

antiseptic cotton wool of the recording studio, Queen tore through their set with a force that could have registered on the Richter Scale...

   '... The lights go up, the crowd go home, their fantasies fulfilled. I enjoyed it considerably more than I thought I would. As an event, a Queen gig is certainly impressive, and however objectively you may view Queen and their music, it is difficult not to be impressed by the spectacle. Impressed, but not necessarily involved. It is a strange feeling to be alone at the heart of a crowd. Queen fans are familiar with, and expect, every cadence and note, variation is permitted within reason, but it is familiarity that breeds content. The kid next to me had come down from Leeds for the gig. 'And it were bloody worth it,' according to him. That is who Queen are playing for.'

   Brian uses a 12 string guitar at this venue which, as he explains during the show, belongs to Roger.

■ *Second night*: Jailhouse Rock / We Will Rock You (fast) / Let Me Entertain You / Play The Game / Medley: Mustapha; Death On Two Legs; Killer Queen; I'm In Love With My Car; Get Down Make Love / Need Your Loving Tonight / Save Me / Now I'm Here / Dragon Attack / Now I'm Here (reprise) / Fat Bottomed Girls / Love Of My Life / Keep Yourself Alive / Instrumental Inferno / Battle Theme / Flash / The Hero / Brighton Rock / Crazy Little Thing Called Love / Bohemian Rhapsody / We Will Rock You (slow) / We Are The Champions / Encore: Another One Bites The Dust / Sheer Heart Attack / 2nd Encore: Tie Your Mother Down / God Save The Queen

December 8 ↗**/9** ↗**/10** ↗
Wembley Arena, London
■ *First night*: Jailhouse Rock / We Will Rock You (fast) / Let Me Entertain You / Play The Game / Medley: Mustapha; Death On Two Legs; Killer Queen; I'm In Love With My Car; Get Down Make Love / Need Your Loving Tonight / Save Me / Now I'm Here / Dragon Attack / Fat Bottomed Girls / Love Of My Life / Keep Yourself Alive / Battle Theme / Flash / The Hero / Brighton Rock / Crazy Little Thing Called Love / Bohemian Rhapsody / We Will Rock You (slow) / We

WEMBLEY ARENA
HARVEY GOLDSMITH ENTERTAINMENTS
presents

Queen

WEDNESDAY, 10 DECEMBER, 1980
at 8 p.m.

ARENA

£6.00 ★

TO BE RETAINED See conditions on back

DECEMBER
10

ENTER AT
SOUTH DOOR
BLOCK
F

ROW
17

SEAT
31

Are The Champions / Encore: *Another One Bites The Dust* / *Sheer Heart Attack* / 2nd *Encore: Tie Your Mother Down* / *God Save The Queen*

Following the opening number, Freddie greets the home town audience with the words: "It's fucking cold in this auditorium, especially for those at the back. Don't worry, we'll soon set your arses on fire!" He then launches into a blistering recitation of 'We Will Rock You'.

❖ On December 8, the *Flash Gordon* soundtrack album is released in the UK. It peaked at number 10. The American release, which reaches number 23 in the *Billboard* charts, is held back until January 27, 1981.

■ *Second night*: *We Will Rock You (fast)* / *Let Me Entertain You* / *Play The Game* / *Medley: Mustapha; Death On Two Legs; Killer Queen; I'm In Love With My Car; Get Down Make Love* / *Save Me* / *Now I'm Here* / *Dragon Attack* / *Now I'm Here* / *Fat Bottomed Girls* / *Love Of My Life* / *Imagine* / *Battle Theme* / *Flash* / *The Hero* / *Brighton Rock* / *Crazy Little Thing Called Love* / *Bohemian Rhapsody* / *We Will Rock You (slow)* / *We Are The Champions* / Encore: *Another One Bites The Dust* / *Sheer Heart Attack* / 2nd Encore: *Tie Your Mother Down* / *God Save The Queen*

Queen play 'Imagine' as a tribute to John Lennon, shot dead by deranged Beatles fan Mark Chapman in New York the previous day. Like everyone touched by Lennon's spirit, the band are devastated at the news and want to pay tribute to one of their greatest heroes in their show. Limited rehearsal time does not permit the best rendition

ever, but the technical quality is secondary to the gesture.

☛ Roger (in 1981): "John Lennon was my ultimate hero. He was the best living songwriter, and one of the best rock'n'roll voices I've ever heard. And when you think of what he did in his life - he stood up for what he thought was right. I just couldn't believe it. I still haven't quite come to terms with the fact that he's not here any more."

■ *Final night*: *Jailhouse Rock* / *We Will Rock You* / *Let Me Entertain You* / *Play The Game* / *Medley: Mustapha; Death On Two Legs; Killer Queen; I'm In Love With My Car; Get Down Make Love* / *Save Me* / *Now I'm Here; Dragon Attack; Now I'm Here (Reprise)* / *Fat Bottomed Girls* / *Love Of My Life* / *Keep Yourself Alive* / *Flash* / *The Hero* / *Brighton Rock* / *Guitar Solo* / *Crazy Little Thing Called Love* / *Bohemian Rhapsody* / *Tie Your Mother Down* / Encore: *Another One Bites The Dust* / *Sheer Heart Attack* / 2nd Encore: *We Will Rock You* / *We Are The Champions* / *God Save The Queen*

December 12/13
Forêst Nationale, Brussels
■ *Second night*: *Jailhouse Rock* / *We Will Rock You* / *Let Me Entertain You* / *Play The Game* / *Medley: Mustapha; Death On Two Legs; Killer Queen; I'm In Love With My Car; Get Down Make Love* / *Save Me* / *Now I'm Here; Dragon Attack; Now I'm Here (Reprise)* / *Fat Bottomed Girls* / *Love Of My Life* / *Keep*

ORIGINAL SOUNDTRACK MUSIC BY QUEEN

Yourself Alive / Instrumental Inferno / Battle Theme / Flash / The Hero / Brighton Rock / Guitar Solo / Crazy Little Thing Called Love / Bohemian Rhapsody / Tie Your Mother Down / Encore: Another One Bites The Dust / Sheer Heart Attack / 2nd Encore: We Will Rock You / We Are The Champions / God Save The Queen

December 14 ♪
Festhalle, Frankfurt

Identical set to previous night, but with 'Imagine' making its second and last appearance in a Queen show, again following 'Love Of My Life'.

December 16
Hall Rheus, Strasbourg

December 18
Olympiahalle, Munich

■ *Jailhouse Rock / We Will Rock You / Let Me Entertain You / Play The Game / Medley: Mustapha; Death On Two Legs; Killer Queen; I'm In Love With My Car; Get Down Make Love / Save Me / Now I'm Here; Dragon Attack; Now I'm Here (Reprise) / Fat Bottomed Girls / Love Of My Life / Keep Yourself Alive / Instrumental Inferno / Battle Theme / Flash / The Hero / Brighton Rock / Guitar Solo / Crazy Little Thing Called Love / Bohemian Rhapsody / Tie Your Mother Down / Encore: Another One Bites The Dust / Sheer Heart Attack / 2nd Encore: We Will Rock You / We Are The Champions / God Save The Queen*

December 19

The band fly back to England to spend Christmas at home. By the end of 1980 they have sold 45 million albums and 25 million singles worldwide.

1981

Japan 1981 - Japan Tour

On February 8, the band leave London and head for Japan for brief rehearsals ahead of five consecutive shows at the vast Budokan Hall in Tokyo. On the same flight as the band is the Nottingham Forest football team who are travelling to Japan to play in the world championships. On a rare day off between shows, Roger, Brian and John attend one of the matches. Forest lose 1-0.

February 10

The Japanese première of the *Flash Gordon* film takes place in Tokyo, to which Queen are invited as honoured guests. The band are interviewed on stage by top Japanese DJ Yuki Okazaki before the film is screened.

February 12/13/16/17/18
Budokan Hall, Tokyo

■ *First night*: *Jailhouse Rock / We Will Rock You / Let Me Entertain You / Play The Game / Medley: Mustapha; Death On Two Legs; Killer Queen; I'm In Love With My Car; Get Down Make Love / Save Me / Now I'm Here; Dragon Attack; Now I'm Here (Reprise) / Fat Bottomed Girls / Love Of My Life / Keep Yourself Alive / Instrumental Inferno / Vultan's Theme / Battle Theme / Flash / The Hero / Brighton Rock / Guitar Solo / Crazy Little Thing Called Love / Bohemian Rhapsody / Tie Your Mother Down / Encore: Another One Bites The Dust / Sheer Heart Attack / 2nd Encore: We Will Rock You / We Are The Champions / God Save The Queen*

Queen perform all five shows here before capacity audiences of 12,000.

Curiously, 'Teo Torriatte' is performed only on the last night.

Second night*: same as previous night, but with 'Need Your Loving Tonight' after the medley and before 'Save Me'.*

■ ***Third night****: Jailhouse Rock / We Will Rock You / Let Me Entertain You / Play The Game / Medley: Mustapha; Death On Two Legs; Killer Queen; I'm In Love With My Car; Get Down Make Love / Rock It / Save Me / Now I'm Here; Dragon Attack; Now I'm Here (Reprise) / Fat Bottomed Girls / Love Of My Life / Keep Yourself Alive / Instrumental Inferno / Vultan's Theme / Battle Theme / Flash / The Hero / Brighton Rock / Guitar Solo / Crazy Little Thing Called Love / Bohemian Rhapsody / Tie Your Mother Down / Encore: Another One Bites The Dust / Sheer Heart Attack / 2nd Encore: We Will Rock You / We Are The Champions / God Save The Queen*

Gary Numan attends all three shows here as he too is in Japan on tour.

While Queen are in Japan for these shows, *Music Life* magazine release a commemorative book entitled *Queen The Miracle* containing 104 pages of beautifully illustrated full colour pictures and text – much of it pertaining to concerts.

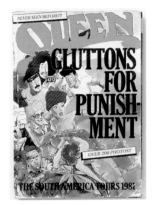

■ ***Final night****: Jailhouse Rock / We Will Rock You (fast) / Let Me Entertain You / Play The Game / Medley: Mustapha; Death On Two Legs; Killer Queen; I'm In Love With My Car; Get Down Make Love / Rock It / Save Me / Now I'm Here / Dragon Attack / Now I'm Here (reprise) / Love Of My Life / Keep Yourself Alive / Instrumental Inferno / Vultan's Theme / Battle Theme / Flash / The Hero / Crazy Little Thing Called Love / Bohemian Rhapsody / Tie Your Mother Down / Encore: Another One Bites The Dust / Sheer Heart Attack / 2nd Encore: We Will Rock You (slow) / We Are The Champions / Teo Torriatte / God Save The Queen*

Note the unusual placing of 'Teo Torriate' in the set, replacing 'Champions' as the closing song. Following this show, Freddie decides to stay on in Japan to undertake crucial last minute shopping. Having left himself the minimum amount of time to reach the airport, when he does eventually arrive for his flight to New York, he boards the wrong aircraft.

SOUTH AMERICA 1981 - Gluttons For Punishment Tour

In mid-February, Queen fly to Rio De Janeiro for final preparations for their first (and only, as it turns out) tour of South America. From here they move on to Buenos Aires where they are greeted

at the airport by their own music playing over the public address system. At the express orders of Argentina's President, the band are also permitted to bypass lengthy arrival procedures,

The obligatory press conference is broadcast live on national television, and such is the interest in the band's progress throughout the tour that local radio and TV companies *Radio Cidade* and *TV Bandeirantes* run frequent Queen news bulletins that interrupt or replace scheduled programmes. Following the press conference, they encounter a phenomenon that will sustain throughout the entire tour.

➧ John Deacon: "We just about made it to our cars in time, rattled and bruised. We had only gone a few hundred yards when the driver stopped for petrol. Within seconds the car was surrounded by girls battering on the windows and roof. The driver had no idea what was going on. They'd never had to deal with anything like that before."

The equipment required to stage these shows – among the biggest Queen will ever perform - consists of 72 specially built speakers, 16 tons of scaffolding100 rolls (three tons) of artificial turf (to protect the sacred football pitches), and 350 aircraft landing lights (which make up the lighting rig). Every square inch of aircraft space is filled. The collective weight of the gear is a

staggering 75 tons. Each concert costs around £25,000 to stage, and the tour entourage involves 34 people.

Because there are no equipment hire firms in South America, 20 tons of sound equipment is shipped in from Japan. Not only is the flight from Tokyo to Buenos Aires hideously expensive, it is also, at 36 hours, the longest air route between capital cities anywhere in the world. A further 40 tons of equipment is flown in from Miami, including additional artificial turf to cover football fields on which the band will perform - plus 16 tons of stage scaffolding from Los Angeles, and five tons of lighting gear.

When the band's production manager Chris Lamb arrives in Buenos Aires after an exhausting eighteen hour flight from Los Angeles, he is promptly arrested for being in possession of 'obscene material'. The offending items are tour stage passes, which feature an illustration of a Japanese girl facing Carmen Miranda. Both are wearing only suggestive grins and native head attire, and one is shown holding a peeled banana in a none too subtle manner. Although Lamb takes an unscheduled detour to the local police station, he is eventually released.

Meanwhile, the equipment, which has thus far survived its mammoth journey from Japan without incident, encounters problems of its own. When one of the forty foot containers falls off the transporter truck into the street, it remains there for two days until a crane large enough to lift it can be located.

● Despite every Customs document being labelled with strict warnings that they be retained at every step along the tour, tour manager Gerry Stickells is somewhat alarmed to observe every last one of them being ripped to shreds and binned by the first Customs official they encounter. Stickells later recalls, "No explanation was forthcoming."

Setting up the monstrous stage structure mostly entails working in extreme temperatures – frequently over 100 degrees, and so many of the crew and the local hired help take to wearing shorts, vests and caps. This seemingly harmless attire causes a problem one day when one of the crew ventures into town on an errand. He is arrested, hauled off to a cell and the alarm is raised when he fails to return. Unbeknown to the

Queen staff, there is a strict law forbidding men to wear shorts in public.

Following a brief spell in jail, the unfortunate individual is released.

February 28 ♫
Velez Sarfield, Buenos Aires, Argentina ①
■ *We Will Rock You / Let Me Entertain You / Play The Game / Somebody To Love / Medley: Mustapha; Death On Two Legs; Killer Queen; I'm In Love With My Car; Get Down Make Love / Need Your Loving Tonight / Rock It / Save Me / Now I'm Here; Dragon Attack; Now I'm Here (Reprise) / Fat Bottomed Girls / Love Of My Life / Keep Yourself Alive / Instrumental Inferno / Flash / The Hero / Brighton Rock / Guitar Solo / Crazy Little Thing Called Love / Bohemian Rhapsody / Tie Your Mother Down / Encore: Another One Bites The Dust / Sheer Heart Attack / 2nd Encore: We Will Rock You / We Are The Champions / God Save The Queen*

● Prior to the tour the band had been apprehensive that fans unfamiliar with their show might be confused by their peculiar concert routines, and Freddie's particular kind of banter. Europe, Australia and America are well accustomed to Queen on stage, but this is an entirely different proposition. How might they react, for instance, to the band walking off stage during 'Bo Rhap', or to Freddie inviting them to sing along with him? There is no way of knowing. They will simply have to suck it and see.

Thankfully, Queen need not have worried. The audience reaction exceeds everyone's best expectations. When it comes time for Freddie and Brian to perform 'Love Of My Life', the excited masses join in with the first to last words, exactly like a London, Liverpool or Paris crowd, without even a hint of a prompt from Freddie – who is stunned. "I stood there blinking away like mad and swallowing hard, with the same feeling that the last night of the proms gives me."

Queen perform before a capacity 54,000 people at this venue, and go on to play sell-out shows at every venue hereafter.

'Jailhouse Rock' no longer kicks off most of the

174

shows, and 'Mustapha' begins the medley only occasionally.

↗ 'DON'T CRY FOR QUEEN ARGENTINA', by Nina Myskow, *The Sun*, March 20, 1981: *'Supergroup numero uno: That is the new title that Queen have been crowned in South America. Amid scenes of Beatle-type adulation and frenzy, the four-man British rock band have sparked another revolution in the turbulent history of Argentina. A rock revolution. In the first of a series of huge outdoor concerts, they conquered new territory with a dazzling display of rock at its best.'*

↗ 'BUENOS ROCKERS', by Mike Reynolds and Mike Ashwell, *Record Mirror*, March 7, 1981: *'QUEEN have brought a whole new meaning to the word revolution in South America. For the British superstars, who are sinking nearly £1 million of their own money into a two-week tour of the Continent, have turned the Latin Americans on their heads with their unique brand of rock.*

'We watched in amazement from the grandstand of the magnificent purpose built Vellez Sarfield soccer stadium in Buenos Aires last Friday, on the opening night of the tour. A happy, swaying crowd of 40,000 Argentineans — ranging from small children to mothers and fathers — applauded politely as the strains of their country's World Cup victory song boomed through the giant speakers.

'Then it was Queen's turn. And if lead singer Freddie Mercury had any doubts about how they would be received they must have disappeared with his first look at the audience. Everywhere, from the top of the stands to the grass near the stage, people were holding up lighters . . . and calling for their favourite Queen songs in English...'

March 1
Velez Sarfield, Buenos Aires
■ We Will Rock You / Let Me Entertain You / Play The Game / Somebody To Love / Medley: Killer Queen; I'm In Love With My Car; Get Down Make Love / Need Your Loving Tonight / Save Me / Now I'm Here; Dragon Attack; Now I'm Here (Reprise) / Fat Bottomed Girls / Love Of My Life / Keep Yourself Alive / Instrumental Inferno / Flash / The Hero / Brighton Rock / Guitar Solo / Crazy Little Thing Called Love / Bohemian Rhapsody / Tie Your Mother Down / Encore: Another One Bites The Dust / Sheer Heart Attack / 2nd Encore: We Will Rock You / We Are The Champions / God Save The Queen

This show is broadcast live on national television and is watched by an incredible 35 million people in Argentina and Brazil. Bootleg audio and video copies are quickly circulated. Many find their way to Europe and North America and quickly become much sought-after collectors' items. The specially adapted set features a running order not played elsewhere, and fans are anxious to familiarise themselves with it.

↗ *Rolling Stone*, by James Henke, February 1981: *'When I return to Velez Sarfield that evening for the show, the stadium is swarming with kids — and cops. These are crusty, corpulent tough guys — not the boot-camp boys I saw at the airport. And it doesn't take long to find out that they mean business. When one American writer snaps a photo of the 20-odd billy-club-wielding policemen who are cordoning off the backstage area, he's pinned against a government owned Falcon and threatened at knife point with the loss of a finger until he yields his film. "No problem." Sure.*

''Un supergrupo numero uno,' the MC announces as the lights dim, and with a burst of smoke, Queen appears on stage and begins hammering out its anthem, 'We Will Rock You.' Mercury – dressed in a

Queen Live '81

white, sleeveless Superman T-shirt, red vinyl pants and a black vinyl jacket – frequently stops singing and dares the audience to carry the weight. And carry the weight they do: the fans seem to know all the lyrics throughout the 110-minute show – which, if for no other reason, is impressive for the number of hits the group is able to offer, such as 'Keep Yourself Alive', 'Killer Queen', 'Bohemian Rhapsody', 'Fat Bottomed Girls' and 'Bicycle Race'.

'Though the band-audience interaction is remarkable, the crowd responds with such unquestioning devotion I get the feeling that if Freddie Mercury told them to shave their heads, they'd do it...

'... For the encore, the band reprises 'We Will Rock You', then bounds into 'We Are The Champions'. Mercury, by this time wearing only a pair of black leather short shorts and a matching policeman's leather hat, struts around the stage like some hybrid of Robert Plant and Peter Allen, climactically kicking over a speaker cabinet and bashing it with his microphone stand. Pretty ridiculous in this day and age, but the kids love it.'

March 4
Estadio Municipal, Mar Del Plata
■ We Will Rock You / Let Me Entertain You / Play The Game / Somebody To Love / Medley: Death On Two Legs; Killer Queen; I'm In Love With My Car; Get

Down Make Love / Need Your Loving Tonight / Save Me / Now I'm Here; Dragon Attack; Now I'm Here (Reprise) / Fat Bottomed Girls / Love Of My Life / Keep Yourself Alive / Instrumental Inferno / Flash / The Hero / Brighton Rock / Guitar Solo / Crazy Little Thing Called Love / Bohemian Rhapsody / Tie Your Mother Down / Encore: Another One Bites The Dust / Sheer Heart Attack / 2nd Encore: We Will Rock You / We Are The Champions / God Save The Queen

March 6
Alletico Rosario Central, Rosario

March 8 ↗
Velez Sarfield, Buenos Aires
■ We Will Rock You / Let Me Entertain You / Play The Game / Somebody To Love / Medley: Death On Two Legs; Killer Queen; I'm In Love With My Car; Get Down Make Love / Need Your Loving Tonight / Rock It / Save Me / Now I'm Here; Dragon Attack; Now I'm Here (Reprise) / Fat Bottomed Girls / Love Of My Life / Keep Yourself Alive / Instrumental Inferno / Flash / The Hero / Brighton Rock / Guitar Solo / Crazy Little Thing Called Love / Bohemian Rhapsody / Tie Your Mother Down / Encore: Another One Bites The Dust / Sheer Heart Attack / 2nd Encore: We Will Rock You / We Are The Champions / God Save The Queen

This show is also broadcast on national television. Much later, it will surface on the *Rare Live* video – as will other footage from this tour.

While in Buenos Aires the band are invited to the home of General Viola (President Designate of Argentina). Most of them attend. Later, they are introduced to footballer Diego Maradona, who joins Queen on stage that night. He says a few words to the startled audience then leaves as the band continue with 'Bites The Dust'.

Before playing the final two shows of the tour, the band take a short break. John and Roger head for London, Freddie flies to New Orleans and Brian remains in Rio.

Additional concerts in Venezuela and Mexico, which are eventually confirmed for September, are not at this time finalised. Concerts in New

Zealand and Australia are also discussed but ultimately do not happen.

Jim Beach would later explain Queen's thinking on playing in South America.

● "The actual cost of appearing there was so enormous that the profit margin for the band was quite small, but the promotion was marvelous. During our last week in Argentina every one of Queen's 10 albums filled the top 10 positions in the charts. In Brazil 50 per cent of the population is under the age of 21, that is a massive potential audience."

Roger Taylor too is asked for his take on the tour: "In some ways I was surprised that we didn't get more criticism for playing South America. I didn't think we were being used as tools by political régimes, although obviously we have to co-operate with them. We were playing for the people. We didn't go there with the wool pulled over our eyes. We know fully what the situation is like in some of those countries. But for a time we made thousands of people happy. Surely that must count for something. We weren't playing for the government, we were playing to lots of ordinary Argentinean people. In fact, we were asked to meet the President, President Viola, and I refused. I didn't want to meet him because that would have been playing into their hands."

March 20♪/21♪
Morumbi Stadium, Sao Paulo, Brazil ①
■ *First night*: *We Will Rock You / Let Me Entertain You / Play The Game / Somebody To Love / Medley: Mustapha; Death On Two Legs; Killer Queen; I'm In Love With My Car; Get Down Make Love / Need Your Loving Tonight / Save Me / Now I'm Here; Dragon Attack; Now I'm Here (Reprise) / Fat Bottomed Girls / Love Of My Life / Keep Yourself Alive / Instrumental Inferno / Flash / The Hero / Brighton Rock / Guitar Solo / Crazy Little Thing Called Love / Bohemian Rhapsody / Tie Your Mother Down / Encore: Another One Bites The Dust / Sheer Heart Attack / 2nd Encore: We Will Rock You / We Are The Champions / God Save The Queen*

Before permission can be granted to use this giant stadium, 40 local people are drafted in to jump up and down on the protective coating covering the sacred turf. It is only after anxious football officials are absolutely satisfied the grass can sustain the stresses of the attending masses that the two shows are confirmed.

Queen break yet more records at this venue, attracting the biggest paying audience in history. There are 131,000 people at the opening, with a further 120,000 the second night.

This stadium is the second biggest in the world. The band had intended to also play the biggest – Maracana Stadium in Rio, but had been refused permission. This would have held 206,000 people.

Second night: same as previous night, but with 'Rock It' instead of 'Need Your Loving Tonight'.
↗ Ray Coleman reports: *'Flanked by the menacing security gorillas as they make their way down the players' tunnel to face the wall of noise emanating from the 130,000 fans before whom they will play, they appear small and fragile. But once on stage, emerging from the billowing clouds of their smoke machine and illuminated by the dazzling colours of their kaleidoscopic lighting equipment, the seductive power of rock music takes its own control, and the armed guards who surrounded Queen watch in bewilderment, as the youth of Sao Paulo open their hearts and lungs to the first rock concerts they have ever seen, in a*

touching non-violent dialogue of music and friendship.'

Immediately after the last show ends, the valuable equipment is hastily dismantled and loaded on to a specially chartered New York-bound 747 cargo plane before local Customs and Excise red tape can delay it, or before it can be confiscated or stolen. Thesa are very real possibilities, because much earlier in the tour Gerry Stickells notices the words EARTH, WIND AND FIRE on spotlights supplied by the local concert organisers. Clearly this represents equipment ghosted away from their shows at some point previously. Gerry is taking no such risk with Queen's equipment.

It now seems that all the problems (and many there were!) encountered on the tour are finally at an end. This is not the case. The jumbo develops compass problems during flight and is forced to land in Puerto Rico. The four crew members left behind to supervise the equipment complete the appropriate paperwork and book into a hotel for the night. When they return the next morning they discover that the airport ground crew have broken the steering gear, and the flight is delayed yet further. Eventually the crew and gear does reach its American destination. The equipment remains in storage there until it is needed for the second leg of the tour, in September.

In his letter to the fan club members (Autumn 1981 issue), John Deacon reflects briefly on the forthcoming shows: *"When you read this we should have finished our recording session in Montreux, Switzerland and be on our way to Caracas, Venezuela. We hope to be playing Rio in Brazil before moving on to Mexico. It's always very exciting to play in a country for the first time, and 1981 has really been our year for discovering new audiences we didn't even know existed. Thank You... John."*

September

The band spend the early part of September working on new material for what will later emerge as the *Hot Space* album. Work is interrupted, however, for the second visit to South America, two Canadian shows and the Christmas break, but it resumes again in the new year. The sessions will eventually end in March 1982.

SOUTH AMERICA 1981 - Gluttons For Punishment Tour (2nd Leg)

On September 15, Queen travel to New Orleans for rehearsals before resuming the South American tour. They then fly to Caracas on September 21. As with the American tour in 1980, the lighting rig used throughout all the South American dates is Fly Swatters.

September 25/26/27
Poliedro De Caracas, Caracas, Venezuela ①
■ *First night: We Will Rock You / Let Me Entertain You / Play The Game / Somebody To Love / Medley: Killer Queen; I'm In Love With My Car; Get Down Make Love / Save Me / Now I'm Here; Dragon Attack; Now I'm Here (Reprise) / Fat Bottomed Girls / Love Of My Life / Keep Yourself Alive / Instrumental Inferno / Flash / The Hero / Brighton Rock / Guitar Solo / Crazy Little Thing Called Love / Bohemian Rhapsody / Tie Your Mother Down / Encore: Another One Bites The Dust / Sheer Heart Attack / 2nd Encore: We Will Rock You / We Are The Champions / God Save The Queen*

Despite a six-month gap between shows, there are no significant changes to the setlist. 'Death On Two Legs' no longer features, with 'Killer Queen' taking its place as the medley opening number.

Two additional shows proposed for this venue, scheduled for September 29 and 30, are cancelled, as is a second show at Monterey on October 10. The concerts in Guadalajara, Mexico on October 15 and 16 are moved to Puebla on the 16th and 17th.

On September 30 the band fly back to New Orleans for final rehearsals. They then travel on to Mexico on October 8.

Two other shows in Venezuela (September 29 and 30) are cancelled when former President Romulo Ethancourt dies and the country's population goes into a period of mourning. Ethancourt's deteriorating health had already jeopardised three shows, but he'd held on long enough for them to go ahead.

☛ When an advance party of crew members attempts to cross the border into Mexico, they are told it is impossible to issue all eighteen with visas. Only six per day can be issued. Threatened with spending six unplanned days awaiting passage into Mexico, and faced with a second refusal the following day, the crew needs a plan – and quick. With inflexible schedules to be met and time running out fast, there is only one alternative - bribery. An 'offer' is made and all eighteen are granted visas and permitted to cross the border together. Gerry Stickells later puts this down to "British ingenuity triumphing yet again."

October 8

Gerry Stickells is contacted at his hotel room by an anxious journalist calling to confirm the time of the Queen interview next morning. The lady has been promised exclusive time with the band by an unscrupulous local promoter who never surfaces again, but rather naïvely she has paid the man 10,000 pesos for the privilege. Queen know nothing of the arrangement. This is not an isolated incident.

October 9

Estadio Universitario de Monterrey, Monterrey Nuevo Leon, Mexico ①

■ *We Will Rock You / Let Me Entertain You / Play*

The Game / Somebody To Love / Medley: Killer Queen; I'm In Love With My Car; Get Down Make Love / Save Me / Now I'm Here; Dragon Attack; Now I'm Here (Reprise) / Fat Bottomed Girls / Love Of My Life / Keep Yourself Alive / Instrumental Inferno / Flash / The Hero / Brighton Rock / Guitar Solo / Crazy Little Thing Called Love / Bohemian Rhapsody / Tie Your Mother Down / Encore: Another One Bites The Dust / Sheer Heart Attack / 2nd Encore: We Will Rock You / We Are The Champions / God Save The Queen

October 16/17

Estadio Zaragoza, Puebla, Mexico (now called Aquiles Serdan)

■ *First night: Jailhouse Rock / We Will Rock You / Let Me Entertain You / Play The Game / Somebody To Love / Medley: Killer Queen; I'm In Love With My Car; Get Down Make Love / Save Me / Now I'm Here; Dragon Attack; Now I'm Here (Reprise) / Love Of My Life / Keep Yourself Alive / Instrumental Inferno / Flash / The Hero / Brighton Rock / Guitar Solo / Crazy Little Thing Called Love / Bohemian Rhapsody / Tie Your Mother Down / Encore: Another One Bites The Dust / Sheer Heart Attack / 2nd Encore: We Will Rock You / We Are The Champions / God Save The Queen*

'Jailhouse Rock' begins the show here for the last time. Thereafter it is performed as an encore song, or as part of the rock'n'roll medley. This is also the first time 'I Go Crazy' features in Brian's solo.

Anyone attending this show with the intention of bootlegging it is aggrieved to find security staff awaiting them as they pass through the turnstile. Each person is thoroughly searched and any batteries are confiscated. However, the Mexican are a step ahead. Once inside the stadium there is a stall selling batteries - newly confiscated 'second hand' batteries – at highly inflated prices.

Second night: same as previous night, but without 'Jailhouse Rock'

These shows are massively succesful and Queen enjoy album and single sales here which no-one foresees.

In early 1983, Jim Beach and Gerry Stickells fly

back to South America for discussions for further gigs. Although venues and dates are pencilled in for the end of year, all are eventually shelved when the enormous costs, and risks, prove too great.

Queen do return to Brazil, however, in January 1985, to perform at the two day Rock In Rio Festival. It will be their last visit to South America.

❖ October 26

A full seven months ahead of the *Hot Space* album release, on which it will appear, 'Under Pressure' is issued in the UK. Coupled with the enigmatic non-album cut 'Soul Brother', the David Bowie joint venture gives Queen their second number one. Surprisingly, the same pairing reaches only number 29 in America.

❖ November 2

Greatest Hits is issued in the UK, having been put back two weeks from an October 12 release. Originally planned for December 1980, *Hits* was shelved to make way for the *Flash Gordon* project. Because of the band's various single successes in different territories, numerous variations of the compilation are issued. 'Love Of My Life' is included on the South American disc, because it had spent many weeks at number one there. Likewise, the Japanese counterpart includes 'Teo Torriatte' for the same reason. Other variations include 'Keep Yourself Alive' on the American, Australian, Canadian and New Zealand editions (in spite of its failure to chart there), 'Sweet Lady' on the Bulgarian and Russian issues, and 'Tie Your Mother Down' on the Canadian, Australian and New Zealand versions. All variations will become collectable.

In conjunction with the album, two sister products are also issued: *Greatest Flix*, an eighteen track video compilation, and a *Greatest Pix* book. This triple marketing concept is repeated for the *Hits II* sequel a decade down the line.

November 22

The band travel to Canada for rehearsals and last minute preparations for two concerts which are to be filmed. The shows are organised purely because the band want to put together a full length film to properly document their live show.

❖ The footage from both shows is edited together to give the impression of just one. On September 10, 1984, a 21-track aptly titled *We Will Rock You* video is released. It is the first commercially available film of Queen in concert.

'Under Pressure' is included in the set for the first time, and 'Need Your Loving Tonight' is dropped.

November 24⏎/25⏎

Forum, Montreal, Quebec

■ *Both nights*: We Will Rock You (fast) / Let Me Entertain You / Play The Game /Somebody To Love / Killer Queen / I'm In Love With My Car /Get Down, Make Love / Save Me /Now I'm Here /Under Pressure /Flash/ The Hero /Keep Yourself Alive / Guitar Solo; Drum Solo/ Crazy Little Thing Called Love / Bohemian Rhapsody /Tie Your Mother Down / 1st Encore: Another One Bites The Dust / Sheer Heart Attack / Jailhouse Rock / 2nd Encore: We Will Rock You (slow) / We Are The Champions / God Save The Queen

Most of the above material appears on the *We Will Rock You* video. Only 'Flash's Theme' and 'The Hero' are absent. Although this video is a welcome addition to Queen collections, many will have preferred something from 1979 instead.

Freddie's opening words: "Hello Montreal... long time no see. You wanna get crazy? Okay let's go!"

November 26

Queen fly home for the Christmas period.

December 6

The band go to Munich to continue sessions for the *Hot Space* album, with the studio's resident producer Mack.

1982

EUROPE 1982 - The Hot Space Tour

Following several day's rehearsals, the band fly to Gothenburg on April 8 for the opening show in Europe. The tour comprises 30 performances in nine cities, at 22 different venues. It would have included other more ulliustrious venues had things gone according to plan.

Although applications to play at Manchester United and Arsenal football grounds (Old Trafford and Highbury) are made, both are turned down. Magistrates refuse to issue licences because of objections from local residents, despite the all-clear being given by the local Council and the Police. Apart from that, there are no chemical toilet facilities available to hire because all have been booked for Pope John Paul II's personal appearances around the country. The proposed Manchester show is replaced by one in Leeds

(May 29), and the Arsenal show by one at Milton Keynes (June 5).

Plans for a show at the Albert Hall are abandoned because of fears that the famous domed ceiling might cave in under the weight of the Queen lighting rig.

The support act for the tour is British band Bow Wow Wow. Regrettably, they will not stay for the duration because fans at one gig decide to pelt them with bottles and food. Brian May is outraged. He later says that he never could have imagined so-called Qeen fans acting in such an appalling way to a guest of the band. He is further disappointed that the group quit before they reach Germany, where they have sold some records and are likely to be well received. Bow Wow Wow's final dates are at Leiden, Holland, on April 24/25.

🗩 Brian: "We liked them very much. There was this certain section in the audience that didn't like them, who found them very modern. Our audience, it's a sad comment, is perhaps a little narrow-minded in that way. It's only a small percentage. Most people gave them a very good hearing. But there were a few people who went so far as to throw things at them, which to be honest I was pretty disgusted at. Unfortunately Bow Wow Wow decided to throw them back, as a matter of policy. On a couple of nights in particular it just snowballed into a big fight, which became very silly."

Annabella of Bow Wow Wow: "The fans were extremely hostile. We decided to come home before one of us got badly hurt. There was no point in carrying on really."

Matthew Ashman's response was more from the heart. "All those tossers wanted to do was kiss Queen's arse... well bollocks to them."

Another British band called Airrace are drafted in for the remaining dates.

For certain numbers Queen are augmented on stage by keyboard player Morgan Fisher, formerly of Love Affair and Mott The Hoople. The set now includes new material from the *Hot Space* album - 'Action This Day', 'Staying Power', 'Body Language' and 'Back Chat'. 'Under Pressure' was already introduced for the two Canadian shows in November, and other material from the album will feature in the set in subsequent concerts, but was for now absent - 'Put Out The Fire', 'Calling All Girls' and 'Life Is Real'.

'Let Me Entertain You' and 'Sheer Heart Attack' are dropped from the set, but 'Liar' and 'Mustapha' make more frequent appearances again. Other material is just shuffled about – as is the norm. Queen moved songs around within the set right from the very first shows in 1970, through to the very last dates on the final tour. 'Jailhouse Rock', 'Bohemian Rhapsody', 'Death On Two Legs', 'Brighton Rock', 'Liar', 'Keep Yourself Alive', 'Fat Bottomed Girls', 'We Will Rock You (slow version)', and especially 'Now I'm Here' and 'Tie Your Mother Down' are all good examples of this. All jumped about all over setlist during their concert lifetime.

April 9
Scandinavium, Gothenburg

April 10 ⌀
Isstadion, Stockholm
■ *Flash / The Hero / Tie Your Mother Down / Action This Day / Play The Game / Somebody To Love / Staying Power / Get Down Make Love / Body Language / Under Pressure / Fat Bottomed Girls / Love Of My Life / Save Me / Guitar Solo / Liar / Crazy Little Thing Called Love / Bohemian Rhapsody / Now I'm Here; Dragon Attack / Now I'm Here (Reprise) / Encore: Another One Bites The Dust / Bohemian Rhapsody / Sheer Heart Attack / 2nd Encore: We Will Rock You / We Are The Champions / God Save The Queen*

At the beginning of 'Save Me' here, Freddie starts to sing, "It started off so well," but Brian does not accompany him on piano, as he cannot hear him properly. Freddie stops, announces "It didn't start THAT fucking well!" laughs, and then begins again. This is typical of Freddie's quick wit. 'Action This Day' features Roger's backing vocals every bit as prominently as on the album version. Although by no means the strongest track on *Hot Space*, it takes on a new life in the concert forum.

April 12
Drammenshallen, Oslo ①

April 16/17 ⌀
Hallenstadion, Zurich

■ *First night*: *Flash / The Hero / Tie Your Mother Down / Action This Day / Play The Game / Somebody To Love / Get Down Make Love / Back Chat / Liar / Love Of My Life / Save Me / Mustapha / Fat Bottomed Girls / Crazy Little Thing Called Love / Bohemian Rhapsody / Now I'm Here / Dragon Attack / Encore: Another One Bites The Dust / Sheer Heart Attack / We Will Rock You / Under Pressure / Staying Power / We Are The Champions /God Save The Queen*

■ *Second night*: *Flash / The Hero / Tie Your Mother Down /. Action This Day / Play The Game / Staying Power / Get Down Make Love / Back Chat / Under Pressure / Love Of My Life / Mustapha / Save Me / Fat*

Bottomed Girls / Crazy Little Thing Called Love / Bohemian Rhapsody / Now I'm Here / Dragon Attack / Now I'm Here (reprise) / 1st Encore: Another One Bites The Dust / Sheer Heart Attack / 2nd Encore: We Will Rock You / We Are The Champions / God Save The Queen

These setlists are correct – as unlikely as they seem.

April 19
Palais De Sport, Paris

■ *First night*: *Flash / The Hero / Tie Your Mother Down / Action This Day / Play The Game / Staying Power / Somebody To Love / Get Down Make Love / Body Language / Back Chat (Rhythm Version) / Under Pressure / Love Of My Life / Save Me / Back Chat / Fat Bottomed Girls / Crazy Little Thing Called Love / Bohemian Rhapsody / Now I'm Here; Dragon Attack; Now I'm Here (Reprise) / Encore: Another One Bites The Dust / Sheer Heart Attack / 2nd Encore: We Will Rock You / We Are The Champions / God Save The Queen*

❖ Also on April 19, the band's twentieth UK single is released. 'Body Language' is the second track to be lifted from *Hot Space*. It fails to make the top 20 and peaks at a lowly number 25. The choice of B-side is universal: Freddie's tribute to John Lennon entitled 'Life Is Real'.

Released on the same day in America too, the pairing fares rather better there than at home, peaking at number11. The accompanying promo video is considered too provocative for TV broadcast and is also annoyingly ignored for the *Greatest Flix 2* video.

April 20
Palais De Sport, Lyon

April 22/23
Forêst Nationale, Brussels

■ *Second night*: *Flash / The Hero / We Will Rock You / Action This Day / Play The Game / Staying Power / Somebody To Love / Get Down Make Love / Instrumental Inferno / Under Pressure / Liar / Love Of My Life / Save Me / Fat Bottomed Girls / Crazy Little*

Thing Called Love / Bohemian Rhapsody / Tie Your Mother Down / Now I'm Here; Dragon Attack; Now I'm Here (Reprise) / Encore: Another One Bites The Dust / Sheer Heart Attack / 2nd Encore: We Will Rock You / We Are The Champions / God Save The Queen

April 24/25
Groenoordhalle, Leiden

■ *Second night*: *Flash / The Hero / Tie Your Mother Down / Action This Day / Play The Game / Somebody To Love / Get Down Make Love / Instrumental Inferno / Under Pressure / Love Of My Life / Save Me / Fat Bottomed Girls / Crazy Little Thing Called Love / Bohemian Rhapsody / Now I'm Here; Dragon Attack; Now I'm Here (Reprise) / Back Chat / Staying Power / Liar / Encore: Another One Bites The Dust / Sheer Heart Attack / 2nd Encore: We Will Rock You / We Are The Champions / God Save The Queen*

Brian plays parts of the intro of "For Your Love", by The Yardbirds, during 'Liar' - using the edge of his six-pence as a plectrum to emulate the tone of the original song.

April 28/29
Festhalle, Frankfurt

■ *First night*: *Flash / The Hero / Tie Your Mother Down / Action This Day / Play The Game /Staying Power / Somebody To Love / Love Of My Life / Save Me / Get Down Make Love / Under Pressure / Fat Bottomed Girls / Crazy Little Thing Called Love / Back Chat (piano improvisation) / Death On Two Legs (part) / Bohemian Rhapsody / Now I'm Here / Dragon Attack / Encore: Another One Bites The Dust / Sheer Heart Attack / 2nd Encore: We Will Rock You / We Are The Champions / God Save The Queen*

Freddie proves once again here that he's not

one to mince his words. Having explained the band have a new album out, he asks if the audience want to hear it. Someone at the front says no, and Freddie's immediate retort is, "You don't want to hear it?... If you don't wanna hear it, fucking go home!" This comment later inspires the title of a bootleg (see Bootlegs section)

One of the two shows here (it's unclear which) is filmed and later broadcast on German television.

May 1 ♫
Westfallenhalle, Dortmund
■ Flash / The Hero / Tie Your Mother Down / Action This Day / Play The Game / Staying Power / Somebody To Love / Love Of My Life / Save Me / Get Down, Make Love / Instrumental Inferno / Under Pressure / Fat Bottomed Girls / Crazy Little Thing Called Love / Death On Two Legs (part) / Bohemian Rhapsody / 16. Now I'm Here / 17. Dragon Attack / 1st Encore: Another One Bites The Dust / Sheer Heart Attack / 2nd Encore: We Will Rock You / We Are The Champions / God Save The Queen

May 3
Palais De Sport, Paris
■ Flash / The Hero / Tie Your Mother Down / Action This Day / Play The Game / Staying Power / Somebody To Love / Love Of My Life / Save Me / Get Down, Make Love / Instrumental Inferno / Under Pressure / Fat Bottomed Girls / Crazy Little Thing Called Love / Bohemian Rhapsody / Now I'm Here / Dragon Attack / Now I'm Here (reprise) / 1st Encore:. Another One Bites The Dust / 2nd Encore: We Will Rock You / We Are The Champions / God Save The Queen

May 5
Eilenriedehalle, Hanover

May 6 ♫ /7
Sporthalle, Cologne

May 9
Carl Diem Halle, Wurzburg
■ Flash / The Hero / We Will Rock You / Action This

Day / Play The Game / Back Chat / Somebody To Love / Now I'm Here; Dragon Attack; Now I'm Here (Reprise) / Love Of My Life / Save Me / Get Down Make Love / Instrumental Inferno / Under Pressure / Fat Bottomed Girls / Crazy Little Thing Called Love / Bohemian Rhapsody / Tie Your Mother Down / Encore: Another One Bites The Dust / Sheer Heart Attack / 2nd Encore: We Will Rock You / We Are The Champions / God Save The Queen

May 10
Sporthalle, Stuttgart

May 12 ♫ /13
Stadthalle, Vienna
■ First night: Flash / The Hero / We Will Rock You (fast) / Action This Day / Play The Game / Staying Power / Somebody To Love / Now I'm Here / Dragon Attack / Now I'm Here (reprise) / Love Of My Life / Save Me / Back Chat / Get Down, Make Love / Instrumental Inferno / Under Pressure / Fat Bottomed Girls / Mustapha (part) / Crazy Little Thing Called Love / Bohemian Rhapsody / Tie Your Mother Down / 1st Encore: Another One Bites The Dust / 2nd Encore: We Will Rock You / We Are The Champions / God Save The Queen

This show is filmed (in its entirety), for a possible local television broadcast. Whether the transmission ever went ahead however, is unclear. The tracks shown in bold feature as bonus material on the 2004 Queen On Fire – Live At The Bowl DVD.

■ Second night: Flash / The Hero / Action This Day / Play The Game / Staying Power / Somebody To Love / Now I'm Here; Dragon Attack; Now I'm Here (Reprise) / Love Of My Life / Save Me / Body Language / Get Down Make Love / Instrumental Inferno / Under Pressure / Fat Bottomed Girls / Crazy Little Thing Called Love / Bohemian Rhapsody / Tie Your Mother Down / Encore: Another One Bites The Dust (Incorporating Back Chat) / Sheer Heart Attack / 2nd Encore: We Will Rock You / We Are The Champions / God Save The Queen

This show is filmed for the band's archive. A

superb segment of 'Dust' is contained on *Rare Live*, and sees Freddie parading around the stage in a hooded towelling robe.

May 15
Waldbuehne, Berlin
■ *Flash / The Hero / We Will Rock You / Action This Day / Play The Game / Staying Power / Somebody To Love / Now I'm Here; Dragon Attack; Now I'm Here (Reprise) / Love Of My Life / Save Me / Get Down Make Love / Instrumental Inferno / Under Pressure / Body Language / Back Chat / Fat Bottomed Girls / Crazy Little Thing Called Love / Bohemian Rhapsody / Tie Your Mother Down / Encore: Another One Bites The Dust / Sheer Heart Attack / 2nd Encore: We Will Rock You / We Are The Champions / God Save The Queen*

May 16
Ernst-Mercke Halle, Hamburg

May 18♫
Eissporthalle, Kassel
■ *Flash / The Hero / Sheer Heart Attack / Action This Day / Play The Game / Staying Power / Somebody To Love / Now I'm Here; Dragon Attack; Now I'm Here (Reprise) / Love Of My Life / Save Me / Guitar Solo / Get Down Make Love / Instrumental Inferno / Under Pressure / Fat Bottomed Girls / Crazy Little Thing Called Love / Bohemian Rhapsody / Tie Your Mother Down / Encore: Another One Bites The Dust / 2nd Encore: We Will Rock You / We Are The Champions / God Save The Queen*

May 21
Olympiahalle, Munich
■ *Flash / The Hero / Sheer Heart Attack / Action This Day / Play The Game / Staying Power / Somebody To Love / Now I'm Here; Dragon Attack; Now I'm Here (Reprise) / Love Of My Life / Save Me / Get Down Make Love / Instrumental Inferno / Under Pressure / Fat Bottomed Girls / Crazy Little Thing Called Love / Bohemian Rhapsody / Tie Your Mother Down / Encore: Another One Bites The Dust / 2nd Encore: We Will Rock You / We Are The Champions / God Save The Queen*

❖ Also on May 21, Queen's eleventh studio album *Hot Space* is released in the UK. It peaks at number four, and number 22 in America.

Three tracks are not included in the live set. The Deacon/Mercury co-composition 'Cool Cat' is not altogether surprising, but the omission of 'Las Parablas De Amor' and 'Dancer' (both Brian May songs) certainly is.

UK 1982 - The Hot Space Tour
May 29♫
Elland Road Football Stadium, Leeds
■ *Flash / The Hero / We Will Rock You / Action This Day / Play The Game / Staying Power / Somebody To Love / Now I'm Here; Dragon Attack; Now I'm Here (Reprise) / Love Of My Life / Save Me / Get Down Make Love / Instrumental Inferno / Under Pressure / Fat Bottomed Girls / Crazy Little Thing Called Love / Bohemian Rhapsody / Tie Your Mother Down / Encore: Another One Bites The Dust / Sheer Heart Attack / 2nd Encore: We Will Rock You / We Are The Champions / God Save The Queen*

This show goes ahead despite local residents' objections. Signed petitions are submitted to the City Council, but given that the site is commonly used as a venue for football matches, the complaints are regarded lightly. A house opposite the ground is commandeered on the night of the concert to monitor Queen's noise level, but it does not exceed noise limitations.

Despite encountering problems with the tuning of his guitar (as is always a problem with open air venues), Brian May later cites this show as one of

Queen's best ever live performances. It is made more enjoyable for him because he has family in Leeds. A capacity 38,000 people witness the show. Brian is interviewed before the show at the Dragonara Hotel, where the band are staying. The interviewer is irritated because a certain band member will not speak with him:

Q: "What's up with fruitcake Fred?"

🖝 Brian: "He's been torn apart and bitten so many times before, that he doesn't want to say anything. It's very difficult being a frontman in a band, because the things you say often get twisted. In my position I can stand away and be objective, Freddie comes in for abuse. He's part of the team and he doesn't like it when he's singled out. Would you?"

'Las Parablas' is played during rehearsals for this gig, but never makes it to the set. It is discarded for the usual reason; the band feel is just doesn't work well enough to fit into the concert.

Support Acts are The Teardrop Explodes, Heart, and Joan Jett & The Blackhearts.

June 1♫/2
Ingliston Showground, Edinburgh
■ **First night**: Flash / The Hero / We Will Rock You / Action This Day / Play The Game / Staying Power / Somebody To Love / Now I'm Here; Dragon Attack; Now I'm Here (Reprise) / Love Of My Life / Save Me / Back Chat / Get Down Make Love / Instrumental Inferno (Incorporating I Go Crazy) / Under Pressure /

Fat Bottomed Girls / Crazy Little Thing Called Love / Bohemian Rhapsody / Tie Your Mother Down / Encore: Another One Bites The Dust / 2nd Encore: We Will Rock You / We Are The Champions / God Save The Queen

❖ Also on June 1, 'Las Palabras De Amor' is released in the UK. Backed with 'Cool Cat', it peaks at a disappointing number 17 – not helped by the absence of an accompanying promo video. The same track is issued in Japan, as B-side to 'Back Chat', but it is not released at all in America.

■ **Second night**: Flash/ The Hero / We Will Rock You (fast) / Action This Day / Play The Game / Staying Power / Somebody To Love / Now I'm Here / Dragon Attack / Now I'm Here (reprise) / Love Of My Life / Save Me / Get Down, Make Love / Instrumental Inferno / Under Pressure / Fat Bottomed Girls / Crazy Little Thing Called Love / Bohemian Rhapsody / Tie Your Mother Down / 1st Encore: Another One Bites The Dust / Sheer Heart Attack / 2nd Encore: We Will Rock You (slow) / We Are The Champions / God Save The Queen

June 5♫
Milton Keynes Bowl, Buckinghamshire
■ Flash / The Hero / We Will Rock You (fast) / Action This Day / Play The Game / Staying Power / Somebody To Love / Now I'm Here; Dragon Attack; Now I'm Here (Reprise) / Love Of My Life / Save Me / Back Chat / Get Down Make Love / Guitar Solo / Drum Solo /

Under Pressure / Fat Bottomed Girls / Crazy Little Thing Called Love / Bohemian Rhapsody / Tie Your Mother Down / Encore: Another One Bites The Dust / Sheer Heart Attack / 2nd Encore: We Will Rock You / We Are The Champions / God Save The Queen

Highlighted tracks feature in the television broadcast. All tracks feature on the 2004 *Queen On Fire – Live At The Bowl* CD and DVD.

The show does not actually begin with 'Flash' proper, but instead with a pre-recorded backing track of the song, designed to affect maximum excitement. 'The Hero' is the first real *performance* piece, and it is utterly breathtaking.

Freddie's first words come after a frenzied recital of 'Rock You'. "Hello ev'rybody... okay? You know it's not very often that we do shows in the daylight... I fucking wish we had before – I can see you all now! ... and there's some beauties here tonight, I can tell you. On with the show... This is 'Action'."

Queen give a superb rendition of 'Play The Game', intro'd by another piano pre-amble from Freddie. "This is your bloody life," he sings, "Don't play hard to get. It's a free world, all you have to do is play the game."

"Hey hey hey!" Freddie is off again, down the 'everything I sing, you sing' road. First he showers the front rows with his drink, then he addresses them: "Now most of you know that we've got some new sounds out, in the last week, and for what it's worth we're gonna do a few songs in the funk/black category... whatever you call it. That doesn't mean we've lost our rock and roll feel, okay!... I mean it's only a bloody record. People get so excited about these things. We just want to try out a few sounds. This is 'Staying Power'."

The amazing Arif Mardin horn arrangement present on the album version of 'Power' is replaced on stage by Freddie's vocal interpretation. This is probably the fans' favourite track from the album in the context of the live show.

Another rather lovely piano pre-amble precedes the next song, 'Somebody To Love'.

Having nailed a particularly tricky high note, conquering it with ease, Freddie turns to the audience and grins. "Are you ready? Huh? Are you ready brothers and sisters?..." An enthusiastic "Yeah" comes back at him, and the song crashes into life. This is Queen – and Freddie in particular – at their very best.

"I feel positively knackered, I tell ya" says Fred after 'Now I'm Here', then he's off again. "Okay everybody, let's play games, huh? "I'm gonna make you sing like Aretha Franklin." This time the singalong-a-Freddie ends with him telling the people they can join the band.

Later, Brian and Freddie are on stage alone again, seated on stools at the front centre of stage. Brian: "This is the guitarist's chance to say a few words. Thank you for coming first of all. Thank you for making this long trip to Milton Keynes. I think it was worth it, what do you think? I'm gonna dedicate this next one – this is a little unusual... I'd like to dedicate this particular song

to all those people who are not like us, who sit here and have a good time listening to music – no matter where they come from – people who have given up their lives for what they believe." 'Love Of My Life' follows.

With no introduction at all, the band slide into another ballad and 'Save Me' begins once more. John's 'Back Chat' follows, again without formal introduction, and 'Get Down Make Love' follows that, complete with lengthy mid-song interlude which is predictably edited out of the television broadcast. Brian then gives a punishing guitar solo which he looks relieved to finish, before Roger comes in with a short drum solo introduction to 'Under Pressure'.

Later on, Brian dashes across the stage during his guitar solo and inadvertently switches off his guitar output. He promptly retraces his steps, as baffled as the audience by the sudden loss of sound, and his trusted roadie (Jobby) spots the problem in a flash and switches Brian live again. This is absent from the television broadcast but does feature in the 2004 *On Fire* DVD.

Freddie's intro to 'Crazy Little Thing' is familiar one: "Ten years ago I only knew about three chords on the guitar, and now in 1982, I know three chords on the guitar. Before this wonderful intro that I'm gonna give you, right now I'd like to introduce to you Mr Morgan Fisher on piano... in that wonderful PINK! He's either AC or he's DC – I don't know. This is for anyone that's *crazy* out there..."

The show nears the end with 'Bo Rhap' and 'Mother Down' (two of the half dozen or so tracks Queen are not permitted to leave the stage without performing), and then 'Bites The Dust' follows as an encore. Another frantic-paced 'Sheer Heart Attack' (which seem out of place in this tour) speeds by, before the band leave the stage and return again for 'Rock You' and 'Champs', second encore.

This show is filmed by Tyne Tees Television (in its entirety), and later broadcast on British TV's *The Tube* programme in January the following year on Channel 4, edited down to 60 minutes.

Gavin Taylor, The Tube's resident director, steers the filming, which so impresses Queen they later invite him to direct the Wembley Stadium (July 12, 1986) show - which is later released on video. The footage receives its American TV première on August 20, 1983, on the MTV network.

The television broadcast also features brief snippets of pre-show interviews with Roger and Brian, as well as with a fan who says he is attending his 23rd Queen concert, and, he adds, up to this point, he has travelled 8,000 miles (over the years) to see them.

● "Why have you travelled all this way to see Queen?", asks a local journalist. The replies are varied.

"Sheer technical brilliance, good songs and a good show" / "I've been waiting four years to see them" / "They're one step ahead of everybody - three steps ahead of everybody" / "Coz we luv 'em... we luv 'em all."

Stage manager Rick O'Brien talks about the lights: "Those cost $9,000 apiece, they are custom built for this show. They've (the manufacturers) taken a standard follow-spot and rebuilt the optics to our specifications, and then built that custom housing for it. It's being used in a very unique application. All the operator has to do is point it at whatever it is he's following, all the

other spotlight controls and colour changing is done by remote – for all the spotlights – so it's an amazing piece of work.

"Once the band is on stage, most of my worries are over – the show really runs itself. We've got a very professional crew, and the band is very professional. It's getting them on stage that is the hard part – getting everything working, and perfect for them. What you want to do is create a 60 by 40 foot universe that never changes for the band. So they just come up, and play – whether it be in Argentina, or in Europe, or in the States, on stage is the same wherever they go. The band shouldn't have anything else to worry about except playing for their fans."

The band arrive at the venue in a helicopter, and then later, immediately prior to the start of the show, they are seen again backstage; nervous and apprehensive and excited, waiting to go on and do their stuff. It is a rare insight, and shows an uncommly anxious looking Roger and John. Freddie, meanwhile, clad in white jeans and striking matching leather jacket, looks fantastic - anything but nervous.

Support acts are the same as Elland Road on May 29, with one extra band: The Anti Nowhere League. The Teardrop Explodes finish their set early when the audience become restless and begin to throw things at the stage - an all too common occurrence on this tour!

After the show Queen hold a 'shorts or suspenders' party at the Embassy club, in London. This is Morgan Fisher's last show with the band, as he is unable to travel to the next legs of the tour due to a fear of flying.

❖ This entire concert is released on DVD (featuring both stereo and 5.1 Surround Sound mixes) and on CD, in November 2004. Titled *Queen On Fire – Live At The Bowl*, the DVD offers all the material not aired by Channel 4, and extensive bonus material too.

❖ **July 19**
'Calling All Girls' / 'Put Out The Fire' is issued

as a single exclusive to America. It precedes Canadian and North American dates by only two days and will eventually reach just No.60 in the Billboard charts.

USA 1982 - Rock'n'America Tour '82

Queen fly to Montreal on July 18 to embark upon what would prove to be their final tour of North America. It entails 40 shows at 29 different venues, performed over a seven week period. Four of the shows are in Canada. It concludes with two concerts at the Inglewood Forum on September 14 and 15.

The support act is Billy Squier, who has become a good friend of the band over the years. Freddie, Brian and Roger have all made appearances on his albums, either by playing their respective instruments or by providing backing vocals.

The show now includes material from *Hot Space* which was previously absent - 'Calling All Girls', 'Life Is Real' and 'Put Out The Fire'. The set is not otherwise much different to that played in Europe, but again is shuffled around a bit.

Fred Mandel (who will later provide 'rip-roaring' piano on *The Works* album, among other things) replaces Morgan Fisher on keyboards/piano. He remains throughout the American and Japanese legs of this tour.

July 21
Forum, Montreal, Quebec

■ Flash / Rock It / We Will Rock You / Action This Day / Play The Game / Staying Power / Now I'm Here; Dragon Attack; Now I'm Here (Reprise) / Save Me / Calling All Girls / Back Chat / Get Down Make Love / Instrumental Inferno / Under Pressure / Fat Bottomed Girls / Crazy Little Thing Called Love / Bohemian Rhapsody / Tie Your Mother Down / Body Language / Encore: Another One Bites The Dust / 2nd Encore: We Will Rock You / We Are The Champions / God Save The Queen

July 23
Boston Gardens, Boston, Massachusetts

July 24
Spectrum, Philadelphia, Pennsylvania

July 25
Capitol Center, Washington DC

July 27/28 ♪
Madison Square Garden, New York

■ **First night**: Flash / Rock It / We Will Rock You / Action This Day / Play The Game / Staying Power / Now I'm Here; Dragon Attack; Now I'm Here (Reprise) / Save Me / Calling All Girls / Back Chat / Get Down Make Love / Instrumental Inferno / Under Pressure / Fat Bottomed Girls / Crazy Little Thing Called Love / Bohemian Rhapsody / Tie Your Mother Down / Body Language / Encore: Another One Bites The Dust / 2nd Encore: We Will Rock You / We Are The Champions / God Save The Queen

Queen make an in-store appearance at Crazy Eddies, the largest in a chain of New York record and audio shops.

■ **Second night**: Flash / Rock It / We Will Rock You / Action This Day / Play The Game / Somebody To Love / Now I'm Here; Dragon Attack / Save Me / Calling All Girls / Get Down Make Love / Instrumental Inferno / Body Language / Under Pressure / Fat Bottomed Girls / Crazy Little Thing Called Love / Bohemian Rhapsody / Tie Your Mother Down / Encore: Another One Bites The Dust / 2nd Encore: We Will Rock You / We Are The Champions / God Save The Queen

Female mud wrestlers are hired backstage for the entertainment of the crew. They are also present at both Madison Square Garden shows.

July 31
Richfield Coliseum, Cleveland, Ohio

August 2
Maple Leaf Gardens, Toronto, Ontario

■ Flash / Rock It / We Will Rock You / Action This Day / Play The Game / Staying Power / Now I'm Here; Dragon Attack / Save Me / Calling All Girls / Get Down Make Love / Instrumental Inferno / Body Language / Under Pressure / Fat Bottomed Girls / Crazy Little Thing Called Love / Bohemian Rhapsody / Tie Your Mother Down / Encore: Another One Bites The Dust / 2nd Encore: We Will Rock You / We Are The Champions / God Save The Queen

August 3
Maple Leaf Gardens, Toronto, Ontario

August 5
Market Square Arena, Indianapolis, Indiana

August 6
Joe Louis Arena, Detroit, Michigan

■ Flash / Rock It / We Will Rock You / Action This Day / Play The Game / Staying Power / Now I'm Here; Dragon Attack; Now I'm Here (Reprise) / Save Me / Calling All Girls / Back Chat / Get Down Make Love / Instrumental Inferno / Body Language / Under Pressure / Fat Bottomed Girls / Crazy Little Thing Called Love / Bohemian Rhapsody / Tie Your Mother Down / Encore: Another One Bites The Dust / 2nd Encore: We Will Rock You / We Are The Champions / God Save The Queen

August 7
Riverfront Coliseum, Cincinnati, Ohio

August 9 ♪
Brendon Burn Coliseum, Meadowlands, New Jersey

■ *Flash / Rock It / We Will Rock You / Action This Day / Play The Game / Somebody To Love / Now I'm Here; Dragon Attack; Now I'm Here (Reprise) / Save Me / Calling All Girls / Get Down Make Love / Instrumental Inferno (Prolonged) / Body Language / Under Pressure / Life Is Real / Fat Bottomed Girls / Crazy Little Thing Called Love / Bohemian Rhapsody / Tie Your Mother Down / Encore: Another One Bites The Dust / 2nd Encore: We Will Rock You / We Are The Champions / God Save The Queen*

During his 'Brighton Rock' solo, Brian breaks a string on his beloved Red Special guitar and is less than amused. He discards it and is quickly handed a John Birch replica replacement. However, when a string breaks on this guitar too, Brian loses patience – a rare occurance. He races past John Deacon to the far side of the stage and over to his wall of Vox amplifiers, and promptly hurls the guitar over the stack into the dark abyss. Dutiful roadie Jobby brings out yet another instrument and Brian finishes the solo. At the end of the song the restrung Red Special appears again and the show goes on as normal. Later, Jobby emerges from behind the stack to show Brian and the audience the result of this episode. He holds up the two pieces of the guitar and the front rows are suitably stunned. This is a unique occurance. After the show the band throw a party at the famous Danceteria Club. It is co-organised by the American record company Elektra and is

attended by a host of famous celebrities including Irene Cara, Andy Warhol, Ian Hunter, Johnny Rotten and Vitas Gueralitis.

❖ Also on August 9. While no single was released in America on this day, in Britain the final track taken from *Hot Space* emerges. 'Back Chat' / 'Staying Power' fails to make much impression on the British public, struggling to reach number 40. Allowing for the generally uninspiring reception given to the second, third and fourth dance orientated *Hot Space* singles, EMI would have been better advised releasing the heavier Brian May songs 'Put Out The Fire' and 'Dancer' (as I wrote and told them at the time!). During a promotional interview for *Hot Space*, Brian is asked by English radio broadcaster Richard Skinner to explain why 'Put Out The Fire' has been placed directly before the John Lennon tribute song 'Life Is Real', in the album's running sequence. Skinner remarks that the message that guns do not kill people, only people do, followed by a song for the assassinated Lennon, is perhaps a little too blatant.

🗨 Brian: "I think it is a good idea to put out the fire in many respects. In some songs you can subtle-out yourself. We've put little things like that in previous albums, and they've been overlooked."

In a separate interview he adds: "It's seldom that people actually pick them up, except the few real close fans who listen very carefully. It was deliberate."

August 10
New Haven Coliseum, Connecticut

August 13/14
Poplar Creek, Chicago, Illinois
■ *Second night: Flash / Rock It / We Will Rock You / Action This Day / Play The Game / Calling All Girls / Now I'm Here; Dragon Attack; Now I'm Here (Reprise) / Save Me / Get Down Make Love / Life Is Real / Body Language / Under Pressure / Fat Bottomed Girls / Crazy Little Thing Called Love / Bohemian Rhapsody / Tie Your Mother Down / Encore: Another*

One Bites The Dust / 2nd Encore: We Will Rock You / We Are The Champions / God Save The Queen

August 15
Civic Center Arena, St Paul, Minnesota

August 19
Civic Center, Biloxi, Mississippi
■ Flash / Rock It / We Will Rock You / Action This Day / Play The Game / Calling All Girls / Now I'm Here; Dragon Attack; Now I'm Here (Reprise) / Save Me / Get Down Make Love / Life Is Real / Body Language / Under Pressure / Fat Bottomed Girls / Crazy Little Thing Called Love / Bohemian Rhapsody / Tie Your Mother Down / Encore: Another One Bites The Dust / 2nd Encore: We Will Rock You / We Are The Champions / God Save The Queen

August 20
Summit, Houston, Texas

August 21
Reunion, Dallas, Texas

August 24
The Omni, Atlanta, Georgia

August 25
Mid South Coliseum, Memphis, Tennessee

August 27
City Myriad, Oklahoma
■ Flash / Rock It / We Will Rock You / Action This Day / Somebody To Love / Calling All Girls / Now I'm Here / Dragon Attack / Love Of My Life / Save Me / Get Down Make Love / Instrumental Inferno / Guitar Solo / Body Language / Back Chat / Under Pressure / Fat Bottomed Girls / Crazy Little Thing Called Love / Saturday Night's Alright For Fighting / Bohemian Rhapsody / Tie Your Mother Down / Jailhouse Rock / Encore: Another One Bites The Dust / 2nd Encore: We Will Rock You / We Are The Champions / God Save The Queen

August 28
Kemper Arena, Kansas City, Missouri

August 30
McNichols Arena, Denver, Colorado

September 2
Portland Coliseum, Portland, Oregon
■ Flash / Rock It / We Will Rock You / Action This Day / Play The Game / Calling All Girls / Now I'm Here; Dragon Attack ; Now I'm Here (Reprise) / Save Me / Get Down Make Love / Instrumental Inferno / Body Language / Under Pressure / Fat Bottomed Girls / Crazy Little Thing Called Love / Bohemian Rhapsody / Tie Your Mother Down / Encore: Another One Bites The Dust / 2nd Encore: We Will Rock You / We Are The Champions / God Save The Queen

September 3
Seattle Coliseum, Seattle, Washington

September 4
PNE Coliseum, Vancouver, British Columbia

September 7
Oakland Coliseum, Oakland, California
■ *Flash / Rock It / We Will Rock You / Action This Day / Play The Game / Calling All Girls / Now I'm Here; Put Out The Fire; Dragon Attack; Now I'm Here (Reprise) / Save Me / Get Down Make Love / Instrumental Inferno / Body Language / Under Pressure / Fat Bottomed Girls / Crazy Little Thing Called Love / Bohemian Rhapsody / Tie Your Mother Down / Encore: Another One Bites The Dust / 2nd Encore: We Will Rock You / We Are The Champions / God Save The Queen*

September 10
ASU Arena, Temple, Texas

September 11/12
Irving Meadows, Irving, Texas
Being a huge Aretha Franklin fan, Freddie breaks into a spontaneous verse from 'Jump To It', during 'Another One Bites The Dust' here.

September 14/15 ♪
The Inglewood Forum, Los Angeles, California
■ *Second night: Flash / Rock It / We Will Rock You / Action This Day / Somebody To Love / Calling All Girls / Now I'm Here ; Put Out The Fire ; Dragon Attack / Love Of My Life / Save Me / Get Down Make Love / Instrumental Inferno / Guitar Solo / Body Language / Back Chat / Under Pressure / Fat Bottomed Girls / Crazy Little Thing Called Love / Saturday Night's Alright For Fighting / Bohemian Rhapsody / Tie Your Mother Down / Encore: Another One Bites The Dust / Jailhouse Rock / 2nd Encore: We Will Rock You / We Are The Champions / God Save The Queen*

Queen are joined on stage by Billy Squier for the 'Jailhouse Rock' encore. Billy has been the support act throughout the American dates. Also in attendance are friends of the band Michael Jackson, Rod Stewart and Donna Summer.

September 25
Queen appear on the American television programme *Saturday Night Live*, in the first of a new series. They perform 'Crazy Little Thing Called Love' and 'Under Pressure'.

JAPAN 1982 - Japan (Hot Space) Tour

Queen fly to Japan once again to begin their fifth tour there - a two week visit entailing only six shows in five cities. Unusually, the vast Budokan Hall venue, in the capital city, is not one of them. The set features 'The Hero' back in its rightful place as the opening track, and other than the inclusion once again of 'Teo Torriatte', there are no significant changes to the set.

The sixth show is filmed and later issued as an exclusively Japanese video. It very soon becomes a difficult to locate collectors' item, and the relatively few copies in circulation increase in value ten fold. However, when the internet and mighty e-bay auction facility arrives, years down the line, concert rarities like this, and other once scarce Queen concert gems, are suddenly in abundance and the market plummets.

October 19/20
Kyuden Taiikukan, Fukuoka

October 24 ♪
Hankyu Nishinomiya-kyujo, Osaka
■ *Flash / The Hero / We Will Rock You / Action This Day / Somebody To Love / Calling All Girls / It's Late (part) / Now I'm Here; Put Out The Fire; Dragon Attack; Now I'm Here (Reprise) / Love Of My Life / Improvisation / Save Me / Get Down Make Love / Instrumental Inferno / Body Language / Under Pressure / Fat Bottomed Girls / Crazy Little Thing Called Love / Saturday Night's Alright For Fighting / Bohemian Rhapsody / Tie Your Mother Down / Encore: Another One Bites The Dust / Jailhouse Rock / 2nd Encore: Teo Torriatte / We Will Rock You / We Are The Champions / God Save The Queen*

'Spread Your Wings' is part of the intended set here, but when Freddie admits to having forgotten the words, it is quickly abandoned in preference to the Elton John cover.

The concert is filmed for the band's own archive. Some of it features on the 1989 *Rare Live* video.

'Crazy Little Thing' is without doubt one of the best renditions ever captured on film. The band are assisted on stage by Fred Mandel on piano again, and it is largely due to him that the song is as good as it is.

While in Osaka, Queen hold a press conference to satisfy the huge demand for their time. So many radio stations, television presenters and journalists have requested time with them that it is decided everyone should attend one big conference.

October 26
Kokusai Tenjijo, Nagoya

October 29
Hokkaidoritsu Sango Kyoshin-kaijo, Sapporo
■ *Flash / The Hero / We Will Rock You / Action This Day / Somebody To Love / Calling All Girls / Now I'm Here; Put Out The Fire; Dragon Attack; Now I'm Here (Reprise) / Love Of My Life / Improvisation / Save Me / Get Down Make Love / Instrumental Inferno / Body Language / Under Pressure / Fat Bottomed Girls / Crazy Little Thing Called Love / Saturday Night's Alright For Fighting / Bohemian Rhapsody / Tie Your Mother Down / Encore: Another One Bites The Dust / Jailhouse Rock / 2nd Encore: Teo Torriatte / We Are The Champions / God Save The Queen*

Queen perform 'Take Me Home' during this set, but it is not known where in the set it features.

November 3 ♫
Seibu Lions Stadium, Tokyo
■ *Flash* / The Hero* / Rock It / We Will Rock You / Action This Day / Now I'm Here*; Improvisation*; Put Out The Fire*; Dragon Attack*; Now I'm Here (Reprise)* / Love Of My Life / Save Me / Get Down Make Love / Guitar Solo (AKA Instrumental Inferno) / Body Language / Back Chat / Under Pressure / Fat Bottomed Girls / Crazy Little Thing Called Love* / Bohemian Rhapsody / Tie Your Mother Down / Encore: Teo Torriatte* / 2nd Encore: We Will Rock You / We Are The Champions / God Save The Queen*

Highlighted tracks feature on the Japanese video. * denotes tracks which feature as bonus material on the 2004 *On Fire* DVD.

This entire show is filmed and later issued (much abridged) on video - exclusive to the Japanese market. *Live In Japan* is the very first commercially available footage of Queen in concert (though 'Greatest Hits' in 1981 did contain some live material). The rest of the world will have to wait until September 1984 for its first Queen concert video - the November 1981, Montreal Forum, Canadain shows, issued as *We Will Rock You*.

Though 'Live In Japan' offers a brutally edited account of the show, it does at least feature the only officially available concert footage of 'Teo Torriatte' and 'Put Out The Fire'.

This is the last night of the tour.

November 4
Brian and John travel home to the UK, while Freddie stays on for further shopping sprees, as usual, in his beloved Japan. Roger flies to Hong Kong for a short holiday before moving on to Bangkok and Thailand.

November 13
Roger screens a 60-minute edited cut of what will become the 'We Will Rock You' live video, at his home during a fireworks party. John and Brian are also in attendance. Freddie is still shopping!

There are no Queen concerts in 1983.

❖ **January 23**

Roger Taylor's 'Radio Ga Ga' is released in the UK as the first single from the forthcoming album *The Works*. It is backed with Brian's non-album gem 'I Go Crazy' and reaches number two. The same pairing is released in America on February 7 and peaks at number16.

February 3 ①

Queen fly to Italy to headline in the annual San Remo Song Festival. The event is broadcast live throughout Europe, and is watched by 30 million people. Other artists on the bill include Paul Young, Bonnie Tyler and Culture Club. It is Queen's first performance in Italy. They perform 'Radio Ga Ga' in front of a studio audience of 2,000 – though it is not played live, but lip-synched. Freddie makes no effort to hide the fact he is miming.

Freddie is impressed by Culture Club's performance and later remarks that Boy George possesses a great talent. He thinks him very brave - referring to his camp image – and sees definite similarities between George and himself during Queen's early days.

❖ **February 27**

Queen release their eleventh studio album *The Works*, in the UK - and a day later in America. The numerous subsequent singles from it yield some rather interesting non-album material, not least the 'Ga Ga' B-side 'I Go Crazy' - in which Freddie protests he "ain't gonna go and see the Rolling Stones no more", and "I ain't gonna go and see Queeeeeen."

The track is an astonishing omission from the album (despite there being ample room to accommodate it) and even more so from the live set. Only a tiny fragment will feature (in Brian's guitar solo), and even then only on rare occasions. Given its concert related theme, the full bone-

QUEEN   THE WORKS

shaking version would have gone down a storm. I cannot imagine why this song was overlooked for the concerts – it is staggering. It is probably *the* most incredible example of a Queen live AWOL of all.

The Works is unprecedented in that it will be the only Queen album to have each and every track issued as a single – be it as an A-side or B-side track. For this reason, 1984 will be an expensive period for collectors. 'Ga Ga', 'Hard Life', 'Break Free' and 'Hammer To Fall' are all issued as main singles, while 'Tear It Up', 'Prowl', 'Machines', 'Windows' and 'World We Created' all appear as B-sides. In addition to that, extended versions of 'Ga Ga', 'Hard Life', 'Prowl', 'Break Free' and 'Windows', instrumentals of 'Ga Ga' and 'Machines', and a Headbanger's version of 'Hammer To Fall' also emerge.

Regardless of the prolific vinyl output, several songs from *Works* do not appear in the live show. As well as 'I Go Crazy', Freddie's 'Keep Passing The Open Windows' and 'Man On The Prowl', and the Taylor/May co-write 'Machines' are also overlooked. Actually, 'Machines' does feature, but only in the form of the pre-recorded introduction tape.

March/April

On March 24 John and Roger leave London for Tokyo where they undertake a gruelling two week tour promoting *The Works*. They cram an average of six radio and television interviews into every day, which includes appearances on Tokyo Rock TV and a *Music Life* magazine special. They move on to Seoul for more interviews, and then fly on to Sydney on April 1. On April 5 they move onwards again, to Melbourne, for yet more appointments, before concluding the tour in Los Angeles, on April 8. Between them, John and Roger give a total of 112 interviews in 16 days.

❖ April 2

'I Want To Break Free' is released as the second single from *The Works*. Coupled with 'Machines (Or Back To Humans)', it provides Queen with a number three hit in the UK.

May 12

Golden Rose Pop Festival, Montreux, Switzerland

■ *Radio Ga Ga / Tear It Up / I Want To Break Free / It's A Hard Life*

This four day event kicks off on May 10 and runs through to the 13th. Queen are the headline act on the 12th. None of the performances are live, and miming to the songs presents Freddie with the usual problems: he forgets the odd lyric, or comes in too late. Freddie hates miming and avoids it whenever possible.

Also featured on the same day as Queen are Adam Ant, Status Quo and Madness.

The event is recorded by both Swiss TV and the BBC, and is eventually broadcast to over forty countries around the world – which is the main reason for Queen's attendance.

Cliff Richard, Shakin' Stevens, Duran Duran, Rod Stewart and Elton John also appear.

May 22

Freddie attends an Elton John concert in Munich. He does not join him on stage, however, as his foot and leg are in plaster following a severe knee ligament injury.

June 28

Queen attend the Music Therapy Awards dinner and are presented with a *Silver Clef* award for outstanding contribution to music.

❖ July 16

The penultimate single from *The Works* is released in the UK. Backed with the acoustic May/Mercury ballad 'Is This The World We Created', 'It's A Hard Life' eventually reaches

My Life', 'Bo Rhap', 'Tie Your Mother Down', 'Under Pressure', 'Brighton Rock' and 'Somebody To Love'. Other concert favourites will be brought out of retirement too: 'Seven Seas Of Rhye', 'Keep Yourself Alive', 'Stone Cold Crazy', part of 'Liar', and Freddie's wondrous 'Great King Rat'.

August 24
Forêst Nationale, Brussels

■ *Machines (intro) / Tear It Up / Tie Your Mother Down / Under Pressure / Somebody To Love / Killer Queen / Seven Seas Of Rhye / Keep Yourself Alive / Liar / It's A Hard Life / Get Down, Make Love(part) / Staying Power / Dragon Attack / Now I'm Here / Is This The World We Created / Love Of My Life / Stone Cold Crazy / Great King Rat / Guitar Solo / Brighton Rock / Radio Ga Ga / Another One Bites The Dust / Crazy Little Thing Called Love / Bohemian Rhapsody / Hammer To Fall / 1st Encore: I Want To Break Free / Sheer Heart Attack / 2nd Encore: We Will Rock You / We Are The Champions / God Save The Queen*

This show is filmed for the 'Hammer To Fall' promotional video. Members of the audience are invited back the following day for additional work. David Mallett is the director.

A photograph taken of the event, depicting the extraordinary lighting display, is used to illustrate the front cover of early 'Hammer To Fall' single sleeves, but these are quickly withdrawn and replaced with a plain red/vlack jacket. A number of the sleeves do circulate, however, and go on to become hugely collectable. The same photograph is later used to promote the *Greatest Hits II* video.

As if by magic, during 'Radio Ga Ga' everyone in the audience unites to recreate the synchronised handclapping that features in the video. An incredible sea of arms are seen to clap twice above heads, and then thrust into the night sky with clenched fists. It is almost as if the audience have arrived hours beforehand, and rehearsed it. This wonderful spectacle will occur at every subsequent Queen live performance.

Freddie's false breasts (his 'falsies') make their debut at this show too, during 'I Want To Break Free'. This eccentric addition to the show will

number six. Issued ten days earlier in America, the same pairing struggles to reach number 72 – not helped by the eccentric (to say the least) promotional video.

EUROPE 1984 - Queen Works! (The Works Tour)

Queen begin what is commonly referred to as The Works Tour. It entails twenty-three shows at fourteen different sites in seven countries. The nine British shows begin on August 28 with two concerts in Dublin and three consecutive gigs at the National Exhibition Centre in Birmingham. Four memorable shows at London's Wembley Arena follow that.

The stage backdrop is based upon scenes from the Fritz Lang silent movie *Metropolis*, made in 1930. Two giant cogwheels rotate slowly in front of immense skyscrapers, partly obscured by clouds of steam. Strobe lights illuminate the entire backdrop during 'Radio Ga Ga'.

The set has undergone a radical facelift to incorporate much of the new material: 'Tear It Up', 'Hard Life', 'World We Created', 'Hammer', 'Ga Ga', 'Break Free' are new additions - and a keyboard version of 'Machines' starts the show.

As might be expected, most of the *Hot Space* and *Game* tracks, as well as other material, is dropped to accommodate the new stuff. A handful of the tried and tested 'faithfuls' (which can never be dropped) are juggled around somewhat: 'Love Of

continue throughout 1984/85 – with varying reactions!

August 28⏎/29
Royal Dublin Society Showgrounds, Dublin
■ *First night*: Machines (Intro) / Tear It Up / Tie Your Mother Down / Under Pressure / Medley: Somebody To Love; Killer Queen; Seven Seas Of Rhye; Keep Yourself Alive; Liar / It's A Hard Life / Staying Power / Dragon Attack / Now I'm Here / Is This The World We Created / Love Of My Life / Stone Cold Crazy / Great King Rat / Machines (Keyboard Improv) / Guitar Solo / Brighton Rock / Another One Bites The Dust / Hammer To Fall / Crazy Little Thing Called Love / Bohemian Rhapsody / Radio Ga Ga / Encore: I Want To Break Free / Sheer Heart Attack / 2nd Encore: We Will Rock You / We Are The Champions / A Day At The Races (Outro)

Because it is considered inappropriate to close the two shows here with 'God Save The Queen', the band instead end with the musical passage from 'A Day At The Races'. On the second night, however, members of the audience improvise and singing the national anthem anyway.

For 'Hammer To Fall' on this tour, the band are joined on stage by Spike Edney, who provides additional guitar. He also plays piano on 'Crazy Little Thing Called Love'.

August 31⏎/September 1/2⏎
NEC, Birmingham
■ *First night*: Machines (Intro) / Tear It Up / Tie Your Mother Down / Under Pressure / Medley: Somebody To Love; Killer Queen; Seven Seas Of Rhye; Keep Yourself Alive; Liar / Improvisation / It's A Hard Life / Staying Power / Dragon Attack / Now I'm Here / Is This The World We Created / Love Of My Life / Stone Cold Crazy / Great King Rat / Machines (Keyboard Improvisation) / Guitar Solo / Brighton Rock / Hammer To Fall / Another One Bites The Dust / Crazy Little Thing Called Love / Bohemian Rhapsody / Radio Ga Ga / Encore: I Want To Break Free / Jailhouse Rock / 2nd Encore: We Will Rock You / We Are The Champions / God Save The Queen

All three shows at this venue are sold out.

Eleven thousand people fill the NEC to its capacity every night.

↗ **'NEC SHOW'S A REAL DAZZLER'**, by Roger Trapp, *Birmingham Evening Mail*, September 1 1984: *'Chart topping rock group Queen began their three-night stand in Birmingham last night with one of the most spectacular shows the NEC Arena has ever seen. Back in Britain for the first time in two years, the four-man group, who have scored numerous hits in the last decade, performed with enormous energy and enthusiasm for nearly two hours.*

'While lead singer Freddie Mercury – clad for much of the show in just skin-tight red Spiderman trousers – strutted and pranced about the stage, the multi-coloured lights on the huge rig rose and fell and gigantic wheels spun against a mechanical landscape backdrop.

'Queen – who have a reputation for producing excessive concerts – had promised their fans something special this time. None of them can havebeen disappointed. The only low point was when guitarist Brian May took a sustained – and by the end rather tedious – solo spot. Otherwise he, Mercury, drummer Roger Taylor and bass player John Deacon – with help from an extra musician and the special effects – held the audience's rapt attention.

'All the favourites - from 'Seven Seas Of Rhye', through 'Killer Queen' and 'Under Pressure' to the recent No.1 'Radio Ga Ga' were there and performed with a staggering panache. So thrilled at their reception were the group that Mercury vowed they would keep playing concerts as long as their records sold.'

■ *Second night*: *Machines (Intro) / Tear It Up / Tie Your Mother Down / Under Pressure / Medley: Somebody To Love; Killer Queen; Seven Seas Of Rhye; Keep Yourself Alive; Liar / Improvisation / It's A Hard Life / Staying Power / Dragon Attack / Now I'm Here / Is This The World We Created / Love Of My Life / Stone Cold Crazy / Great King Rat / Machines (Keyboard Improvisation) / Guitar Solo / Brighton Rock / Hammer To Fall / Another One Bites The Dust / Crazy Little Thing Called Love / Saturday Night's Alright For Fighting / Bohemian Rhapsody / Radio Ga Ga / Encore: I Want To Break Free / Sheer Heart Attack / 2nd Encore: We Will Rock You / We Are The Champions / God Save The Queen*

The support act is General Public, a group consisting of two former members of The Beat – Dave Wakeling and Ranking Roger. They also support at the four London shows.

The concerts are attended by a variety of celebrities, including Andy Taylor (Duran Duran), Tony Hadley (Spandau Ballet) and Jim Lea and Dave Hill from Slade.

■ *Final night*: *Machines (Intro) / Tear It Up / Tie Your Mother Down / Under Pressure / Medley: Somebody To Love; Killer Queen; Seven Seas Of Rhye; Keep Yourself Alive; Liar / Improvisation / It's A Hard Life / Staying Power / Dragon Attack / Now I'm Here / Is This The World We Created / Love Of My Life / Stone Cold Crazy / Great King Rat / Machines (Keyboard Improvisation) / Guitar Solo / Brighton Rock / Hammer To Fall / Another One Bites The Dust / Crazy Little Thing Called Love / Saturday Night's Alright For Fighting / Bohemian Rhapsody / Radio Ga Ga / Encore: I Want To Break Free / Sheer Heart Attack / 2nd Encore: We Will Rock You / We Are The Champions / God Save The Queen*

Freddie's opening words: "Hello - how you doing? Listen, I must say it's nice to be back on the road again after two years of absence. It seems kind of different, but as long as you guys are here, it'll be alright.

"A lot of people are saying that this is gonna be our last tour. That is completely untrue, okay. If we wanted to break up we'd let you know, but as long as you buggers buy the records, we're gonna be here. Just to prove it, this is 'Staying Power'."

When the audience begin singing the opening lines of 'Love Of My Life' without Freddie, he stops Brian from continuing and suggests that they start again from the top. Just then, an audience member gives two hoots on a hand-held air horn.

"Don't mess about," Freddie snaps, then he jokingly chastises the culprit. "How dare you sing without my command." Before he is permitted to resume though, he must first face a barrage of "We love you Freddie", repeated about twenty times. "That's what I like – a really intelligent bunch," he adds, laughing. "Look, shall we sing this bugger or not?" The song eventually gets under way – it is faultless.

Most audio bootlegs of this concert include the pre-show soundcheck tracks, but the sound quality is abysmal.

September 4♪/5/7♪/8
Wembley Arena, London

■ **First night**: *Machines (Intro) / Tear It Up / Tie Your Mother Down / Under Pressure / Medley: Somebody To Love; Killer Queen; Seven Seas Of Rhye; Keep Yourself Alive; Liar / Improvisation / It's A Hard Life / Staying Power / Dragon Attack / Now I'm Here / Is This The World We Created / Love Of My Life / Stone Cold Crazy / Great King Rat / Machines (Keyboard Improvisation) / Guitar Solo / Brighton Rock / Hammer To Fall / Another One Bites The Dust / Not Fade Away / Crazy Little Thing Called Love / Bohemian Rhapsody / Radio Ga Ga / Encore: I Want To Break Free / Jailhouse Rock / 2nd Encore: We Will Rock You / We Are The Champions / God Save The Queen*

When the band return for their first encore here, Freddie is dressed in the wig he wore for the infamous 'I Want To Break Free' video. He also has an enormous pair of false breasts poking through his pink jumper. He then takes great delight in lifting up his top and exposing his new assets to the already uproarious onlookers. Freddie grins from ear to ear and the fans love it.

'Not Fade Away' is not performed in its entirety, Freddie merely sings a few opening verses as a segue to 'Crazy Little Thing'.

■ **Second night**: *Machines (Intro) / Tear It Up / Tie Your Mother Down / Under Pressure / Medley: Somebody To Love; Killer Queen; Seven Seas Of Rhye; Keep Yourself Alive; Liar / Improvisation / It's A Hard Life / Staying Power / Dragon Attack / Now I'm Here / Is This The World We Created / Love Of My Life / Stone Cold Crazy / Great King Rat / Machines (Keyboard Improvisation) / Guitar Solo / Brighton Rock / Hammer To Fall / Another One Bites The Dust / Crazy Little Thing Called Love / Bohemian Rhapsody / Radio Ga Ga / Encore: I Want To Break Free / Jailhouse Rock / 2nd Encore: We Will Rock You / We Are The Champions / God Save The Queen*

Following 'Dragon Attack' the audience sings 'Happy Birthday' to Freddie, who is thirty-eight. He acknowledges this with a smile, bows, and proceeds to shower the front rows with the contents of a plastic beaker. He then opens a card

handed to him from the audience. "I can't read this," he declares. Then, after a couple of minutes of improvised vocal ad-libbing, the band break into 'Now I'm Here'.

During the 'Break Free' encore, Freddie shows off his huge 'breasts' again, strutting about the stage showing them to anyone who will look, before finally thrusting them into John Deacon's face. Both laugh, as cameras flash in every direction.

Later, Freddie takes the opportunity to respond to yet more tedious tabloid misrepresentation. "You've all been reading a lot of things in the press today. Let me just say that the stories about us splitting up are all unfucking true, alright." The audience seems relieved, and roar their appreciation. "We love you!" he adds, and the show continues.

Rick Parfitt joins Queen on stage to assist with additional guitar backing and vocals on 'Shake Rattle And Roll'. Freddie's thirty-eighth birthday ensures that spirits are high throughout.

After the show the band and friends make their way to the Xenon nightclub in Piccadilly. Celebrations last well into the next morning, and Freddie is presented with two huge cakes – one a superbly decorated Rolls Royce with FM 1 as its licence number.

■ **Third night**: *Machines (Intro) / Tear It Up / Tie Your Mother Down / Under Pressure / Medley: Somebody To Love; Killer Queen; Seven Seas Of Rhye;*

Keep Yourself Alive; Liar / Improvisation / It's A Hard Life / Staying Power / Dragon Attack / Now I'm Here / Is This The World We Created / Love Of My Life / Stone Cold Crazy / Great King Rat / Machines (Keyboard Improvisation) / Guitar Solo / Brighton Rock / Another One Bites The Dust / Hammer To Fall / Crazy Little Thing Called Love / Saturday Night's Alright For Fighting / Bohemian Rhapsody / Radio Ga Ga / Encore: I Want To Break Free / Jailhouse Rock / 2nd Encore: We Will Rock You / We Are The Champions / God Save The Queen

'TEN YEARS AFTER' *(an uncredited revue): Roll up! Roll up! Step this way!*

'For a mere £9 you too can visit Mercury's Amazing Time Machine and be whisked back to a time when you could play and enjoy heavy metal and not be ashamed of it.

'The band are ten minutes late and plenty of eyes are being cast down at watches. Suddenly the lights dimmed and the Arena erupts. The impressive backdrop of pulleys and cogs ('The Works' – geddit?) springs into life, flashpots ignite and with a bang they're onstage at last...

'It was obvious that Freddie's overworked vocal chords were suffering, but with an impressive light show and the band on such form, there weren't any complaints. "You sing it!" he invites the crowd before 'Somebody To Love', and they dutifully obliged. His control over the crowd throughout was almost frightening to behold. One word was the signal for a roar of almost atomic proportions.'

■ ***Final night***: *Machines (Intro) / Tear It Up / Tie Your Mother Down / Under Pressure / Medley: Somebody To Love; Killer Queen; Seven Seas Of Rhye; Keep Yourself Alive; Liar / It's A Hard Life / Staying Power / Dragon Attack / Now I'm Here / Is This The World We Created / Love Of My Life / Stone Cold Crazy / Great King Rat / Machines (Keyboard Improvisation) / Guitar Solo / Brighton Rock / Another One Bites The Dust / Hammer To Fall / Crazy Little Thing Called Love / Saturday Night's Alright For Fighting / Bohemian Rhapsody / Radio Ga Ga / Encore: I Want To Break Free / Sheer Heart Attack / 2nd*

Encore: We Will Rock You / We Are The Champions / God Save The Queen

Following the acoustic guitar introduction to 'Love Of My Life', Freddie misses Brian's cue to begin singing, and general confusion ensues. Freddie ponders a while and then exclaims: "Well, we fucked that up between us," and both give a good humoured grin and restart the song. The audience erupts into laughter.

As with the shows in Birmingham, all four nights at this venue are sold out, each attended by capacity audiences of 8,000. Similarly, they are attended by numerous celebrities, including John Taylor of Duran Duran, racing driver Jackie Stewart, various members of Def Leppard, and actor John Hurt and his new wife. The Hurts have been guests at Freddie's birthday party, and are married the next morning.

Due largely to the seven NEC and Wembley Arena shows, in the week ending September 21, 1984, no less than nine Queen albums appeared in the UK Top 200 album chart: *The Works* (number nine), *Greatest Hits* (22), *A Night At The Opera* (85), *A Day At The Races* (123), *Sheer Heart Attack* (134), *The Game* (138), *Queen II* (148), *Live Killers* (160), *News Of The World* (161).

❖ **September 10**

'Hammer To Fall (Edit)' / 'Tear It Up' (both penned by Brian) is issued in the UK. Though two other tracks, 'Man On The Prowl' and 'Keep Passing The Open Windows', later accompany the non-album 'Thank God It's Christmas' single, this is the last track to be released as a main single from *The Works*. It peaks in the charts at number 13, due largely to the promotional film filmed in Brussels two weeks earlier.

The two tracks are a universal coupling although, surprisingly, Japan is overlooked. In America the disc is released a month later.

❖ Also released on September 10, is the first officially available worldwide Queen concert video (bootleg videos had surfaced before this, and the official *Live In Japan* was exclusive to that territory).

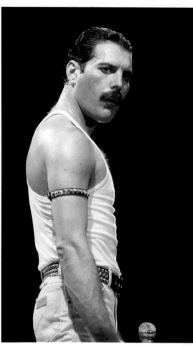

September 12
Westfallenhalle, Dortmund

September 14⟋/15⟋
Sportspalace, Milan ①

■ *First night*: Machines (Intro) / Tear It Up / Tie Your Mother Down / Under Pressure / Medley: Somebody To Love; Killer Queen; Seven Seas Of Rhye; Keep Yourself Alive; Liar / It's A Hard Life / Staying Power / Dragon Attack / Now I'm Here / Is This The World We Created / Love Of My Life / Stone Cold Crazy / Great King Rat / Machines (Keyboard Improvisation) / Guitar Solo / Brighton Rock / Another One Bites The Dust / Hammer To Fall / Crazy Little Thing Called Love / Bohemian Rhapsody / Radio Ga Ga / Encore: I Want To Break Free / Jailhouse Rock / 2nd Encore: We Will Rock You / We Are The Champions / God Save The Queen

■ *Second night*: Machines (Intro) / Tear It Up / Tie Your Mother Down / Under Pressure / Somebody To Love / Medley: Killer Queen; Seven Seas Of Rhye; Keep Yourself Alive; Liar / It's A Hard Life / Mustapha (part) / Dragon Attack / Now I'm Here / Is This The World We Created / Love Of My Life / Stone Cold Crazy / Great King Rat / Machines (Keyboard Improvisation) / Guitar Solo / Brighton Rock / Another One Bites The Dust / Hammer To Fall / Crazy Little Thing Called Love / Bohemian Rhapsody / Radio Ga Ga / Encore: I Want To Break Free / Jailhouse Rock / 2nd

'We Will Rock You' is a long awaited 21-track visual documentation of the two Montreal shows of November 1981. It enters the UK video charts in true Queen style, at number one. The video is directed by Saul Swimmer, who is also responsible for co-producing The Beatles *Let It Be* film. Originally scheduled for a Christmas 1982 release, *WWRY* was delayed because of problems with the eight-track Dolby sound system. The footage is also shown at selected British cinemas throughout September and October, and continues showing until early March 1985 - as attendance figures are better than anticipated. The promotional videos for 'Ga Ga', 'Hard Life', 'Break Free' and 'Hammer To Fall' accompany the film as the support programme.

Encore: We Will Rock You / We Are The Champions / God Save The Queen

September 16
Olympic Hall, Munich

September 18 ⚐
Omnisports, Paris

■ *Machines (Intro) / Tear It Up / Tie Your Mother Down / Under Pressure / Medley: Somebody To Love; Killer Queen; Seven Seas Of Rhye; Keep Yourself Alive; Liar / Improvisation / It's A Hard Life / Dragon Attack / Now I'm Here / Is This The World We Created / Love Of My Life / Stone Cold Crazy / Great King Rat / Machines (Keyboard Improvisation) / Guitar Solo / Brighton Rock / Another One Bites The Dust / Hammer To Fall / Crazy Little Thing Called Love / Bohemian Rhapsody / Radio Ga Ga / Encore: I Want To Break Free / Jailhouse Rock / 2nd Encore: We Will Rock You / We Are The Champions / God Save The Queen*

September 20
Groenoordhalle, Leiden

■ *Machines (Intro) / Tear It Up / Tie Your Mother Down / Under Pressure / Medley: Somebody To Love; Killer Queen; Seven Seas Of Rhye; Keep Yourself Alive; Liar / It's A Hard Life / Dragon Attack / Now I'm Here / Is This The World We Created / '39 / Love Of My Life / Stone Cold Crazy / Great King Rat / Machines (Keyboard Improvisation) / Guitar Solo / Brighton Rock / Another One Bites The Dust / Hammer To Fall / Crazy Little Thing Called Love / Bohemian Rhapsody / Radio Ga Ga / Encore: I Want To*

Break Free / Jailhouse Rock / 2nd Encore: We Will Rock You / We Are The Champions / God Save The Queen* Queen performs an impromptu recital of '39' here. They sing only a small segment of it, in response to the audience's prompting.

September 21 ⚐
Forêst Nationale, Brussels

■ *Machines (Intro) / Tear It Up / Tie Your Mother Down / Under Pressure / Somebody To Love / Medley: Killer Queen; Seven Seas Of Rhye; Keep Yourself Alive; Liar / Improvisation / It's A Hard Life / Dragon Attack / Now I'm Here / Is This The World We Created / Love Of My Life / Stone Cold Crazy / Great King Rat / Machines (Keyboard Improvisation) / Brighton Rock / Guitar Solo / Another One Bites The Dust / Hammer To Fall / Crazy Little Thing Called Love / Mustapha (Intro) / Bohemian Rhapsody / Radio Ga Ga / Encore: I Want To Break Free / Jailhouse Rock / 2nd Encore: We Will Rock You / We Are The Champions / God Save The Queen*

September 22
Europhalle, Hanover

During 'Hammer To Fall', Freddie falls heavily on the stage ladder and further damages his already injured knee. He is helped to the piano and performs three more songs. Two songs are abandoned and the show concludes prematurely with Freddie still seated at the piano. The 'show must go on' philosophy is never more true.

When the lights go down, Freddie is carried straight to a waiting car and driven to hospital. He performs the remaining five European shows with his leg heavily bandaged.

September 24
Deutschlandhalle, Berlin

September 26
Festhalle, Frankfurt

■ *Machines (Intro) / Tear It Up / Tie Your Mother Down / Under Pressure / Medley: Somebody To Love; Killer Queen; Seven Seas Of Rhye; Keep Yourself Alive; Liar / Improvisation / It's A Hard Life / Dragon Attack / Now I'm Here / Is This The World We Created / Love Of My Life / Stone Cold Crazy / Great King Rat / Machines (Keyboard Improvisation) / Brighton Rock / Guitar Solo / Another One Bites The Dust / Hammer To Fall / Crazy Little Thing Called Love / Bohemian Rhapsody / Radio Ga Ga / Encore: I Want To Break Free / Jailhouse Rock / 2nd Encore: We Will Rock You / We Are The Champions / God Save The Queen*

September 27 ⟋
Schleyerhalle, Stuttgart

■ *Machines (Intro) / Tear It Up / Tie Your Mother Down / Under Pressure / Medley: Somebody To Love; Killer Queen; Seven Seas Of Rhye; Keep Yourself Alive; Liar / It's A Hard Life / Dragon Attack / Now I'm Here /Is This The World We Created / Love Of My Life / Stone Cold Crazy / Great King Rat / Machines (Keyboard Improvisation) / Brighton Rock / Guitar Solo / Another One Bites The Dust / Hammer To Fall / Crazy Little Thing Called Love / Saturday Night's Alright For Fighting / Bohemian Rhapsody / Radio Ga Ga / Encore: I Want To Break Free / Jailhouse Rock /*

2nd Encore: We Will Rock You / We Are The Champions / God Save The Queen

September 29/30
Stadthalle, Vienna

■ *First night: Machines (Intro) / Tear It Up / Tie Your Mother Down / Under Pressure / Medley: Somebody To Love; Killer Queen; Seven Seas Of Rhye; Keep Yourself Alive; Liar / Improvisation / It's A Hard Life / Dragon Attack / Now I'm Here / Is This The World We Created / Love Of My Life / Stone Cold Crazy / Great King Rat / Machines (Keyboard Improvisation) / Brighton Rock / Guitar Solo / Another One Bites The Dust / Hammer To Fall / Crazy Little Thing Called Love / Saturday Night's Alright For Fighting / Bohemian Rhapsody / Radio Ga Ga / Encore: I Want To Break Free / Jailhouse Rock / 2nd Encore: We Will Rock You / We Are The Champions / God Save The Queen*

■ *Final night: Machines (Intro) / Tear It Up / Tie Your Mother Down / Under Pressure / Medley: Somebody To Love; Killer Queen; Seven Seas Of Rhye; Keep Yourself Alive; Liar / Improvisation / It's A Hard Life / Dragon Attack / Now I'm Here / Is This The World We Created / Love Of My Life / Stone Cold Crazy / Great King Rat / Machines (Keyboard Improvisation) / Brighton Rock / Guitar Solo / Another One Bites The Dust / Hammer To Fall / Crazy Little Thing Called Love / Bohemian Rhapsody / Radio Ga Ga / Encore: I Want To Break Free / Jailhouse Rock / 2nd Encore: We Will Rock You / We Are The Champions / God Save The Queen*

⟋ **'Ministry Of Works',** *Record Mirror, August 25, 1984: 'After the European tour, Queen will be taking the whole shebang down to South America, headlining a 10-day festival in Rio. The place they will be playing is an amphitheatre down by the sea that can seat 300,000 people a night. It all makes Castle Donington seem like just another night at the Marquee. A local radio station in Rio held a survey to see who the most popular bands were and them some local promoters went out and booked them for the extravaganza. Naturally Queen came out on top.*

'Queen will also be doing some shows in South Africa. This is more than a little controversial. Especially with the memory of Nelson Mandella still very warm.

'"We've thought about the morals of it a lot and it's something we've decided to do," says Brian May "This band is not political, we are not out to make statements, we play to anybody who comes to listen. The show will be in Botswana in front of a mixed audience."

'The band wanted to play Russia but the authorities objected. This situation may change though, considering that Iron Maiden have been let into Poland to wreak havoc.

'"The Russians still think we're very decadent," confides Roger Taylor. "We want to play China as well, and Korea and it's a fascinating place. They're finishing work on the Olympic Stadium for the next games!"'

SOUTH AFRICA 1984 - The Works Tour

Having concluded the European tour, Queen fly home for a few days before their controversial

South African shows begin.

The concerts have provoked a media storm since being announced in early May, and the band are naturally apprehensive.

Twelve shows are scheduled in all, but only seven will actually happen because Freddie again encounters problems with his throat. The cancelled shows will be those scheduled for October 6, 7, 9 and 12.

October 5/10/13/14/18/19/20
Super Bowl, Sun City, Bophuthatswana, South Africa ①
(now known as Northern Transvaal)

■ Machines (Intro) / Tear It Up / Tie Your Mother Down / Under Pressure / Medley: Somebody To Love; Killer Queen; Seven Seas Of Rhye; Keep Yourself Alive; Liar / Improvisation / It's A Hard Life / Dragon Attack / Now I'm Here / Is This The World We Created / Love Of My Life / Stone Cold Crazy / Great King Rat / Machines (Keyboard Improvisation) / Guitar Solo / Brighton Rock / Another One Bites The Dust / Hammer To Fall / Crazy Little Thing Called Love / Bohemian Rhapsody / Radio Ga Ga / Encore: I Want To Break Free / Jailhouse Rock / 2nd Encore: We Will Rock You / We Are The Champions / God Save The Queen

The sets differs hardly at all throughout the seven shows. This is the most common set performed.

When Freddie walks back on stage for the 'Break Free' encore, wearing the wig and proudly thrusting his plastic bosoms for all to admire, he is greeted with contempt. John Deacon's song has become widely recognised by South Africans as a stand against apartheid and dictatorship generally. This is not something to be taken lightly or in any way mocked or ridiculed. Freddie's comic attire is innappropriate, so the audience responds by hurling cans at him. Not meaning to offend, Freddie discards his assets and the show continus without further incident.

● An article published in *The Sun*, April 1986, refers to a remark made by Radio One presenter John Peel, about Queen's South African shows. Peel had referred to the band as "Sun City Boys

Queen", and Roger Taylor takes exception to this:

"I was totally disgusted by that remark. Peel is an ageing hypocrite trying to jump on some moral bandwagon. Now millions of people might think that we are racists, which is far from the case, because of some glib remark."

The article goes on to redress the balance, however, pointing out that Queen have repeatedly stated that they played Sun City specifically because it was a mixed audience. They *only* perform to non-segregated audiences.

"Our songs are very popular in South Africa," adds Roger. "'I Want To Break Free' is an unofficial anthem among the African National Congress Movement. And 'Another One Bites The Dust' is one of the biggest-selling songs in South African black history. It was ridiculous of Peel to say what he did."

In a separate article in *Smash Hits*, March 1986, Brian comments: "The criticisms are absolutely and definitely not justified. We're totally against apartheid and all it stands for, but I feel that by going there we did a lot of bridge building. We actually met musicians of both colours. They all welcomed us with open arms. The only criticism we got was from outside South Africa."

🔊 Jim Beach: "Some people have questioned whether or not we are right to play countries like these at all, and whether or not we seem to be supporting the political system. If we took that attitude there would be very few countries in the world outside Western Europe and North America where we would ever be able to play."

❖ As a result of the Sun City visit, EMI South Africa issue an edited version of the *Live Killers* album. All proceeds from the album (including EMI's) are donated to the Kutlwamong School for deaf and blind children. The money goes towards purchasing a new wing for the school.

This edited album was also issued in numerous other countries. Details of all of them are contained in the Live Discography section of this book.

❖ **November 26**
EMI release Queen's 28th UK single. 'Thank God It's Christmas', backed with the only two remaining unissued tracks from *The Works*, is timed to exploit the Christmas market. The three track disc fails to make the Top 20, however, missing it by only one place.

Brazil 1985 – Rock In Rio

January 12⌗/19⌗
Rock In Rio Festival, Rio De Janeiro

■ *Both nights: Machines (Intro) / Tear It Up / Tie Your Mother Down / Under Pressure / Medley: Somebody To Love; Killer Queen; Seven Seas Of Rhye; Keep Yourself Alive; Liar / Rock In Rio Blues / It's A Hard Life / Dragon Attack / Now I'm Here / Is This The World We Created / Love Of My Life / Improvisation (incorporating Let Me Out) / Brighton Rock / Guitar Solo / Another One Bites The Dust / Hammer To Fall / Crazy Little Thing Called Love / Bohemian Rhapsody / Radio Ga Ga / Encore: I Want To Break Free / Jailhouse Rock / 2nd Encore: We Will Rock You / We Are The Champions / God Save The Queen*

Highlighted tracks appear on the video.

Queen are the headline act for the huge Rock In Rio Festival. Though the festival runs for ten days, Queen perform on only two nights, the 12th and the 19th. The warm-up bands for Queen are Iron Maiden and Def Leppard for the first show and The Go Go's and B52's for the second.

An estimated audience of between 250,000 and 300,000 attends each show. Queen take to the stage at 2.00 a.m. for both their appearances. Edited highlights are later shown on Globo television throughout South America, and are watched by nearly 200 million people.

'Rock In Rio Blues' is similar to the piano improvisation played at previous European dates, but is reworked to incorporate lyrics written exclusively for the South American audience.

Brian: "You want to sing with us? Alright. Well, this is especially for you. I have to tell you that this song is very special to the people of South America, and we thank you very much for making it special throughout the world. This is called 'Love Of My Life'."

Freddie starts the ballad off, but the audience are anxious to show off their newly acquired English vocabulary. They almost drown him out before he allows them to continue without him.

Freddie is visibly moved, as is everyone on stage. He blows them a kiss, and Brian remarks "You sing very nicely."

When Freddie stops singing to let Brian begin his acoustic solo, a barrage of "Brian, Brian, Brian" fills the vast stadium, and now it is his turn to swallow hard. Later, he incorporated parts of 'Let Me Out' from the 1983 *Star Fleet* solo project into the guitar solo.

When Freddie appears with the wig and false boobs for 'I Want To Break Free', there is a similar response to that encountered in South Africa. This time, half expecting the reaction, Freddie laughs and abruptly discards the offending items. He later remarks: "I may have been stoned like the Queen of Sheba, but I'm not giving up my boobs for anyone."

Following 'Rock You', at the end of the show, Freddie emerges holding a large Union Jack flag above his head. He walks to the front of the stage and turns 180 degrees to reveal the Argentinean equivalent on the reverse side. A quarter of a million people cheer and applaud the gesture. Freddie then throws it into the audience. A fireworks display begins as 'God Save The Queen' plays out. In the next seconds the band are hurrying to their cars for their usual high-speed exit.

Apart from Globo Television's coverage of the festival, the second Queen show is filmed with the

intention of issuing it on home video, if all goes well - which it does. A 16-track video (as highlighted above) is eventually released on May 13, 1985.

While Queen are in Brazil, EMI throw a huge party in their honour around the swimming pool which Freddie's suite overlooks, at the Copacabana Palace Hotel in Rio. Every artist playing at the festival is invited, and many attend. Meanwhile, down on the beach near to the hotel, local Queen fans enjoy a party of their own. They place five hundred lighted candles in the sand spelling out the band's name. Brian hears about it and he and his daughter leave the official party for a while and join the fans on the beach. The gesture is much appreciated.

NEW ZEALAND 1985

On April 5 Queen fly to New Zealand for their very first show there. Despite what they consider to have been a blatant anti-apartheid gesture in performing in South Africa, they will soon find themselves in trouble with the Musicians' Union, and here they are met at the airport by anti-apartheid demonstrators. They will encounter

similar problems later, when they arrive at their hotel.

Again, the set is that already performed in Europe, South Africa and Brazil. Nothing is dropped or added. The sequence of songs played towards the latter part of the show varies slightly sometimes, but not significantly.

April 13 ⊘
Mount Smart Stadium, Auckland, New Zealand
①
■ *Machines (Intro) / Tear It Up / Tie Your Mother Down / Under Pressure / Medley: Somebody To Love; Killer Queen; Seven Seas Of Rhye; Keep Yourself Alive; Liar / Improvisation / It's A Hard Life / Dragon Attack / Now I'm Here / Is This The World We Created / Love Of My Life / Improvisation / Brighton Rock / Another One Bites The Dust / Hammer To Fall / Crazy Little Thing Called Love / Bohemian Rhapsody / Radio Ga Ga / Encore: I Want To Break Free / Jailhouse Rock / 2nd Encore: We Will Rock You / We Are The Champions / God Save The Queen*

When the band discover that Tony Hadley of Spandau Ballet has flown in from Australia especially to see their show, they invite him to join them on stage for the 'Jailhouse Rock' encore. Due

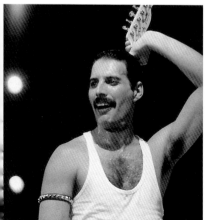

211

Your Mother Down / Under Pressure / Medley: Somebody To Love; Killer Queen; Seven Seas Of Rhye; Keep Yourself Alive; Liar / Improvisation / It's A Hard Life / Dragon Attack / Now I'm Here / Is This The World We Created / Love Of My Life / Improvisation / Brighton Rock / Another One Bites The Dust / Hammer To Fall / Crazy Little Thing Called Love / Bohemian Rhapsody / Radio Ga Ga / Encore: I Want To Break Free / Jailhouse Rock / 2nd Encore: We Will Rock You / We Are The Champions / God Save The Queen

Because the band have no show on April 18 they go instead to watch Phil Collins in concert. He duly returns the compliment by attending the Queen show on April 20.

■ *Third night*: *Machines (Intro) / Tear It Up / Tie Your Mother Down / Under Pressure / Medley: Somebody To Love; Killer Queen; Seven Seas Of Rhye; Keep Yourself Alive; Liar / Improvisation / It's A Hard Life / Dragon Attack (Guitar Version) / Now I'm Here / Is This The World We Created / Love Of My Life / Improvisation / Brighton Rock / Guitar Solo / Another One Bites The Dust / Hammer To Fall / Crazy Little Thing Called Love / Bohemian Rhapsody / Radio Ga Ga / Encore: I Want To Break Free / Jailhouse Rock / 2nd Encore: We Will Rock You / We Are The Champions / God Save The Queen*

■ *Final night*: *Machines (Intro) / Tear It Up / Tie Your Mother Down / Under Pressure / Medley: Somebody To Love; Killer Queen; Seven Seas Of Rhye; Keep Yourself Alive; Liar / Improvisation / It's A Hard Life / Dragon Attack / Now I'm Here / Is This The World We Created / Love Of My Life / Improvisation / Brighton Rock / Guitar Solo / Another One Bites The Dust / Hammer To Fall / Crazy Little Thing Called Love / Bohemian Rhapsody / Radio Ga Ga / Encore: I Want To Break Free / Jailhouse Rock / 2nd Encore: We Will Rock You / We Are The Champions / God Save The Queen*

This show is marred not only by the lighting rig, which gives up the ghost mid-way through the concert, but also re-occurring sound problems. Having been handed various microphones that don't work, Freddie becomes increasingly

not least to the alcohol he and Freddie have imbibed before the show, Hadley confuses lyrics of the song with those of 'Tutti Frutti', but muddles through it well enough.

Parts of this show are filmed and later broadcast throughout New Zealand. It yields a number of bootlegs.

AUSTRALIA 1985

Queen undertake a short two-week, two-venue mini tour of Australia, their first since 1976, performing four consecutive shows in Melbourne and Sydney. They fly into Melbourne hoping their concerts will be accepted rather better than had been the case almost a decade previously.

The band hope to perform concerts in the Far East following the eight shows here, but for a multitude of reasons no such shows will ever materialise.

April 16/17/19⌐/20⌐
Sports & Entertainment Centre, Melbourne
■ *First night*: *Machines (Intro) / Tear It Up / Tie*

While in Sydney, Brian and John attend the Opera House as guests of John Reid - Elton John's manager and Queen's ex-manager.

■ *Third night*: Machines (Intro) / Tear It Up / Tie Your Mother Down / Under Pressure / Medley: Somebody To Love; Killer Queen; Seven Seas Of Rhye; Keep Yourself Alive; Liar / Improvisation / It's A Hard Life / Dragon Attack / Now I'm Here / Is This The World We Created / Love Of My Life / Improvisation / Brighton Rock / Guitar Solo / Another One Bites The Dust / Hammer To Fall / Crazy Little Thing Called Love / Bohemian Rhapsody / Radio Ga Ga / Encore: I Want To Break Free / Jailhouse Rock / 2nd Encore: We Will Rock You / We Are The Champions / God Save The Queen

On April 30 Queen return home to London for a few days off, and to prepare for what will be their final visit to Japan.

JAPAN 1985

May 7/9
Budokan Hall, Tokyo

■ *First night*: Machines (Intro) / Tear It Up / Tie Your Mother Down / Under Pressure / Medley: Somebody To Love; Killer Queen; Seven Seas Of Rhye; Keep Yourself Alive; Liar / Fooling Around (Instrumental Jam) / It's A Hard Life / Dragon Attack / Now I'm Here / Is This The World We Created / Love Of My Life / Improvisation / Brighton Rock / Guitar Solo / Another One Bites The Dust / Hammer To Fall / Crazy Little Thing Called Love / Bohemian Rhapsody / Radio Ga Ga / Encore: I Want To Break Free / Jailhouse Rock / 2nd Encore: We Will Rock You / We Are The Champions / God Save The Queen

An identical show to that played in Melbourne the preceding month, but with the addition of the 'Fooling Around' jam. This experimental song is later included in the 1986 'Magic' tour set.

■ *Second night*: Machines (Intro) / Tear It Up / Tie Your Mother Down / Under Pressure / Medley: Somebody To Love; Killer Queen; Seven Seas Of Rhye; Keep Yourself Alive; Liar / Fooling Around

irritated. He finally snaps at a member of the audience whose request for 'Mustapha' is badly timed. "Fuck it! You don't get it," he barks.

Due to the technical difficulties the show starts so late that it does finish until 12.30am, hence Freddie telling the crowd, "We'll see you again tonight."

April 25/26/28/29
Entertainments Centre, Sydney

■ *First and second nights*: Machines (Intro) / Tear It Up / Tie Your Mother Down / Under Pressure / Medley: Somebody To Love; Killer Queen; Seven Seas Of Rhye; Keep Yourself Alive; Liar / Improvisation / It's A Hard Life / Dragon Attack / Now I'm Here / Is This The World We Created / Love Of My Life / Improvisation / Brighton Rock / Guitar Solo / Another One Bites The Dust / Hammer To Fall / Crazy Little Thing Called Love / Bohemian Rhapsody / Radio Ga Ga / Encore: I Want To Break Free / Jailhouse Rock / 2nd Encore: We Will Rock You / We Are The Champions / God Save The Queen

(Instrumental Jam) / It's A Hard Life / Dragon Attack / Now I'm Here / Is This The World We Created / Love Of My Life / Improvisation / Brighton Rock / Guitar Solo / Another One Bites The Dust / Hammer To Fall / Crazy Little Thing Called Love / Bohemian Rhapsody / Radio Ga Ga / Encore: I Want To Break Free / Jailhouse Rock / 2nd Encore: We Will Rock You / We Are The Champions / God Save The Queen

May 10/11⍈
Yoyogi Kyogijo (Swimming Pool Auditorium), Tokyo

■ *Second night*: Machines (Intro) / Tear It Up / Tie Your Mother Down / Under Pressure / Medley: Somebody To Love; Killer Queen; Seven Seas Of Rhye; Keep Yourself Alive; Liar / Fooling Around (Instrumental Jam) / It's A Hard Life / Dragon Attack / Now I'm Here / Is This The World We Created / Love Of My Life / Improvisation / Brighton Rock / Guitar Solo / Another One Bites The Dust / Hammer To Fall / Crazy Little Thing Called Love / Bohemian Rhapsody / Radio Ga Ga / Encore: I Want To Break Free / Jailhouse Rock / 2nd Encore: We Will Rock You / We Are The Champions / God Save The Queen

This is another of Queen's most widely bootlegged shows.

May 13
Aichi-ken Taiikukan, Nagoya

■ Machines (Intro) / Tear It Up / Tie Your Mother Down / Under Pressure / Medley: Somebody To Love; Killer Queen; Seven Seas Of Rhye; Keep Yourself Alive; Liar / Improvisation / It's A Hard Life / Dragon Attack / Now I'm Here (incorporating Johnny B. Goode) / Is This The World We Created / Love Of My Life / Improvisation / Brighton Rock / Guitar Solo / Another One Bites The Dust / Hammer To Fall / Crazy Little Thing Called Love / Saturday Night's Alright For Fighting / Bohemian Rhapsody / Radio Ga Ga / Encore: I Want To Break Free / Jailhouse Rock / 2nd Encore: We Will Rock You / We Are The Champions / God Save The Queen

A Concert Documentary

❖ Picture Music International release *Live In Rio*. The 16-track video offers an edited account of Queen's second concert at the Rock In Rio Festival, recorded on January 19. As *We Will Rock You* had done before it, the video enters the British video charts at number one.

May 15

Osaka-jo Hall, Osaka

■ *Machines (Intro) / Tear It Up / Tie Your Mother Down / Under Pressure / Medley: Somebody To Love; Killer Queen; Seven Seas Of Rhye; Keep Yourself Alive; Liar / Improvisation / It's A Hard Life / Dragon Attack / Now I'm Here / Is This The World We Created / Love Of My Life / Improvisation / Brighton Rock / Guitar Solo / Another One Bites The Dust / Mustapha / Hammer To Fall / Crazy Little Thing Called Love / Saturday Night's Alright For Fighting / Bohemian Rhapsody / Radio Ga Ga / Encore: I Want To Break Free / Jailhouse Rock (incorporating Whole Lotta Shakin Going On) / 2nd Encore: We Will Rock You / We Are The Champions / God Save The Queen*

May 17

Queen fly home.

June 21

Brian attends a trade fair in New Orleans to promote and demonstrate a newly produced copy of his guitar, by Guild. During his stay he visits a local club and ends up on stage playing in a jam session with John Entwistle and Eddie Van Halen.

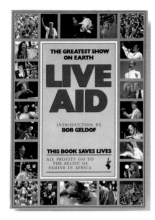

July 13

Live Aid, Wembley Stadium, London

■ *Bohemian Rhapsody / Radio Ga Ga / Hammer To Fall / Crazy Little Thing Called Love / We Will Rock You / We Are The Champions*

London line up: (in order of appearance) Status Quo, The Style Council, The Boomtown Rats, Adam Ant, Ultravox, Spandau Ballet, Elvis Costello, Nik Kershaw, Sade, Sting, Phil Collins, Howard Jones, Bryan Ferry, Paul Young, Alison Moyet, U2, Dire Straits (with Sting), Queen, David Bowie, The Who, Elton John, Kiki Dee, Wham, Brian May & Freddie Mercury, Paul McCartney, Finale.

This concert is conceived by Bob Geldof, as was the Band Aid charity single that preceded it in late 1984. Geldof was so appalled by the images he saw on Michael Buerke's harrowing television famine news reports from Ethiopia that he immediately set about contacting every established name in the music industry to secure their services for the event. He eventually gets Queen by tracking down Jim Beach in New Zealand, having first made contact in Japan and then again in Australia. Geldof's tenacity will become legendary.

The entire show is broadcast live by BBC TV

and Radio One, and is beamed via satellite to over 160 countries, reaching a combined audience of one and a half billion people (a third of the Earth's population) on 80 per cent of the televisions on the planet. It is the perfect audience for Freddie Mercury.

The event proves to be an unparalleled technical and logistical nightmare, but is ultimately a fantastic and unprecedented success, raising over £50 million for the starving people of Ethiopia and neighbouring African countries.

Queen are introduced on stage by comedians Mel Smith and Griff Rhys Jones, both of whom are dressed in police uniforms: "Her Majesty... Queen." Queen bound onto stage. The time is precisely 6.44 pm. Because of the time difference, Queen are the first act to be seen in Philadelphia, where the parallel concert is taking place. This is no accident!

Freddie seats himself at the piano and 'Bo Rhap' begins immediately. Before the operatic part begins, he is handed his microphone and struts around the vast Wembley stage singing 'Radio Ga Ga'. Despite a throat infection and doctor's advice not to perform, he looks and sounds his very best. During the main verses of the song, the audience once again unites in a wave of overhead clapping. It is executed, as ever, with military type precision.

Freddie walks to centre stage and indulges the crowd with some of his vocal improvisation. They respond gladly. Then he initiates 'Hammer To Fall'... Queen's Live Aid pièce de résistance. When Freddie is pursued across the stage by a cameraman, he stops and spins around him, his face only inches from the lens. When the impromptu play-acting is over, Freddie walks away with his thumb pointing backwards over his shoulder – as if to gesture that the cameraman is mad. This is truly wonderful stuff.

"This next song is only dedicated to beautiful people here tonight – that means all of you. Thank you for coming along and making this such a great occasion." 'Crazy Little Thing' begins. Freddie remains static for the most part, standing at the microphone. When Brian takes his guitar solo, a horrible feedback squeal accompanies the first half. The band finishes its 20 minute 'global jukebox' show with 'Rock You' segueing into 'Champions' and Freddie is once again back at the piano. For the final verse he gets up on his feet again inciting the audience to sing along with him. They do. Even the once reluctant anti-Queenists are persuaded to sing, and they too give it everything.

Queen's performance is devastating. As will soon be widely documented, the band truly have stolen the show – the biggest show on earth. Not only has this mighty performance guaranteed more record sales, and reminded the world that Queen is still one of the planet's biggest rock music forces, but it has confirmed in the minds of the band members that Queen is too important to end.

Freddie and Brian later return to the stage (at 9.48 pm), just prior to the finale. Introduced by actor John Hurt, they perform the acoustic *Works* track 'Is This The World We Created', a song they composed together which features lyrics as appropriate to the occasion as anything performed this day. Unfortunately, again the performance is marred by recurring feedback.

Prior to this show, there had been speculation about Queen's future. An article in *The Sun* in April 1986 focused on just that. Entitled 'How Live Aid Saved Our Queen', Martin Dunn's feature included numerous quotes from Roger on the general mood and feeling within the band prior to receiving the telephone call from Bob Geldof:

💬 "Whenever we have a band meeting, it's like World War III. We had been living in each others' pockets for months and I had frequently argued with Brian over everything. Our act had become jaded and stale. We were all determined to get away from Queen for a long while."

"Live Aid proved a fantastic tonic for us. Now we can't wait to hit the stage again.

"It was a great idea. It was a great day, great show, and it also proved, for us, that we could be quite effective with virtually no lights, because it was daylight, and absolutely no effects or anything, and it, you know, all we had was sound really."

Brian: "We had to go on Live Aid naked, more or less. We didn't have any lights. It was daylight, middle of the day. We didn't have our sound system. We didn't have a lot of our regular guys. We had a thrown together back line, because it had to be thrown on the stage and thrown off again, and we went on in jeans and shirts, as us, and the fact that it worked and the whole stadium rose to it, was a big confidence booster."

In the same interview, Roger also recalled an amusing Freddie anecdote: "We were playing at the huge San Remo festival in Italy and were due on stage in five minutes. I was really screaming at everyone, especially Brian. I hated some of the things he'd chosen to play in the concert, and he hated the stage settings we'd dreamed up. The atmosphere was so highly charged anything could have happened.

"Then someone realised that Freddie wasn't there. They burst into his changing room and found him still sitting in his underpants and vest, eating a bowl of cornflakes. We just all collapsed in hysterics. And that's Freddie's secret, he will always do the most unexpected thing and bring us back together."

Queen's performance at Live Aid is a triumph of colossal proportions that both revitalises the band and gains them thousands of new fans. The rehearsals at the Shaw Theatre have paid off and Queen is a tight unit once more.

Live Aid featured sixty-three different acts, performing in London and Philadelphia at no cost. All 72,000 tickets for the show sold out within four hours of going on sale, each at a cost of £25 – no small sum in 1985.

In 2004, Live Aid was released on DVD for the very first time (officially). It marked the 20th anniversary of the Band Aid single, and raised further funds for Africa.

❖ November 4

Queen's only single of the year is released. Preceding the album *A Kind Of Magic* by almost exactly six months, 'One Vision' provides an unexpectedly positive conclusion to the year by reaching number seven in the UK charts. Backed with the non-album mish-mash track 'Blurred Vision', the disc is another universal pairing. Once again though, the American sales figures do little to inspire confidence, when the disc peaks at a miserable number 61.

❖ December 2

The Complete Works boxed set is released only in the UK. It comprises all the albums up to *The Works* (excluding *Greatest Hits*), and an extra seven-track rarities album called *Complete Vision*. Every disc is repackaged in a plain white embossed sleeve and contains digitally remastered material for the first time.

The tracks on the bonus album were: 'See What A Fool I've Been', 'A Human Body'. 'Soul Brother', 'I Go Crazy', 'Thank God It's Christmas', 'One Vision', 'Blurred Vision'.

❖ **March 17**

Roger Taylor's 'A Kind Of Magic' single is released from the soon to follow album of the same name. Backed with the non-album instrumental track 'A Dozen Red Roses For My Darling' (also written by Roger), it goes on to be a number three hit in the UK. The American release (June 4) is instead coupled with the frantic Brian May gem 'Gimme The Prize'. It reaches number 42. EMI in Japan also issue this Roger Taylor pairing. The single is aided greatly by a superb, partially animated promotional video, something not done by Queen since 'Save Me', in 1980.

❖ **April 7**

'Princes Of The Universe' / 'A Dozen Red Roses For My Darling' is released in America. Apart from Japan, where it is coupled with 'Who Wants To Live Forever', it is completely overlooked for release elsewhere, despite being one of the *Magic* album's standout tracks, and having the support of one of Queen's finest promotional videos, in which Christopher Lambert makes a cameo appearance. The track is

never employed in the live set; one of the most notable concert absentees of all.

May 15

The promotional video for 'Friends Will Be Friends' is filmed at a studio in Wembley which Queen are using for rehearsals. Some 850 Queen fans are drafted in to assist. Following the filming, the band perform an impromptu live set by way of a thank you.

May

Golden Rose Pop Festival, Montreux, Switzerland
■ *One Vision / Friends Will Be Friends / Hammer To Fall*

Queen return to the annual Golden Rose rock festival in Montreux, as they had done in 1984. This time they mime to three tracks from the *Magic* album.

❖ **June 2**

A Kind Of Magic Queen's twelfth studio album is released in the UK. Though the material is written for Russel Mulcahy's Highlander film, it is not regarded as a soundtrack album - as *Flash Gordon* had been six years earlier.

Of the nine tracks, five will never appear in the live set. John Deacon must have been most

frustrated as two of the five oversights are his songs. 'Pain Is So Close To Pleasure' (co-written with Freddie) is the most heavily dance-oriented song on the album, and probably accounts for its exclusion, but why 'One Year Of Love' is not incorporated, is baffling. The remaining tracks are among the most extraordinary omissions of Queen's entire concert history. Written by Brian, Roger and Freddie respectively, 'Gimme The Prize', 'Don't Lose Your Head' and 'Princes Of The Universe' all contain classic Queen trademarks, and would have converted brilliantly to the stage environment. None are played even once!

EUROPE 1986 - The Magic Tour

Following an unusually long period of rehearsal in London during May, Queen travel to Stockholm for the first Magic Tour shows. Roger Taylor tells journalists that the tour will feature the most elaborate lighting set-up ever seen in a Queen show. It is the most expensive stage production ever undertaken too.

🗨 "We are going to play on the biggest stage ever built at Wembley, with the greatest light show ever seen. I think we are probably the best live band in the world at the moment, and we are going to prove it. No one who comes to see us will be disappointed." His comments will prove not to be exaggerated.

The Magic Tour incorporates the UK and nine European countries only. It is never taken to America, Japan or Canada, as were most other tours. It consists of 26 performances at twenty separate locations, played over an eight-week

period. It includes Queen's first and only show in Budapest, Hungary (which is filmed and later issued on video), and also their only concert at the beautiful Knebworth Park site, in Hertfordshire. The 15th century mansion house would be a fitting location for what would sadly prove to be Queen's very last concert.

The stage is 64 feet long and has two wings each side which add another 40 feet each and covers 6,000 sq ft in total. For the Wembley and Knebworth Park shows, two 60 x 15 feet Starvision screens are used, which alone weigh twenty tons. They are supported by a custom made two-piece bridge-like structure, made by an engineering company normally involved in motorway and bridge construction. Six trucks are required to transport it. Such is the weight of the completed structure that it is counterbalanced behind the stage by a vast water tank. Nine trucks in all are required to transport the stage equipment.

The lighting rig weighs in at nine and a half tons and by itself occupies four of the 40 feet trucks. The PA system consists of 180 Claire Brothers S4 speaker cabinets, 150 Carver amplifiers, sixty-four input channels (on two Audio mixing desks), and four racks of electronics, which put out a combined total of 245,000 watts of power.

During the tour the trucks which transport the equipment cover just over 165,000 miles, the equivalent of nearly seven times around the Earth.

The set has now changed drastically. Although the previous album (*The Works*) is still well represented by 'Tear It Up', 'Break Free', 'Is This The World', 'Hammer To Fall' and 'Ga Ga', the new one is represented rather less than might have been expected. While 'One Vision', 'Who Wants To Live Forever', 'Friends Will Be Friends' and 'A Kind Of Magic' all now feature, five others do not.

'One Vision' opens the show, 'Machines' disappears completely, as do 'Killer Queen', 'Somebody To Love', 'Dragon Attack', 'Great King Rat', 'Jailhouse Rock' and 'Keep Yourself

223

Alive', but an exciting new rock'n'roll medley now includes '(You're So Square) Baby I Don't Care', 'Tutti Frutti', 'Hello Mary Lou', and occasional renderings of 'Gimme Some Lovin'' and 'Saturday Night's Alright For Fighting', as well as snippets of 'Stupid Cupid' and 'Shake Rattle & Roll'. 'Liar' is gone from the set too, but riffs from it do feature, fleetingly, towards the end of 'Seven Seas'.

June 7
Rasunda Fotbollstadion, Stockholm

■ *One Vision / Tie Your Mother Down / Medley: In The Lap Of The Gods (Revisited); Seven Seas Of Rhye; Tear It Up / A Kind Of Magic / Under Pressure / Another One Bites The Dust / Who Wants To Live Forever / I Want To Break Free / Improvisation / Now I'm Here / Love Of My Life / Is This The World We Created / Medley: (You're So Square) Baby I Don't Care; Hello Mary Lou; Tutti Frutti / Bohemian Rhapsody / Hammer To Fall / Crazy Little Thing Called Love / Radio Ga Ga / Encore: We Will Rock You / We Are The Champions / God Save The Queen*

Not for the first time, the band encounters anti-apartheid protesters outside the stadium. They are responding to comments Brian had made for a Swedish magazine article. Typically, he had been quoted out of context.

During this show, a sound engineer conducts a noise check on the audience. The startling news emerges that the audience vocal output is only one decibel less than that put out by Queen's vast bank of loudspeakers.

The support act is Gary Moore.

❖ June 9
'Friends Will Be Friends' coupled with 'Seven Seas Of Rhye', from 1974, is released in the UK. Assisted by a promotional video which featured fan club members interacting with Queen, it achieves a number 14 chart placing. In America and Japan 'Pain Is So Close To Pleasure' and 'Princes Of The Universe' respectively, were issued instead.

June 11/12 ♪
Groenoordhalle, Leiden

■ *First night: One Vision / Tie Your Mother Down / Medley: In The Lap Of The Gods (Revisited); Seven Seas Of Rhye; Tear It Up / A Kind Of Magic / Under Pressure / Another One Bites The Dust / Who Wants To Live Forever / I Want To Break Free / Improvisation*

/ Now I'm Here / Love Of My Life / Is This The World We Created / Medley: (You're So Square) Baby I Don't Care; Hello Mary Lou; Tutti Frutti / Bohemian Rhapsody / Hammer To Fall / Crazy Little Thing Called Love / Radio Ga Ga / Encore: We Will Rock You / Friends Will Be Friends / We Are The Champions / God Save The Queen

■ *Second night*: One Vision / Tie Your Mother Down / Medley: In The Lap Of The Gods (Revisited); Seven Seas Of Rhye; Tear It Up / A Kind Of Magic / Under Pressure / Another One Bites The Dust / Who Wants To Live Forever / I Want To Break Free / Improvisation / Gimme Some Lovin' / Now I'm Here / Love Of My Life / Is This The World We Created / Medley: (You're So Square) Baby I Don't Care; Hello Mary Lou; Tutti Frutti / Bohemian Rhapsody / Hammer To Fall / Crazy Little Thing Called Love / Radio Ga Ga / Encore: We Will Rock You / Friends Will Be Friends / We Are The Champions / God Save The Queen

The band play 'Gimme Some Lovin' at this show. Again, this song very rarely features in the set.

June 14
Hippodrome De Vincennes, Paris
■ *One Vision / Tie Your Mother Down / Medley: In The Lap Of The Gods (Revisited); Seven Seas Of Rhye;*

Tear It Up / A Kind Of Magic / Under Pressure / Another One Bites The Dust / Who Wants To Live Forever / I Want To Break Free / Improvisation / Now I'm Here / Love Of My Life / Is This The World We Created / Medley: (You're So Square) Baby I Don't Care; Hello Mary Lou; Tutti Frutti / Bohemian Rhapsody / Hammer To Fall / Crazy Little Thing Called Love / Radio Ga Ga / Encore: We Will Rock You / Friends Will Be Friends / We Are The Champions / God Save The Queen

The support acts here are Level 42 and

Marillion – and also for the shows on June 21 and 26, and July 19.

June 17
Forêst Nationale, Brussels

■ *One Vision / Tie Your Mother Down / Medley: In The Lap Of The Gods (Revisited); Seven Seas Of Rhye; Tear It Up / A Kind Of Magic / Under Pressure / Another One Bites The Dust / Who Wants To Live Forever / I Want To Break Free / Improvisation / Now I'm Here / Love Of My Life / Is This The World We Created / Medley: (You're So Square) Baby I Don't Care; Hello Mary Lou; Tutti Frutti / Bohemian Rhapsody / Hammer To Fall / Crazy Little Thing Called Love / Radio Ga Ga / Encore: We Will Rock You / Friends Will Be Friends / We Are The Champions / God Save The Queen*

June 19
Groenoordhalle, Leiden

■ *One Vision / Tie Your Mother Down / Medley: In*

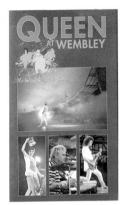

The Lap Of The Gods (Revisited); Seven Seas Of Rhye; Tear It Up / A Kind Of Magic / Under Pressure / Another One Bites The Dust / Who Wants To Live Forever / I Want To Break Free / Improvisation / Now I'm Here / 39 (part) / Love Of My Life / Is This The World We Created / Medley: (You're So Square) Baby I Don't Care; Hello Mary Lou; Tutti Frutti / Bohemian Rhapsody / Hammer To Fall / Crazy Little Thing Called Love / Radio Ga Ga / Encore: We Will Rock You / Friends Will Be Friends / We Are The Champions / God Save The Queen

Brian performs a short extract of '39 at this concert. Why? Because July 19th 1986 is his 39th birthday.

June 21 ♪
Maimarktgelande, Mannheim

■ *One Vision / Tie Your Mother Down / Medley: In The Lap Of The Gods (Revisited); Seven Seas Of Rhye; Tear It Up / A Kind Of Magic / Under Pressure / Another One Bites The Dust / Who Wants To Live Forever / I Want To Break Free / Improvisation (incorporating Gimme Some Lovin') / Improvisation / Now I'm Here / Love Of My Life / Is This The World We Created / Medley: (You're So Square) Baby I Don't Care; Hello Mary Lou; Tutti Frutti / Bohemian Rhapsody / Hammer To Fall / Crazy Little Thing Called Love / Radio Ga Ga / Encore: We Will Rock You*

/ *Friends Will Be Friends* / *We Are The Champions* / *God Save The Queen*

During the soundcheck Freddie decides to make his initial entrance on stage via a metal bucket which will be lowered down by a crane. The equipment is drafted in, but soon returned when Freddie discovers that being crammed into a metal bucket and hoisted up high is somewhat undignified, not to mention terrifying. The idea is abandoned.

Fish (from Marillion) joins the band on stage for

'Tutti Frutti'. This concert is broadcast live on German radio, British national anthem and all, and also later features on a US radio series *Off The Record*, titled 'Done Under Pressure'. The show has since become widely bootlegged, and is available in countless different forms, on various formats.

June 26

Waldbuehne, Berlin

■ *One Vision* / *Tie Your Mother Down* / *Medley: In The Lap Of The Gods (Revisited); Seven Seas Of Rhye; Tear It Up* / *A Kind Of Magic* / *Under Pressure* / *Another One Bites The Dust* / *Who Wants To Live Forever* / *I Want To Break Free* / *Immigrant Song* / *Improvisation* / *Now I'm Here* / *Love Of My Life* / *Is This The World We Created* / *Medley: (You're So Square) Baby I Don't Care; Hello Mary Lou; Tutti Frutti* / *Bohemian Rhapsody* / *Hammer To Fall* / *Crazy Little Thing Called Love* / *Radio Ga Ga* / *Encore: We Will Rock You* / *Friends Will Be Friends* / *We Are The Champions* / *God Save The Queen*

Queen perform an extremely rare rendition of Led Zeppelin's 'Immigrant Song' at this show. Bootleg copies, of which there are at least two, are worth purchasing just for this, even if both do offer relatively poor sound reproduction.

June 28/29

Olympiahalle, Munich

■ **First night**: *One Vision* / *Tie Your Mother Down* /

Medley: In The Lap Of The Gods (Revisited); Seven Seas Of Rhye; Tear It Up / A Kind Of Magic / Under Pressure / Another One Bites The Dust / Who Wants To Live Forever / I Want To Break Free / Improvisation / Now I'm Here / Love Of My Life / Is This The World We Created / Medley: (You're So Square) Baby I Don't Care; Hello Mary Lou; Tutti Frutti / Bohemian Rhapsody / Hammer To Fall / Crazy Little Thing Called Love / Radio Ga Ga / Encore: We Will Rock You / Friends Will Be Friends /We Are The Champions / God Save The Queen

July 1/2
Hallenstadion, Zurich
First night: set same as June 28, but with 'Mustapha (Intro)' after 'Tutti Fruitti'.

Second night: set same as June 28, but with no 'In The Lap Of The Gods (Revisited)' or 'Who Wants To Live Forever'.

July 5 ♫
Slane Castle, Dublin
■ *One Vision / Tie Your Mother Down / Medley: In The Lap Of The Gods (Revisited); Seven Seas Of Rhye; Tear It Up / A Kind Of Magic / Under Pressure / Another One Bites The Dust / Who Wants To Live Forever / I Want To Break Free / Improvisation / Gimme Some Loving / Guitar Solo / Now I'm Here / Love Of My Life / Is This The World We Created / Medley: (You're So Square) Baby I Don't Care; Hello Mary Lou; Tutti Frutti / Bohemian*

Rhapsody / Hammer To Fall / Crazy Little Thing Called Love / Radio Ga Ga / Encore: We Will Rock You / Friends Will Be Friends / We Are The Champions.

The 95,000 crowd begins to descend on the ground here, at 9 am, as soon as the gates open, and nine hours before Queen are due on stage.

As 'Seven Seas Of Rhye' nears its end, Freddie is forced stop the show when an inebriated member of the audience staggers over a cable and rips it out. The cable is one of many linking the stage mixing desk to a 24-track mobile recording studio the band are using to record the show.

Later on, after being hit by a can thrown from the audience, an outraged Brian threatens not to return to the stage for an encore. Reluctantly he and the band return, without further incodent.

Brian later describes this as his worst ever moment on stage.

The show finishes early due to the lack of lights on site and the possible hazard to those making their way out of the grounds. The National Anthem is not played.

The support acts are The Bangles, Fountainhead and Chris Rea.

July 9 [♪]
St James Park, Newcastle-Upon-Tyne
■ *One Vision / Tie Your Mother Down / Medley: In The Lap Of The Gods (Revisited); Seven Seas Of Rhye; Tear It Up / A Kind Of Magic / Under Pressure / Another One Bites The Dust / Who Wants To Live Forever / I Want To Break Free / Improvisation / Now I'm Here / Love Of My Life / Is This The World We Created / Medley: (You're So Square) Baby I Don't Care; Hello Mary Lou; Tutti Frutti / Bohemian Rhapsody / Hammer To Fall / Crazy Little Thing Called Love / Radio Ga Ga / Encore: We Will Rock You*

/ *Friends Will Be Friends / We Are The Champions / God Save The Queen*

The show is the largest ever staged in Newcastle. The queue for tickets is longer than that seen in 1974, when Newcastle United reached the FA Cup Final. All 38,000 tickets are sold within an hour. The proceeds are donated to the Save The Children Fund. Many local children who have benefited from projects run by the charity, attend the show and meet the band afterwards. Brian dedicates 'Is This The World We Created' to the fund during the show.

Jim Beach later recalls that Queen are so overwhelmed by Newcastle's enthusiasm to see them that they want to offer some token of appreciation here. Princes Anne's dedication to Save The Children provided the perfect opportunity.

July 11/12 [♪]
Wembley Stadium, London
■ *First night: One Vision / Tie Your Mother Down / Medley: In The Lap Of The Gods (Revisited); Seven Seas Of Rhye; Tear It Up / A Kind Of Magic / Under Pressure / Another One Bites The Dust / Who Wants To Live Forever / I Want To Break Free / Improvisation / Now I'm Here / Love Of My Life / Is This The World We Created / Medley: (You're So Square) Baby I Don't Care; Hello Mary Lou; Tutti Frutti / Bohemian Rhapsody / Hammer To Fall / Crazy Little Thing Called Love / Radio Ga Ga / Encore: We Will Rock You / Friends Will Be Friends / We Are The Champions / God Save The Queen*

When major problems are encountered attempting to fit the stage into position, the crew are baffled and somewhat panic stricken. On investigation it is discovered that the architectural plans for Wembley Stadium are precisely four feet out, making it impossible to fit the already designed stage construction into place. Working from the plans, the crew had designed a stage to fit into one complete end of the stadium. When it proved to be over a yard too long, everyone pulls together to rebuild one which does fit in time for the show. An apparently minor oversight very nearly resulted in Queen's first home town gig since Live Aid being cancelled.

Support acts were Status Quo, The Alarm and INXS. Attendance each night is 72,000

As Queen begin 'A Kind Of Magic', four huge inflatable caricature dummies of the band (as depicted on the LP artwork) are released into the air. While two of them are quickly dragged into the audience and punctured, the others escape into the night air. Though this author cannot recall exactly what happened to John, I vividly remember watching Freddie's grinning face floating higher and higher into the London sky until it was visible no more. A somewhat startled lady several miles away apparently found the half deflated Queen frontman in her garden the next morning.

'Is This The World' as recorded here is later used for the *Live Magic* album, as is 'Hammer To Fall' from the following evening's performance.

■ *Second night*: One Vision / Tie Your Mother Down / Medley: In The Lap Of The Gods (Revisited); Seven Seas Of Rhye / A Kind Of Magic / Under Pressure / Another One Bites The Dust / Who Wants To Live Forever / I Want To Break Free / Improvisation / Now I'm Here / Love Of My Life / Is This The World We Created / Medley: (You're So Square) Baby I Don't Care; Hello Mary Lou; Tutti Frutti / Gimme Some Loving / Bohemian Rhapsody / Hammer To Fall / Crazy Little Thing Called Love / Big Spender / Radio Ga Ga / Encore: We Will Rock You / Friends Will Be Friends / We Are The Champions / God Save The Queen

This show is filmed by Tyne Tees Television, and later broadcast as their first ever radio / television simulcast, transmitted to all 48 stations in the Independent Radio Network. The stereo radio sound is beamed via satellite to the stations and requires a quarter second delay to ensure it synchronises exactly with the television pictures. Satellites are used only because no land lines exist to carry the signals.

As at the June 1982 Milton Keynes Bowl show, Gavin Taylor is employed to direct the programme. He ultimately uses fifteen different cameras, which are not only situated in every conceivable place on and around the stage, but are mounted on cranes outside the stadium and operated by remote control. As an extra touch, he sites a hidden 35mm stills camera on the stage. Still shots from this are incorporated into the programme during final editing.

When the show is finally broadcast, on October 25 (on Channel 4), it is a wonderfully produced and entertaining programme – even for non-Queen enthusiasts – and is watched by 3.5 million people. The programme is titled *Real Magic* and it is also broadcast in America as part of Westwood One's *Superstar Concert* series. To confuse matters further, some unofficial recordings of the TV/radio broadcasts circulate under the guise of *Don't Lose Your Seat*. Due to public demand Channel 4 eventually repeat the programme, on January 2, 1987.

↗ The following morning's *Sun* carries this report by Mydrim Jones:

'*Freddie Mercury, the outrageous leader of Queen, reigned supreme at Wembley Stadium as he brought the house down amid plumes of smoke and brilliantly coloured lights. He whipped up the fans to fever pitch for the second night running and put himself among the all-time rock'n'roll greats.*

'*Only The Rolling Stones and Bruce Springsteen have ever had two consecutive sell-out concerts at Wembley. Before last night's show Freddie had feared his voice would fail. But once on stage – it was covered in 6,000 sq. ft. of expensive carpet – he pranced around in his king's crown and cloak, singing encore after encore.*

'*Five electrical generators pumped 500,000 watts along miles of cable to operate the sound and lighting systems. And the fans loved every marvellous minute of it. Among them were Minder star Dennis Waterman, his girlfriend Rula Lenska and EastEnders actress Anita 'Angie' Dobson. And sitting in the middle of the swaying, waving fans was the old king himself – Mick Jagger. He quietly watched the performance with his daughter Jade. And clearly he saw a new ruler in the magic kingdom of rock.*'

This entire concert was released on DVD in June 2003 (featuring both stereo and 5.1 Surround Sound mixes). The second disk contains various bonus material including extremely rare rehearsal footage - discovered by a fan in a discarded box at a car boot sale!

July 16 ♪
Maine Road, Manchester

■ One Vision / Tie Your Mother Down / Medley: In The Lap Of The Gods (Revisited); Seven Seas Of Rhye; Tear It Up / A Kind Of Magic / Under Pressure / Another One Bites The Dust / Who Wants To Live Forever / I Want To Break Free / Piano Solo / Guitar Solo / Now I'm Here / Love Of My Life / Is This The World We Created / Medley: (You're So Square) Baby I Don't Care; Hello Mary Lou; Tutti Frutti / Bohemian Rhapsody / Hammer To Fall / Crazy Little Thing Called Love / Radio Ga Ga / Encore: We Will Rock You / Friends Will Be Friends / We Are The Champions / God Save The Queen

July 19
Muengersdorfer Stadion, Cologne

■ One Vision / Tie Your Mother Down / Medley: In The Lap Of The Gods (Revisited); Seven Seas Of Rhye; Tear It Up / A Kind Of Magic / Under Pressure / Another One Bites The Dust / Who Wants To Live Forever / I Want To Break Free / Improvisation / Now I'm Here / Love Of My Life / Is This The World We

Created / Medley: (You're So Square) Baby I Don't Care; Hello Mary Lou; Tutti Frutti / Saturday Night's Alright For Fighting / Bohemian Rhapsody / Hammer To Fall / Crazy Little Thing Called Love / Radio Ga Ga / Encore: We Will Rock You / Friends Will Be Friends / We Are The Champions / God Save The Queen

July 21 ♪/22
Stadthalle, Vienna

■ **First night**: One Vision / Tie Your Mother Down / Medley: In The Lap Of The Gods (Revisited); Seven Seas Of Rhye; Tear It Up / A Kind Of Magic / Under Pressure / Another One Bites The Dust / Who Wants To Live Forever / I Want To Break Free / Improvisation / Now I'm Here / Love Of My Life / Is This The World We Created / Medley: (You're So Square) Baby I Don't Care; Hello Mary Lou; Tutti Frutti / Bohemian Rhapsody / Hammer To Fall / Crazy Little Thing Called Love / Radio Ga Ga / Encore: We Will Rock You / Friends Will Be Friends / We Are The Champions / God Save The Queen

■ **Second night**: One Vision / Tie Your Mother Down / Medley: In The Lap Of The Gods (Revisited); Seven Seas Of Rhye; Tear It Up / A Kind Of Magic / Under Pressure / Another One Bites The Dust / Who Wants To Live Forever / I Want To Break Free / Improvisation / Now I'm Here / Love Of My Life / Is This The World We Created / Medley: (You're So Square) Baby I Don't Care; Hello Mary Lou; Tutti Frutti / Bohemian Rhapsody / Hammer To Fall / Crazy Little Thing Called Love / Radio Ga Ga / Encore: We Will Rock You / Friends Will Be Friends / We Are The Champions / God Save The Queen

July 27 ♪
Nepstadion, Budapest, Hungary ①

■ One Vision / Tie Your Mother Down / Medley: In The Lap Of The Gods; Seven Seas Of Rhye; Tear It Up / A Kind Of Magic / Under Pressure / Another One Bites The Dust / Who Wants To Live Forever / I Want To Break Free / Guitar Solo / Now I'm Here / Love Of My Life / Tavaszi Szel Vizet Araszt / Is This The World We Created / Medley: You're So Square; Hello Mary Lou; Tutti Frutti / Bohemian Rhapsody /

Hammer To Fall / Crazy Little Thing Called Love / Radio Ga Ga / Encore: We Will Rock You / Friends Will Be Friends / We Are The Champions / God Save The Queen

Highlighted tracks are those featured on the *Live In Budapest* video.

This performance – Queen's first and last in Hungary – is filmed by the Hungarian Film State company Mafilm Dialog, as is the soundcheck. The filming necessitates using nearly every available 35mm television camera in the country, seventeen in all.

An edited 85-minute account is eventually broadcast in December throughout the Communist Bloc, including China, Poland, Czechoslovakia, East Germany, Yugoslavia and Mongolia, as well as to 59 Hungarian cinemas for general release on New Year's Day 1987. The director is Janos Zsombolyai. Other footage of the band – on and of stage in addition to that available on the video – is used to complement television news reports.

The 60-strong crew members arrived some days prior to the band. Having driven across Europe in 15 trucks, with the huge custom-designed 180-foot long stage, they then spent two full days piecing it all together. Two 60-foot towers were constructed, which were then fitted with searchlights to dazzle the audience from both sides of the stadium during the show. Eight miles of cables are required to connect everything.

Unlike audiences in every other nation in which Queen had played, the Hungarians were unfamiliar with the many customary Queen concert traditions. This is, after all, the first ever such event in that territory; indeed, it is the first such undertaking anywhere behind the Iron Curtain. For this reason, local newspapers published guides to rock concert etiquette and protocol in the days leading up to the show.

The band themselves were equally apprehensive and, ultimately, the fans would exceed all expectations, and play their part in the proceedings as efficiently as any of the audiences before them. It is like Sao Paulo, Brazil, all over

again, with 80,000 pairs of hands united in a 'Radio Ga Ga' promo video revisited.

Freddie's introduction is unorthodox. Instead of the usual "Good evening everybody," he sang his opening words: "Hello everybody... it's really nice to be here today... it's really nice to be here tonight."

For the opening of 'Who Wants To Live Forever', Brian sat at an electronic keyboard, as he would throughout all the shows on the Magic tour, leaving it for the first guitar solo. 'Now I'm Here' contained an especially nice, although brief, vocal improvisation from Freddie.

Unusually, there is no proper introduction to 'Love Of My Life'. Instead Brian merely commented: "This is a night that we're never gonna forget." Brian, sat on a stool, played the opening segment of the ballad, and Freddie, who is not seated, offers a lovely version of the song. Next, he walked over to Brian, and with a big grin upon his face, comments: "Now comes the difficult bit... tonight, for the very first time... this is a very special song from Queen... to you." Reading from the scribbled lyrics on his hand, he then sang a modest rendering of an old Hungarian folk song. The audience are impressed by the gesture and join in with him. For a second verse, Freddie instead hums the melody, and prompts the crowd to sing. 'Tavaszi Szel Vizet Araszt' roughly translates as 'Spring wind shields the rain'. Remaining in acoustic vane, Freddie then performed 'Is This The World' to a sea of illuminated matches and cigarette lighters.

Roger and John then returned to stage, Roger with a tambourine, for a short good humoured ad-libbed jam, before segueing into 'Tutti Frutti'. For the song's conclusion, Roger sneaks back to the drum kit and Brian exchanges guitars again. Spike Edney assists with piano backing.

'Bo Rhap' brings the house down. Even the Hungarians know this track, and sing along like any other audience, but they seem confused when Queen leave the stage for the mid-section. The extraordinary light show keeps them occupied until the band return, having changed their

clothes. Queen ally Spike Edney again helps out on 'Hammer To Fall', but this time with guitar.

For 'Crazy Little Thing', Freddie walks around the stage with his guitar. At one point he sits on the edge of the piano stool with Edney, before setting off again.

Queen then leave the stage again, but return to revive 'Ga Ga' which is curiously absent from the *Live In Budapest* video credits.

The set concludes in a similar fashion to other shows of the tour: 'Rock You' merges into 'Friends' which in turn segues into 'Champions': "Good night. Thank you very much you beautiful people. We love you. God bless you." The support is provided by a local group called Z'Zi Labor, who perform a curious rendition of The Rolling Stones' 'Honky Tonk Woman' (backed by a choir of women dressed in peasant costumes) in their set, and Dutch band Craaft.

In the book *Queen – A Magic Tour*, Peter Hillmore wrote: *'Darkness fell, the noise of the crowd rose, the stage lights flashed even more brightly and the smoke billowed even more violently – and out of the mist, Queen came on stage. Freddie Mercury began to flash like the lights and chase the smoke around the stage. Roger Taylor crouched behind his drums*

233

pounding out the rhythm, seemingly intent on smashing them to oblivion; John Deacon's face was tight with concentration as he played his bass, and Brian May fought a musical duel with Freddie Mercury. 'One Vision' was an apt title for the opening number.'

❖ In February 1987, the performance was issued as the band's fourth live video *Live In Budapest* (MVN 99 1146 2). It enters the UK video chart straight at number one. Unlike its predecessors, the video also includes footage of the band offstage. Freddie is seen on stage inside an empty

arena, rehearsing material which later features in the show, and John is seen talking with a young English girl he encounters walking around the city.

'A Kind Of Magic' and 'Under Pressure' from this show, are used for the *Live Magic* album.

July 30
Amphitheatre, Fréjus
■ *One Vision / Tie Your Mother Down / Medley: In The Lap Of The Gods (Revisited); Seven Seas Of Rhye; Tear It Up / A Kind Of Magic / Under Pressure / Another One Bites The Dust / Who Wants To Live Forever / I Want To Break Free / Improvisation / Now I'm Here / Love Of My Life / Is This The World We Created / Medley: You're So Square; Hello Mary Lou; Tutti Frutti / Bohemian Rhapsody / Hammer To Fall / Crazy Little Thing Called Love / Radio Ga Ga / Encore: We Will Rock You / Friends Will Be Friends / We Are The Champions / God Save The Queen*

August 1
Monumental Plaza De Toros, Barcelona

August 3
Rayo Vallecano, Madrid

August 5
Estadio Municipal, Marbella
This was to have been the last show of the tour, but due to the huge interest in the tour and because virtually every show had sold out so quickly, a further British date is added. Promoter Harvey Goldsmith had foreseen the possibility of an extra show, and had provisionally booked the venue anyway.

August 9
Knebworth Park, Stevenage, Hertfordshire
■ *One Vision / Tie Your Mother Down / Medley: In The Lap Of The Gods (Revisited); Seven Seas Of Rhye; Tear It Up / A Kind Of Magic / Under Pressure / Another One Bites The Dust / Who Wants To Live Forever / I Want To Break Free / Improvisation / Now I'm Here / Love Of My Life / Is This The World We*

Created / Medley: You're So Square; Hello Mary Lou; Tutti Frutti / Bohemian Rhapsody / Hammer To Fall / Crazy Little Thing Called Love / Radio Ga Ga / Encore: We Will Rock You / Friends Will Be Friends / We Are The Champions / God Save The Queen

The highlighted tracks later appear on the band's penultimate live album *Live Magic*, issued in December 1986. Segments of 'We Are The Champions' also appear on the 1989 *Rare Live* video.

Support acts for this day-long show are Belouis Some, Status Quo and Big Country. As in London, the concert is shown on a huge (600 square foot) screen, above the stage, for those who are too far from the front to see everything. One hundred and eighty speakers throw out 500,000 watts of power, the equivalent of approximately 10,000 home hi-fi systems.

No-one knows it yet but this is to be Queen's last ever public performance, and it seems appropriate now that it took place in the heart of the English countryside on a beautiful summer's day and not on some distant foreign stage. Before an audience variously estimated at between 160,000 and 200,000, Queen certainly went out in style.

They also arrived in style too, descending from cloudless skies in a custom decorated helicopter, provoking a massive cheer from the audience during Big Country's set as they flew overhead. A stunning photograph depicting the scene is later used for the inside illustration of the tour's commemorative live album (*Live Magic*). The helicopter is pictured as it approaches the two hundred acre 15th century grounds of the house.

Following a dazzling opening to Queen's set and 'Tie Your Mother Down' on which it seemed everyone had joined in, Freddie addressed the audience: "Hello... This is what you wanted, this is what you're gonna get. Is everybody okay, and having a nice day?... Yeah, not too bad huh! Now you gotta put up with us!" During 'In The Lap Of The Gods' there's a deafening chorus' of "Wo wo la la wo" from the audience which drowns out Freddie. Someone in the crowd begins to sing,

heartily, an extra verse, before he realises his mistake and feigns a somewhat embarrassed cough, and shuts up. Moments later the opening piano chords of 'Seven Seas' ring out, and Freddie is joined again by the masses for a rendition of Queen's first ever hit.

Brian plays an intriguing segue into the next song. A riff from 'Liar' misleads the fans into expecting Freddie singing "I have sinned dear Father" but it doesn't come. A brief riff from 'Dragon Attack' follows just to confuse matters further, and then he's into 'Tear It Up', and the fans at last know where they are. The track starts with the main chorus instead of the proper album cut opening, but even those unfamiliar with the song can join in with the "Oh yeah" bits - and they do.

A few unusual sounds baffle the audience once again. Then Freddie enlightens them: "It's a kinda magic - it's a kinda magic." After a typically big finish to Roger's 'Magic', Freddie speaks again: "This is an ENORRRRRMOUS place, even by our standards – I tell you. It looks beautiful from up here, it's frightening." After a pause, Freddie is off down the crowd participation road again: "Da da da da da da da do" – the audience repeat it. Freddie continues, they again repeat, and similar lines follow, higher and lower. He makes it as difficult for the crowd to repeat as he can, but eventually submits: "You fuckers are good, I tell you! I'll get you after a couple of songs though, you wait!"

Roger begins 'Under Pressure' with a simple cymbal introduction, and John's instantly recognisable bass line lets everyone know exactly what song is next. There were rumours that David Bowie might turn up to join Queen, especially as this is the last show on the tour. He didn't.

"This next song calls for a boogie. It means I throw my c**t around the stage even more than I've done." That's the cue for 'Another One Bites The Dust'. When the first verse comes up Freddie invites the crowd to sing it. They do, and Freddie says "Thank you", in time to the beat. Thereafter they sing everything with him. This version of

'Dust' is probably the best ever recorded, and can be found on the *Live Magic* album with the introductory expletives excised. The audience are in brilliant voice, but Freddie is in even better form. The *Live At Wembley* cut also features an improvised vocal section. "I told you I was gonna get you," Freddie says as the song reaches the halfway point. Again he invites the masses to repeat all that he sings. They cope admirably.

"I think most of you know that is the last stop on our tour... you know that don't you? It's such a beautiful way to end it, I mean look at them (points to the mass of heads, as far back as the eye can see) the lot of you. I might also add that this has been the best European tour for us, thanks to every single one of you. And earlier on there were rumours of us splitting up, but I mean – fuck 'em – I mean really, look at this. How can you split up when you have an audience like this... I mean really. We're not that stupid. So now we're gonna do a song called 'Who Wants To Live Forever'." An especially poignant version follows.

'I Want To Break Free' starts without an introduction from Freddie. The audience sing the opening line before Freddie comes in. The band perform a semi-improvised operatic interlude next which resembles 'Rock In Rio Blues' from 1985. This segues into an unusual guitar solo from Brian that forms the opening of 'Now I'm Here', and Freddie reappears on stage. Roger and John join in together and Knebworth rocks to a stunning version of one of Queen's oldest and best loved anthems.

As is always the case, Roger and John leave the stage at this point, leaving Brian and Freddie to perform alone. The two sit on stools at the front centre of stage, with just one spotlight on them. While checking the tuning of the guitar he has just been handed, Brian says: "I would just like to say that you're a joy to play to. You are great. This is it." A moving acoustic version of 'Love Of My Life' begins, and Freddie is joined by a 100,000 voice choir.

They remain seated. Brian speaks again: "As some of you may know, the proceeds of this concert are going to the Save The Children people. So we would like to dedicate this to you and to all the people who work for Save The Children the whole year round. 'Is This The World We Created' follows.

"Okay, it's time to fool around a little, come on... everybody." The band then begin their Fifties style rock'n'roll medley. Elvis Presley's '(You're So Square) Baby I Don't Care' sees Roger at the forefront of the stage with the other three, returning to his drums when 'Tutti Frutti' calls for an extra punch. "This next one is a Ricky Nelson song. See if you know it," says Freddie. They obviously do, and many sing along with him. Freddie gets carried away with an extra line of "Awopbopalubop awopbamboom", as Roger crashes in over him with a ferocious thrashing drum roll intro.

Freddie walks around the stage briefly, sipping a drink, and then seats himself at the piano again. The very first notes he plays provoke the audience into roars of encouragement. 'Bo Rhap' begins. Afterwards, cries of "Freddie, Freddie, Freddie," begin somewhere in the front rows, and soon spread to every corner of the park. His reaction is simply... "And it's... 'Hammertafall'."

With a frenzied 'Hammer To Fall' behind them, the band settle down to a less physically demanding attempt at 'Crazy'. Freddie is handed a guitar but he seems indifferent to it. "This guitar only plays three chords for me... who gives a shit!" he says. "This is a... sort of a crazy kind of song." He seems far more at home later in the song, when he abandons the guitar and settles down at the piano.

As ever, 'Radio Ga Ga' features the traditional synchronised hanclapping from the audience, made even more impressive by the sheer volume of numbers that participate. A massive sea of hands above heads accompanies the main verse, exactly as in the promo video. After this song, Queen leave the stage, and the lights dim.

When 'We Will Rock You' begins, the crowd know that the show is rapidly nearing its conclusion. What they do not know, however, is that Queen are performing it for the very last time. 'Rock You' is followed not by 'Champions' but by 'Friends Will Be Friends'. 'Champions' follows that, after which Freddie addresses his fans: "Thank you lovely people, you've been a wonderful audience - God bless you. Good night, thank you."

After the show departing fans created one of the biggest traffic jams in British recorded history. The situation is made worse because the local authorities had chosen to close parts of the main A1 near Stevenage.

During the show a woman in the audience goes into labour, and actually gives birth within the grounds, in a St. John's ambulance. However, a Status Quo fan in the audience is stabbed, and bleeds to death before medical personnel can reach him. Queen are extremely upset by the news, which mars an otherwise spectacular climax to their concert career.

Since the tour began, on June 7, the band have played to a fraction over one million people. The millionth fan - whoever it is, is present at this show.

❖ September 15

The last single from *A Kind Of Magic* is released in the UK. Once again nothing new is offered as the B-side, even though numerous extended mixes exist. Brian May's 'Who Wants To Live Forever' is instead backed with 'Killer Queen'. It reaches number 24. On the 12" vinyl disc, however, a beautiful piano version of 'Forever' is contained as a bonus track, in addition to both single and album cuts of the main track.

❖ December 1

EMI release the band's second live album *Live Magic* in the UK. It is not issued in America. Consisting of material recorded between July and August during the Magic tour, the 15-track album goes on to peak at number three in the charts. It is produced by Queen and Trip Khalaf, Queen's concert sound engineer of ten years.

Because the band are reluctant to issue another double album, some of the tracks are heavily edited, to their detriment. The compact disc, however, did offer the full versions of 'A Kind Of Magic', 'Another One Bites The Dust' and 'Hammer To Fall'. Considering the huge volume of li ve Queen recordings known to exist, this comes as a big disappointment to fans.

April 20
Wembley Stadium, London

The Freddie Mercury Tribute Concert - For Aids Awareness
Part 1: Various Artists:

■ *Metallica: Enter Sandman / Sad But True / Nothing Else Matters. Extreme: Medley: Mustapha / Bohemian Rhapsody / Keep Yourself Alive / I Want To Break Free / Bicycle Race / Another One Bites The Dust / We Will Rock You / Radio Ga Ga / Stone Cold Crazy / Radio Ga Ga / Love Of My Life / More Than Words. Def Leppard: Animal / Let's Get Rocked / Now I'm Here (with Brian). Bob Geldof & The Happy Club: Too Late God. Spinal Tap: Infinity / The Majesties Of Rock. Guns n' Roses: Paradise City / Knockin' On Heaven's Door. Mango Groove: Special Star (Dedicated to Freddie) live via satellite from an Aids awareness concert in Johannesburg, South Africa. Liz Taylor: Speech.*

Part 2: Queen provide backing for:

■ *Brian May, Joe Elliott and Slash: Tie Your Mother Down. Tony Iommi & Roger Daltrey: I Want It All. Zucchero: Las Parablas De Amor. Gary Cherone & Tony Iommi: Hammer To Fall. James Hetfield & Tony Iommi: Stone Cold Crazy. Robert Plant: Innuendo /*

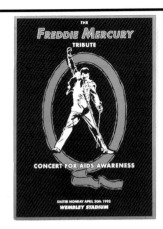

Kashmir / Thank You / Crazy Little Thing Called Love. Brian May & Spike Edney: Too Much Love Will Kill You. Paul Young: Radio Ga Ga. Seal: Who Wants To Live Forever. Lisa Stansfield: I Want To Break Free. Annie Lennox & David Bowie: Under Pressure. David Bowie, Ian Hunter & Mick Ronson: All The Young Dudes. David Bowie & Mick Ronson: Heroes. David Bowie: The Lord's Prayer. George Michael: '39. George Michael & Lisa Stansfield: These Are The Days Of Our Lives. George Michael: Somebody To Love. Elton John & Axl Rose: Bohemian Rhapsody. Elton John: The Show Must Go On. Axl Rose: We Will Rock You. Liza Minnelli: We Are The Champions. Backing vocalists are Maggie Ryder, Chris Thompson & Miriam Stockley.

The tribute concert was conceived on the night that Freddie lost his fight for life, on November 24, 1991. The three remaining members of Queen assembled at Roger Taylor's house in Surrey, and eventually decided to organise some kind of tribute to their colleague – though at the time they did not know exactly what form it should take. That was decided later.

Roger formally announced the event at the Brit Awards ceremony on February 12, after he and

especially those relating to the artists who would appear, all of whom they selected themselves. Every artist approached accepted their invitation to perform.

Among the first to be confirmed for the concert were Guns'n'Roses. Axl Rose contacted the Queen office immediately after hearing of Freddie's death, and offered the services of his band for any event which might be organised. He was a huge Queen fan, and later went on to host an American television tribute documentary entitled *These Are The Days Of Our Lives*.

Rehearsals commenced in mid-March at a studio near Shepherds Bush in London. The three Queen members spent the first week sifting through and playing material, deciding which tracks to perform themselves and which to offer to the other acts on the bill. When the setlist is established, the other performers attend to rehearse alongside Queen. Each arrival is eagerly observed by the world's press.

As April 20 loomed closer, the rehearsals moved on to Bray Studios near Windsor, Berkshire where the significantly larger sound stage provided a more realistic simulation of Wembley Stadium. The final soundchecks took place at Wembley on Sunday, the 19th.

Brian collected an award on Queen's behalf for their Outstanding Contribution To Music. During his acceptance speech, Brian became very emotional and had to pause for a moment to compose himself. It was equally emotional for the many fans watching the event at home, as well as an immensely proud one. The award was presented to them in fond memory of Freddie. The two received a standing ovation.

The show was co-ordinated from the London based Queen Offices in Pembridge Road. Gerry Stickells and promoter Harvey Goldsmith conducted meetings with television and radio representatives, lighting and sound technicians, merchandising personnel, stage hands, crew members and roadies. Roger, Brian and John were present at many of the meetings, and were involved in every stage of the arrangements,

➤ Roger Taylor (in a letter to the fans): *"The concert however is looking tremendously exciting, with an unbelievable line up, and hopefully some real surprises. We are keeping much of it a secret to provide us with more flexibility up to the last minute and maximum entertainment and surprise factor on the day. Therefore please keep an open mind brothers and sisters!*

"We see the concert as primarily a tribute to our friend and colleague, but also as a way of using the tragedy of his death to good effect, in bringing an awareness of the fact that AIDS AFFECTS ALL of us, to a wider range of people – by using a wide and weighty spectrum of the very best in serious contemporary popular music.

"This is such an important message, especially for the younger people of the world – and especially – NOW! If Freddie can posthumously help that

awareness, it will be a major addition to the already wonderful achievements of his life.

"In advance, the band and myself, Jim Beach, Gerry & Sylvia Stickells – Julie & the staff, would like to thank all the brilliant people helping and participating in the event. Names will be named! See you April 20th – fingers crossed for a great day! Love Roger."

When Roger, Brian and John walked out on stage they were greeted by a deafening roar. Brian's first words are obscured by the din, but he continues anyway: "Good evening Wembley – and the world (it's daytime really). We are here today to celebrate the life, and work, and dreams of one Freddie Mercury. We're gonna give him the biggest send off in history!"

Brian then made way for Roger: "Today is for Freddie, it's for you, it's to tell everybody around the world that Aids affects us all – that's what these red ribbons are all about... You can cry as much as you like! And John's got something to tell you..."

John: "Hello. First of all, Brian, Roger and myself would like to thank all the artists who we have performing here today, in London. They've given their time and energy to make this tribute to Freddie a reality, and to happen today. First of all – the show must go on – and we'll start with an American band, three times Grammy Award winners – please welcome Metallica."

ARTIST 2

● The section of the show which features U2 was recorded live on April 18, at the Oakland Coliseum, in California, as part of their Zoo TV Tour. During that show Bono dedicates 'Dancing Queen' and 'Satellite Of Love' to Freddie. He explains to the audience: "We're sending some of tonight's show down the wire to Freddie Aid in London. He was a very cool guy. He was exceptionally cool to me." Bono made numerous other references to Freddie during the show also. 'Until The End Of The World' was the song which was shown on the Wembley screens, on the day.

When Freddie himself suddenly appeared midway through the show on the huge 20 by 30 ft video screens addressing a concert audience from yesteryear, there was a stunned silence. "Are you ready?" he asks, as large as life. "YEAH," the masses respond. "Huh, are you ready brothers and sisters?" he asks again, courtesy of a recording of his voice from the June 1982 Milton Keynes gig. No one had expected Freddie to be present at his own tribute but, then again, he'd always been in his element before big crowds and this was Queen's biggest ever.

During the concert Neil James of Radio One spoke to Brian and Roger backstage...

Brian: "We thought it would be nice to do something which would give Freddie the proper

send off, when the right time came. The concert came out of that really. But it was a long road from that point to this. At some points I think we almost decided that it couldn't be done. But I think we're extremely glad we pressed on, at this point - eh Rog?"

Roger: "Yes, there was a lot of work, and a lot of talking to be done, and a lot of logistics to overcome – from the fact of using a lot of people. We had a lot of encouragement in the early days, from I must say – to single out two people – Elton John and Guns n'Roses, who were behind the idea of doing something from the beginning, and offered their services from the beginning – along with everyone else.

"It's not a marathon and it's not a telethon, it's not even entirely about raising money. It's a celebration of Freddie's life and Freddie's work, and it's a raising of awareness about the fact that Aids affects all of us, and what a terrible hidden threat it is."

Brian: "We've had positive feelings from everybody – everybody's been great. Most people said do whatever you like. It might be worth saying that artistically this is different from your average sort of charity concert I think. In Live Aid for instance – which was a wonderful success – you had people coming on doing their thing, then they're off, then the next person comes on and does his thing. This, from the point where the three of us hit the stage, is a very co-operative thing – it's not Queen – it's the three of us

combined with a lot of other people, in various capacities. It's almost like one band. Every song you see will be a one-off. You'll never see the likes of this happening again - well not this week anyway."

Neil James: "As far as Queen is concerned, is this the last show for Queen?"

Brian: "I think the last show for Queen was 1986. Truly. The Knebworth show on the end of the Magic tour was the last time you saw Queen as a band. I don't think it can ever exist, as such, again. The spirit is still alive – as you'll see. And I think the three of us definitely still work together great – there's no question about that. This is just my own personal view (Roger agrees), the last chapter has already been written, and I think we're very proud of the whole book. It has a beginning, and a lot of good stuff in the middle - a good catalogue - and it has an ending, and I think that's where we are."

↗ **'YOU WERE WONDERFUL, MY DEARS!'** Q magazine: *'Bowie burst into prayer; Axl sang his 'buns' off; George & Lisa went for the Peters & Lee vote; Ian Hunter arose and appeared to many; while Brian, Roger and 'Deaky' played themselves sore. The Freddie Mercury Tribute Concert for Aids Awareness... they laughed, they cried, they hurled.'*

On a technical level, 1,000 people were involved in producing the show; 5,000 stage lights, 30 tons

of scaffolding, 175 microphones, 400 miles of cable, and 13 satellite link-ups (including the first ever such link to South Africa) are used. A record breaking £600,000 worth of merchandising material was sold: £50,000 in programmes, £100,000 in T-shirts, £50,000 in badges, £40,000 in baseball caps and £40,000 in posters. Furthermore, 5,000 cans of beer and 2,000 bottles of wine were laid on by the Hard Rock Café for the performing artists, while the audience drank and ate their way through 26,000 pints of lager, 64,000 Cokes, 20,000 burgers, 15,000 hot dogs, a quarter of a ton of chips and 3,000 boxes of popcorn. 100,000 red ribbons and 40,000 red scarves were given away free at the turnstiles on the day, as a symbol of Aids awareness. Ultimately £12 million is raised for Aids research.

Of all the many images that day, the ones I recall most vividly were two home made banners. The first featured a huge black double posted flag, with the words "Freddie... Pure Genius" in gold stencilled letters, a concept lifted from the Guinness television commercials. The other was more poignant: "How I loved you – how I cried", it read. The line from Brian May's 'Save Me' seemed to summarise the mood of most of us Queen aficionados, as we shuffled expectantly towards entrance gate 'C'.

The atmosphere outside the stadium was electric, the sense of camaraderie fantastic. In whichever direction you chose to look, there was a British, or American, or Dutch, or Canadian fan sharing sandwiches, crisps and pork pies with fellow Japanese or Australian fans, who only hours beforehand had been total strangers. When Roger invited us all to cry as much as we liked, it struck me that for many fans the advice had probably come too late.

"Freddie had great strength of will, and actually used the effort of getting to work in the last three years or so, as a kind of focus to help him through all the pain he was going through.

"We felt that just by being involved with him – working closely together in the studio, we were actually helping him as much as we could.

"In fact, I think the rest of the band feel that his best vocal performances – in terms of range, power and emotion, were on the last album.

"He was warm, and generous to a fault, and work was always fun. We were honoured to work with him, and we'll never forget him."

Roger Taylor, November 1991

TYPICAL QUEEN CONCERT SETLISTS; 1973–1986: A SUMMARY

The following are summaries of the songs played on each Queen tour (or leg thereof). Each setlist represents a typical show. The songs listed in square brackets are those performed less frequently - some were only played once.

■ **1973:** *Procession / Father To Son / Son And Daughter / Ogre Battle / Hangman / Keep Yourself Alive / Liar / Jailhouse Rock / Shake Rattle And Roll / Stupid Cupid / Be Bop A Lul a / Jailhouse Rock (reprise) / Big Spender / Bama Lama Bama Loo.*

[*Stone Cold Crazy / Great King Rat / Doing All Right / Modern Times Rock'n'Roll / See What A Fool I've Been*]

■ **1974:** *Procession / Father To Son / Ogre Battle / White Queen / Doing All Right / Son And Daughter / Keep Yourself Alive / Liar / Jailhouse Rock / Shake Rattle And Roll / Stupid Cupid / Be Bop A Lula / Jailhouse Rock (reprise) / Big Spender / Modern Times Rock'n'Roll.*

[*Great King Rat / Hangman / Seven Seas Of Rhye / Bama Lama Bama Loo / See What A Fool I've Been*]

■ **1975:** *Procession / Now I'm Here / Ogre Battle / Father To Son / White Queen / Flick Of The Wrist / In The Lap Of The Gods / Killer Queen / March Of The Black Queen / Bring Back That Leroy Brown / Son & Daughter / Keep Yourself Alive / Seven Seas Of Rhye / Stone Cold Crazy / Liar / In The Lap Of The Gods... revisited / Big Spender / Modern Times Rock'n'Roll / Jailhouse Rock / God Save The Queen*

[*Hangman / Great King Rat / Doing All Right / See What A Fool I've Been / Stupid Cupid / Be Bop A Lula*]

■ **1976:** *Bohemian Rhapsody / Ogre Battle / Sweet Lady / White Queen / Flick Of The Wrist / Bohemian Rhapsody / Killer Queen / March Of The Black Queen / Bohemian Rhapsody (reprise) / Bring Back That Leroy Brown / Son And Daughter / The Prophet's Song / Stone Cold Crazy / Doing All Right / Keep Yourself Alive / Seven Seas Of Rhye / Liar / In The Lap Of The Gods... revisited / Now I'm Here / Big Spender / Jailhouse Rock / God Save The Queen*

[*Big Spender / Modern Times Rock'n'Roll / See What A Fool I've Been / Hangman / Shake Rattle And Roll / Stupid Cupid / Be Bop A Lula / Saturday Night's Alright For Fighting / Father To Son*]

■ **1977**: (North America): *A Day At The Races intro / Tie Your Mother Down / Ogre Battle / White Queen / Somebody To Love / Killer Queen / The Millionaire Waltz / You're My Best Friend / Bring Back That Leroy Brown / Sweet Lady / Brighton Rock / '39 / You Take My Breath Away / White Man / The Prophet's Song / Bohemian Rhapsody / Stone Cold Crazy / Keep Yourself Alive / Liar / In The Lap Of The Gods... revisited / Now I'm Here / Big Spender / Jailhouse Rock / God Save The Queen*

[*Saturday Night's Alright For Fighting / Stupid Cupid / Be Bop A Lula*]

■ **1977 (Europe):** *A Day At The Races intro / Tie Your Mother Down / Ogre Battle / White Queen / Somebody To Love / Killer Queen / Good Old Fashioned Lover Boy / The Millionaire Waltz / You're My Best Friend / Bring Back That Leroy Brown / Death On Two Legs / Sweet Lady / Brighton Rock / '39 / You Take My Breath Away / White Man / The Prophet's Song / Bohemian Rhapsody / Stone Cold Crazy / Keep Yourself Alive / In The Lap Of The*

Gods... revisited / Now I'm Here / Liar / Jailhouse Rock / God Save The Queen

[Big Spender / I'm A Man / Mannish Boy / Doing All Right / Lucille / Mull Of Kintyre / Saturday Night's Alright For Fighting / Stupid Cupid / Be Bop A Lula]

■ **1977 (North America, revisited):** We Will Rock You (slow/fast) / Brighton Rock / Somebody To Love / Death On Two Legs / Killer Queen / Good Old Fashioned Lover Boy / I'm In Love With My Car / Get Down Make Love / Millionaire Waltz / You're My Best Friend / Spread Your Wings / Liar / Love Of My Life / '39 / My Melancholy Blues / White Man / Instrumental Inferno / The Prophet's Song (reprise) / Now I'm Here / Stone Cold Crazy / Bohemian Rhapsody / Tie Your Mother Down / We Will Rock You / We Are The Champions / Sheer Heart Attack / Jailhouse Rock / God Save The Queen

[It's Late / Keep Yourself Alive / Doing All Right / Sleeping On The Sidewalk / White Christmas]

■ **1978 (Europe):** We Will Rock You (slow/fast) / Brighton Rock / Somebody To Love / Death On Two Legs / Killer Queen / Good Old Fashioned Lover Boy / I'm In Love With My Car / Get Down Make Love / Millionaire Waltz / You're My Best Friend / Spread Your Wings / It's Late / Now I'm Here / Love Of My Life / '39 / My Melancholy Blues / White Man / Instrumental Inferno / The Prophet's Song (reprise) / Stone Cold Crazy / Bohemian Rhapsody / Keep Yourself Alive / Tie Your Mother Down / We Will Rock You / We Are The Champions / Sheer Heart Attack / Jailhouse Rock / God Save The Queen

[Liar / Big Spender]

■ **1978 (North America):** We Will Rock You (fast) / Let Me Entertain You / Somebody To Love / If You Can't Beat Them / Death On Two Legs / Killer Queen / Bicycle Race / I'm In Love With My Car / Get Down Make Love / You're My Best Friend / Now I'm Here / Spread Your Wings / Dreamer's Ball / Love Of My Life / '39 / It's Late / Brighton Rock / Fat Bottomed Girls /

Keep Yourself Alive / Bohemian Rhapsody / Tie Your Mother Down / Sheer Heart Attack / We Will Rock You / We Are The Champions / God Save The Queen

[Jailhouse Rock / Big Spender]

■ **1979 (Europe and Japan):** We Will Rock You (fast) / Let Me Entertain You / Somebody To Love / If You Can't Beat Them / Death On Two Legs / Killer Queen / Bicycle Race / I'm In Love With My Car / Get Down Make Love / You're My Best Friend / Now I'm Here / Don't Stop Me Now / Spread Your Wings / Dreamer's Ball / Love Of My Life / '39 / It's Late / Brighton Rock / Keep Yourself Alive / Bohemian Rhapsody / Tie Your Mother Down / Sheer Heart Attack / We Will Rock You / We Are The Champions / God Save The Queen

[Fat Bottomed Girls / If You Can't Beat Them / Fun It (part only) / Teo Torriatte / Mustapha (intro) / Jailhouse Rock / Big Spender]

■ **1979 (Crazy Tour of the UK):** Intro / Jailhouse Rock / We Will Rock You (fast) / Let Me Entertain You / Somebody To Love / Mustapha / Death On Two Legs / Killer Queen / I'm In Love With My Car / Get Down Make Love / You're My Best Friend / Save Me / Now I'm Here / Don't Stop Me Now / Spread Your Wings / Love Of My Life / '39 / Keep Yourself Alive / Drums solo / Guitar Solo / Brighton Rock reprise / Crazy Little Thing Called Love / Bohemian Rhapsody / Tie Your Mother Down / Sheer Heart Attack / We Will Rock You / We Are The Champions / God Save The Queen

[If You Can't Beat Them / Liar / Fat Bottomed Girls / Silent Night / Jailhouse Rock / Danny Boy]

■ **1980 (North America):** Intro / Jailhouse Rock / We Will Rock You (fast) / Let Me Entertain You / Play The Game / Mustapha / Death On Two Legs / Killer Queen / I'm In Love With My Car / Get Down Make Love / Save Me / Now I'm Here / Dragon Attack / Now I'm Here (reprise) / Fat Bottomed Girls / Love Of My Life / Keep Yourself Alive / Instrumental Inferno / Brighton Rock reprise / Crazy Little Thing Called Love

/ Bohemian Rhapsody / Tie Your Mother Down / Another One Bites The Dust / Sheer Heart Attack / We Will Rock You / We Are The Champions / God Save The Queen

[You're My Best Friend / Need Your Loving Tonight / Somebody To Love / '39 (part)]

■ **1980 (Europe):** *Intro / Jailhouse Rock / We Will Rock You (fast) / Let Me Entertain You / Play The Game / Mustapha / Death On Two Legs / Killer Queen / I'm In Love With My Car / Get Down Make Love / Save Me / Now I'm Here / Dragon Attack / Now I'm Here (reprise) / Fat Bottomed Girls / Love Of My Life / Keep Yourself Alive / Instrumental Inferno / Flash's Theme / The Hero / Brighton Rock reprise / Crazy Little Thing Called Love / Bohemian Rhapsody / Tie Your Mother Down / Another One Bites The Dust / Sheer Heart Attack / We Will Rock You / We Are The Champions / God Save The Queen*

[Battle Theme / Need Your Loving Tonight / Imagine]

■ **1981 (Japan):** *Intro / Jailhouse Rock / We Will Rock You (fast) / Let Me Entertain You / Play The Game / Mustapha / Death On Two Legs / Killer Queen / I'm In Love With My Car / Get Down Make Love / Save Me / Now I'm Here / Dragon Attack / Now I'm Here (reprise) / Fat Bottomed Girls / Love Of My Life / Keep Yourself Alive / Instrumental Inferno / Battle Theme / Flash's Theme / The Hero / Crazy Little Thing Called Love / Bohemian Rhapsody / Tie Your Mother Down / Another One Bites The Dust / Sheer Heart Attack / We Will Rock You / We Are The Champions / God Save The Queen*

[Need Your Loving Tonight / Vultan's Theme / Rock It / Teo Torriatte]

■ **1981 (South America):** *Intro / We Will Rock You (fast) / Let Me Entertain You / Play The Game / Somebody To Love / Mustapha / Death On Two Legs / Killer Queen / I'm In Love With My Car / Get Down Make Love / Save Me / Now I'm Here / Dragon Attack / Now I'm Here (reprise) / Fat Bottomed Girls / Love Of*

My Life / Keep Yourself Alive / Instrumental Inferno / Flash / The Hero / Crazy Little Thing Called Love / Bohemian Rhapsody / Tie Your Mother Down / Another One Bites The Dust / Sheer Heart Attack / We Will Rock You / We Are The Champions / God Save The Queen

[Rock It / Need Your Loving Tonight / Jailhouse Rock]

■ **1982 (Europe):** *Flash's Theme (tape intro) / The Hero / Tie Your Mother Down / Action This Day / Play The Game / Staying Power / Somebody To Love / Get Down Make Love / Instrumental Inferno / Under Pressure / Love Of My Life / Save Me / Fat Bottomed Girls / Crazy Little Thing Called Love / Bohemian Rhapsody / Now I'm Here / Dragon Attack / Now I'm Here (reprise) / Another One Bites The Dust / Sheer Heart Attack / We Will Rock You / We Are The Champions / God Save The Queen*

[We Will Rock You (fast) / Back Chat / Body Language / Mustapha (intro) / Death On Two Legs (intro) / Not Fade Away / Liar / I Go Crazy (part in guitar solo)]

■ **1982 (USA, Canada, Japan):** *Flash's Theme / Rock It / We Will Rock You (fast) / Action This Day / Play The Game / Now I'm Here / Dragon Attack / Now I'm Here (reprise) / Save Me / Calling All Girls / Back Chat / Get Down Make Love / Instrumental Inferno / Body Language / Under Pressure / Fat Bottomed Girls / Crazy Little Thing Called Love / Bohemian Rhapsody / Tie Your Mother Down / Another One Bites The Dust / We Will Rock You / We Are The Champions / God Save The Queen*

[Somebody To Love / Life Is Real / Staying Power / Put Out The Fire / Teo Torriatte / Saturday Night's Alright For Fighting / Spread Your Wings (intro) / Death On Two Legs (intro)]

■ **1984 (Europe and South Africa):** *Machines (intro) / Tear It Up / Tie Your Mother Down / Under Pressure / Somebody To Love / Killer Queen / Seven Seas Of Rhye / Keep Yourself Alive / Liar / Freddie Improvisation / It's A Hard Life / Dragon Attack /*

Now I'm Here / Is This The World We Created? / Love Of My Life / Stone Cold Crazy / Great King Rat / Guitar solo / Brighton Rock finale / Another One Bites The Dust / Hammer To Fall / Crazy Little Thing Called Love / Bohemian Rhapsody / Radio Ga Ga / I Want To Break Free / Jailhouse Rock / We Will Rock You / We Are The Champions / God Save The Queen

[*Staying Power / Saturday Night's Alright For Fighting / Mustapha (intro) / Sheer Heart Attack / Not Fade Away / '39*]

■ **1985 (Rio Festival, Australia, Japan):** *Machines (intro) / Tear It Up / Tie Your Mother Down / Under Pressure / Somebody To Love / Killer Queen / Seven Seas Of Rhye / Keep Yourself Alive / Liar / It's A Hard Life / Dragon Attack / Now I'm Here / Is This The World We Created? / Love Of My Life / Guitar solo / Brighton Rock finale / Another One Bites The Dust / Hammer To Fall / Crazy Little Thing Called Love / Bohemian Rhapsody / Radio Ga Ga / I Want To Break Free / Jailhouse Rock / We Will Rock You / We Are The Champions / God Save The Queen*

[*Rock In Rio Blues (improvisation) / Saturday Night's Alright For Fighting / Mustapha (intro) / Whole Lotta Shakin' Goin' On / My Fairy King (part) / March Of The Black Queen (part)*]

■ **1986 (Europe):** *One Vision / Tie Your Mother Down / In the Lap Of The Gods... revisited / Seven Seas Of Rhye / Tear It Up / A Kind Of Magic / Freddie Improvisation / Under Pressure / Another One Bites The Dust / Who Wants To Live Forever / I Want To Break Free / Impromptu / Brighton Rock solo / Now I'm Here / Love Of My Life / Is this the World We Created? / (You're So Square) Baby I Don't Care / Hello Mary Lou (Goodbye / Tutti Frutti / Bohemian Rhapsody / Hammer To Fall / Crazy Little Thing Called Love / Radio Ga Ga / We Will Rock You / Friends Will Be Friends / We Are The Champions / God Save The Queen*

[*Big Spender / Saturday Night's Alright For Fighting / Immigrant Song / Gimme Some Lovin' / Mustapha (intro) / Tavaszi Szel Viset Araszt / Keep Yourself Alive (part) / Get Down Make Love (part during guitar solo) / Chinese Torture (part during guitar solo) / I Feel Fine (guitar riff only)*]

QUEEN LIVE DISCOGRAPHY

UK SINGLES

❖ Love Of My Life (Live) / Now I'm Here (Live)
EMI 2959 (29/06/79)

❖ Crazy Little Thing Called Love / We Will Rock You (Live)
EMI 5001 (05/10/79)

❖ Save Me / Let Me Entertain You (Live)
EMI 5022 (25/01/80)

❖ The Miracle / Stone Cold Crazy (Live)
QUEEN 15 (7") (27/11/89)

❖ The Miracle / Stone Cold Crazy (Live) / My Melancholy Blues (Live)
12 QUEEN 15 (12") (27/11/89)

❖ The Miracle / Stone Cold Crazy (Live) / My Melancholy Blues (Live)
CD QUEEN 15 (CD Single) (27/11/89)

❖ Somebody To Love / Killer / Papa Was A Rollin' Stone / These Are The Days Of Are Lives / Calling You
PARCO 8 805502 (1993)

JAPANESE SINGLES

❖ Love Of My Life (Live) / Now I'm Here (Live)
P-423E (05/79)

❖ We Will Rock You (Live) / Let Me Entertain You (Live)
P-486E (10/79)

❖ Crazy Little Thing Called Love / Spread Your Wings (Live)
P-529E (01/80)

❖ Save Me / Sheer Heart Attack (Live)
P-550E (04/80)

AMERICAN SINGLES

❖ We Will Rock You (Live) / Let Me Entertain You (Live)
E46532 (24/08/79)

❖ Crazy Little Thing Called Love / Spread Your Wings (Live)
E46579 (07/12/79)

DUTCH SINGLE

❖ We Will Rock You (Live) / We Are The Champions (Live) / We Will Rock You (Studio Version) / We Are The Champions (Studio Version)
Issued only in Holland (1992)

Albums (LPs and CDs)
Worldwide Releases

❖ Live Killers
Double LP/CD
UK LP
EMSP 330
Released (22/06/79)
Reached No.3

❖ UK CD
CDS 7 462118
Running time: 47.11/43.12

❖ US LP
BB 702
Released (26/06/79)
Reached No.16

❖ US CD
HR 61066 2
Running time: 47.11/43.10

❖ Japanese LP
Elektra P5567E 1/4
Green/red vinyl

❖ Japanese CD
Elektra CP28 5316/7
Running time: 47.11/43.10
Side 1: We Will Rock You (3.18) / Let Me Entertain You (3.15) / Death On Two Legs (3.31) / Killer Queen (1.59) / Bicycle Race (1.28) / I'm In Love With My Car (2.01) / Get Down Make Love (4.31) / You're My Best Friend (2.08)
Side 2: Now I'm Here (8.42) / Dreamers Ball (3.44) / Love Of My Life (4.57) / '39 (3.26) / Keep Yourself Alive (4.02)
Side 3: Don't Stop Me Now (4.28) / Spread Your Wings (5.22) / Brighton Rock (12.13)
Side 4: Bohemian Rhapsody (6.02) / Tie Your Mother Down (3.40) / Sheer Heart Attack (3.35) / We Will Rock You (2.48) / We Are The Champions (3.27) / God Save The Queen (1.31)

❖ Queen Live
Japanese single album
Elektra P13117E
Edited version of *Live Killers*
Side 1: We Will Rock You (3.23) / Let Me Entertain You (3.17) / Killer Queen (2.00) / Bicycle Race (1.13) / You're My Best Friend (2.05) / Spread Your Wings (5.29) / Keep Yourself Alive (4.00)
Side 2: Don't Stop Me Now (4.26) / Bohemian Rhapsody (6.03) / Tie Your Mother Down (3.40) / Sheer Heart Attack (3.33) / We Are The Champions (3.34)

❖ Live Killers
South African single album
EMI EXTRA5
Edited version of *Live Killers*
Marketed and distributed by EMI. Music South Africa (PTY) Limited. Issued after the six Sun City shows in October 1985. It contains an edited tracklisting and different front cover sleeve to the 1979 UK counterpart. All proceeds were donated to charity. It was also issued on audio cassette.

Side 1: We Will Rock You (3.23) / Let Me Entertain You (3.17) / Killer Queen (2.00) / Bicycle Race (1.13) / You're My Best Friend (2.05) / Spread Your Wings (5.29) / Keep Yourself Alive (4.00)
Side 2: Don't Stop Me Now (4.26) / Bohemian Rhapsody (6.03) / Tie Your Mother Down (3.40) / Sheer Heart Attack (3.33) / We Are The Champions (3.34)

❖ Queen Live
Australian single album
Elektra 60343/1
Edited version of *Live Killers*
Side 1: We Will Rock You (3.23) / Let Me Entertain You (3.17) / Killer Queen (2.00) / Bicycle Race (1.13) / You're My Best Friend (2.05) / Spread Your Wings (5.29) / Keep Yourself Alive (4.00)
Side 2: Don't Stop Me Now (4.26) / Bohemian Rhapsody (6.03) / Tie Your Mother Down (3.40) / Sheer Heart Attack (3.33) / We Are The Champions (3.34)

❖ Live In Concert
New Zealand single album
Elektra 60343/1
Edited version of *Live Killers*
Side 1: We Will Rock You (3.23) / Let Me Entertain You (3.17) / Killer Queen (2.00) / Bicycle Race (1.13) / You're My Best Friend (2.05) / Spread Your Wings (5.29) / Keep Yourself Alive (4.00)
Side 2: Don't Stop Me Now (4.26) / Bohemian Rhapsody (6.03) / Tie Your Mother Down (3.40) / Sheer Heart Attack (3.33) / We Are The Champions (3.34)

❖ Concert For The People Of Kampuchea
Double LP / Cassette)
Atlantic K 60153.
Released April 1981
This LP includes 'Now I'm Her' (as screened on TV) recorded on December 26, 1979, at the Hammersmith Odeon, London.

❖ **Queen Live: Rock In Rio**
Brazilian single album
4047224
Released in 1985
This material does not relate to the January 1985 Brazilian Rock In Rio Festival, as the title suggests. It was merely issued at the time of the Festival. It is actually an edited version of Live Killers, although the album sleeve is different.
Side 1: *We Will Rock You (3.23) / Let Me Entertain You (3.17) / Killer Queen (2.00) / Bicycle Race (1.13) / You're My Best Friend (2.05) / Spread Your Wings (5.29) / Keep Yourself Alive (4.00)*
Side 2: *Don't Stop Me Now (4.26) / Bohemian Rhapsody (6.03) / Tie Your Mother Down (3.40) / Sheer Heart Attack (3.33) / We Are The Champions (3.34)*

❖ **Live Magic**
UK LP
EMC 3519
Released (01/12/86)
Reached No.3

❖ **UK CD**
CDP 746413 2
Running time: 49.22

❖ **Japanese CD**
CP32 5173
Running time: 49.22
Not issued in USA, on either format
Side 1: *One Vision (5.09) / Tie Your Mother Down (2.59) / Seven Seas Of Rhye (1.21) / A Kind Of Magic (5.30) / Under Pressure (3.49) / Another One Bites The Dust (5.50)*
Side 2: *I Want To Break Free (2.40) / Is This The World We Created (1.31) / Bohemian Rhapsody (4.42) / Hammer To Fall (5.20) / Radio Ga Ga (4.27) / We Will Rock You (1.33) / Friends Will Be Friends (1.09) / We Are The Champions (2.01) / God Save The Queen (1.19)*

❖ **Live At Wembley '86**
Double LP/CD

UK LP
799594 1
Released (26/05/92)
Reached No.2

❖ **UK CD**
CDPCSP 725
Running time: 60.34/50.28

❖ **US CD**
HR 61104 2
Released (26/05/92)
Reached No. 53
Running time: 60.32/50.27
Side 1: *One Vision (5.50) / Tie Your Mother Down (3.52) / In The Lap Of The Gods (2.44) / Seven Seas Of Rhye (1.19) / Tear It Up (2.12) / A Kind Of Magic (8.41) / Under Pressure (3.41) / Another One Bites The Dust (4.54)*
Side 2: *Who Wants To Live Forever (5.16) / I Want To Break Free (3.34) / Impromptu (2.55) / Brighton Rock Solo (9.11) / Now I'm Here (6.19)*
Side 3: *Love Of My Life (4.47) / Is This The World We Created (2.59) / (You're So Square) Baby I Don't Care (1.34) / Hello Mary Lou (Goodbye Heart) (1.24) / Tutti Frutti (3.23) / Gimme Some Lovin' (0.55) / Bohemian Rhapsody (5.50) / Hammer To Fall (5.36)*
Side 4: *Crazy Little Thing Called Love (6.27) / Big Spender (1.07) / Radio Ga Ga (5.57) / We Will Rock You (2.46) / Friends Will Be Friends (2.08) / We Are The Champions (4.05) / God Save The Queen (1.27)*

❖ **Queen On Fire - Live At The Bowl**
Double CD (picture CDs)
7243 5 4418792
Released (25/10/04)
Recorded at Milton Keynes Bowl, June 5th 1982.
Disc 1: *Flash / The Hero / We Will Rock You (Fast) / Action This Day / Play The Game / Staying Power / Somebody To Love / Now I'm Here / Dragon Attack / Now I'm Here (Reprise) / Love Of My Life / Save Me / Back Chat.*
Disc 2: *Get Down Make Love / Guitar Solo / Under Pressure / Fat Bottomed Girls / Crazy Little Thing*

Called Love / Bohemian Rhapsody / Tie Your Mother Down / Another One Bites The Dust / Sheer Heart Attack / We Will Rock You / We Are The Champions / God Save The Queen.

❖ We Will Rock You (Fast)
Promo CD Single CD
PCD-3030
Released (October 04)
We Will Rock You (Fast) (5.51)
This one track CD was issued in Japan only to promote the forthcoming 'Queen On Fire - Live At The Bowl' album.

VIDEOS & DVDs

❖ Greatest Flix: Volume I
MVP 99 1011 2
Released (19/10/81)
Essentially a collection of promotional videos which accompanied the band's
singles up to 'Flash', though it also includes live footage of 'We Will Rock You' (fast version) and 'Love Of My Life'.

❖ Live In Japan
APVG-4004
Released in Japan only in 1983 (on Japanese video system). Watanabe Music Publishing 1983. Produced by Raincloud Productions. Recorded at the Seibu Lions Stadium, Tokyo, Japan (03/11/82)
Flash's Theme; The Hero / Now I'm Here; Put Out The Fire; Dragon Attack; Now I'm Here / Love Of My Life / Save Me / Guitar Solo / Under Pressure / Crazy Little Thing Called Love / Bohemian Rhapsody / Tie Your Mother Down / Teo Torriatte / We Will Rock You / We Are The Champions

❖ We Will Rock You
PVM 6122
Released September 10, 1984. Reissued October 1989 MC 2032
Recorded at the Forum, Montreal, Canada (24-25/11/81)

We Will Rock You / Let Me Entertain You / Play The Game / Somebody To Love / Killer Queen / I'm In Love With My Car / Get Down Make Love / Save Me / Now I'm Here / Dragon Attack / Love Of My Life / Under Pressure / Keep Yourself Alive / Crazy Little Thing Called Love / Bohemian Rhapsody / Tie Your Mother Down / Another One Bites The Dust / Sheer Heart Attack / We Will Rock You / We Are The Champions / God Save The Queen

❖ Live In Rio
MVP 99 1079 2
Released (13/05/85)
Recorded at the Rock In Rio Festival, Rio De Janeiro, Brazil (19/01/85)
Tie Your Mother Down / Seven Seas Of Rhye / Keep Yourself Alive / Liar / It's A Hard Life / Now I'm Here / Is This The World We Created / Love Of My Life / Brighton Rock / Hammer To Fall / Bohemian Rhapsody / Radio Ga Ga / I Want To Break Free / We Will Rock You / We Are The Champions / God Save The Queen

❖ Live In Budapest
MVN 99 1146 2
Released (16/02/87)
Recorded at the Nepstadion, Budapest, Hungary (27/07/86)
Tavaszi Szel Vizet Araszi / One Vision / Tie Your Mother Down / In The Lap Of The Gods... Revisited / Seven Seas Of Rhye / Tear It Up / A Kind Of Magic / Tavaszi Szel Vizet Araszi / Under Pressure / Who Wants To Live Forever / I Want To Break Free / Now I'm Here / Love Of My Life / Tavaszi Szel Vizet Araszi / Is This The World We Created /Tutti Frutti / Bohemian Rhapsody / Hammer To Fall / Crazy Little Thing Called Love / Radio Ga Ga / We Will Rock You / Friends Will Be Friends / We Are The Champions / God Save The Queen

❖ The Magic Years
MVB 991157 2
Released (30/11/87)
Sold as a three video boxed set, and individually:
Volume I: The Foundations
Volume II: Live Killers In The Making

Volume III: Crowned In Glory

As the title suggests, the second collection contains numerous snippets of live performances. It covers the progression of Queen's live concerts from 1974 to 1984.

❖ Rare Live: A Concert

Through Time And Space
MVP 9911893
Released (21/08/89)

I Want It All (Title track / credits, 1989) / Crazy Little Thing Called Love (Osaka, Japan, 1982) / Liar (Rehearsal in London, 1973 & Rainbow Theatre, London, 1974) / Another One Bites The Dust (Buenos Aires, Argentina, 1981 & Vienna, Austria 1982) / Big Spender (Hammersmith Odeon, London 1975) / Jailhouse Rock (Hammersmith Odeon, London, 1975) / Stupid Cupid (Hammersmith Odeon, London, 1975) / My Melancholy Blues (Houston, Texas, USA, 1977) / Hammer To Fall (Wembley Stadium, London, 1986) / Killer Queen (Earls Court, London, 1977) / We Will Rock You (Live Aid, London, 1985) / Somebody To Love (Milton Keynes Bowl, 1982) / Tie Your Mother Down (Paris, France, 1979 & Rio De Janeiro, Brazil, 1985) / Keep Yourself Alive (Hammersmith Odeon, London, 1975 & Tokyo, Japan, 1985) / Love Of My Life (Sao Paulo, Brazil, 1981) / Stone Cold Crazy (Rainbow Theatre, London, 1974) / Radio Ga Ga (Sydney, Australia, 1985) / You Take My Breath Away (Earls Court, London, 1977) / Sheer Heart Attack (Houston, Texas, USA, 1977) / We Are The Champions (Knebworth Park, Stevenage, 1986 & Frankfurt, Germany, 1982)

Additional excerpts from Tokyo 1985, Hyde Park 1976, Hammersmith Odeon 1979, Montreal, Canada 1980, Newcastle 1986 and Budapest, Hungary 1986.

Trawling through the various and best researched fan-*atical* web sites (something I could not do in 1995, but could do for this revised edition), I can confirm I'm not alone in my low opinion of this muddled compilation. The general consensus 'out there' ranges from abysmal and incompetent, to disastrous - one site even has it renamed 'Rare Crap'!

A sample of opinion... *The worst edited tripe ever committed to celluloid / A brilliant idea on paper, but a wasted opportunity / A disaster of gargantuan proportions... watch with sunglasses and headache pills / What did these DoRo's (the Producers) think; that no-one would notice the changing clothes, guitars, drums and everything? / Most of the Hammersmith pictures have been replaced with the old promo video – it's really just a huge, disgusting mess! / 'Saying it's (Liar) a rehearsal when it's quite clearly from 'Box Of Flix', is just lame.*

There's no escaping it; there a few redeeming features here. *Rare Live* is a sorry attempt at offering the best of Queen live. Even the great footage (of which there is much) is offered in an unwatchable way. What could and should have been a stunning collection, is a tediously edited mishmash riddled with errors from beginning to end.

Too harsh? No, I think not; 'Liar' is clearly not rehearsal footage, as the band are seen miming to the standard studio recording (available on GVH DVD 1 now). And live pictures of this song are from the widely known Rainbow theatre with an audience that would obviously not have been in attendance at a band rehearsal. The rock'n'roll medley is not from Hammy Odeon '75, as stated, but also from the Rainbow gig, and with a further eight or nine niggling errors in dates and venues which could so easily have been checked, this video is pretty well disregarded by those who expected an entertaining trip down memory lane, but whom got rather less.

This concept - a compilation of Queen's most exceptional concert recitals - will be revisited one day soon, I am certain, and executed with the research, respect and care it deserves.

❖ Queen Live At Wembley

MVP 9912593
Released (03/12/90)

Brighton Rock / One Vision / Tie Your Mother Down / In The Lap Of The Gods... Revisited / Seven Seas Of Rhye / A Kind Of Magic / Under Pressure / Another One Bites The Dust / Who Wants To Live Forever / I

Want To Break Free / Is This The World We Created / Tutti Frutti / Bohemian Rhapsody / Hammer To Fall / Crazy Little Thing Called Love / Radio Ga Ga / We Will Rock You / Friends Will Be Friends / We Are The Champions / God Save The Queen

For reasons best known to Queen and Picture Music International, this video is considerably shorter in length than its CD and LP counterparts. The following tracks appear on the disc formats but not on this video: *Tear It Up / Impromptu, Brighton Rock / Now I'm Here / Love Of My Life / You're So Square / Hello Mary Lou / Big Spender / Gimme Some Lovin.*

Note: *Brighton Rock* appears here in its studio recorded form (not as a live version). It provides the background music to the opening credits, and footage of the speeded up stage construction.Recorded at Wembley Stadium, London, July 12, 1986.

❖ Live At The Rainbow

Released May 1992 as part of the Box Of Tricks boxed set (The video has no catalogue no.)
Recorded at the Rainbow Theatre, London (20/12/74)
Procession / Now I'm Here / Ogre Battle / White Queen / In The Lap Of The Gods / Killer Queen / March Of The Black Queen / Bring Back That Leroy Brown / Son & Daughter / Father To Son / Keep Yourself Alive / Liar / Son & Daughter / Stone Cold Crazy / In The Lap Of The Gods... Revisited / Jailhouse Rock / God Save The Queen.

❖ Freddie Mercury Tribute Concert Double Video

MVB 4910623
Released (23/11/92)
Recorded at Wembley Stadium, London (20/04/92)
Running time: Video 1: 90 mins. Video 2: 117 mins
Produced by Queen and Jim Beach Directed and re-edited by David Mallet Remixed by David Richards
Some artists who took part in the concert declined permission for their performances to be included on this edited double video. Most, however, did give their permission. The majority of fans recorded the show directly from television, and so have the missing performances anyway.

❖ We Will Rock You

2 DVD set
11554
Released (30/10/01)
Recorded at The Forum, Montreal, Canada, November 24/25, 1981.
Sound formats: Dolby digital 5.1 Surround Sound DTS
Disc 1: We Will Rock You / Let Me Entertain You / Play The Game / Somebody To Love / Killer Queen / I'm In Love With My Car / Get Down And Make Love / Save Me / Now I'm Here / Dragon Attack / Love Of My Life / Under Pressure / Keep Yourself Alive / Drum Solo / Guitar Solo / Crazy Little Thing Called Love / Jailhouse Rock / Bohemian Rhapsody / Tie Your Mother Down / Another One Bites The Dust / Sheer Heart Attack / We Will Rock You (Reprise) / We Are The Champions / God Save The Queen.
Disc 2 contained various special features.

❖ Freddie Mercury Tribute Concert

2 DVD set
7243 4 92869 93
Released (13/05/02)
Recorded at Wembley Stadium, London, England, April 20, 1992.
Sound format: DTS
Disc 1: Tie Your Mother Down - Queen, Joe Elliott & Slash / I Want It All - Queen, Roger Daltrey & Tony Iommi / Las Palabras De Amor - Queen & Zucchero / Hammer To Fall - Queen, Gary Cherone & Tony Iommi / Stone Cold Crazy - Queen, James Hetfield & Tony Iommi / Innuendo, Kashmir - Queen & Robert Plant / Thank You, Crazy Little Thing Called Love - Queen & Robert Plant / Too Much Love Will Kill You - Brian May & Spike Edney / Radio Ga Ga - Queen & Paul Young / Who Wants To Live Forever - Queen & Seal / I Want To Break Free - Queen & Lisa Stansfield / Under Pressure - Queen & David Bowie & Annie Lennox / All The Young Dudes - Queen & Ian Hunter

& Mick Ronson & David Bowie / Heroes - Queen, David Bowie & Mick Ronson / '39 - Queen & George Michael / These Are The Days Of Our Lives – Queen, George Michael & Lisa Stansfield / Somebody To Love - Queen & George Michael / Bohemian Rhapsody – Queen, Elton John & Axl Rose / The Show Must Go On - Queen & Elton John / We Will Rock You - Queen & Axl Rose / We Are The Champions – Queen, Liza Minelli & all stars.

Disc 2. Extras: Featurettes: Behind The Scenes - Rehearsals footage, Made for TV Documentary, Freddie Mercury inserts / Gallery-Photo - 2x Photo Slideshow / Gallery - 2x Facts Slideshow.

❖ Live At Wembley Stadium

2 DVD set

4904719

Released (09/06/03)

Recorded at Wembley Stadium, London, England, July 12, 1986.

Sound formats: Dolby digital 5.1 Surround Sound DTS

Disc 1: One Vision / Tie Your Mother Down / In The Lap Of The Gods / Seven Seas Of Rhye / Tear It Up / A Kind Of Magic / Under Pressure / Another One Bites The Dust / Who Wants To Live Forever / I Want To Break Free / Impromptu / Brighton Rock Solo / Now I'm Here / Love Of My Life / Is This The World We Created? / (You're So Square) Baby I Don't Care / Hello Mary Lou (Goodbye Heart) / Tutti Frutti / Gimme Some Lovin' / Bohemian Rhapsody / Hammer To Fall / Crazy Little Thing Called Love / Big Spender / Radio Ga Ga / We Will Rock You / Friends Will Be Friends / We Are The Champions / God Save The Queen.

Disc 2 contained special features; Wembley Unseen Including: New interviews with Brian

May and Roger Taylor/Multi Angle Feature/Rehearsal and Friday concert excerpts/Backstage documentary.

❖ Queen On Fire - Live At The Bowl

2 DVD set

7243 5 4418792

Released 25/10/04

Sound formats: Dolby digital 5.1 Surround Sound / DTS

Recorded at Milton Keynes Bowl, June 5, 1982.

Disc 1: Flash / The Hero / We Will Rock You (Fast) / Action This Day / Play The Game / Staying Power / Somebody To Love / Now I'm Here / Dragon Attack / Now I'm Here (Reprise) / Love Of My Life / Save Me / Back Chat / Get Down Make Love / Guitar Solo / Under Pressure / Fat Bottomed Girls / Crazy Little Thing Called Love / Bohemian Rhapsody / Tie Your Mother Down / Another One Bites The Dust / Sheer Heart Attack / We Will Rock You / We Are The Champions / God Save The Queen.

Disc 2: Interview with Brian May & Roger Taylor (recorded on the day of the concert)

Interview with Freddie Mercury (recorded in Munich, 1982)

Interview with Brian May & Roger Taylor (recorded in Munich, 1982).

Tour Highlights (Seibu Lions Stadium, Tokyo, Japan, November 3, 1982) (25 mins): Flash / The Hero / Now I'm Here / Improvisation / Put Out The Fire / Dragon Attack / Now I'm Here (Reprise) / Crazy Little Thing Called Love / Teo Torriatte.

Tour Highlights (Stadhalle, Vienna, Austria, May 12, 1982) (11 mins): Another One Bites The Dust / We Will Rock You / We Are The Champions / God Save The Queen.

QUEEN'S BBC SESSIONS

Session 1:
◁¶ *My Fairy King / Keep Yourself Alive / Doing All Right / Liar*
Recorded at Langham 1 Studio, London (05/02/73)
Producer: Bernie Andrews
Engineer: John Etchells
Broadcast: John Peel (Radio One) (15/02/73)
Released as Side One of 'Queen At The Beeb' (4/12/89)

Session 2:
◁¶ *See What A Fool I've Been / Liar / Son And Daughter / Keep Yourself Alive*
Recorded at Langham 1 Studio, London (25/07/73)
Producer: Jeff Griffin/Chris Lycett Engineer: John Etchells
Broadcast: Bob Harris (Radio One) (13/08/73)
'Keep Yourself Alive' was broadcast (24/09/73)

Session 3:
◁¶ *Ogre Battle / Great King Rat / Modern Times Rock'n'Roll / Son And Daughter*
Recorded at Langham 1 Studio, London: (03/12/73)
Producer: Bernie Andrews
Engineer: Nick Griffiths/Mike Franks
Broadcast: John Peel (Radio One) (06/12/73)
Released as Side Two of 'Queen At The Beeb' (04/12/89)

Session 4:
◁¶ *Modern Times Rock'n'Roll / March Of The Black Queen / Nevermore / White Queen*
Recorded at Langham 1 Studio, London 03/04/74
Producer: Pete Ritzema
Engineer: Unknown
Broadcast: Bob Harris (Radio One) (15/04/74)

Session 5:
◁¶ *Now I'm Here / Stone Cold Crazy / Flick Of The Wrist / Tenement Funster*
Recorded at Maida Vale 4 Studio, London (16/10/74)
Producer/Engineer: Jeff Griffin
Broadcast: Bob Harris (Radio One) (04/11/74)

Session 6:
◁¶ *Spread Your Wings / It's Late / My Melancholy Blues / We Will Rock You*
Recorded at Maida Vale 4 Studio, London (28/10/77)
Producer: Jeff Griffin
Engineer: Mike Robinson
Broadcast: John Peel (Radio One) (14/11/77)

❖ Queen At The Beeb
LP: Band Of Joy Records BOJ 001
Released (04/12/89)
CD: BOJCD 001
Running time: 37.43
Not issued in USA at time of going to press
Side 1: My Fairy King (4.06) / Keep Yourself Alive (3.47) / Doing All Right (4.11) / Liar (6.28)
Side 2: Ogre Battle (3.56) / Great King Rat (5.57) / Modern Times Rock'n'Roll (2.00) / Son And Daughter (7.08)
Side 1 relates to Session 1. Side 2 to session 3. Both sessions were recorded at Langham 1 studio, London. Produced by Bernie Andrews.
The album reached No.67 in the UK album charts. It was not issued elsewhere. The possibility of issuing an *At The Beeb* sequel album is under consideration.
Queen At The Beeb has since been issued in america, on the Hollywood Record label, retitled *Queen At The BBC*. It is also available as a 12" promo picture disc limited edition.

QUEEN BOOTLEGS

Queen's live performances were always widely bootlegged, and since Freddie's death the number of unauthorised compact discs has grown dramatically. Prior to 1991 there were perhaps a dozen bootleg CDs on the market but in the two years that followed, that figure has increased almost tenfold, with 1993/94 releases pushing the number into treble figures.

What follows is a summary of all the discs known to me which are currently available, or which have at one time been in circulation around the world. The vast majority are not worth seeking out, for reasons detailed below. Many unofficial compact discs are purchased purely as additions to collections, and in many cases remain unplayed or even removed from their packaging; in which case the content is immaterial.

Very few discs are worth the generally exorbitant price, but the good ones are very good and should be regarded as a must for collectors.

The location and date of each recording, as advised immediately before each disc's tracklist, is exactly as it appears on the sleeve notes. Many are inaccurate. Additional notes have been added by the author (in italics beneath each setlist), to clarify any particularly misleading, inaccurate, humorous or plainly absurd points of interest. The numerous spelling inaccuracies which invariably accompany bootleg releases have been corrected.

A Day At The Stadium
KTS 039, Kiss The Stone Records, Italy, 1992
Recorded live in London, summer, 1985
Running time: 77.05
Queen played only one show in the summer of 1985 – Live Aid on July 13. The material on this disc is actually from the Magic tour of 1986.

A Night At The Court
Double CD, TNT 007/008, Tarantula Records, 1991

Tracks 1-26 Earls Court, London, June 6, 1977. Tracks 27-32 Town Hall, Birmingham, November 21, 1973
Running times: 73.29/59.53
Queen did not play Birmingham Town Hall on the date indicated on the sleeve notes. They played that venue on November 27, 1973, and Preston Guildhall on the 21st. While the sleeve notes advise that both discs contain sixteen tracks each, in fact they both feature only eleven. A number of songs on each disc are grouped together as one complete medley. Curiously no recording from the second night at this venue, has ever materialised.

A Tribute To Freddie Mercury
P910012, Dicid Records, Germany, 1992
Wembley Stadium, London (20/04/92)
Running time: 58.00

Absolutely Perfect
MNS 0292, Make Me Smile Records, Italy, 1992
Live in Brussels
Running time: 77.07
This disc actually contains material recorded in Japan, and not Belgium as the sleeve notes claim. It is yet another variation of the May 11, 1985 Yogishi Swimming Pool Auditorium gig. The double CD set Le Fleur Du Mal is by far a superior and more sensible alternative, not least as it offers four more tracks.

Absolutely Rare
Double CD, QUCD 9202, 1992
Various shows
Running times: 59.29/59.16
Yet another disc which doesn't contain all the material it purports to. Track 14 on Disc 2 is not a rare unissued song, as unfamiliar fans might be forgiven for presuming, but merely Freddie's recorded message for the 1987 fan club convention. Each member of the band would record a message which would be played in their

absence at the beginning of the convention. This track is such an example.

All Your Love Tonight
RC 2106, Rock Calender Records, Luxembourg, 1993
Live in Milwaukee Arena,
September 10, 1980
Running time: 67.15
The writing credits for track 3 are very curiously attributed to J. Styne & S. Sondheim instead of Freddie; Julie Styne & Steven Sondheim presumably. The disc title comes from a line from Brian May's 'Tie Your Mother Down'.

Best Selection
VC 3024, Echo Industry Co Limited, Japan, 1992
Various shows
Running time: 66.21
Collectors need not get too excited at the apparent inclusion of live versions of 'Nevermore', 'You And I' and 'Who Needs You'. They are not what they purport to be. Regrettably all are merely the familiar *Queen II*, *Races* and *N.O.T.W* album cuts, as can be seen by their running times. I made the same mistake as did many collectors who purchased this disc, by assuming that the set offered predominately live renditions – it does not.

Big In Japan
Double CD, NRG 010/11, Energy Records, Italy, 1994
Recorded live in Japan in May 1985. Extra tracks from 13-17 recorded live in UK in 1985
Running times: 68.18/71.39
Some tracks actually originate from the July 1986 Wembley Stadium shows. Tracks 11 and 12 relate to the June 1973 Phil Spector inspired Larry Lurex single, for which Freddie sang lead vocals (EMI 2030).

By Request: The Ultimate
Collection (Volume II), Double CD, RM002/003, Royalty Music, 1991

Running times: 73.24/73.55
The details in brackets are as they appear on the sleeve notes. This double set is yet another example of the packaging and sleeve notes not living up to expectations. For example: only one version of 'Thank God It's Christmas' is available, so to suggest that this CD contains the "twelve inch version", is absurd.

Coverin'
COW 100, Ugly Records, Italy, 1994
Various shows
Running time: 58.37
With the exception of track 4 (September 4) in fact relating to 1984, not 1980, the remaining date and venue details are correct.

Crowning Glory
KTS 071, Kiss The Stone Records, Italy, 1992
Recorded live in Europe, 1986
Running time: 78.06
This set is actually that of July 11, 1986 – the first of the Wembley Stadium shows. Curiously, the sleeve notes advise that all tracks are written by Freddie, unless otherwise stated. In fact only four tracks on the disc are Freddie compositions, the other fourteen are made up of cover versions, other band member songs, or were written by Queen collectively. Nothing is 'otherwise stated' anyway.

Cry Argentina
Double CD, OH BOY 2-9145, Oh Boy Records, Streamway Limited, Germany, 1992
Recorded live in Buenos Aires, Argentina, 1981, except tracks 9-12 (Disc 2), recorded in London 1973
Running times: 59.29/52.48
All the material purporting to have been recorded in Argentina has actually been lifted straight from the September 1984 home video release 'We Will Rock You' (PVM 6122). The video consists of a mixture of two shows, recorded in Montreal, Canada, on November 24 & 25, 1981.

Domo Arigato

Double CD, A 2157, Aulica Records, Italy, 1993
Recorded at Nishinoimiya Stadium, Osaka, October 24, 1982
Running times: 48.30/58.08
The inclusion of some rare *Hot Space* material makes this disc a welcome addition to any live CD collection. While the date of this show is accurate, the spelling of the venue is not.

Done Under Pressure

Double CD, LCD 115-2, Leopard Records, Italy, 1992
Live in Germany, 1986
Running times: 50.13/49.15
There are so many excellent quality audio tape copies of this show currently in circulation, all of them easily accessible, that there seems little point in paying out the best part of £15 just for a compact disc alternative. An attractive and neatly assembled eight page booklet, is perhaps the only reason many people seek out this set. The audio and vinyl sister products remain much more sought after.

18 Greatest Hits Live

From Queen, STEN 91.005, Stentor Records, Germany, 1991
Recorded live in Zurich '82/86 Hallen Stadium
Running time: 70.54
In typical bootleg fashion, the writing credits for tracks 14 and 17 are attributed to a Mr 'Tawler'!

Eve Of Christmas

TR 256, Turtle Records, Australia, 1992
Live at the Hammersmith Odeon, December 24, 1975
Running time: 55.53

Flash Freddie

Double CD , BM 051/052, Beech Marten Records, Italy, 1992
Recorded live at Wembley Arena, London (UK) July 5, 1986
Running times: 42.28/43.48

Apart from the venue actually being Wembley Stadium, and not the Arena, and the fact that Queen played Slane Castle, Dublin on July 5, 1986, the other glaring error on the sleeve notes, is that all the tracks are attributed to Freddie and Brian only.

Freddie Mercury Is Alive

Double CD, WR CD 001/2, World Records, Italy, 1994
Various shows
Running times: 68.49/30.35
This provocative title warrants no comment from me.

From The Beeb To Tokyo

CD 17, RS Records, France, 1990
Live studio sessions for *The Sound Of The Seventies* BBC radio show. Tracks 1-4 from '73, 5-8 from '77. 9-12 Tokyo, Japan '75
Running time: 69.46
The first four tracks relate to Queen's first BBC session, recorded February 5, 1973, and the latter material would seem to originate from other vinyl bootleg sources. As far as the session material is concerned, the 1989 *At The Beeb* collection (BOJCD 001) is a far more sensible alternative. It is an official release, and so offers a sound quality which befits the work.

God Save The Queen

OS CD 4, Onstage Records, Italy 1992
Recorded live during '80
Running time: 44.48
This disc offers only the second half of a (1986 London) show. Why this isn't a double CD is absurd and typical of bootlegs.

Golden Demos 1973/76

STECK 001, Steck Records, Germany, 1993
Various oddities
Running time: 61.28
Collectors will not be entirely surprised to learn that with only one exception, not one track on this

deliberately misleading titled compilation is actually a Queen demo. The only reason that even one is included is because the version of 'The Night Comes Down' from the band's 1973 début album, was lifted straight from a De Lane Lea Studios demo tape. As the track could not not be bettered in the time available during recording sessions at Trident Studios, it appeared in this form. For that reason alone, it is the only true demo track on this bootleg, but obviously not a rare one.

The remaining fifteen tracks on the disc are made up of either BBC session material, a brief live snippet ('Ogre Battle'), or more often, simply the regular album cuts recorded without the output to one speaker, thus effectively bypassing the stereo effect and muting the main vocals – an experiment which most school boy music enthusiasts will have attempted at some stage.

This insultingly transparent ploy is most evident on 'Misfire', 'Father To Son', 'Killer Queen', 'Sunday Afternoon' and 'Bo Rhap'. Every track in this category is further given away by the fact that the running times are all but exactly the same as their respective mother album versions.

Goodbye

Double Disc, Limited edition anniversary CD in presentation folder, NE2211, Never End Records By Abraxas, Italy, 1992
Disc 1: Tracks 1 and 2 live in London (05/02/73) 3-5 and 6-17 (25/12/75). Disc 2: live in Tokyo (05/11/85).
Running times: 75.20/61.03

Queen did not play any shows at all after Live Aid in 1985, and the material on the second disc relates to Japanese shows from May 1985 – of which there were six.

Greatest Hits USA

GH 1826, Mikasa & Tsusho Limited, Japan, 1992
Various shows
Running time: 46.30
No details relating to venue or dates are contained on this set. Not all the material originates from American shows (as the title implies) – especially track six, which was only ever performed in Japan.

I Want To Break Free

CD/ON 2223, On Stage Records, 1994
Recorded September 14, 1984, Palazzo Dello Sport / July 26, 1986, Nep Stadium, Budapest
Running time: 51.14
Only tracks 1-3 and 14 relate to the Milan show. The remaining material has been recorded directly from the 'Live In Budapest' video.

I'm In Love With Freddie

MLP 2, Music Lovers Production, Italy, 1992
Running time: 65.22
Recorded live in Chicago, USA (19/09/80)
As numerous good quality bootleg alternatives already exist from this show, this miserably titled set is hardly worth parting with hard earned cash for.

Immortal

G53203, NCB Records, 1993
Country of origin: unknown
Various shows
Running time: 48.44
The notes on the sleeve laughably advise: 'This is a professional digital remixed and remastered recording which was originally realized by a member of the audience.'
Since this is obviously a live performance, one wonders what material it was necessary to 'remix' and 'remaster', and why. The notes conclude with the contradictory point: "Possible variations in audio quality are not due to the performance of the artist."

In The Lap Of The Gods

SCM 01, Splat Cat Records, 1994
Recorded at the Rainbow Theatre, London (20/12/74)
Running time: 50.38
Since this material has obviously been recorded directly from the *Live At The Rainbow* video, from

May 1992's *Box Of Tricks* boxed set, it is that collection, and not this, that should be recommended, albeit significantly higher in price.

In The Lap Of The Queen

CO 25153, Chapter One Digital Recordings, Germany, 1991

Recorded live in Seattle, USA (17/03/77). Track 9: unreleased Queen/Bowie song, 1981

Running time: 48.03

Queen played Seattle Arena on March 13, not 17 as stated on the sleeve notes. Track 9 is the *Hot Space* album track, in an early form which was not released. It features an ad-libbed vocal from David Bowie and occasional backing from Freddie. My guess is that Queen were working on the track during the sessions which spawned 'Under Pressure', and played the backing track to Bowie, who ended up recording a crude version himself, though probably only for fun.

Japan 1985 Highlights

TCS CD 001, The Concert Series, Luxembourg, 1991

Running time: 70.36

Queen performed six shows in Japan between May 7 and 15, 1985. It is unlikely that this disc represents material from any of them. Although it is not – as might be expected – yet another copy of the May 11 Yogishi Swimming Pool Auditorium show, much of the material has been lifted straight from the official *Live At Wembley '86* release. This would obviously account for the excellent sound quality, which the sleeve notes have the gall to attribute to: A Sonic Solutions Nonoise System, apparently used by a fan to record the show from a live American radio station broadcast.

An identical CD bearing a very similar name (Japan '85 Highlights) and identical catalogue number, but packaged differently, is also available. The disc predictably offers the same sound quality as its counterpart.

Killers

FLASH 09.90.0130, Flashback World Products, Luxembourg, 1990

All songs recorded live in London 1973, 1974 and 1975

Running time: 46.25

This is yet another European bootleg which refers to 'Ogre Battle' as 'Orge Battle'. At least four separate discs include the same error - proving conclusively that the manufacturers of such material rely on previous issues for sleeve note information, instead of conducting their own research, or indeed, consulting any number of books. As a consequence they repeat some, or all, the errors which appear time and time again.

Le Fleur Du Mal

Double CD, WORK 5538.2, Men At Work Records, Italy, 1992

Distributed by Vox Populi, issued in gatefold sleeve

Recorded live in Tokyo Swimming Pool Auditorium (11/05/85)

Running Times: 48.06/40.10

'Now I'm Here' is incorrectly credited as a Freddie Mercury composition. In fact Brian wrote it – from his bed, during a spell of recuperation from hepatitis and an ulcer in 1975. The song was inspired by Mott The Hoople, hence the reference to them in the lyrics.

The nearest translation of the title, is *The Flower Of Evil* which is borrowed from the classic French novel *Les Fleurs Du Mal*.

Live Dates: Volume 17

STONED 012, Stoned Records, 1992

Xmas 1975

Running time: 52.40

Live In Cologne

PRCD 1033, Golden Stars Records, Italy, 1990

Live in Cologne, (01/02/79)

Running time: 79.24

This was Queen's seventh concert in Germany in 1979. They played 13 in all, but just the one in

Cologne. This disc is one of the best representations available – in any bootleg format. It is a pity that so much of the show was overlooked. A double disc would have been far better.

The writing credits for ''39'' are incorrectly attributed to John Deacon, instead of Brian.

Live In Montreal
Double CD, CS CD 10006, Continental Sounds, Italy, 1993
Montreal (01/12/78)
Running times: 73.31/48.49
This disc offers a tracklist which again closely resembles that of the *Live Killers* album. It also contains four popular tracks of the period which were not included on the album – 'Somebody To Love', 'If You Can't Beat Them', 'It's Late' and 'Fat Bottomed Girls', and for that reason is popular with fans and collectors alike.

An unrelated front cover picture (from 1981) spoils it somewhat.

Live In USA 1977
HL CD014, Headliner Records, Germany, 1993
Running time: 48.03
This is a copy of *In The Lap Of The Queen*. While the original disc featured sleeve pictures of the band with Elizabeth II lookalike Jeanette Charles, and a portrait photograph from 1976 (available through the fan club at the time), this one features a decidedly dull sleeve.

The incorrect date advice which accompanied the first disc has been rectified for this issue. The material was recorded on March 13, 1977, in Seattle, USA.

Live USA
IMT 900.076, Imtrat Records, Germany, 1992
Recorded live in USA in 1977 and 1982
Running time: 50.29
Six other tracks appear on this disc, but are ignored on the sleeve notes. 'Father To Son' follows the first track, a four song medley ('Killer Queen', 'Millionaire Waltz', 'Best Friend', 'Leroy Brown') follows track 2, and 'White Man' merges with 'The Prophet's Song'. While 'Calling All Girls' makes an uncredited appearance on this disc, 'Action This Day' is not featured at all.

Live USA
Triple CD, IMT 920.076/083/084
Imtrat Records, Germany, 1992
Recorded live in USA in 1977 and 1982.
Running times: 50.34/41.21/42.02
A lack of continuity in catalogue numbering here suggests that discs two and three were probably intended to be issued on their own, as a double set only (they are packaged in identical sleeves). The third disc is not only packaged entirely differently, but its catalogue number is inconsistent too. I can find no good explanation, however, as to why all three actual discs are similar in appearance. If a triple CD set was always the intended proposition, why weren't all three packaged the same?

To sequence any track after 'God Save The Queen' – widely known as the one which for so long concluded Queen's concerts – demonstrates gross ignorance on the part of the manufacturer.

London 1975
FBCD 1146, Golden Stars Records, EEC, 1991
Recorded live at Hammersmith Odeon, (24/12/75)
Running time: 59.37
Yet another disc which offers a variation of the legendary Christmas Eve concert of 1975. An unusual pencil drawing on the front cover sleeve, makes this disc fractionally more attractive to collectors than it might otherwise have been.

London 1986
PSCD 1170, Red Line Records, EEC, 1992
Recorded live at Wembley Arena during the European tour
Running time: 73.05
The manufacturers have once again made the mistake of confusing London's Wembley Stadium

with the much smaller Arena venue, on the sleeve advise notes.

Made In Heaven

P&L 1992, Peace & Love Music, EEC, 1992
Alternative demo versions of the classic Queen songs
Running time: 57.41

These tracks are most definitely not alternative demo versions of classic Queen songs, but just the standard album takes with Freddie's lead vocals somewhat muted. This is one of many discs that was hastily issued soon after Freddie's death – hence the pretentious title and much over-used front cover illustration (Freddie on stage with regal cloak and crown).

An extremely collectable cassette version of this bootleg is also available, although strangely it's titled *Exposed For Now*. The material featured is the same as this CD. 'Who Needs You' is incorrectly attributed to Freddie, instead of John Deacon.

Made In Heaven was also one of the many proposed titles for the forthcoming final Queen studio album for which Freddie recorded lead and backing vocals and to which the three remaining band members subsequently laid down instrumental tracks. The title was discarded and Fan Club members were invited to suggest alternatives.

Made In Japan

RS 9210, Rarities Special, Italy, 1992
Live in Japan, 1985
Running time: 70.31

This is yet another variation of the *Japan 1985/'85 Highlights* CD's, but is again packaged differently, and the track timings are slightly different.

A reference to Roger 'Tailor' mars the otherwise error free sleeve notes.

Merry Christmas

GDR CD 9108, Great Dane Records, Italy, 1991
Recorded Christmas 1975, Hammersmith Odeon, London, England

Running time: 53.12

This is by far the most common bootleg, though not necessarily in this form. The same show has cropped up under several names and in several formats over the years with varying sound quality and tracklistings.

Other compact disc bootlegs related to this show include: *Eve Of Christmas, London 1975, Rhapsody In Red, Command Performance, X'Mas 1975, Live Dates Volume17, Christmas At The Beeb* and *Unauthorised*. In addition to discs which offer this show exclusively, many others contain segments of it alongside material recorded elsewhere. 'Goodbye', 'Thanks' and 'Noblesse Oblige' are three such examples.

My Favourite Dance Tracks

MMS 0892, Make Me Smile, Italy, 1992
Recorded Buenos Aires, 1981
Running time: 68.03

Queen played the Velez Sarfield, Buenos Aires, on February 28 and March 1, 1981. The two shows were their first, and only, gigs in Argentina.

According to the sleeve notes, 'Let Me Entertain You' was written not by Freddie Mercury, but by J. Styne and S. Sondheim, a mistake which is not uncommon. 'All Your Love Tonight' includes an identical oversight.

Nihon

Double CD, NSCD 0014/15
Record label: unknown, made in Italy, 1993
Running Times: 47.47/55.03

Although the sleeve notes contain no details of where this material was recorded, it is evident that disc one and most of the second revisits the Tokyo show (May 11, 1985), and the remainder originates from London, July 1986.

Nikon

Double CD, LSCD 5250051/2, Live Storm Records, Italy, 1994
Running times: 47.48/55.03

This is a reissue of the above CD, but in a repackaged form. Perhaps it was put out as a result of the Italian manufacturers discovering the date and venue information, which is included here but was absent from the first release.

Although this disc was issued through the so called Live Storm label, it does not necessarily follow that the *Nihon* disc was distributed by the same people. The catalogue number prefix however, would seem to point to that being likely.

Instead of Roger Taylor, the writing credits for 'A Kind Of Magic' are wrongly attributed to Freddie, although it is generally excepted that Freddie took a shine to the song in its early stages, and contributed substantially to the arrangement.

No More Heroes

POET 9212, Poetry In Motion Records, Italy, 1992
Date and venue unknown, though probably various
Running time: 57.28
Despite the sleeve notes advising this to be a thirteen track disc, there are only ten. Tracks 10-13 are all recognised as one track – hence a ten and a half minute running time.

Noblesse Oblige

LLRCD 149, Living Legend Records, Italy, 1992
Recorded live in concert 1973-86
Running Time: 74.42
Some of the material here relates to the Christmas Eve 1975 show (yet again), and the Wembley Stadium July 11, 1986 show (yet again). The first track however, is a strange mixture of 'Rock You' album cut, mixed with the *Live Killers* rendition!

Although track 8 might seem to be a misspelled and extremely rare live version of 'Coming Soon' from *The Game* album – indeed, it would have been the only live version in existence – sadly it is not. It is another semi-improvised instrumental piece featuring Freddie's wonderful nonsense vocal ad-libbing, with guitar support from Brian.

On Fire

1018, New Keruac Line, Italy, 1993
Limited Edition CD (issued in 5" round tin with numbered certificate)

Running time: 70.07
Recorded July 11, 1986 Wembley Stadium. The tracklist sequence is erratic to say the least. An extremely attractive round tin makes this disc more collectable than it would otherwise have been, since the musical content is far from exciting.

Opera Omnia

4-CD Boxed Set, RPBX 012/13/14/15, Red Phantom Records, Italy, 1992
Limited edition of 2,000
Running times: 79.20/75.56/78.33/72.20 Various shows, dates and venues unknown
Although it is impossible to say for certain when and where each track was recorded, much of the material (like most bootlegs) is instantly recognisable. Some of the better known shows represented on this set include: Earls Court (June 6, 1977), Milton Keynes Bowl (June 5, 1982), Tokyo (May 11, 1982) and the two Buenos Aires shows in Feb/Mar 1981.

The sound quality of some of the material featured on this set is absolutely superb, and must surely have been compiled using original mixing desk tapes. Furthermore, much of the music is extremely rare. 'Love Of My Life' (disc 2) is truly outstanding. 'White Man' (on disc 2) does not appear as a whole song, instead it is the conclusion of the preceding song, 'The Prophet's Song'. This is without doubt the *creme de la creme* of all compact disc bootlegs.

Over The Best Or Worst (The Greatest Tribute)

Double CD, 5556 2/1, Men At Work Records, Italy, 1992
Various shows
Running times: 65.52/68.52
This extremely lavish double CD package is let down by disappointing musical content, all of which is available elsewhere. The attractive sleeve design is similar to the *Le Fleur Du Mal* set, which is not entirely surprising, as each was issued by the Italian Men At Work record label. The overall package is marred by tasteless illustrations of a

syringe and an identification label tied to the toe of a human corpse.

Pearly Queen
BGS 018, Future Music, Italy, 1994
Recorded live in Rio De Janeiro, Brazil, (12/02/85)
Running time: 59.26
This disc is an exact copy of *Regina De Ipanema*, though packaged differently. Regina was issued in January 1994, and this followed it only two months later. So clichéd is the title, it could only have come from a non-English source!

Queen
Double CD, NE1122
Never End Records, Italy, 1992
Running times: 75.20/61.03
This double CD set is an extremely rare advance copy of *Goodbye*, housed in a lilac and white cardboard sleeve with a printed sticker. The tracklisting and running times are obviously the same.

Queentessance:
In Memoriam Of Frederick Bulsara, LL CD 9214
Live Life Records, Luxembourg, 1992
Running time: 75.14
The details of where and when each recording was made are riddled with inaccuracies – too numerous to note.

   An introduction to this disc on the back sleeve, begins: "We wants to eat Hamburgers every day when variety is the spice of life", and continues in an equally nonsensical vane. Thankfully, such sleeve notes are uncommon.

Queen Reigns The World
Double CD, TCC 028/029, Three Cool Cats, 1991
Exact country of origin is unknown Recorded live in concert 1986
Running times: 55.34/47.11
Amazingly, the sleeve notes have 'Robert' Taylor credited with drums and vocals, and neglect to mention track 9 on disc 1 at all. Of less interest, perhaps, is the failure of the disc manufacturer to correctly spell the name of their own record label. While the discs themselves carry the Three Cool Cats reference, the sleeve notes conflict with Three 'Cole' Cats.

Radio Ga Ga
HS 29104, Hotshot Records, Germany, 1992
Live in Japan '85
Running time: 70.33
Well, surprise surprise, this is not a Japanese show at all, but the umpteenth visit to London's Wembley Stadium, July 11, 1986.

Regina Versus Freddie And The Boys
Double CD, OTR 75517/18, Off The Record, Italy, 1994
Recorded Seattle Arena (13/03/77) / Brussels, Vorst National (20/09/84)
Running times: 57.28/77.07
This rather expensive and dubiously titled double set merely brings together two already available CDs – *Saturday Night's Alright For Fighting* (Disc 1) and *Absolutely Perfect* (Disc 2). Issued this time as a limited edition of 1,000, it was probably a final attempt at promoting sales.

Regina De Ipanema
BC 008, Future Music, Italy, 1994
Recorded live in Rio De Janeiro, Brazil (11/01/85)
Running time: 59.26
Identical musical content to *Pearly Queen* disc. Sorry, I have no idea as to how the title translates.

Rhapsody In Gold
Double CD, LIMES 3001
Limited edition of 300
Record label: unknown, made in Italy, 1993
Running times: 68.03/77.03
Recorded in Buenos Aires, Argentina (March 1, 1981) and Brussels, Belgium (September 21, 1984). Another bootleg which attributes the writing credits for 'Let Me Entertain You' to J. Styne and S. Sondheim, instead of F. Mercury. Both discs are packaged in an unusual triangular box, which also contains a T-shirt and numbered authentication card.

Rhapsody In Red

BUC 033, Buccaneer Records, Italy, 1991

Running time: 75.04

Tracks 1-4 recorded live in Middlesex, UK (10/76), tracks 5-17 recorded at Hammersmith Odeon '76 (Christmas Concert).

Tracks 1-4 feature Queen's final BBC session, as recorded in October 1977. It includes the fabricated audience overdubs. Queen did not play the Hammersmith Odeon in 1976, hence tracks 5-17 in fact relate to the 1975 Christmas Eve show – yet again.

Rock In Japan

Double CD, FLASH 07.91.0156/1/2

Flashback World Productions, Luxembourg, 1991

Tracks 1-13 (Disc 1) and 1-11 (Disc 2) recorded live in Osaka (15/05/85), tracks 12-15 recorded live in San Diego, 1977

Running times: 42.36/63.22

Contrary to the sleeve notes, tracks 12-15 (Disc 2) were not recorded in San Diego, in 1977, but are once again the tracks Queen recorded for the BBC in October 1977.

Rocking Osaka In 1982

BIG 067, Big Music Records, Italy, 1993

Recorded live at the Tiger Stadium, Osaka, Japan (25/10/82) (second night)

Running time: 57.35

Although Queen were in Japan during late October 1982, they did not play a show on the 25th. They were in fact en route to Nagoya on that day, having performed a show in Osaka on the 24th, which was not at the Tiger Stadium. In fact Queen have never played at a venue of that name, if indeed it exists. As a matter of interest, the only occasion which saw the band play two consecutive nights at an Osaka venue (as the sleeve notes suggest is the case here), was on April 19 and 20, 1979. This material was recorded directly from the 1982 *Live In Japan* video.

Saturday Night's Alright For Fighting

BOD CD 214, Buy Or Die Records, Italy, 1991

Recorded live during the 1977 tour

Running time: 57.28

Most of this material (tracks 1-3 and 9-13) relates to the March 13 Seattle Arena show of 1977. The remaining tracks (4-8) come from the March 31, 1974 Rainbow Theatre show. Although 13 tracks are listed on the sleeve notes, the disc actually comprises only ten. The four rock'n'roll medley songs which conclude the set are recognised as one track, as is frequently the case on unauthorised discs.

Shivers Down My Spine

XX1, Luhjaa Records, Germany, 1992

Live Munich, Olympia Hall (29/06/86)

Running time: 63.52

This is perhaps the most intriguing of all the bootleg compact discs currently in circulation. Each song has been retitled using a line from its lyrics, a practice commonly used on vinyl bootlegs of The Beatles which appeared during the Seventies. Although the example on track 13 displays a sense of humour on the part of whoever produced the disc, it's a pity he did not have the foresight to have the sleeve notes printed after the actual disc production. He would have realised that tracks 18-21 (as described on the notes) do not actually appear on the disc. Apparently there wasn't room for them.

Tavaszi Szel

Double CD, LCD 109-2, Leopard Records, Italy, 1992

Live in Europe (27/07/86)

Running times: 44.36/37.27

This disc is merely a copy of the *Live In Budapest* video, but with the various interludes taken out.

Thanks!!!

Triple CD, 9320.23, Aulica Records, Italy, 1993

Limited edition CD of 1000 presented in silk box

Running times: 75.20/61.03/20.41

Various shows

This uninspiring set contains Queen's first and third BBC sessions (probably lifted directly from

1989's *At The Beeb* album) on Disc 1, the May 1985 Yogishi Swimming Pool show on Discs 2 & 3, and, tediously, the Christmas Eve 1975 gig again, which makes its umpteenth live CD appearance on Disc 1.

Thank You Freddie

Triple CD, PWCD 101/1/2/3, Power Records, Italy, 1993
Recorded live in London (20/04/92)
Running times: 61.11/60.20/66.08
The discs are packaged in a 12" x 12" box – usually associated with vinyl boxed sets – which contains a beautifully presented 24-page book of colour photographs from the memorial concert.

The Carriage Of Mystery

REX DISCS, Royal Amusement Records, Germany, 1993
Recorded at St. Pauls, London, 1986
Running time: 69.13
Never in their career did Queen perform live at St. Pauls, London. This disc relates to the Mannheim, Germany, show of June 21, 1986.

The Freddie Mercury Tribute

Triple CD, TFKRL 9204-3 CD. TFKRL Records, Germany, 1993
Recorded Easter Monday (20/04/92), Wembley Stadium - Concert for AIDS Awareness
Running times: 69.45/48.17/44.06
The musical content here differs slightly from the Italian *Thank You Freddie* triple set: while that set offers 43 tracks collectively, this one offers 33. The packaging is similar to that of the official tribute video release (MVB 4910623). The failure to issue a proper CD of this, one of the most important Queen related live performances ever, ensured the inevitable arrival of this bootleg, and others like it, though some would no doubt have emerged regardless.

The Jewels

Double CD, IST 31/32
Insect Records, Italy, 1994

Running times: 61.50/44.27
It could have been worse. I imagine that *The Crown Jewels* must have at some point been toyed with as the title.

The Mercury Is Rising

ARC 003,Alternative Recording Company, Germany, 1993
Limited edition of 1500
Recorded live in London, Earls Court, (14/06/74) except for tracks 8, 9 and 10, Santa Monica Auditorium (22/03/74) and tracks 11, 12, 13, 14 and 15, Seattle Arena (13/03/77)
Running time: 74.45
While the inner sleeve notes offer the information given above, the outer notes contradict them. They advise instead that tracks 1-7 relate to an American Cleveland Arena show (June 14). In fact Queen did not perform any show at all on June 14, 1974, nor on March 22, 1975. They did, however, play the Seattle Arena show on March 13, 1977, as stated. The individual track timings displayed on the sleeve notes are also inaccurate. Again, such glaring oversights are common on bootleg releases.

The Ultimate Collection:

Rarities, Oddities and Cover Versions, Double CD, RMCD 001, Royalty Music, Germany, 1992
Various shows
Running times: 65.07/68.30
Note: The details in brackets are as they appear on the sleeve notes. At first glance this CD would seem to be the most exciting collectors' set ever. However, as much of the material on it is not what it purports to be, it is a huge disappointment. Tracks described as first takes, alternate versions, forgotten intro's and demos, are labelled as such purely to deceive collectors into buying the discs. Needless to say, many of the date and venue references are incorrect. The set does at least offer an idea as to what rare live and pre-Queen tracks do exist, and when they were recorded, though the fan club biography provides that information in far greater detail. In typical bootleg fashion, the

compact disc catalogue numbers and main title are different to those which appear on the accompanying sleeve notes. It is most likely that what was originally intended to be a predominantly pre-Queen rarities set – Larry Lurex is the credited artist on each CD – was later changed into this curious mishmash compilation.

The Ultimate Queen

Back Catalogue: Volume 1
No catalogue number or year of release details are contained on the disc or sleeve
Running time: 76.20

The Smile, Larry Lurex and non-album B-side material here offer newcomers to the band's music a welcome introduction to some rare songs, many of which are still awaiting an official release. It is increasingly likely that Freddie's superb vocal performance as Larry lurex will be released at some point as part of a long overdue rarities set, but nothing could be confirmed at the time of writing. 'I Can Hear Music' / 'Going Back' is a vastly underrated pairing, one of Freddie's finest recorded moments. All in all, this disc is a sensible investment.

The Ultimate Queen Back Catalogue: Volume 2

ODY 022m Record label unknown, Italy, 1994
Running time: 77.01

Though this disc (and Volume 1) clearly do not offer live material, it is included here for its informative and interest value. Following the success of Queen's penultimate studio album *The Miracle* in 1989, a follow up set containing non-album B-side material and the augmented cuts of 'Breakthru' (track 11), 'Scandal' and 'The Invisible Man' was considered. Tentatively titled *Another Miracle*, the idea was shelved and later cancelled – like numerous other Queen related projects. Had it emerged, however, it would have contained the other two non-album B-sides ('My Life Has Been Saved' and 'Hijack My Heart'), in addition to 'Stealin' (track 10). While tracks 1 and 2 have still

not been made officially available on CD, tracks 3, 4, 5, 6, 9 and 11 were all included on the 1992 *Box Of Tricks* 12-track compilation CD *The 12" Collection* (CDQTEL 0001).

Track 6 is the stunning instrumental version which had previously only been available on vinyl as flip the side to the American 'I Want To Break Free' single release in April 1984 (B5350). Tracks 7 and 8 are both logical additions to this disc, but neither one is particularly rare or difficult to locate

Tracks 12-16 have been lifted straight from a March 1991 Hollywood Records promotional disc. Issued through the Hollywood owned Basic label, the disc contains five alternative mixes of 'Rock You' and 'Champions' – all are dreadful, and offer collectors nothing very significant. [I refuse to accept that any Queen song should have a Zulu Scratch A Capella label attached to it... it simply doesn't feel right.]

Tribute: Rare Live And Unreleased Tracks
MF284, Mercury Records, 1991
Tracks 1-4: BBC Sessions 1973 / tracks 5-8: BBC Sessions 1977 / tracks 9 and 10: Smile 1969 / tracks 11-17: Live Aid, July 1985
Running time: 72.07

The first four tracks feature Queen's second BBC session, as recorded on July 25, 1973. Tracks 5-8 are once again the band's sixth and final BBC session (October 1977) which is by far the most widely available of all six sessions, though this time it is heard in its proper form, without the overdubbed fake audience. This material is also available as *Queen Tribute* which offers an identical tracklisting and bears the same catalogue number, but is packaged differently.

The front cover features a picture from the 'It's A Hard Life' promotional video.

Tokyo '85

APR 92.006, Arriba Records, Germany, 1992
Recorded live in Japan,1985
Running time: 49.20

This is yet another tedious offering of the July 11,

1986, London show, despite the sleeve note's claim to the contrary.

Tokyo 1985
TKCD 1120, Golden Stars Records, EEC, 1991
Recorded live in Tokyo (05/11/85)
Running time: 72.00
Not to be confused with the above disc (as some collectors seem to do) for this 17-track set is the better option. Although both offer material already available in various forms elsewhere, this one does at least include a two-page booklet. We must once again disregard the sleeve notes.

Queen did not play any live shows in November 1985. In fact they performed no shows at all that year after Live Aid. It would seem that whoever set out the sleeve artwork for this disc mistook 11/5/85 to mean the fifth day of the eleventh month, instead of the eleventh day of the fifth month, which is the correct date. This set comprises material recorded at the Yogishi Swimming Pool, Tokyo, Japan.

Unauthorised: Live: Volume 1
JOK 015-A, Joker Records, Australia, 1993
Running time: 55.53
If it's originality you're looking for, you won't find it here. This disc merely covers well trodden ground in offering the festive 1975 performance. This limited edition disc (of 1,500) is the only one I have come across that originates from Australia. There no doubt are other examples, but none as yet seem to have found their way onto the European market, though that is certain to change.

Two other similarly titled discs exist, with the addition of a 'We Will Rock You' sub-title, but because both discs offer yet again the Christmas Eve 1975 and Yoshigi, Tokyo, May 1985, shows, full details are unnecessary.

Unforgettable Music
Double CD, 10201, Red Line Records, Italy, 1993
Running Times: 50.19/53.19
This is one of the most difficult Queen CD

bootlegs to locate – and one of the most expensive. It is presented in 10" x 10" box and includes a 12-page booklet, numbered certificate of authentication and – what no Queen fan should be without – a medallion! The significance of the rather tacky medallion remains a mystery.

I would suggest that it is the untypical packaging that attracts the attention of collectors, because it can't be the music which has been lifted straight from Discs 2 and 3 of the German *Freddie Mercury Tribute* bootleg CD (TFKRL 9204-3 CD), as already outlined. The set is limited to 3,000.

Waiting On A Death Trip
TGP 137, Grand Prix Records, Italy, 1991
Live in Argentina, 1981
Running time: 68.03
This set offers an extremely good representation of 1981's infamous South American tour. Recorded in Buenos Aires on March 1, it contains most of the material that Queen chose to perform there. Only the familiar concluding few songs are absent.

We Still Rock You
ROLA 009, Rockland Records, Germany, 1993
Live in Europe, 1986
Running time: 73.52
Track 15 is a ten and a half minute semi-heavy improvisation, which mostly features Brian. Having only read the sleeve notes, but not actually heard the music, I cannot confirm that this featured in the show. It may well have been introduced onto the disc from an entirely unrelated gig.

As if the title of this disc wasn't guaranteed to arouse extreme prejudice, the two-page accompanying booklet included the words "In Memory of Brian Mercury". There are literally hundreds of errors on bootlegs but this takes the cake.

We Will Love You
Double CD, SKCD 2063
Skeleton Records, Italy, 1992

Recorded live at Palazzo Dello Sport, Milan (14/09/84) & Wembley Stadium, London (13/07/85)

Running times: 69.52 / 59.25

Although it would be reasonable to assume that Queen's illustrious Live Aid performance would have made copious bootleg appearances, curiously it has made surprisingly few. Tracks 9-15 on Disc 2 offer not only the main six song set, but also Brian and Freddie's finale. The inclusion of the Italian material is also uncommon.

We Will Rock You

CD 12018, On Stage Records, EEC, 1992

Date and venue (of tracks 5-14) unknown

Running time: 65.10

There are two identical CDs with this title, both issued by the On Stage label with the same catalogue number. Only the front cover pictures differ. Unsuspecting collectors invariably end up with a copy of each.

Who Wants To Live Forever

PLR CD 9201, Pluto Records, Italy, 1992

Recorded live in Paris, France Hippodrome De Vincennes (14/06/86)

Running time: 76.14

Though Queen did perform at this venue on the day indicated, this disc does not relate to it. Instead it features the July 12 Wembley Stadium show. When the concert was televised on ITV, the show opened with speeded up footage of the stage being constructed. The track which accompanied the film was the studio version of 'Brighton Rock'. Had the producers of this disc been aware of that, and omitted it, the deception might not have been discovered quite so quickly.

X-mas 1975

SR 012, Stoned Records, Korea, 1989

Queen – X-Mas 1975

Running time: 53.11

The sleeve notes claim that this was the first ever Queen CD bootleg release. An advanced copy (packaged in a black sleeve) also exists, though neither one is as early an issue as it purports to be.

Year Of The Opera

AAF 014, All About Fame Records, Germany, 1993

Various shows

Running time: unknown

You're My Best Friend

CD 12030

On Stage Records, EEC, 1992

Recorded live between 1975 and 1979 on the European Tour

Running time: 60.01

As the sleeve notes correctly observe, the first ten tracks do indeed originate from the European tour of 1979. Whoever compiled this disc need only to have looked at the 'Live Killers' sleeve notes to establish this... all ten tracks are the versions contained on that album. They appear in a different running order to the album, probably in an attempt to deceive fans. This song sequence, however, would never have been performed.

This bootleg does offer one of Roger Taylor's finest recorded moments – 'I'm In Love With My Car' – which he sings himself while simultaneously drumming. Other than the writing credits of 'Killer Queen' being attributed to Freddie, all the rest are incorrectly credited to Queen collectively. Nonspecific venue and date details - as presented here – usually indicate that the material featured, originates from numerous other bootleg recordings. They are essentially cocktails of various shows mixed together.

The following bootlegs have emeged post-1996, covering the intervening period up to 2004

A Day At The Apollo

2 CD, GE 145/146, Japan, 2000

Recorded 30/05/77

A Day At The Stadium
QUE 062201, Italy, 2001
Recorded 11/07/86

A Night At The Court
SPANK 201/2, Italy, 2000
Recorded 6/6/77 & 27/11/73

A Night At The Rainbow
No Cat Number, Germany, 2002
Recorded from original video *Live At The Rainbow*

A Tribute To Freddie Mercury
P 910012, Germany, 1992
Recorded 20/04/92

Absolutely Enthusiastic
Q-81, Italy, 1997
Recorded from original video *We Will Rock You*

Action And More Action
2 CD, HB 939, Japan, 1999
Recorded 24/10/82

Action This Night
2 CD, GE 104/105, Japan, 1999
Recorded 01/05/82

Back To Queen
No Cat Number, Bulgaria, 1998
Recorded Various live & Studio

Bonsoir Paris
2 CD, GE 179/180, Japan, 2001
Recorded 28/02/79

Bring It Back Alive
Planet X PLAN 023, Italy, 1999
Recorded 11/05/85

Cardiac Arrest
HIP 001, Japan, 1997
Recorded 29/03/74 & 04/04/76

Christmas At The Beeb
No Cat Number, Japan, 1997
Recorded 24/12/75

Cinema Cut
No Cat Number, Japan, 1997
Recorded from original video *Live At The Rainbow*

Command Performance
CPCD-8375-3100-0, Germany, 1997
Recorded 05/06/82

Complete Kampuchea Concert
2 CD, GE137/138, Japan, 2000
Recorded 26/12/79

Complete Rare Demo & Studio Live
2 CD, No cat no., Japan, 1996
Recorded Various

Complete Rare Remix
2 CD, No cat no., Japan, 1996
Recorded: Various

Complete Rare Singles
2 CD, No cat no., Japan, 1996
Recorded: Various

Crazy Tour
2 CD, CT 001/002, Japan, 1998
Recorded 26/12/79

Don't Cry For Me
2 CD, TB.95.1027, Italy, 1995
Recorded 24/25/11.81 & 11/05/85

Done Under Pressure In Germany
2 CD, GE 141/142, Japan, 2000
Recorded 21/06/86

Dynasty
3 CD, QN 1-6, Japan. 1997
Recorded 27/09/84

Eastern Tits
CDP 74262882, Germany, 1998
Recorded 27/07/86

Electric Magic
2 CD, AMS 728, Japan, 1997
Recorded 09/08/86

Expert Sky Cabinet
2 CD, GE 201/202, Japan, 2002
Recorded 29/03/76 (afternoon)

Final Live In Japan
2 CD, RMU-98, Italy, 1998
Recorded 11/05/85 & 11/07/86

First Live Attack
2CD, PM 007/8, Japan, 1998
Recorded 01/05/75

First Procession
GE, Japan, 2002
Recorded 13/9/73 & 27/11/73

Ga Ga
2 CD, Qu 001/002, Japan, 1998
Recorded 01/09/84

Get Down
2 CD, 141-RC, Japan, 1997
Recorded 24/10/82

Golden Demos 1973-1976
AML7, Italy, 1996
Recorded Various

Gonna Get Game
2 CD, GE 033/034, Japan, 1998
Recorded from original video *We Will Rock You* &
28/11/77 + Studio

Great King Hang Man
BS-7, Japan, 1996
Recorded 19/04/75 & 01/05/75

Great Queen In Vienna
2 CD, GE 152/153
Japan, 2001
Recorded 29/09/84

Greatest Hits Live In Concert
ABS 1789, Australia, 1999
Recorded 11/07/86

He Made It On His Own
GE 144, Japan, 2000
Recorded 13/7/85 & 14/04/76

Her Majesties Jewels
HMJCD, Germany, 1997
Recorded Various

Hot Space Tour '82
3CD, HAST-001
Japan, 1997
Recorded 15/9/82 & 05/06/82

Hyde Park '76
GE 158, Japan, 2000
Recorded 18/09/76

Imagine
2 CD, GE162/163, Japan, 2001
Recorded 14/12/80

Immigrant Magic
2 CD, GE148/149, Japan, 2000
Recorded 26/06/86

In Concert '74
2 CD, GE 156/157, Japan, 2000
Recorded 06/12/74

In Nuce
1LP (Pic Disc), Cosmic MS 1001, Italy, 2000
Recorded Various

In The Lap Of The Gods
QUE 061901, Italy, 2001
Recorded from original video *Live At The Rainbow*

Invite You To A Night At The Warehouse
2CD, STONED-5, Japan, 1997
Recorded 12/05/77

Jazz Final
2 CD, No Cat Number, Japan, 1996
Recorded 06/05/79

Killers In The Forum
P-rec 25, Italy, 2003
Recorded from original video *We Will Rock You*

Last European News
2CD, GE 222/223, Japan, 2002
Recorded 02/05/78

Lazing On A Sunday Evening
MARC TQ-76042, Japan, 1997
Recorded 04/04/76

Let Me Show In
2 CD, GE 013/014, Japan, 1997
Recorded 15/09/84

Let Sao Paulo Entertain You
2CD, GE 132/133, Japan, 2001
Recorded 01/03/81

Life Is Real
2 CD, GE 154/155, Japan, 2000
Recorded 09/08/82

Live – A Beautiful Album
QB-1002, Japan, 1997
Recorded 19/04/75 & 01/05/75

Live Achievements
2 CD, GE 090/091, Japan, 1999
Recorded 01/12/78

Live Aids
1 LP, QCP 1992, Germany, 1992
Recorded 13/07/85 & 20/04/92

Live In Leiden
1Lp (Picture Disk), R LP Q1, Holland, 2000
Recorded 27/11/80

London 1986
LSCD 51170, Italy, 1996
Re-Release of *A Day At The Stadium*

Long Life To The Queen
2 CD, No Cat Number, Japan, 1998
Recorded 16/04/82

Magic In Stockholm
2 CD, GE 217/ 218, Japan, 2001
Recorded 07/06/86

Master Of "Sheetkeeckers"
No Cat Number, Japan, 1997
Recorded 31/03/74 & 13/09/73

Melbourne 1985
2 CD, KF 98020/21, Japan, 2000
Recorded 19/04/85

Need You Loving Rock
2 CD, GE 206/207, Japan, 2002
Recorded 13/02/81

Not Authorized
Ban, Australia, 1995
Recorded 11/07/86 & Various Live & Studio

Not Fade Away
2 CD, GE 175/176. Japan, 2001
Recorded 04/09/84

Over The Best Or Worse
2 CD, WORK 5556*2, Italy, 1992
Recorded 20/04/92 and various venues

Play The Game
3 CD, PR 01032003, Italy, 2003
Recorded 15/09/82 & 11/07/86

Pre Ordained
FLCD 7500, Italy, 1996
Recorded Various

Procession
GE 178, Japan, 2001
Recorded 29/11/73

Queen Live (Unlicensed)
SW8, Australia, 1995
Re-release of *Who Wants To Live Forever*

Queens Last Stand
2 CD, ETS 2563/64, Japan, 1997
Recorded 15/05/85

Rarities
EB-75, Germany, 2000
Recorded Demos BBC Sessions and Various

Real Dazzler
2CD, GE 197/198, Japan, 2002
Recorded 02/09/84

Rock 'N' Roll Night Tonight, Okay !!
2 CD, GE123/124, Japan, 1999
Recorded 13/04/1978

Rock It To The Bowl
DH-006, Japan, 1997
Recorded 05/06/82

Rogues and Scandals
QR 10001, Japan, 1998
Recorded 13/9/73 & 24/12/75

Savage Young Mercury
GE 2112, Japan, 2001
Recorded 21/4/74 & 09/9/69

Seven Seas Of Tsumagoi
2 CD, SW-004/5, Japan, 2001
Recorded 29/04/75

Sheetkeeckers
OUTSIDE-001, Japan, 1996
Recorded 31/03/74

South America
LR 61247-2, Germany, 1997
Recorded 28/02/81

Standing On The Arena
2 CD, GE 135/136, Japan, 2000
Recorded 08/12/80

Staying Power And Glory
2 CD, GE 213/214, Japan, 2002
Recorded 12/05/82

Supporting Mott The Hoople
No cat No., Japan, 1997
Recorded 07/05/74 & 20/11/73

Sweet Rhapsody
2 CD, GE 047/048, Japan, 1998
Recorded 26/11/75

Thank You Freddie
3 CD, PWCD 101, Italy, 1992
Recorded 20/04/92

The Eye
2 CD, No cat no., Japan, 2000
Recorded Audio Tracks from the video game

The Fly Swatters
2 CD, GE 159/160, Japan, 2001
Recorded 19.12.80

The Freddie Mercury Memory Concert
SBC 027, Italy, 1997
Recorded 20/04/92

The Freddie Mercury Tribute
3 CD, FM-Tribute CD, Italy, 1992
Recorded 20/04/92

The Freddie Mercury Tribute
3 CD, TFKRL 9204, Germany, 1992
Recorded 20/04/92

The Royal American Tour 1975
DOCTOR-01, Japan, 1996
Recorded 29/03/75

The Royal Countdown
JAG 002, Italy, 1996
Recorded Various Live & Studio

The Ultimate Collection Vol. Three
2 CD, RMCD007/008, Germany, 1995
Recorded 24/10/73 & 13/9/73

The Ultimate Queen Back-Catalogue Volume III
No cat No., Germany, 1997
Recorded Various

The Ultimate Rarities Collection
FBCD 001, Germany, 1996
Re-release of *Ultra Rare Trax*

Under Pressure
7", LIVE, UK, 1993
Recorded 20/04/92

Unforgettable Music
2 CD, 10201, Italy, 1992
Recorded 20/04/92

Waiting On A Death Trip
TGP 137, Italy, 1996
Recorded 28/02/81

When You Don't Wanna Here It...Fuckin' Go Home
2 CD, THWS-001/002, Germany, 1998
Recorded 28/4/82 & 15/9/82 & 14-15.9/82

White Queen Night
GE 134, Japan, 2000
Recorded 24/12/75

LIVE BOOTLEG LPs
Prior to the advent of compact discs, there was a thriving trade in vinyl bootlegs. Most collectors now consider these obsolete but there will always be a number of fans who will continue to collect vinyl, though the choice on offer to them is steadily decreasing.

What follows is as comprehensive a list as is possible to provide. As with all bootleg formats, it is constantly being updated, and will be out of date almost immediately.

A Day In Munich
QMU
(26/06/86)

Absolutely Enthusiastic
Double Album, TFKRL 9002-2
(11/05/85)

Absolutely Rare
Double Album, TFKRL 9201
Various Shows

Black & White Queen
EEN 98
(24/12/75)

Cardiac Arrest
HIP 001
Various Shows

Command Performance
TAKRL 1997
(24/12/75)

Crazy Duck
DR 481
(26/12/79)

Crazy Tour
Double Album, 26Q
(26/12/79)

Crowning Glory
FLAT 8218
(04/04/76)

Dear Friend Goodbye
TFMML 001
(07/05/75)

Done Under Pressure
Double Album
(21/06/86)

Don't Stop Us Live
(02/02/79)

Duck Soup
SLA 007
(13/03/77)
Also available as 'Somebody To Love'
RRL 6900
Part 2 issued as PNW ODD 3

Dynasty
Double Album, QN 1-6
(27/09/84)

Elizabeth II
(14/09/84)

En Viva Pueblo
(16/10/81)
Also available as *No More Mananas*

Flash Alive
Double Album, Q 80128
(08/12/80)

Falklands Are Rocking
STQ 231082
(03/81)

Falklands II - The Sequel
KQ001
(03/81)

Freddie's Boys At The Beeb [*** see note at bottom]
JOKE 40 HO, BBC sessions

Freddie's Last Journey
Double Album
(24-25/11/81)
Copy of *We Will Rock You* video, PAN 648-09

Free In The Park
MARC
(18/09/76)

Ga Ga
Double Album, ETS 2563/64
(01/09/84)

Geisha Boys
SLA 001
(04/04/76)
Copy of Japanese bootleg *Lazing On A Sunday Afternoon*

Get Down
Double Album, LR 140RC
(24/10/82)

Gonna Rock
Side 1 is first side of *No News Is Good News* and Side 2 is first side of *Sheetkickers*
QLS 1957

Halfpence
EEN 98 (24/12/75)
Same as *Black & White Queen*. Same catalogue no. also

Her Majesties Secret Service
Double Album, TFKRL 9001
Unknown venue and date

High Voltage
Double Album, SR 25 703
(24/12/75)
Re-release of *Sheetkickers* and *Command Performance*

Hot Space Tour '82
Triple Album, ETS 2511
(14/09/82)

I've Just Got To Have It Now
Unknown venue, date and catalogue no.

Kimono My Place Live
MARC 75122
(01/05/75)

King's Favourite
Double Album, 141RC
(20/09/84)

Lazing On A Sunday Evening
MARC TQ-76042
(04/04/76)

Live
OG-860
(19/04/75)

Live At Budokan
TAB 001
(24/12/75)
Recorded in London, not Japan. Copy of Royal Rock Us

Live In Japan
Double Album, S3004
(Japan 1982)

Long Life To The Queen
Triple Album
(April 1982)

Magic At Knebworth
Double Album, RSR 250
(09/08/86)

Mania
EGF 1200 (13/03/77)

Mercury Poisoning [** see note at bottom]
IMP 1118
(31/04/76)

Moet & Chandon
TFKRL 9101
Unknown venue and date

No More Mananas
SLA 0009, Reissued as KWIN 101
1981 tour, Unknown cat no.

No News Is Good News
BBC session and live material

Queen At St. James' Park
Double Album
(09/07/86)
Extremely Limited Edition

Queen Elizabeth II
(14/09/84)

Queen Invite You To A Night At The Budokan
MARC TQ-76059
(31/04/76)

Queen Invite You To A Night At The Warehouse
Double Album , STONED 5
(12/05/77)
Reissued as QUO 012

Queen Reigns The World
Double Album, Miles Records
(21/06/86)

Queen's Last Stand
Double Album, ETS 2583/84
(15/05/85)

Rogues And Scoundrels
AFTERMATH 8
Usually advertised as *Rogues And Scandals*
Various shows

Royal American Tour
WRMB 307
(22/03/75)

Royal Rock Us
TAKRL 927
(24/12/75)

Save Me
Double Album
(01/02/79)

Sheetkickers
2 sleeves, TAKRL 1957
Various Shows from 1974
Includes 'Ballroom Blitz' by Sweet!

Stunning
BRR 006
(01/05/75)
Copy of *Kimono My Place Live* reissued by Rodan
Records in a colour cover

Tie Your Mother Down
KQ 001
(28/02/81)

Tokyo Rampage
TKRWM 1801
Various Shows

Tornado In The Far East
(Part 1) TFKRL 9002 2
Unknown venue and date
Part 2 - same catalogue no.

Zoom Queen
Double Album, LLX 314
(Japan 1976)

*** There seems to be much confusion about an album called *Freddie's Boys At The Beeb*. As the catalogue number implies (Bulsara: Freddie's real surname), it is a bootleg disc which features session material recorded for the BBC on both sides. The eight-track disc was issued in three different coloured vinyls (yellow, blue and red), though I have yet to see a red copy. The material on Side 1 relates to Queen's second BBC session (25/7/73), and Side 2 to the final one (28/10/77). See the Live discography section for tracklist details.

** Mercury Poisoning (IMP 1118): Some copies of this album were mispressed, and contained Side 2 of Paul McCartney's *Wings From The Wings* album, on the B-side (IMP 1117-1119).

VINYL ALBUM BOOTLEGS ORIGINATING FROM ONE CONCERT ONLY

Like their compact disc equivalents, many vinyl bootlegs contain sleeve note errors and incorrect date and venue advice. *Dear Friend Goodbye* is a good example. Queen did not play a concert on May 7, 1975. The eight shows they performed in Japan that year concluded on May 1.

The following list is an at-a-glance summary of the information outlined above. It contains only those discs which relate to one specific show, not those which feature material from various sources.

A Day In Munich (26/6/86)
Absolutely Enthusiastic (11/5/85)
Black & White Queen (24/12/75)
Command Performance (24/12/75)
Crazy Duck (26/12/79)
Crowning Glory (04/04/76)
Dear Friend Goodbye (07/05/75)
Done Under Pressure (21/06/86)
Don't Stop Us Live (02/02/79)
Duck Soup (13/03/77)

Dynasty (27/09/84)
Elizabeth II (14/09/84)
En Viva Pueblo (16/10/81)
Flash Alive (08/12/80)
Falklands Are Rocking (03/81)
Falklands II - The Sequel (03/81)
Free In The Park (18/09/76)
Ga Ga (01/09/84)
Geisha Boys (04/04/76)
Get Down (24/10/82)
Halfpence (24/12/75)
Hot Space Tour '82 (14/09/82)
High Voltage (24/12/75)
Kimono My Place Live (01/05/75)
King's Favourite (20/09/84)
Lazing On A Sunday Evening (04/04/76)
Live (19/04/75)
Live At Budokan (24/12/75)
Magic At Knebworth (09/08/86) Mania
(13/03/77)
Queen At St. James' Park (09/07/86)
Queen Elizabeth II (14/09/84)
**Queen Invite You To A Night At The
Warehouse** (12/05/77)
Queen Reigns The World (21/06/86)
Queen's Last Stand (15/05/85)
Royal American Tour (22/03/75)
Royal Rock Us (24/12/75)
Save Me (01/02/79)
Stunning (01/05/75)
Tie Your Mother Down (28/02/81)

AUDIO CASSETTE RECORDINGS

The most effective way new fans can familiarise themselves with Queen's live performances is to respond to fan club or *Record Collector* advertisements.

Most collectors who start and build up their collections in this way (myself included), prefer not to sell copies of shows they have, but instead swap them for shows they do not have.

In addition to live recordings, fans also exchange Queen related press conference, biography, documentary, American radio show, tribute and interview tapes. There are well over a thousand of these, and it would be impossible and impractical to summarise them all here.

Although Queen performed a total of 704 documented shows in their career, almost exactly a quarter of that number (approximately 150), have at some stage emerged in audio cassette form.

The following chronological list details only the tapes which most frequently appear on sale and swap lists.

Marquee
Marquee Club, London, England (20/12/72)
Queen On The Green
Golders Green Hippodrome, London, England (13/09/73)
Paris Theatre
London, England (20/10/73)
Oxford New Theatre
Oxford, England (20/11/73)
Opera House
Manchester, England (26/11/73)
Birmingham Town Hall
Birmingham, England (27/11/73)
Bristol Colston
Colston Hall, Bristol, England (29/11/73)
Rainbow Theatre
London, England (31/03/74)
Mott Tour
Uris Theatre, New York, USA (07/05/74)
At The Palace
Manchester, England (30/10/74)
St Georges Hall
Bradford, England (06/11/74)
Live At The Rainbow
Rainbow Theatre, London, England (20/11/74)
Sheetkickers
Various shows from 1974 (originally known as 'Shitkickers')
Rogues And Scoundrels
Various shows from 1974
Cardiac Arrest
Various shows from 1974/75

Tokyo Rampage
Various shows from 1974/75
Royal American Tour
Santa Monica Civic Auditorium, USA (29/03/75)
Kimono My Place Live
Budokan Hall, Tokyo, Japan (01/05/75)
Stunning Live In Tokyo
Various shows in Tokyo, Japan (19-30/04/75)
Budokan
Budokan Hall, Tokyo, Japan (19/04/75)
Liverpool Empire
Liverpool, England (15/11/75)
Coventry Theatre
Coventry, England (16/11/75)
Manchester
Manchester, England (26/11/75)
Halfpence
Hammersmith Odeon, London (24/12/75)
Command Performance
Hammersmith Odeon, London (24/12/75)
Christmas At The Beeb
Hammersmith Odeon, London (24/12/75)
Merry Christmas
Hammersmith Odeon, London (24/12/75)
Los Angeles
Santa Monica Civic Auditorium, USA (03/76)
Fukuoka
Kyden Gymnasium, Fukuoka, Japan (26/03/76)
Kosei Nenkin
Osaka, Japan (29/03/76)
Mercury Poisoning
Budokan, Tokyo, Japan (01/04/76)
Geisha Boys
Nichidai Kodo, Tokyo, Japan (04/04/76)
Crowning Glory
Nichidai Kodo, Tokyo, Japan (04/04/76)
Lazing On A Sunday Afternoon
European copy of above
Adelaide
Apollo Stadium, Adelaide, Australia (15/04/76)
Playhouse Theatre
Edinburgh, Scotland (02/09/76)
Free In The Park
Hyde Park, London, England (18/09/76)

Queen At The Races
College Park, Maryland, USA (04/02/77)
Vancouver
PNE Coliseum, Vancouver, Canada (11/03/77)
Pacific North Western
Seattle Arena, USA (13/03/77) (aka PNW)
Duck Soup
Seattle Arena, USA (13/03/77)
Queen Mania
Seattle Arena, USA (13/03/77) (similar to above – different listing)
Stockholm
Ice Stadium, Stockholm, Sweden (08/05/77)
Sheer Bloody Poetry
Scandanavium, Gothenburg, Sweden (10/05/77)
Queen Invite You To A Night At The Warehouse
Broendby Hall, Copenhagen, Denmark (12/05/77)
Bristol Hippodrome
Bristol, England (24/05/77)
Glasgow
Glasgow Apollo, Scotland (30/05/77)
Glasgow Apollo
Glasgow, Scotland (30/05/77)
Apollo II
Glasgow, Scotland (31/05/77)
Empire Theatre
Liverpool, England (03/06/77)
Earls Court
London, England (06/06/77)
Copenhagen
Falkoner Theatre, Copenhagen, Denmark (13/04/78)
Rotterdam
Ahoy Hall, Rotterdam, Holland (19/04/78)
Paris Pavillion
Paris, France (23/04/78)
Vienna
Stadhalle, Vienna, Austria (02/05/78)
Bingley Hall
Stafford, England (06/05/78)
Dallas
Convention Centre, Dallas, USA (28/10/78)

Queen Play The Square
Madison Square Garden, New York, USA (17/11/78)

The Forum
Montreal, Canada (01/12/78)

Deutchlandhalle
Berlin, Germany (24/01/79)

Back On The Road Again
Sportshalle, Cologne, Germany (01/02/79)

Don't Stop Us Live
Festhalle, Frankfurt, Germany (02/02/79)

Zurich
Hallenstadium, Zurich, Switzerland (04/02/79)

Basketball Halle
Munich, Germany (11/02/79)

Pavillion De Paris
Paris, France (28/02/79)

Pavillion De Paris II
Paris, France (01/03/79)

Tokyo Budokan
Budokan Hall, Tokyo, Japan (23/04/79)

Budokan
Budokan Hall, Tokyo, Japan (24/04/79)

Saarbruken
Ludwigsparkstadion, Saarbruken, Germany (18/08/79)

City Hall
Newcastle, England (03/12/79)

Mack Attack
Newcastle, England (04/12/79)

Queen Go Crazy
Hammersmith Odeon, London, England (26/12/79)

A Silent Night At The Odeon
Hammersmith Odeon, London, England (26/12/79)

Crazy Tour
Various shows from European leg of the Crazy Tour 1979

LA Forum
Los Angeles, USA (11/07/80)

Oakland
Oakland Coliseum, USA (14/07/80)

Rhode Island
Civic Centre, Providence, USA (26/08/80)

Mecca
Milwaukee, USA (10/09/80)

Chicago Plays The Game
Horizon Theatre, Chicago, USA (19/09/80)

Paris
Le Bourget La Retonde, Paris, France (25/11/80)

Leiden
Groenoordhalle, Leiden, Germany (27/11/80)

Essen Germany
Grudhalle, Essen, Germany (29/11/80)

Berlin
Deutchlandhalle, Berlin, Germany (30/11/80)

NEC Birmingham
National Exhibition Centre, Birmingham, England (05/12/80)

NEC Revisited
National Exhibition Centre, Birmingham, England (06/12/80)

Flash Alive
Wembley Arena, London, England (08/12/80)

Wembley Arena
London, England (09/12/80)

Flash Bites The Big One
Wembley Arena, London, England (10/12/80)

Frankfurt
Festhalle, Germany (14/12/80)

Falklands Are Rocking
Various South American shows (Feb-Mar 81)

Falklands II (The Sequel)
Buenos Aires, Argentina (28/02-01/03/81)

Gluttons For Punishment
Sarfield Stadium, Buenos Aires, Argentina (08/03/81)

Buenos Aires Revisited
Sarfield Stadium, Buenos Aires, Argentina (08/03/81)

Save Us
Morumbi Stadium, Sao Paulo, Brazil (20/03/81)

Puebla Mexico
Estadion Cuahtermoc, Puebla (17/10/81)

Stockholm
Isstadion, Stockholm, Sweden (10/04/82)

Long Life To The Queen
Hallenstadion, Zurich, Switzerland (17/04/82)

Forest Nationale
Brussels, Belgium (23/04/82)
Frankfurt
Feathalle, Frankfurt, Germany (28/04/82)
Dortmund
Westallenhalle, Dortmund, Germany (01/05/82)
Hamburg
Ernst-Mercke Halle, Hamburg, Germany (16/05/82)
Kassel
Eisspdorthalle, Kassel, Germany (18/05/82)
Elland Road
Football Ground, Leeds, England (29/05/82)
Edinburgh
Ingliston Showground, Edinburgh, Scotland (01/06/82)
Live At The Bowl
Milton Keynes Bowl, Buckinghamshire, England (05/06/82)
Montreal
Forum, Montreal, Canada (21/06/82)
Queen Rock The Square
Madison Square Garden, New York, USA (28/06/82)
Rock It Over America
Madison Square Garden, New York, USA (28/06/82)
New Jersey
Brendon Burn Coliseum, New Jersey, USA (09/08/82)
The Forum
Los Angeles, California, USA (15/09/82)
Get Down
Hankyu Nishinomiyakyujo, Osaka, Japan (24/10/82)
Seibu
Seibu Lions Stadium, Tokyo, Japan (03/11/82)
Dublin Eire
Royal Dublin Society Hall, Dublin, Eire (28/08/84)
Live At The NEC
National Exhibition Centre, Birmingham, England (31/08/84)

NEC Revisited
National Exhibition Centre, Birmingham, England (01/09/84)
Break Free At Birmingham
National Exhibition Centre, Birmingham, England (02/09/84)
Queen Give Em The Works
Wembley Arena, London, England (04/09/84)
Wembley London
Wembley Arena, London, England (05/09/84)
Wembley London
Wembley Arena, London, England (07/09/84)
Wembley London
Wembley Arena, London, England (08/09/84)
Queen Elizabeth II
Sportspalace, Milan, Italy (14/09/84)
Queen Elizabeth II – Second Night
Sportspalace, Milan, Italy (15/09/84)
Paris
Omnisports, Paris, France (18/09/84)
Kings Favourite
Forest Nationale, Brussels, Belgium (21/09/84)
Let Us Entertain You
Forest Nationale, Brussels, Belgium (21/09/84)
Stuttgart
Schleyerhalle, Stuttgart, Germany (27/09/84)
Rock In Rio Festival
Roi De Janeiro, Brazil (12-19/01/85)
Melbourne
Sports & Entertainment Centre, Melbourne, Australia (19/04/85)
Melbourne (Last Night)
Sports & Entertainment Centre, Melbourne, Australia (20/04/85)
Sydney Australia
Entertainments Centre, Sydney, Australia (26/04/85)
Twisting By The Pool
Yogishi Swimming Pool Auditorium, Tokyo, Japan (11/05/85)
In A Sticky Situation
Yogishi Swimming Pool Auditorium, Tokyo, Japan (11/05/85)
Jo Hall
Osaka, Japan (15/05/85)

Live Aid
Wembley Stadium, London, England (13/07/85)
There Can Be Only One
Stockholm, Sweden (07/06/86)
Leiden
Groenoordhalle, Leiden, Germany (12/06/86)
Done Under Pressure
Mannhiem, Germany (21/06/86)
Queen Reign The World
Mannhiem, Germany (21/06/86)
Berlin
Waldbuehne, Berlin, Germany (26/06/86)
Slane Castle
Dublin, Eire (05/07/86)
Magic Moments
St James Park, Newcastle, England (09/07/86)
A Night Of Summer Magic
Wembley Stadium, London, England (12/07/86)
(aka Real Magic)
Don't Lose Your Seat
(USA Radio Broadcast - As Above) Superstar
Concert (Westwood One) (12/07/86)
Maine Road Magic
Maine Road, Manchester, England (16/07/86)
Vienna
Stadhalle, Vienna, Austria (21/07/86)
Vienna (2nd Night)
Stadhalle, Vienna, Austria (22/07/86)
Live In Budapest
Nepstadion, Budapest, Hungary (27/07/86)
Amphitheatre France
Frejus, France (30/07/86)
Magic At Knebworth
Knebworth Park, Hertfordshire, England
(09/09/86)

**SUMMARY OF MOST COMMON AUDIO
BOOTLEG RECORDINGS
RELATING TO ONE SHOW ONLY - NOT
VARIOUS SHOWS**
Marquee (20/12/72)
Queen On The Green (13/09/73)
Paris Theatre (20/10/73)
Oxford New Theatre (20/11/73)
Opera House (26/11/73)

Birmingham Town Hall (27/11/73) Bristol
Colston (29/11/73)
Rainbow Theatre (31/03/74)
Mott Tour (07/05/74)
At The Palace (30/10/74)
St Georges Hall (06/11/74)
Live At The Rainbow (20/11/74)
Royal American Tour (29/03/75)
Budokan (19/04/75)
Kimono My Place Live (01/05/75)
Liverpool Empire (15/11/75)
Coventry Theatre (16/11/75)
Manchester (26/11/75)
Halfpence (24/12/75)
Command Performance (24/12/75)
Christmas At The Beeb (24/12/75)
Merry Christmas (24/12/75)
Fukuoka (26/03/76)
Kosei Nenkin (29/03/76)
Mercury Poisoning (01/04/76)
Geisha Boys (04/04/76)
Crowning Glory (04/04/76)
Lazing On A Sunday Afternoon (04/04/76)
Adelaide (15/04/76)
Playhouse Theatre (02/09/76)
Free In The Park (18/09/76)
Queen At The Races (04/02/77)
Vancouver (11/03/77)
Pacific North Western (13/03/77)
PNW (13/03/77)
Duck Soup (13/03/77)
Queen Mania (13/03/77)
Stockholm (08/05/77)
Sheer Bloody Poetry (10/05/77)
**Queen Invite You To A Night At The
Warehouse** (12/05/77)
Bristol Hippodrome (24/05/77)
Glasgow (30/05/77)
Glasgow Apollo (30/05/77)
Apollo II (31/05/77)
Empire Theatre (03/06/77)
Earls Court (06/06/77)
Copenhagen (13/04/78)
Rotterdam (19/04/78)
Paris Pavillion (23/04/78)

Vienna (03/05/78)
Bingley Hall (06/05/78)
Dallas (28/10/78)
Queen Play The Square (17/11/78)
The Forum (01/12/78)
Deutchlandhalle (01/01/79)
Back On The Road Again (01/02/79)
Don't Stop Us Live (02/02/79)
Zurich (04/02/79)
Basketball Halle (11/02/79)
Pavillion De Paris (28/02/79)
Pavillion De Paris II (01/03/79)
Tokyo Budokan (23/04/79)
Budokan (24/04/79)
Saarbruken (18/08/79)
City Hall (03/12/79)
Mack Attack (04/12/79)
Queen Go Crazy (26/12/79)
A Silent Night At The Odeon (26/12/79)
LA Forum (11/07/80)
Oakland (14/07/80)
Rhode Island (26/08/80)
Mecca (10/09/80)
Chicago Plays The Game (19/09/80)
Paris (25/11/80)
Leiden (27/11/80)
Essen Germany (29/11/80)
Berlin (30/11/80)
NEC Birmingham (05/12/80)
NEC Revisited (06/12/80)
Flash Alive (08/12/80)
Wembley Arena (09/12/80)
Flash Bites The Big One (10/12/80)
Frankfurt (14/12/80)
Gluttons For Punishment (08/03/81)
Buenos Aires Revisited (08/03/81)
Save Us (20/03/81)
Puebla Mexico (17/11/81)
Stockholm (10/04/82)
Long Life To The Queen (17/04/82)
Forest Nationale (23/04/82)
Frankfurt (28/04/82)
Dortmund (01/05/82)
Hamburg (16/05/82)
Kassel (18/05/82)
Elland Road (29/05/82)

Edinburgh (01/06/82)
Live At The Bowl (05/06/82)
Montreal (21/07/82)
Queen Rock The Square (28/07/82)
Rock It Over America (28/07/82
New Jersey (09/08/82)
The Forum (15/09/82)
Get Down (24/10/82)
Seibu (03/11/82)
Dublin Eire (28/08/84)
Live At The NEC (31/08/84)
NEC Revisited (01/09/84)
Break Free At Birmingham (02/09/84)
Queen Give Em The Works (04/09/84)
Wembley London (05/09/84)
Wembley London (07/09/84)
Wembley London (08/09/84)
Queen Elizabeth II (14/09/84)
Queen Elizabeth II - Second Night (15/09/84)
Paris (18/09/84)
Kings Favourite (21/09/84)
Let Us Entertain You (21/09/84)
Stuttgart (27/09/84)
Melbourne (19/04/85)
Melbourne (Last Night) (20/04/85)
Sydney Australia (26/04/85)
Twisting By The Pool (11/05/85)
In A Sticky Situation (11/05/85)
Jo Hall (15/05/85)
Live Aid (13/07/85)
There Can Be Only One (07/06/86)
Leiden (12/06/86)
Done Under Pressure (21/06/86)
Queen Reign The World (21/06/86)
Berlin (26/06/86)
Slane Castle (05/07/86)
Magic Moments (09/07/86)
A Night Of Summer Magic (12/07/86)
Don't Lose Your Seat (12/07/86)
Maine Road Magic (16/07/86)
Vienna (21/07/86)
Vienna (2nd Night) (22/07/86)
Live In Budapest (27/07/86)
Amphitheatre France (30/07/86)
Magic At Knebworth (09/08/86)

QUEEN LIVE BOOKS

Predictably, there is a dearth of written matter relating to Queen's live performances The few which have emerged through the years offer brief details and summaries. Unofficial publications generally offer fans and collectors most information, and the following summary is made up of both official and unofficial books.

❖ Queen - An Official Biography Plus Their Recent U.S. Royal Tour

Written by Larry Pryce and published by Star Books, in 1976, this 124-page paperback, though hard to find now, is an informative and worthwhile read.

❖ Gluttons For Punishment

Published in 1982 (by Peter Lubin), this 82-page souvenir book tells the often amusing, sometimes ridiculous, but always true, story of the 1981 South American tour, from the view point of the tour organisers and crew members. An amusing text (by Mike Reynolds) details many of the behind the scenes mishaps which plagued almost the entire tour.

❖ A Magic Tour

Published in 1987 (by Sidgwick & Jackson), this 98-page book provides technical and logistic information relating to the Magic tour of 1986. The book commences with several pages of text, but is made up for the most part of on and off stage photographs. The text is provided by Peter Hillmore, and the photography by Denis O'Regan.

❖ Live Aid

Published in 1985 (by Sidgwick & Jackson), almost 200 pages of text and photographs detail every artist who performed on the day, and in the order in which they appeared. The main text is courtesy of Peter Hillmore, and Bob Geldof provides the introduction. Four pages relate to Queen (Freddie mostly), and one to Brian and Freddie's acoustic finale.

❖ The First Ten Years / The First Twelve Years

First published in 1981 (by Babylon Books), an entirely reworked and updated edition appeared later in 1984. Compiled by Mike West, the original book contained 112 pages of factual band history, discography and bootleg information. By 1984 however, the retitled work had been condensed down to only 90 pages, and sported a different cover.

To my knowledge, this was the very first publication of its kind. It is certainly the earliest documentation I have come across which relates to Queen bootlegs. It was unauthorised and fan club members were politely asked not to buy it, nor others like it. Inevitably the request inspired the reverse. Curious fans who were previously unaware of this book went straight out in search of it.

The quality of photographic reproduction in the amended edition is vastly superior to the first edition, as is the binding.

The earlier edition fell to pieces within a month of buying it. Both books are recommended to serious collectors.

❖ The Bootleg CDs

Not so much published, as compiled and independently issued, this A4 size booklet was originally made available in March 1994, but was updated and issued again in October the same year.

No author is credited, though its copyright (if one is appropriate) is attributed to Johnny The Limiter. The book originates from Holland, and is most definitely worth seeking out. It is concise, informative and has been meticulously researched. The grammar leaves much to be desired, often making little or no sense at all, but you get the general idea of what the Dutch author is driving at.

As the title suggests, the book concentrates solely upon the many Queen related bootleg compact discs. It also includes details of four Brian May band discs, and The Cross's May 29, 1990 and December 22, 1992 shows.

Having heard almost every disc the book mentions, a few minor discrepancies are apparent. In fairness, most are due to the editor's unfamiliarity with the finer points of the English language, but others are the result of poor research. The book includes a guide to prices as well as an illustration of each one.

❖ As It Began

First published in 1985 (by Sidgewick & Jackson) and reprinted in paperback form in 1993 (by Pan Books). Co-written by Jim Jenkins and Jacky Gunn (now Smith).

Authorised by Queen, and written with their full cooperation, this book offers a great deal of previosly unpublished information and anecdotes, and concludes with full UK (non live) single, album and video discographies, all of which have been meticulously researched by Jim.

As outlined in the opening Preface to this book, *As It Began* is the perfect example of a book from which seemingly every other music journalist has borrowed material for their own projects. The text reappears almost word for word in some cases.

Collectors should extend their search to the original hard back edition, which is already proving troublesome to locate.

NON ALBUM MATERIAL

The following were all issued as single A or B-side tracks, but do not appear on any album, and were never featured in any concert.

A Human Body
B-side of Play The Game, 1980.
Soul Brother
B-side of Under Pressure, 1981.
I Go Crazy
B-side of Radio Ga Ga, 1984.
[*Brian played only guitar riffs from this. The whole song was never performed*]
Thank God It's Christmas
Single A-side, 1984.

Blurred Vision
B-side of One Vision, 1985.
A Dozen Red Roses For My Darling
B-side of A Kind Of Magic, 1986.
Mad The Swine
Extra track on Headlong CD and 12″ singles. Originally recorded for the debut album but ultimately not included, 1991.

Note: Blurred Vision and A Dozen Red Roses are instrumental tracks.

GROUPS THAT HAVE PLAYED AS SUPPORT ACT TO QUEEN

Kid Abelha and Os Aboboras Selvagens (1985) / After The Fire (1982) / Airrace (1984) / The Alarm (1986) / Alvin Lee & Ten Years After (1979) / Angel Child (?) / Argent (1975) / The Bangles (1986) / Belouis Some (1986) / B-52s (1985) / Big Country (1986) / Bow Wow Wow (1982) / Bullitt (?) / Ray Burton Band (1976) / Cate Brothers (1976) / Cheap Trick (1977) / Chris Rea (1986) / Cold Chisel (1976) / Craaft (1986) / Dakota (1980) / Eduardo Dusek (1985) / Erasmo Carlos (1985) / Exploited (1982) / Andy Fairweather-Low (1976) / Foghat (1976) / Fountainhead (1986) / Rory Gallagher (1979) / General Public (1984) / The Go-Go's (1985) / Pepeu Gomes and Baby Consuelo (1985) / Molly Hatchet (1979) / Head East (1977) / Heart (1985) / Steve Hillage (1976) / Hustler (1974) / INXS (1986) / Iron Maiden (1985) / Joan Jett And The Blackhearts (1982) / Kansas (1975) / Kiki Dee (1976) / Level 42 (1986) / Lucifer (1976) / Lynyrd Skynyrd (1974) / Lulu Santos (1985) / Mahogany Rush (1975) / Manfred Mann (1976) / Marillion (1986) / Frankie Miller's Full House (1976) / Gary Moore (1986) / Mr. Big (1975) / The Narcs (1985) / Ney Matogrosso (1985) / Nutz (1974) / The Outlaws (1977) / Sea Level (1980) / Rainbow (1976) / Red Baron (1979) / The Royal Dragoon Guards (1976) / Rufus (1976) / Bob Seger & Silver Bullet Band (1976) / Solution (?) / Billy Squier (1982) / Status Quo (1986) / Straight 8 (1980) / Storm (1974) / Styx

(1975) / Supercharge (1976) / Taste (1976) / Teardrop Explodes (1982) / Thin Lizzy (1977) / Tombstone (1974) / Treat (1986) / Voyager (1979) / Whitesnake (1985) / Yesterday And Today (?) / Zas (1981) / Zeno (1986) / Z'Zi Labor (1986).

Once they were signed to a major label, Queen played support for only one band - Mott The Hoople.

SUMMARY OF WHERE AND WHEN QUEEN PERFORMED

Listed Alphabetically (except that UK is always listed first)
* Denotes Queen played their first show in that country in this year. (excluding the Freddie Mercury Tribute Concert)

Year	Country		
1970	UK	12	12
1971	UK	20	20
1972	UK	5	5
1973	UK	34	36
	Germany *	1	
	Luxembourg *1		
1974	UK	41	71
	Australia *	1	
	Belgium *	1	
	Finland *	1	
	Germany	5	
	Holland *	1	
	Spain *	1	
	Sweden *	1	
	USA *		19
1975	UK	25	71
	Canada *	2	
	Japan *	8	
	USA		36
1976	UK	4	56
	Australia	8	
	Japan		11
	USA		33
1977	UK	12	87
	Canada	8	
	Denmark *	1	
	Germany	3	
	Holland	1	
	Sweden	2	
	Switzerland *	1	
	USA	59	
1978	UK	5	55
	Austria *	1	
	Belgium	3	
	Canada	5	
	Denmark	1	
	France *	2	
	Germany	4	
	Holland	2	
	Sweden	1	
	Switzerland	1	
	USA	30	
1979	UK	19	64
	Belgium	2	
	Eire *	1	
	France	5	
	Germany	13	
	Holland	2	
	Japan	15	
	Spain	4	
	Switzerland	1	
	Yugoslavia *	2	
1980	UK	5	63
	Belgium	2	
	Canada	3	
	France	1	
	Germany	8	
	Switzerland	1	
	USA	43	
1981	Argentina *	5	20
	Brazil *	2	
	Canada	2	
	Japan	5	
	Mexico *	3	
	Venezuela * 3		
1982	UK	4	70
	Austria	2	
	Belgium	2	
	Canada	4	
	France	3	

Year	Country	No.	Total
1982	Germany	12	
	Holland	2	
	Japan	6	
	Norway *	1	
	Sweden	2	
	Switzerland	2	
	USA	30	
1983	No Shows		
1984	UK	7	30
	Austria	2	
	Belgium	2	
	Eire	2	
	France	1	
	Germany	7	
	Italy *	2	
	South Africa *7		
1985	UK	1	18
	Australia	8	
	Brazil	2	
	Japan	6	
	New Zealand 1		
1986	UK	5	26
	Austria	2	
	Belgium	1	
	Eire	1	
	France	2	
	Germany	5	
	Holland	3	
	Hungary *	1	
	Spain	3	
	Sweden	1	
	Switerland 2		
Total		704	

LIVE SONGS/ALBUM BREAKDOWN

A: No of tracks on album.
B: No of tracks performed live.
C: No of tracks not performed live.
D: Percentage played live/not played.

Queen's 12 studio recorded albums contain 137 tracks, 79 of which were performed in concert, and 58 were not. Queen performed 58% of their entire album catalogue.

	A	B	C	D
A Night At The Opera	12	10	2	83/17
Hot Space	11	8	3	73/27
A Day At The Races	10	7	3	70/30
The Game	10	7	3	70/30
The Works	9	6	3	67/33
News Of The World	11	7	4	64/36
Sheer Heart Attack	13	8	5	62/38
Queen	10	6	4	60/40
Queen II	11	6	5	55/45
Jazz	13	7	6	54/46
A Kind Of Magic	9	4	5	44/56
Flash Gordon	18	3	15	17/83
Total	137	79	58	58/42

SONGS QUEEN PERFORMED LIVE (ORIGINAL MATERIAL)

The following tracks were all performed by Queen during their 15 years of touring. The number in brackets relates to the album on which each track can be found.

1. *Queen* (1973)
2. *Queen II* (1974)
3. *Sheer Heart Attack* (1974)
4. *A Night At The Opera* (1975)
5. *A Day At The Races* (1976)
6. *News Of The World* (1977)
7. *Jazz* (1978)
8. *The Game* (1980)
9. *Flash Gordon* (1980)
10. *Hot Space* (1982)
11. *The Works* (1984)
12. *A Kind Of Magic* (1986)

NA	Does not appear on any album
*	An Instrumental track
+	See Below

A Kind Of Magic (Taylor) (12)
Action This Day (Taylor) (10)
Another One Bites The Dust (Deacon) (8)
Back Chat (Deacon) (10)
Battle Theme (May) (9)
Bicycle Race (Mercury) (7)
Body Language (Mercury) (10)
Bohemian Rhapsody (Mercury) (4)
Brighton Rock (May)(3)
Bring Back That Leroy Brown (Mercury) (3)
Calling All Girls (Taylor) (10)
Crazy Little Thing Called Love (Mercury) (8)
Death On Two Legs (Mercury) (4)
Doing All Right (May Staffel) (1)
Don't Stop Me Now (Mercury) (7)
Dragon Attack (May) (8)
Dreamer's Ball (May) (7)
Fat Bottomed Girls (May) (7)
Father To Son (May) (2)
Flash (May) (9)
Flick Of The Wrist (Mercury) (3)
Friends Will Be Friends (FM & JD) (12)
Fun It [part only] (Taylor) (7)
Get Down Make Love (Mercury) (6)
God Save The Queen (Arr. May) (4)
Good Old Fashioned Lover Boy (Mercury) (5)
Great King Rat (Mercury) (1)
Hammer To Fall (May) (11)
Hangman (unknown) (NA) +
The Hero (May) (9)
I Want To Break Free (Deacon) (11)
I Go Crazy [part only] (May) (NA)
If You Can't Beat Them (Deacon) (7)
Impromptu (Queen) (NA) +
Improvisation (Queen) (NA) +
I'm In Love With My Car (Taylor) (4)
In The Lap Of The Gods (Mercury) (3)
In The Lap Of The Gods... Revisited (Mercury) (3)
Instrumental Inferno (Queen) (NA) +
Is This The World We Created (FM & BM) (11)
It's A Hard Life (Mercury) (11)
It's Late (May) (6)
Jesus (Mercury) (1)
Keep Yourself Alive (May) (1)

Killer Queen (Mercury) (3)
Lazing On A Sunday Afternoon (Mercury) (4)
Let Me Entertain You (Mercury) (7)
Liar (Mercury) (1)
Life Is Real (Mercury) (10)
Love Of My Life (Mercury) (4)
Machines (Or Back To Humans) [taped intro only] (BM & RT) (11) *
The March Of The Black Queen (Mercury) (2)
The Millionaire Waltz (Mercury) (5)
Modern Times Rock'n'Roll (Taylor) (2)
Mustapha (Mercury) (7)
My Melancholy Blues (Mercury)(6)
Need Your Loving Tonight (Deacon) (8)
The Night Comes Down (May) (1)
Now I'm Here (May) (3)
Ogre Battle (Mercury) (2)
One Vision (Queen) (12)
Play The Game (Mercury) (8)
Procession (May) (2) *
The Prophet's Song (May) (4)
Put Out The Fire (May) (10)
Radio Ga Ga (Taylor) (11)
Rock In Rio Blues (Queen) (NA) +
Rock It (Prime Jive) (Taylor) (8)
Save Me (May) (8)
See What A Fool I've Been (May) (NA)
Seven Seas Of Rhye (Mercury) (2)
Shag Out (?) (NA) +
Sheer Heart Attack (Taylor) (6)
Somebody To Love (Mercury) (5)
Son & Daughter (May) (1)
Spread Your Wings (Deacon) (6)
Staying Power (Mercury) (10)
Stone Cold Crazy (Queen) (3)
Sweet Lady (May) (4)
Tear It Up (May) (11)
Tie Your Mother Down (May) (5)
Teo Torriatte (May) (5)
39 (May) (4)
Tokyo Blues (Queen) (NA) +
Under Pressure (Q & DB) (10)
Vultan's Theme (Mercury) (9)
We Are The Champions (Mercury) (6)
We Will Rock You (May) (6)

White Man (May) (5)
White Queen (As It Began) (May) (2)
Who Wants To Live Forever (May) (12)
You're My Best Friend (Deacon) (4)
You Take My Breath Away (Mercury) (5)

See What A Fool I've Been
Single B-side. Played live, but not on any album.
Hangman
Played live, but not on any album nor even recorded in the studio.
Shag Out
No such track. It is part of above track.
Rock In Rio Blues
Jamming type Improvisation, not recorded and not on any album.
Tokyo Blues
Jamming type Improvisation, not recorded and not on any album.
Impromptu
Jamming type Improvisation. not on any studio album, but on 'Live At Wembley 86' album.
Improvisation
Jamming type Improvisation, not recorded and not on any album. Usually a vocal or guitar (or both) ad-libbed piece.
Instrumental Inferno
Jam type Improvisation, not recorded and not on any album.

DATE OF DÉBUT SHOW IN EACH COUNTRY
(Number in bracket denotes total amount of shows performed in that country)

Argentina	28 February 1981 (5)
Austria	2 May 1978 (7)
Australia	2 February 1974 (17)
Belgium	1 December 1974 (13)
Brazil	20 March 1981 (4)
Canada	2 April 1975 (24)
Denmark	12 May 1977 (2)
Eire	22 November 1979 (4)
Finland	25 November 1974 (1)
France	23 April 1978 (14)

Germany	13 October 1973 (58)
Holland	8 December 1974 (11)
Hungary	27 July 1986 (1)
Italy	3 February 1984 (3)
Japan	19 April 1975 (51)
Luxembourg	14 October 1973 (1)
Mexico	9 October 1981 (3)
New Zealand	13 April 1985 (1)
Norway	12 April 1982 (1)
South Africa	5 October 1984 (7)
Spain	10 December 1974 (8)
Sweden	23 November 1974 (7)
Switzerland	19 May 1977 (8)
UK	27 June 1970 (199)
USA	16 April 1974 (250)
Venezuela	25 September 1981 (3)
Yugoslavia	6 February 1979 (2)
Total	704

Queen's first ever public live performance (UK - 27/6/70) is the first recorded show.

ALBUM TRACKS WHICH NEVER FEATURED IN ANY QUEEN LIVE SHOW (or which featured only once)

Throughout the fifteen years in which Queen toured, a significant volume of album material did not feature in the live set. While many songs were included repeatedly and often remained in the repertoire for numerous tours, others did not appear even once. What follows is a summary of the tracks never to have featured in any Queen concert – or those which featured only once.

* denotes songs only performed once (as far as can be ascertained)

Queen (1973)
My Fairy King (Mercury) / The Night Comes Down* (May) / Jesus* (Mercury)

Queen II (1974)
Someday One Day (May) / The Loser In The End (Taylor) / Nevermore (Mercury) / Funny How Love Is (Mercury)

Sheer Heart Attack (1974)
Tenement Funster (Taylor) / Lily Of The Valley (Mercury) / Dear Friends (May) / Misfire (Deacon) / She Makes Me (May)

A Night At The Opera (1975)
Seaside Rendezvous (Mercury) / Good Company (May)*

A Day At The Races (1976)
Long Away (May) / You And I (Deacon) / Drowse (Taylor)

News Of The World (1977)
All Dead All Dead (May) / Fight From The Inside (Taylor) / Who Needs You (Deacon)

Jazz (1978)
Jealousy (Mercury) / Dead On Time (May) / In Only Seven Days (Deacon) / Fun It (Taylor) / Leaving Home Ain't Easy (May) / More Of That Jazz (Taylor)

The Game (1980)
Don't Try Suicide (Mercury) / Sail Away Sweet Sister (May) / Coming Soon (Taylor)

Flash Gordon (Soundtrack) (1980)
With the exception of Flash's theme,The Battle Theme, Vultan's Theme and The Hero, no other material from the album was considered appropriate for inclusion in the live set - it is after all a soundtrack project.

Hot Space (1982)
Dancer (May) / Las Parablas De Amor (May) / Cool Cat (Deacon/Mercury)

The Works (1984)
*Man On The Prowl (Mercury) / Keep Passing The Open Windows (Mercury) / Machines (Or Back To Humans)**

**Machines* was featured in the 1984 Intro tape only. Queen never actually performed the song properly

A Kind Of Magic (1986)
One Year Of Love (Deacon) / Pain Is So Close To Pleasure (Mercury/Deacon) / Gimme The Prize (May) / Don't Lose Your Head (Taylor) / Princes Of The Universe (Mercury)

SONGS QUEEN HAVE PERFORMED LIVE - BUT DID NOT WRITE

Bama Lama Bama Loo
Reached No. 37 in July 1977 for Little Richard.
Written by Penniman (Little Richard) and Collins.

Be Bop A Lula
Reached number 30 in July 1956 for Gene Vincent.
Re-entered the charts on two more occasions.
Written by G. Vincent and T. Davis.

Big Spender
Reached number 21 in October 1967 for Shirley Bassey.
Written by C. Coleman and D. Fields.

Danny Boy
Written in 1913 by Fred Weatherly; original recording by Madame Schumann. Has become an Irish favourite.

Gimme Some Lovin
Reached number 2 in November 1966 for Spencer Davis Group.
Written by Steve Winwood, Muff Winwood and Spencer Davis.

Hello Mary Lou (Goodbye Heart)
Reached number 2 in June 1961 for Rick Nelson.
Written by Gene Pitney.

I'm A Man
Reached number 9 in January 1967 for Spencer Davis Group.
Written by Steve Winwood and Jimmy Miller.

Imagine
Reached number 6 in November 1975 and number 1 in December 1980 for John Lennon. Written by John Lennon.

Immigrant Song
Recorded by Led Zeppelin on the *Led Zeppelin III* album in 1970. Not issued as a single.
Written by Jimmy Page and Robert Plant.

Jailhouse Rock
Reached number 1 in January 1958 and January 2005 for Elvis Presley. Also issued in December 1971, September 1977 and February 1983.
Written by Jerry Leiber and Mike Stoller.

Lucille
Reached number 10 in June 1957 for Little Richard.
Written by Penniman (Little Richard) and Collins.

Mannish Boy
Reached number 51 in July 1988 for Muddy Waters.
Written by Muddy Morganfield (Muddy Waters), E. McDaniel and M. London.

Mull Of Kintyre
Reached number 1 in 1977 for Wings.
Written by Paul McCartney.

Not Fade Away
Reached number 3 in February 1964 for The Rolling Stones.
Written by Buddy Holly.

Saturday Night's Alright For Fighting
Reached number 7 in July 1973 for Elton John.
Written by Elton John and Bernie Taupin.

Shake, Rattle & Roll
Originally recorded by Big Joe Turner. Reached number 4 in December 1954 for Bill Haley & His Comets. Also covered by Elvis Presley, Buddy Holly, Carl Perkins and Cliff Richard, amongst others.
Written by Jessie (Charlie Calhoun) Stone.

Silent Night
Reached number 8 in December 1952 for Bing Crosby, number 47 in 1978 for The Dickies, and number 2 in 1988 for Bros. Originally a German hymn.
Written by Joseph Mohr.

Stupid Cupid
Reached number 1 (B-side of Carolina Moon) in August 1958 for Connie Francis. Written by Sedaka and Greenfield.

Take Me Home
Essentially a Brian guitar ad-lib, it crops up on numerous bootleg compilations.

Tavaszi Szel Vizet Araszt
Hungarian folk song.
Composer unknown.

Tutti Frutti
Reached number 29 in February 1957 for Little Richard. Also covered by Elvis Presley.
Written by Lubin, LaBostrie and Penniman (Little Richard).

White Christmas
A hit for numerous artists between 1952 and 1985, most familiarly Bing Crosby - number 5 in December 1977. Reissued in December 1985 (number 69).
Written by Irving Berlin.

You're So Square (Baby I Don't Care)
Originally recorded by Elvis Presley for his movie
Jailhouse Rock. Reached No. 12 in July 1961 for
Buddy Holly.
Written by Jerry Leiber and Mike Stoller.